Reading STREET

Grade K, Unit 4

Let's Explore

PEARSON

Scott Foresman

scottforesman.com

Editorial Offices: Glenview, Illinois • Parsippany, New Jersey • New York, New York
Sales Offices: Boston, Massachusetts • Duluth, Georgia • Glenview, Illinois
Coppell, Texas • Sacramento, California • Mesa, Arizona

We dedicate Reading Street to
Peter Jovanovich.

His wisdom, courage,
and passion for education
are an inspiration to us all.

This work is protected by United States copyright laws and is provided *solely for the use of teachers and administrators* in teaching courses and assessing student learning in their classes and schools. Dissemination or sale of any part of this work (including the World Wide Web) will destroy the integrity of the work and is *not* permitted.

Cover Rob Hefferan

About the Cover Artist
Rob likes to reminisce about the simple life he had as a child growing up in Cheshire, when his biggest worry was whether to have fish fingers or Alphabetti Spaghetti for tea. The faces, colors, and shapes from that time are a present-day inspiration for his artwork.

ISBN-13: 978-0-328-24359-4
ISBN-10:   0-328-24359-0

Copyright © 2008 Pearson Education, Inc.

All Rights Reserved. Printed in the United States of America. This publication is protected by Copyright, and permission should be obtained from the publisher prior to any prohibited reproduction, storage in a retrieval system, or transmission in any form by any means, electronic, mechanical, photocopying, recording, or likewise. For information regarding permission(s), write to: Permissions Department, Scott Foresman, 1900 East Lake Avenue, Glenview, Illinois 60025.

Many of the designations used by manufacturers and sellers to distinguish their products are claimed as trademarks. Where those designations appear in this book, and Scott Foresman was aware of a trademark claim, the designations have been printed with initial capitals and in cases of multiple usage have also been marked with either ® or ™ where they first appear.

2 3 4 5 6 7 8 9 10 V064 16 15 14 13 12 11 10 09 08 07

CC: N1

Reading STREET

Where the Love of Reading Begins

Reading Street Program Authors

Peter Afflerbach, Ph.D.
Professor, Department of
Curriculum and Instruction
University of Maryland at
College Park

Camille L.Z. Blachowicz, Ph.D.
Professor of Education
National-Louis University

Candy Dawson Boyd, Ph.D.
Professor, School of Education
Saint Mary's College of California

Wendy Cheyney, Ed.D.
Professor of Special Education
and Literacy, Florida
International University

Connie Juel, Ph.D.
Professor of Education, School of
Education, Stanford University

Edward J. Kame'enui, Ph.D.
Professor and Director, Institute for
the Development of Educational
Achievement, University of Oregon

Donald J. Leu, Ph.D.
John and Maria Neag Endowed
Chair in Literacy and Technology
University of Connecticut

Jeanne R. Paratore, Ed.D.
Associate Professor of Education
Department of Literacy
and Language Development
Boston University

P. David Pearson, Ph.D.
Professor and Dean,
Graduate School of Education
University of California, Berkeley

Sam L. Sebesta, Ed.D.
Professor Emeritus,
College of Education,
University of Washington, Seattle

Deborah Simmons, Ph.D.
Professor, College of Education
and Human Development
Texas A&M University
(Not pictured)

Sharon Vaughn, Ph.D.
H.E. Hartfelder/Southland
Corporation Regents Professor
University of Texas

Susan Watts-Taffe, Ph.D.
Independent Literacy Researcher
Cincinnati, Ohio

Karen Kring Wixson, Ph.D.
Professor of Education
University of Michigan

Components

Student Editions (1–6)

Teacher's Editions (PreK–6)

Assessment
Assessment Handbook (K–6)

Baseline Group Tests (K–6)

DIBELS™ Assessments (K–6)

ExamView® Test Generator CD-ROM (2–6)

Fresh Reads for Differentiated
Test Practice (1–6)

Online Success Tracker™ (K–6)*

Selection Tests Teacher's Manual (1–6)

Unit and End-of-Year
Benchmark Tests (K–6)

Leveled Readers
Concept Literacy Leveled Readers (K–1)

Independent Leveled Readers (K)

Kindergarten Student Readers (K)

Leveled Reader Teaching Guides (K–6)

Leveled Readers (1–6)

Listen to Me Readers (K)

Online Leveled Reader Database (K–6)*

Take-Home Leveled Readers (K–6)

Trade Books and Big Books
Big Books (PreK–2)

Read Aloud Trade Books (PreK–K)

Sing with Me Big Book (1–2)

Trade Book Library (1–6)

Decodable Readers
Decodable Readers (K–3)

Strategic Intervention
Decodable Readers (1–2)

Take-Home Decodable Readers (K–3)

Phonics and Word Study
Alphabet Cards in English and Spanish
(PreK–K)

Alphabet Chart in English and Spanish
(PreK–K)

Animal ABCs Activity Guide (K)

Finger Tracing Cards (PreK–K)

Patterns Book (PreK–K)

Phonics Activities CD-ROM (PreK–2)*

Phonics Activities Mats (K)

Phonics and Spelling Practice Book (1–3)

Phonics and Word-Building Board and Letters
(PreK–3)

Phonics Songs and Rhymes Audio CD (K–2)

Phonics Songs and Rhymes Flip Chart (K–2)

Picture Word Cards (PreK–K)

Plastic Letter Tiles (K)

Sound-Spelling Cards and Wall Charts (1–2)

Strategies for Word Analysis (4–6)

Word Study and Spelling Practice Book (4–6)

Language Arts
Daily Fix-It Transparencies (K–6)

Grammar & Writing Book and
Teacher's Annotated Edition, The (1–6)

Grammar and Writing Practice Book
and Teacher's Manual (1–6)

Grammar Transparencies (1–6)

Six-Trait Writing Posters (1–6)

Writing Kit (1–6)

Writing Rubrics and Anchor Papers (1–6)

Writing Transparencies (1–6)

Practice and Additional Resources
AlphaBuddy Bear Puppet (K)

Alphasaurus Annie Puppet (PreK)

Amazing Words Posters (K–2)

Centers Survival Kit (PreK–6)

Graphic Organizer Book (2–6)

Graphic Organizer Flip Chart (K–1)

High-Frequency Word Cards (K)

Kindergarten Review (1)

Practice Book and Teacher's Manual (K–6)

Read Aloud Anthology (PreK–2)

Readers' Theater Anthology (K–6)

Research into Practice (K–6)

Retelling Cards (K–6)

Scott Foresman Research Base (K–6)

Skill Transparencies (2–6)

Songs and Rhymes Flip Chart (PreK)

Talk with Me, Sing with Me Chart (PreK–K)

Tested Vocabulary Cards (1–6)

Vocabulary Transparencies (1–2)

Welcome to Reading Street (PreK–1)

ELL
ELL and Transition Handbook (PreK–6)

ELL Comprehensive Kit (1–6)

ELL Posters (K–6)

ELL Readers (1–6)

ELL Teaching Guides (1–6)

Ten Important Sentences (1–6)

Digital Components
AudioText CDs (PreK–6)

Background Building Audio CDs (3–6)

ExamView® Test Generator
CD-ROM (2–6)

Online Lesson Planner (K–6)

Online New Literacies Activities (1–6)*

Online Professional Development (1–6)

Online Story Sort (K–6)*

Online Student Editions (1–6)*

Online Success Tracker™ (K–6)*

Online Teacher's Editions (PreK–6)

Phonics Activities CD-ROM (PreK–2)*

Phonics Songs and Rhymes
Audio CD (K–2)

Sing with Me/Background Building
Audio CDs (PreK–2)

Songs and Rhymes Audio CD (PreK)

My Sidewalks Early Reading Intervention (K)

My Sidewalks Intensive Reading Intervention (Levels A–E)

Reading Street for the Guided Reading Teacher (1–6)

* INTERACTIVE WHITEBOARD READY

v

Kindergarten
Priority Skills

Priority skills are the critical elements of reading—phonemic awareness, phonics, fluency, vocabulary, and text comprehension—as they are developed across and within grades to assure that instructional emphasis is placed on the right skills at the right time and to maintain a systematic sequence of skill instruction.

Key
- ● = Taught/Unit priority
- ◑ = Reviewed and practiced
- ○ = Integrated practice

	UNIT 1		UNIT 2	
	Weeks		Weeks	
	1–3	4–6	1–3	4–6
Phonemic Awareness				
Recognize and produce rhyming words	●	◑	○	○
Count words in sentences	●	○	○	○
Count syllables in words	●	◑	○	○
Identify sounds that are the same or different		●	●	●
Segment and blend onset and rime				●
Identify and isolate initial and final sounds in spoken words		●	●	●
Identify and isolate medial sounds in spoken words			●	●
Blend sounds orally to make words			●	●
Segment a word into sounds			●	●
Add, delete, or substitute phonemes				●
Phonics				
Know most common sound associated with individual letters		●	●	●
Blend sounds of letters to decode one-syllable words			●	●
Consonants		●	●	●
Consonant blends				
Short vowels			●	●
Phonograms/Word families			●	●
Fluency				
Listen to models read aloud with accuracy, comprehension, and appropriate rate	●	●	●	●
Read irregular high-frequency words automatically	●	●	●	●
Oral Vocabulary				
Develop vocabulary through direct instruction, concrete experiences, reading, and listening to text read aloud	●	●	●	●
Use words to describe location, size, color, and shape	●	●	◑	◑
Use new oral vocabulary words in context to reinforce meaning	●	●	●	●

UNIT 3		UNIT 4		UNIT 5		UNIT 6	
Weeks		**Weeks**		**Weeks**		**Weeks**	
1–3	4–6	1–3	4–6	1–3	4–6	1–3	4–6
○	○	○	○	○	○	○	○
○	○	◑	○	◑	○	○	○
●	◑	◑	○	○	○	○	○
●	●	●	●	●	●	○	○
●	●	●	●	●	●	◑	◑
●	●	●	●	●	●	○	○
●	●	●	●	●	●	○	○
●	●	●	●	●	●	○	○
●	●	●	●	●	●	◑	◑
●	●	●	●	●	●	●	●
●	●	●	●	●	●	●	●
		●	◑	○	○	○	○
●	●	●	●	●	●	●	●
●	●	●	●	●	●	●	●
●	●	●	●	●	●	●	●
●	●	●	●	●	●	●	●
●	●	●	●	●	●	●	●
○	○	○	○	○	○	○	○
●	●	●	●	●	●	●	●

Kindergarten
Priority Skills

Key

● = Taught/Unit priority
◑ = Reviewed and practiced
○ = Integrated practice

Text Comprehension	UNIT 1 Weeks		UNIT 2 Weeks	
	1–3	4–6	1–3	4–6
Strategies				
Preview the text	●	●	●	●
Set purpose for reading	●	●	●	●
Activate and use prior knowledge	●	●	●	●
Make and confirm predictions	●	●	●	●
Monitor own comprehension				
Use fix-up strategies				
Use graphic organizers to focus on text structure, to represent relationships in text, or to summarize text				
Answer questions	●	●	●	●
Generate questions				
Recognize story structure			●	●
Retell stories, including characters, setting, and plot	●	●	●	●
Retell/summarize selections, identifying main ideas			●	○
Visualize; use mental imagery				
Make connections: text to self, text to text, text to world	●	●	●	●
Skills				
Cause and effect				
Classify and categorize		●	◑	○
Compare and contrast			●	○
Draw conclusions				
Main idea			●	○
Realism and fantasy				●
Sequence of events	●	◑	◑	◑
Literary Elements				
Character	●	●	◑	◑
Plot				
Setting	●	◑	●	◑

UNIT 3		UNIT 4		UNIT 5		UNIT 6	
Weeks		Weeks		Weeks		Weeks	
1–3	4–6	1–3	4–6	1–3	4–6	1–3	4–6

You Are Here

Unit 6
Building Our Homes

Unit 1
All Together Now

UNIT
4

Let's Explore

Where will our adventures take us?

Unit 4
Skills Overview

	WEEK 1	WEEK 2	WEEK 3
	1–61 **Bunny Day** — ANIMAL FANTASY	63–125 **My Lucky Day** — ANIMAL FANTASY	127–187 **One Little Mouse** — RHYMING/ CONCEPT STORY

Oral Language

	WEEK 1	WEEK 2	WEEK 3
Build Concepts	*What adventures do you have throughout the day?*	*What adventures can you have on a lucky day?*	*What adventures can an animal have?*
Oral Vocabulary	*chores, tidy, bustle, race, story, hungry*	*piglet, fox, lucky, filthy, cook, scrubber*	*woodland, nest, vale, hollow, comfortable, shadows*

Shared Reading

	WEEK 1	WEEK 2	WEEK 3
Reading Strategies	Preview and Predict Recall and Retell	Use Illustrations Recall and Retell	Preview and Predict Recall and Retell
Listening Comprehension	**T** ⟳ Sequence **REVIEW** Compare and Contrast	⟳ Cause and Effect **T** **REVIEW** Plot	**T** ⟳ Sequence **REVIEW** Draw Conclusions

Word Work

	WEEK 1	WEEK 2	WEEK 3
Phonemic Awareness	**T** Phoneme Isolation /h/ Oral Blending Phoneme Segmentation	**T** Phoneme Isolation /l/ Oral Blending Phoneme Segmentation	**T** Phoneme Isolation: Consonant Blends Phoneme Discrimination Phoneme Segmentation
Phonics	**T** ⟳ Connect /h/ to *Hh* **T** **REVIEW** Connect /o/ to *Oo*	**T** ⟳ Connect /l/ to *Ll* **T** **REVIEW** Connect /h/ to *Hh*	**T** ⟳ Consonant Blends **T** **REVIEW** Connect /l/ to *Ll*
High-Frequency Words	**T** *are, that, do*	**T** *are, that, do*	**T** *one, two, three, four, five*

Language Arts

	WEEK 1	WEEK 2	WEEK 3
Grammar	Naming Parts	Action Parts	Complete Sentences
Writing	Shared, Modeled, Interactive, and Independent	Shared, Modeled, Interactive, and Independent	Shared, Modeled, Interactive, and Independent
Speaking, Listening, Viewing	Give Directions	Compare and Contrast	Retell a Story

Integrate Science and Social Studies Standards	Economics, Government, Culture, History	History	Life Science

⟳ Target Skill   **T** Tested Skill

Let's Explore

WEEK 4	WEEK 5	WEEK 6
189–251 **Goldilocks and the Three Bears** CLASSIC TRADITIONAL TALE	253–313 **If You Could Go to Antarctica** INFORMATIONAL TEXT	315–377 **Abuela** FICTION
What kind of adventure can a little girl have?	*What would it be like to take an adventure to the Antarctic?*	*What kind of adventures can you have in the city?*
bears, porridge, cottage, big, middle-sized, small	*Antarctica, continent, icebergs, penguins, seals, whales*	*abuela, adventure, flock, city, airport, harbor*
Preview and Predict Recall and Retell	Text Features Recall and Retell	Preview and Predict Recall and Retell
T Character **T REVIEW** Setting	Classify and Categorize **T REVIEW** Main Idea	**T** Setting **REVIEW** Realism and Fantasy
T Phoneme Isolation /g/ Oral Blending Phoneme Segmentation	**T** Phoneme Isolation /e/ Phoneme Segmentation Phoneme Discrimination	**T** Phoneme Isolation /e/ Phoneme Segmentation Phoneme Discrimination
T Connect /g/ to *Gg* **T REVIEW** Consonant Blends	**T** Connect /e/ to *Ee* **T REVIEW** Connect /g/ to *Gg*	**T** Connect /e/ to *Ee* **T REVIEW** Connect /g/ to *Gg*
T *one, two, three, four, five*	**T** *here, go, from*	**T** *here, go, from*
Telling Sentences	Uppercase Letters and Periods	Pronoun *I*
Shared, Modeled, Interactive, and Independent	Shared, Modeled, Interactive, and Independent	Shared, Modeled, Interactive, and Independent
Discuss Authors and Illustrators	Listen for Story Elements: Character	Listen to Poems

 Government   Earth Science    Transportation, Culture

Ready, Teddy?

(On Reading Street, you're ready for everything and anything!)

Honey is yummy in my tummy.

Student Editions (1–6)

Teacher's Editions (PreK–6)

Assessment
Assessment Handbook (K–6)
Baseline Group Tests (K–6)
DIBELS™ Assessments (K–6)
Examview® Test Generator CD-ROM (2–6)
Fresh Reads for Differentiated
Test Practice (1–6)
Online Success Tracker™ (K–6)*
Selection Tests Teacher's Manual (1–6)
Unit and End-of-Year
Benchmark Tests (K–6)

Leveled Readers
Concept Literacy Leveled Readers (K–1)
Independent Leveled Readers (K)
Kindergarten Student Readers (K)
Leveled Reader Teaching Guides (K–6)
Leveled Readers (1–6)
Listen to Me Readers (K)
Online Leveled Readers Database (K–6)*
Take-Home Leveled Readers (K–6)

Trade Books and Big Books
Big Books (PreK–2)
Read Aloud Trade Books (PreK–K)
Sing with Me Big Book (1–2)
Trade Book Library (1–6)

*

Decodable Readers

Decodable Readers (K–3)

Strategic Intervention
Decodable Readers (1–2)

Take-Home Decodable Readers (K–3)

Phonics and Word Study

Alphabet Cards in English and Spanish
(PreK–K)

Alphabet Chart in English and Spanish
(PreK–K)

Animal ABCs Activity Guide (K)

Finger Tracing Cards (PreK–K)

Patterns Books (PreK–K)

Phonics Activities CD-ROM (PreK–2)*

Phonics Activities Mats (K)

Phonics and Spelling Practice Book (1–3)

Phonics and Word-Building Board and Letters
(PreK–3)

Phonics Songs and Rhymes Audio CD (K–2)

Phonics Songs and Rhymes Flip Chart (K–2)

Picture Word Cards (PreK–K)

Plastic Letter Tiles (K)

Sound-Spelling Cards and Wall Charts (1–2)

Strategies for Word Analysis (4–6)

Word Study and Spelling Practice Book (4–6)

Language Arts

Daily Fix-It Transparencies (K–6)

Grammar & Writing Book and
Teacher's Annotated Edition, The (1–6)

Grammar and Writing Practice Book
and Teacher's Manual (1–6)

Grammar Transparencies (1–6)

Six-Trait Writing Posters (1–6)

Writing Kit (1–6)

Writing Rubrics and Anchor Papers (1–6)

Writing Transparencies (1–6)

Practice and Additional Resources

AlphaBuddy Bear Puppet (K)

Alphasaurus Annie Puppet (PreK)

Amazing Words Posters (K–2)

Centers Survival Kit (PreK–6)

Graphic Organizer Book (2–6)

Graphic Organizer Flip Chart (K–1)

High-Frequency Word Cards (K)

Kindergarten Review (1)

Practice Book and Teacher's Manual (K–6)

Read Aloud Anthology (PreK–2)

Readers' Theater Anthology (K–6)

Research into Practice (K–6)

Retelling Cards (K–6)

Scott Foresman Research Base (K–6)

Skill Transparencies (2–6)

Songs and Rhymes Flip Chart (PreK)

Talk with Me, Sing with Me Chart (PreK–K)

Tested Vocabulary Cards (1–6)

Vocabulary Transparencies (1–2)

Welcome to Reading Street (PreK–1)

ELL

ELL and Transition Handbook (PreK–6)

ELL Comprehensive Kit (1–6)

ELL Posters (K–6)

ELL Readers (1–6)

ELL Teaching Guides (1–6)

Ten Important Sentences (1–6)

Digital Components

AudioText CDs (PreK–6)

Background Building Audio CDs (3–6)

ExamView® Test Generator
CD-ROM (2–6)

Online Lesson Planner (K–6)

Online New Literacies Activities (1–6)*

Online Professional Development (1–6)

Online Story Sort (K–6)*

Online Student Editions (1–6)*

Online Success Tracker™ (K–6)*

Online Teacher's Editions (PreK–6)

Phonics Activities CD-ROM (PreK–2)*

Phonics Songs and Rhymes
Audio CD (K–2)

Sing with Me/Background Building
Audio CDs (PreK–2)

Songs and Rhymes Audio CD (PreK)

My Sidewalks Early Reading Intervention (K)

My Sidewalks Intensive Reading Intervention (Levels A–E)

Reading Street for the Guided Reading Teacher (1–6)

Grouping for AYP

STEP 1

Diagnose and Differentiate

Diagnose
To make initial grouping decisions, use the Baseline Group Test or another initial placement test. Depending on children's ability levels, you may have more than one of each group.

Differentiate

If . . . a child's performance is **Below-Level** **then . . .** use the regular instruction and the daily Strategic Intervention, pp. DI·1–DI·30.

If . . . a child's performance is **On-Level** **then . . .** use the regular instruction for On-Level learners throughout each week.

If . . . a child's performance is **Advanced** **then . . .** use the regular instruction and the daily instruction for Advanced learners, pp. DI·1–DI·30.

Group Time

On-Level

- Explicit instructional routines teach core skills and strategies.
- Ample practice for core skills.
- Independent activities provide practice for core skills
- Kindergarten Student Readers and Decodable Readers provide additional reading and practice with core skills.

Strategic Intervention

- Daily Strategic Intervention provides more intensive instruction, more scaffolding, more practice with critical skills, and more opportunities to respond.
- Decodable Readers practice word reading skills.
- Reteach lessons (pp. DI·31–DI·36) provide additional instructional opportunities with target skills.
- Listen to Me Readers practice target skills and high-frequency words.

Advanced

- Daily Advanced lessons provide compacted instruction for accelerated learning, options for independent investigative work, and challenging reading content.
- Independent Leveled Readers provide additional reading tied to lesson concepts and skills.

Additional opportunities to differentiate instruction:
- Reteach Lessons, pp. DI·31–DI·36
- Leveled Reader Instruction and Leveled Practice, pp. LR1–LR13
- *My Sidewalks on Scott Foresman Reading Street* Early Reading Intervention Program

4-Step Plan for Assessment

1. **Diagnose and Differentiate**
2. **Monitor Progress**
3. **Assess and Regroup**
4. **Summative Assessment**

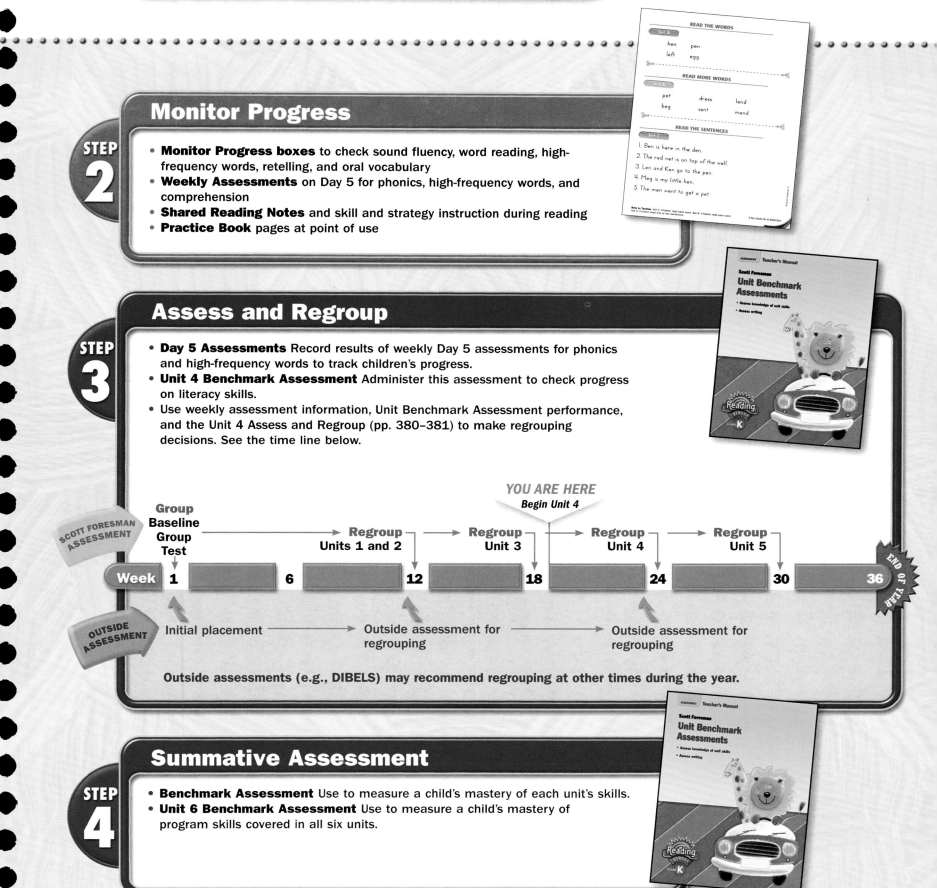

Monitor Progress

STEP 2

- **Monitor Progress boxes** to check sound fluency, word reading, high-frequency words, retelling, and oral vocabulary
- **Weekly Assessments** on Day 5 for phonics, high-frequency words, and comprehension
- **Shared Reading Notes** and skill and strategy instruction during reading
- **Practice Book** pages at point of use

Assess and Regroup

STEP 3

- **Day 5 Assessments** Record results of weekly Day 5 assessments for phonics and high-frequency words to track children's progress.
- **Unit 4 Benchmark Assessment** Administer this assessment to check progress on literacy skills.
- Use weekly assessment information, Unit Benchmark Assessment performance, and the Unit 4 Assess and Regroup (pp. 380–381) to make regrouping decisions. See the time line below.

YOU ARE HERE
Begin Unit 4

SCOTT FORESMAN ASSESSMENT

Group Baseline Group Test

Regroup Units 1 and 2 — Regroup Unit 3 — Regroup Unit 4 — Regroup Unit 5

Week | 1 | 6 | 12 | 18 | 24 | 30 | 36

END OF YEAR

OUTSIDE ASSESSMENT

Initial placement → Outside assessment for regrouping → Outside assessment for regrouping

Outside assessments (e.g., DIBELS) may recommend regrouping at other times during the year.

Summative Assessment

STEP 4

- **Benchmark Assessment** Use to measure a child's mastery of each unit's skills.
- **Unit 6 Benchmark Assessment** Use to measure a child's mastery of program skills covered in all six units.

Unit 4
Theme Launch

Discuss the Big Idea

Read and discuss the theme question: *Where will our adventures take us?* Explain to children that they will be reading stories and doing projects about adventures. Discuss:

- **What are some places you have explored?**
- **What stories do you know of animal adventures?**
- **Where would you like to go on an adventure?**

Display the Big Books and Read Aloud Trade Books from this unit and preview the stories. Read the titles together and look at the cover illustrations. Ask children what they think each story might tell about "Let's Explore."

Finger Play

Animal Friends

I saw a little rabbit come. Hop, hop, hop!
(jump, with hands like paws in front)
A friendly duck came too. Quack, quack, quack!
(open and close hand in front of mouth)
A squirrel scurried down the tree,
(motion upward)
With a bird the color blue. Tweet, tweet, tweet!
(flap arms)
I said to all the animals, "Won't you please stay?"
(palms up, questioning)
But when it started raining—pitter, pitter, pat,
(wiggle fingers down)
They all ran away.
(make fingers "run" outward)

UNIT **4**

Read It Online
PearsonSuccessNet.com

Let's Explore
Where will our adventures take us?

CONNECTING CULTURES

You can use the following selection to help children learn about their own and other cultures and explore common elements of each.

Abuela Explain to children that there are many different languages that people speak. *Abuela* is the Spanish word for "grandma." Ask the children what other languages they know. They can ask their families about what other languages they can speak. As a class, you can find out how to say *grandma* in many languages.

connect to SOCIAL STUDIES
connect to SOCIAL STUDIES
connect to SCIENCE
connect to SOCIAL STUDIES
connect to SCIENCE
connect to SOCIAL STUDIES

Unit Project

Remember When Album

Children can work individually and in groups to create a memory album of adventures they have had in their lives.

PROJECT TIMETABLE

WEEK	ACTIVITY/SKILL CONNECTION
1	**MY PASSPORT** Give each child a stapled booklet to make a passport. They can make the cover and draw pictures of themselves inside. Have children recall places they have visited and draw and label them on the pages of the passport.
2	**REMEMBER WHEN . . .** Have children bring photos or draw and label themselves on special family outings, adventures, or trips. Children can make scrapbook pages and decorate them for their albums.
3	**I WANT TO GO TO . . .** Have children think about somewhere new they would like to explore. They can use cut paper, paint, or fabric to make album pages depicting their future adventures.
4	**MAP IT** Give children an outline of a map of your town, state, or country or the world. Children can mark and label places they have been, with teacher or parent assistance. Add this page to the album.
5	**COVER ART** Children can illustrate covers for their albums, making a pouch for the passport on the inside cover.
6	**PUBLISH** Albums can be hole punched and then bound with yarn or ribbon. Children can present their finished books to the class.

Reflect on theme and connect unit content with questions on p. 378.

CONCEPT DEVELOPMENT

Unit 4
Let's Explore

CONCEPT QUESTION

Where will our adventures take us?

Week 1

Expand the Concept

What adventures do you have throughout the day?

Connect the Concept

Develop Language
chores, tidy, bustle, race, story, hungry

Teach Content
Economics
Government
Culture
History

Time for SOCIAL STUDIES

Literature
Bunny Day

Week 2

Expand the Concept

What adventures can you have on a lucky day?

Connect the Concept

Develop Language
piglet, fox, lucky, filthy, cook, scrubber

Teach Content
History

Time for SOCIAL STUDIES

Literature
My Lucky Day
Keiko Kasza

Week 3

Expand the Concept

What adventures can an animal have?

Connect the Concept

Develop Language
woodland, nest, vale, hollow, comfortable, shadows

Teach Content
Life Science

Time for Science

Literature
ONE LITTLE MOUSE
by Dori Chaconas
illustrated by LeUyen Pham

Week 4

Expand the Concept

What kind of adventure can a little girl have?

Connect the Concept

Develop Language
bears, porridge, cottage, big, middle-sized, small

Teach Content
Government

Time for SOCIAL STUDIES

Literature
Goldilocks and the Three Bears
Retold and illustrated by Valeri Gorbachev

Week 5

Expand the Concept

What would it be like to take an adventure to the Antarctic?

Connect the Concept

Develop Language
Antarctica, continent, icebergs, penguins, seals, whales

Teach Content
Earth Science

Time for Science

Literature
If You Could go to Antarctica

Week 6

Expand the Concept

What kinds of adventures can you have in the city?

Connect the Concept

Develop Language
abuela, adventure, flock, city, airport, harbor

Teach Content
Transportation
Culture

Time for SOCIAL STUDIES

Literature
Abuela
by Arthur Dorros
illustrated by Elisa Kleven

Unit 4
Let's Explore

CONCEPT QUESTION

Where will our adventures take us?

Week 1

EXPAND THE CONCEPT
What adventures do you have throughout the day?

CONNECT THE CONCEPT

▶ **Build Background**

chores	*bustle*	*story*
tidy	*race*	*hungry*

Get Up, Get Up, It's a Beautiful Day

Get up, get up, it's a beautiful day,
We have so much to do!
Let's tidy up and do our chores,
It's so much fun with you!

▶ **Social Studies Content**
Economics, Government, Culture, History

Preview Your Week

What adventures do you have throughout the day?

Big Book

Audio CD

Genre Animal Fantasy

🔊 **Phonics** *Hh/h/*

🔊 **Comprehension Skill** Sequence

Meet the Author

Rick Walton

Rick Walton says he became a children's book writer because "after trying almost every other career in the book, I realized that writing for kids was one of the few things that I both enjoyed and was good at." He has written over fifty books for children, including joke books, picture books, and a poetry collection.

Read another book by Rick Walton.

Bunnies on the Go

Read It
ONLINE
PearsonSuccessNet.com

- Kindergarten Student Readers
- Listen to Me Readers
- Independent Leveled Readers
- Decodable Readers

Books for All Children

Listen to Me Reader

Emergent

- **Develop oral language**
- **Develop phonemic awareness**
- **Read decodable words**
- **Read high-frequency words**

Kindergarten Student Reader

On-Level

- **Read connected text**
- **Apply phonics skills**
- **Read high-frequency words in context**

Leveled Reader K.4.1

Independent Leveled Reader

Independent

- **Practice comprehension skill:** sequence
- **Extend concepts**
- **Connect to Social Studies**

Apply Phonics

Decodable Reader

Phonics Story

Integrate Social Studies Standards

- **Economics**
- **Government**
- **Culture**
- **History**

Read

Big Book *Bunny Day*

Independent Leveled Reader *Fish Can Swim*

Build
Concept Vocabulary
Adventures You Have Throughout the Day,
pp. 13, 23, 36, 45, 53

Apply
Social Studies
Cooperation, p. 61

Teach
Science Concepts

Animal Characteristics, p. 21
Tools and Machines, p. 34
Camouflage, p. 51
Plant Characteristics, p. 61

Weekly Plan

READING

60-90 minutes

TARGET SKILLS OF THE WEEK

🔁 **Phonics Skill**
Hh/h/

🔁 **Comprehension Skill**
Sequence

DAY 1   PAGES 12-21

Oral Language/Vocabulary

QUESTION OF THE WEEK, 12
What adventures do you have throughout the day?

Build Background, 13
Talk with Me, Sing with Me Chart 19A, 19B

Amazing Words, 13
chores, tidy, bustle, race, story, hungry

Comprehension

Shared Reading, 14-15

Read Big Book

Preview and Predict
Reader Response
🔁 Sequence **T**

Word Work

Phonemic Awareness, 16
Introduce /h/

Phonics, 17
🔁 Connect /h/ to *Hh* **T**

High-Frequency Words, 17
Introduce *do, are, that*

Reread Decodable Reader 18

Grouping Options 6-7

DAY 2   PAGES 22-34

Oral Language/Vocabulary

QUESTION OF THE DAY, 22
What are some adventures your family has had?

Build Background, 23
Talk with Me, Sing with Me Chart 19A, 19B

Let's Learn Amazing Words, 23
chores, tidy

Comprehension

Shared Reading, 24-29

Read Big Book

Recall and Retell
🔁 Sequence **T**

Word Work

Phonemic Awareness, 30
Practice /h/

Phonics, 30
🔁 Connect /h/ to *Hh* **T**

High-Frequency Words, 31
Review *are, that, do*

Read Phonics Story

Grouping Options 6-7

LANGUAGE ARTS

20 minutes

Shared Writing, 19
Grammar: Introduce Naming Parts
Connect to Grammar

Speaking and Listening, 20
Introduce Giving Directions

Modeled Writing, 32
Grammar: Practice Naming Parts
Respond to Literature

Speaking and Listening, 33
Let's Review Amazing Words *hide, scampered*

DAILY JOURNAL WRITING

Day 1 *Draw and label a job you do at home every day.*

Day 2 *Draw and label a job you do at school every day.*

EXTEND YOUR DAY   *30 minutes*
Additional Activities for Full-Day Classrooms

Day 1, 21
Time for Science: Animal Characteristics
Grammar: Naming Parts
Comprehension: Sequence

Day 2, 34
Time for Science: Tools and Machines
Phonics: Initial Sounds
Comprehension: Sequence/Retell

DAILY SUCCESS PREDICTORS
for Adequate Yearly Progress

Monitor Progress and Corrective Feedback

Phonemic Awareness
Check Sound Fluency, *16*
Spiral REVIEW Phonics,
High-Frequency Words

Retelling and Phonics
Check Retelling, *29*
Check Letter-Sound Knowledge, *30*
Spiral REVIEW Phonics,
High-Frequency Words

RESOURCES FOR THE WEEK
- Practice Book K.4, *pp. 3–10*
- Talk with Me Chart 19A
- Sing with Me Chart 19B
- Phonics Songs and Rhymes Chart 19

Grouping Options for Differentiated Instruction
Turn the page for the small group lesson plan.

DAY 3 PAGES 35–43

Oral Language/Vocabulary

QUESTION OF THE DAY, 35
What adventures can we find at school?

Build Background, 36
Talk with Me, Sing with Me Chart 19A, 19B

Let's Learn Amazing Words, 36
bustle, race

Comprehension

Shared Reading, 37
Read Big Book
REVIEW Compare and Contrast **T**
Sequence **T**

Word Work

Phonemic Awareness, 38
Practice /h/

Phonics, 38
Connect /h/ to *Hh* **T**

High-Frequency Words, 39
Practice *are, that, they, do, you, see, look, of*

Read Kindergarten Student Reader K.4.1

Grouping Options 6–7

Modeled Writing, 41
Grammar: REVIEW Sentences
Connect to Phonics

Speaking and Listening, 42
Practice Giving Directions

Day 3 *Draw and label five words that begin with Hh/h/.*

Day 3, 43
Time for Math: Time
Phonics: Making Short *o* Words
Comprehension: Sequence

DAY 4 PAGES 44–51

Oral Language/Vocabulary

QUESTION OF THE DAY, 44
What do you do every night?

Build Background, 45
Talk with Me, Sing with Me Chart 19A, 19B

Let's Learn Amazing Words, 45
story, hungry

Comprehension

Shared Reading, 46
Reread Read Aloud Trade Book
Sequence **T**

Word Work

Phonemic Awareness, 47
REVIEW /o/

Phonics, 47
Connect /h/ to *Hh* **T**

High-Frequency Words, 48
Practice *are, that, see, is, a, they, do*

Read Decodable Reader 19

Grouping Options 6–7

Interactive Writing, 49
Grammar: Practice Naming Parts
Connect to Phonics

Speaking and Listening, 50
Practice Giving Directions

Day 4 *Draw and label three naming words.*

Day 4, 51
Time for Science: Camouflage
Drama: Dramatize the Song
Writing: Labels

DAY 5 PAGES 52–61

Oral Language/Vocabulary

QUESTION OF THE WEEK, 52
What adventures do you have throughout the day?

Build Background, 53
Talk with Me, Sing with Me Chart 19A, 19B

Amazing Words, 53
Check *chores, tidy, bustle, race, story, hungry*

Comprehension

Shared Reading, 54, 58
Read *Read Aloud Anthology "A Day Like Every Other Day"*
Monitor Progress
Check Sequence **T**

Word Work

Phonemic Awareness, 55
Review /h/

Phonics, 55
Connect /h/ to *Hh* **T**

High-Frequency Words, 55
Practice *are, that, do*

Grouping Options 6–7

Monitor Progress, 56–57
Read the Words
Read the Sentences

Shared Writing, 59
Grammar: Review Naming Parts
This Week We...

Speaking and Listening, 60
Review Giving Directions

Day 5 *Draw or write about something you will do this weekend.*

Day 5, 61
Time for Math: Graphing
Time for Science: Plant Characteristics
Time for Social Studies: Cooperation

KEY = Target Skill **T** = Tested Skill

 Word Reading
Check High-Frequency Words and Word Reading, *39*
Spiral REVIEW Phonics, High-Frequency Words

 Phonemic Awareness
Check Phoneme Segmentation, 47
Spiral REVIEW Phonics, High-Frequency Words

Oral Vocabulary
Check Oral Vocabulary, *53*
Assess Phonics and Comprehension, *56–58*

SUCCESS PREDICTOR

Small Group Plan *for Differentiated Instruction*

Daily Plan
AT A GLANCE

Reading
Whole Group
- Oral Language/Vocabulary
- Comprehension
- Word Work

Group Time

Meet with small groups to provide:
- Skill Support
- Reading Support
- Skill Application

Read

This week's lessons for daily group time can be found behind the Differentiated Instruction (DI) tab on pp. DI·1–DI·5.

Language Arts
- Grammar
- Writing
- Speaking and Listening

Use *My Sidewalks on Reading Street* for early reading intervention.

DAY 1

On-Level	Strategic Intervention	Advanced
Teacher-Led *Page 18*	**Teacher-Led** *Page DI·1*	**Teacher-Led** *Page DI·1*
• Blend Sounds to Read Words • **Reread** Decodable Reader 18	• More Practice with *h/h/* • **Read** Listen to Me Reader K.4.1	• **Reread** Independent Leveled Reader K.3.6 • **Reread** for Fluency

(*i*) Independent Activities
While you meet with small groups, have the rest of the class...
- Read self-selected reading
- Complete Practice Book K.4 p. 3
- Visit the Literacy Centers
- Write in their journals

DAY 2

On-Level	Strategic Intervention	Advanced
Teacher-Led *Page 31*	**Teacher-Led** *Page DI·2*	**Teacher-Led** *Page DI·2*
• Practice Word Reading • **Read** Phonics Story	• More Practice with *h/h/* • **Read** Phonics Story	• Apply Phonics Skills • **Read** Decodable Reader 19

(*i*) Independent Activities
While you meet with small groups, have the rest of the class...
- Read self-selected reading
- Complete Practice Book K.4 p. 4
- Visit the Literacy Centers
- Write in their journals

DAY 3

On-Level	Strategic Intervention	Advanced
Teacher-Led *Pages 39–40*	**Teacher-Led** *Page DI·3*	**Teacher-Led** *Page DI·3*
• Practice Word Reading • **Read** Kindergarten Student Reader K.4.1	• Practice Reading Words with *h/h/* • **Read** Kindergarten Student Reader K.4.1	• Extend Word Reading • **Read** Kindergarten Student Reader K.4.1

(*i*) Independent Activities
While you meet with small groups, have the rest of the class...
- Read self-selected reading
- Complete Practice Book K.4 pp. 7, 8
- Visit the Literacy Centers
- Write in their journals

DAY 4

On-Level
Teacher-Led
Page 48
- Blend and Read Words with /h/h/
- **Read** Decodable Reader 19

Strategic Intervention
Teacher-Led
Page DI·4
- Blend and Read Words with /h/h/
- **Read** Decodable Reader 19

Advanced
Teacher-Led
Page LR1
- Extend Word Reading
- **Read** Independent Leveled Reader K.4.1

ⓘ Independent Activities

While you meet with small groups, have the rest of the class...

- Read self-selected reading
- Complete Practice Book K.4 pp. 9, 10
- Visit the Literacy Centers
- Write in their journals

DAY 5

On-Level
Teacher-Led
Pages 56–58
- Word Reading, Sets A and B
- Check Phonics
- Check Comprehension

Strategic Intervention
Teacher-Led
Pages 56, 58, DI·5
- Check Phonics
- Check Comprehension
- Alternate Assessment

Advanced
Teacher-Led
Pages 56–58
- Word Reading, Set B
- Sentence Reading, Set C
- Monitor Comprehension

ⓘ Independent Activities

While you meet with small groups, have the rest of the class...

- Read self-selected reading
- Visit the Literacy Centers
- Write in their journals

ELL

Grouping Group English language learners by their reading ability in English.

Take It to the NET ONLINE
PearsonSuccessNet.com

Peter Afflerbach
For ways to assess engagement, see the article "Engaged Assessment of Engaged Readers" by Scott Foresman author Peter Afflerbach.

TEACHER TALK

A **phonogram** is a vowel and ending consonant(s) found in several words, such as *-at*. **Word families** are words that rhyme and share the same phonogram *(cat, bat, hat)*.

Be sure to schedule time for children to work on the theme project *"Remember When* Album." This week children should make a passport.

Looking Ahead

Name _____ Date _____

My Work Plan

Put an ☒ next to the activities you complete.

Listening
☐ Listen to a story.

Writing
☐ Write about bunnies.
☐ Write in your journal.

Word Work
☐ Connect letter *h* to its sound.

Social Studies
☐ Draw a picture of a chore.

Art
☐ Make a bunny.

Math
☐ Make a pasta pattern.

Wrap Up Your Week Turn your paper over. Draw or write about what you did at school this week. What did you read? What did you learn about your daily adventures?

Unit 4 · Week 1 · *Bunny Day*   35

▲ **Group-Time Survival Guide** p. 35, Weekly Contract

ORAL LANGUAGE

Concept Development

What adventures do you have throughout the day?

 *to build oral vocabulary*

chores	bustle	story
tidy	race	hungry

BUILD

☐ **Question of the Week** Use the Message Board to introduce and discuss the question of the week. This week children will talk, sing, read, and write about the adventures of a bunny family. DAY 1 12

☐ **Let's Talk** Use the Talk with Me Chart to introduce Amazing Words in a visual context. DAY 1 13

Talk with Me, Sing with Me Chart 19A

☐ **Let's Listen** Use the Sing with Me/Background Building Audio CD to build background, vocabulary, and concepts. DAY 1 13

☐ **Let's Sing** Use the Sing with Me Chart to sing a song about things people do every day. DAY 1 13

Talk with Me, Sing with Me Chart 19B

DEVELOP

☐ **Question of the Day/Week** Use the questions in the Message Boards to discuss lesson concepts and how they relate to the unit theme, Let's Explore. DAY 2 22, DAY 3 35, DAY 4 44, DAY 5 52

☐ **Let's Talk** Use the Talk with Me Chart to build background, vocabulary, and concepts. DAY 2 23, DAY 3 36, DAY 4 45, DAY 5 53

☐ **Let's Sing** Use the Sing with Me Chart to sing a song about things people do every day. Ask children to stand up and sing along with you, listening for the Amazing Words as they sing. DAY 2 23, DAY 3 36, DAY 4 45, DAY 5 53

CONNECT

☐ **Wrap Up Your Week!** Connect concepts and vocabulary to next week's lesson. DAY 5 60

CHECK

☐ **Check Oral Vocabulary** To informally assess children's oral vocabulary, have children use each word in a complete sentence. DAY 5 53

PHONEMIC AWARENESS

TEACH

☐ **Introduce /h/** Introduce /h/. DAY 1 16

PRACTICE/APPLY

☐ **Listen for Sounds** Use the Phonics Songs and Rhymes Chart to listen for initial /h/. DAY 2 30

☐ **Practice /h/** Discriminate /h/. DAY 3 38

Phonics Songs and Rhymes Chart 19

RETEACH/REVIEW

☐ **Review** Review /o/. DAY 4 47

☐ **Review** Review /h/. DAY 5 55

☐ **Reteach Lesson** If necessary, reteach /h/. DAY 5 DI-31

① Use assessment data to determine your instructional focus.

② Preview this week's instruction by strand.

③ Choose instructional activities that meet the needs of your classroom.

PHONICS

⊙ CONNECT /h/ to Hh

TEACH

☐ **Connect /h/ to Hh** Introduce *Hh*/h/. **DAY 1** *17*

PRACTICE/APPLY

☐ **Connect /h/ to Hh** Practice *Hh*/h/.
DAY 2 *30*, **DAY 3** *38*

☐ **Phonics Story** Practice reading words with *Hh*/h/ in context. **DAY 2** *31*

☐ **Kindergarten Student Reader K.4.1** Practice reading words with *Hh*/h/ in context. **DAY 3** *40*

☐ **Decodable Reader 19** Practice reading words with *Hh*/h/ in context. **DAY 4** *48*

☐ **Homework** Practice Book K.4, pp. 3, 8.
DAY 1 *17*, **DAY 3** *38*

☐ **Word Work Center** Connect /h/ to *Hh*.
ANY DAY *10*

Phonics Story

Kindergarten Student Reader K.4.1

Decodable Reader 19

RETEACH/REVIEW

☐ **Review** Review words with this week's phonics skill. **DAY 5** *55*

☐ **Reteach Lesson** If necessary, reteach *Hh*/h/. **DAY 5** *DI·31*

☐ **Spiral REVIEW** Review previously taught phonics skills. **DAY 1** *18*, **DAY 2** *31*, **DAY 3** *39*, **DAY 4** *47*

ASSESS

☐ **Word and Sentence Reading** Assess children's ability to read words with *Hh*/h/. **DAY 5** *56-57*

HIGH-FREQUENCY WORDS

HIGH-FREQUENCY WORDS
do   are   that

TEACH

☐ **Introduce** Introduce this week's high-frequency words and add them to the Word Wall. **DAY 1** *17*

PRACTICE/APPLY

☐ **Words in Context** Read high-frequency words in the context of the Phonics Story and Decodable Reader 19.
DAY 2 *31*, **DAY 4** *48*

☐ **Word Wall** Use the Word Wall to review and practice high-frequency words throughout the week. **DAY 3** *39*
DAY 4 *48*, **DAY 5** *55*

☐ **Kindergarten Student Reader K.4.1** Practice this week's high-frequency words in context of reader.
DAY 3 *39-40, DI·3*

☐ **Differentiated Text** Practice this week's high-frequency words in the context of differentiated text. **DAY 1** *DI·1*, **DAY 4** *LR1*

☐ **Homework** Practice Book K.4, p. 4.
DAY 2 *31*

Phonics Story **Decodable Reader 19**

Kindergarten Student Reader K.4.1

Listen to Me Reader K.4.1 **Independent Leveled Reader K.4.1**

RETEACH/REVIEW

☐ **Spiral REVIEW** Review previously taught high-frequency words.
DAY 2 *31*, **DAY 3** *39*, **DAY 4** *48*, **DAY 5** *55*

ASSESS

☐ **Word Reading** Assess children's ability to read this week's high-frequency words. **DAY 5** *56-57*

☑ Customize Your Plan *by Strand*

COMPREHENSION

◉ SKILL SEQUENCE In a story, something happens first, something happens next, and something happens last.

TEACH

❏ **Skill Lesson** Introduce and model *sequence.* DAY 1 *15*

PRACTICE/APPLY

❏ **Skill in Context** Model how to identify *sequence.* Then read *Bunny Day*, guiding children as they identify *sequence.* **DAY 2** *24-29*

❏ **Skill in Context** Reread *Hide, Clyde!* and apply *sequence.* **DAY 4** *46*

❏ **Leveled Text** Apply *sequence* to leveled text. DAY 4 *LR1*

Big Book

Trade Book

Independent Leveled Reader K.4.1

ASSESS

❏ **Check** Read "A Day Like Every Other Day." Then have children practice *sequence.* DAY 5 *54*

❏ **Assess** Use the blackline master on p. 58 to assess children's understanding of *sequence.* DAY 5 *54, 58*

Read Aloud Anthology

RETEACH/REVIEW

❏ **Review Compare and Contrast** Review definition of compare and contrast and apply to *Bunny Day*. **DAY 3** *37*

❏ **Reteach Lesson** If necessary, reteach *sequence.* **DAY 5** *DI·31*

WRITING

TEACH

❏ **Write Together** Engage children in writing activities that develop language, grammar, and writing skills and practice phonics skills. Include independent writing as an extension of group writing activities.

Shared Writing
❏ **Connect to Grammar** DAY 1 *19*
❏ **This Week We...** DAY 5 *59*

Modeled Writing
❏ **Respond to Literature** DAY 2 *32*
❏ **Connect to Phonics** DAY 3 *41*

Interactive Writing
❏ **Connect to Phonics** DAY 4 *49*

PRACTICE/APPLY

❏ **Daily Journal Writing** Have children write about concepts and literature in their journals. **EVERY DAY** *4-5*

❏ **Writing Center** Write about bunnies. **ANY DAY** *11*

7c Let's Explore • Week 1

GRAMMAR

TEACH

❑ **Introduce** Introduce naming parts. DAY 1 *19*

PRACTICE/APPLY

❑ **Practice** Practice naming parts. DAY 2 *32*, DAY 4 *49*

❑ **Daily Fix-It** Have children find and correct errors in capitalization and punctuation. DAY 1 *19*, DAY 2 *32*, DAY 3 *41*, DAY 4 *49*, DAY 5 *59*

RETEACH/REVIEW

❑ **Review** Review last week's grammar skill, sentences. DAY 3 *41*

❑ **Review** Review naming parts. DAY 5 *59*

SPEAKING AND LISTENING

TEACH

❑ **Give Directions** Introduce and model giving directions. DAY 1 *20*

PRACTICE/APPLY

❑ **Practice** Have children practice giving directions. DAY 3 *42*, DAY 4 *50*

REVIEW

❑ **Review** Review giving directions. Then have children sing two-step directions. DAY 5 *60*

INQUIRY PROJECT

TEACH

❑ **Unit Inquiry Project** Allow time for children to work on the theme project "*Remember When* Album." Have children make a passport. **ANY DAY** *xxiii*

Resources for Differentiated Instruction

Readers

Emergent

Listen to Me Reader

▶ **Oral Language**
Develop oral vocabulary.

▶ **Phonemic Awareness**
/h/ in initial position

Decodable Words
Hap   hop   hot

▶ **High-Frequency Words**
are   that   do   is
a   you

On-Level

Kindergarten Student Reader

▶ **Connected Text**
Realistic Fiction

Phonics: *Hh*/h/
hit   hot

▶ **High-Frequency Words**
are   that   do

▶ **Spiral Review:**
Decodable Words
and   in   Nan   Nat
can   top   bin   it
tin   fan   nap   man
at   sip   not

High-Frequency Words
a   you   see   the
of   they   look

Independent

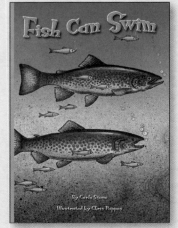

Leveled Reader K.4.1
Independent Leveled Reader

Comprehension: Sequence
Identify beginning, middle, and end in order.

▶ **Concept**
What adventures you have in a day

▶ **Social Studies Standards**
Wants and needs

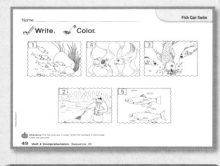

Leveled Reader, TE, LR2

ELL Resources

- ELL Poster 19
- ELL and Transition Handbook
- ELL Notes in Teacher's Edition, pp. 12–61

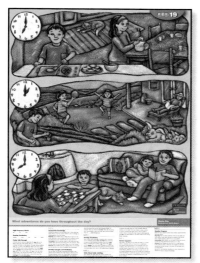

ELL Poster 19

ELL and Transition Handbook

My Sidewalks Early Reading Intervention

For students who need intensive intervention

- Effectiveness proved by scientific research
- Instruction focused on early reading success predictors
- 30 minutes of daily small-group instruction

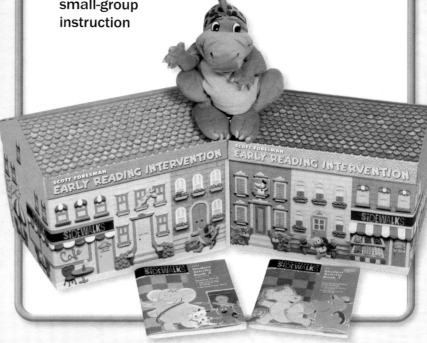
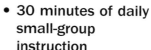

ONLINE

PearsonSuccessNet.com

Use the Online Database of over 600 books to

- Download and print additional copies of this week's leveled readers
- Listen to the readers being read online
- Search for more titles focused on this week's skills, topic, and content

Readers' Theater Anthology

Readers' Theater Anthology

- Six scripts to build fluency
- Poetry for oral interpretation

School + Home

Homework

- Family Times Newsletter

Take-Home Books

- Kindergarten Student Readers
- Decodable Readers
- Listen to Me Readers
- Independent Leveled Readers

Literacy Centers

Listening

Let's Read Along

- *Bunny Day*
- AudioText CD

Audio CD

Journal Writing

- **Day One** Draw and label a job you do at home every day.

- **Day Two** Draw and label a job you do at school every day.

- **Day Three** Draw and label five words that begin with *Hh*/h/.

- **Day Four** Draw and label three naming words.

- **Day Five** Draw or write about something you will do this weekend.

Word Work

Feed the Horse

MATERIALS
a large paper grocery bag, Patterns Book p. 18: *haystack* and *horse,* haystack patterns (4–5 per child), crayons

Connect /h/ to *Hh*

1. Glue the horse cutout to the paper grocery bag.
2. Have children draw and label objects that begin with h/h/ on each haystack.
3. Then have them place their "/h/ haystack" in the bag.

CENTER TIP You may wish to provide some pictures of things that begin with /h/.

Phonics Activities CD — This interactive CD provides additional practice.

Art

Paper Bunny

MATERIALS
an outline of a bunny, white construction paper, cotton balls, crayons

Make a Bunny

1. Have children cut out a bunny.
2. Then have children tear white paper into small pieces.
3. Have children glue the torn white paper to the bunny so it is completely covered.
4. Add eyes, nose, and mouth with crayons. Last, add a cotton ball for its tail.

CENTER TIP Have an example hanging for children to see. You may also wish to have baby wipes available for children to wipe their fingers.

Scott Foresman Reading Street Centers Survival Kit
Use the *Bunny Day* materials from the Reading Street
Centers Survival Kit to organize this week's centers.

 Writing

Bunny Facts

MATERIALS
a variety of writing paper and
utensils, a word poster,
Patterns Book pp. 23, 59

Write About Bunnies
1. Make a word poster specific to rabbits by copying the following patterns in the Patterns Book: *rabbits, carrots, radishes, rake, flowers.*
2. Color and cut out the patterns and mount them on a large poster.
3. Then label the pictures so children can use the words in their writing.
4. Have children write about bunnies.

bunny
carrots
bunnies
radishes
flowers
rake

 Social Studies

Helping Hands

MATERIALS
card stock hand tracers,
various colors of construction
paper, scissors, crayons

Chores at Home
1. Have each child trace a hand onto construction paper and cut it out.
2. Have children illustrate a job they do to help at home.
3. Then have them write or dictate a label describing their job.

CONNECT TO MATH You may wish to create a "hand graph" to compare and contrast jobs at home.

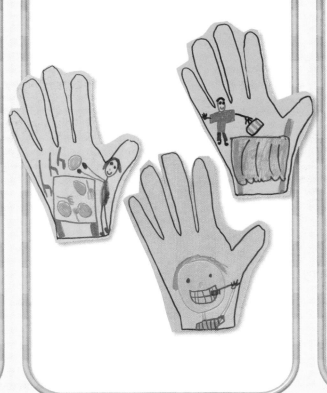

₁₂3 Math

Pasta Patterns

MATERIALS
strips of construction paper
or sentence strips; three
different types of pasta—
wheels, shells, and rotini; glue

Make a Pattern
1. Place pasta in three separate bowls.
2. Have children make a pattern by placing the three types of pasta on their strip of paper. You may wish to provide examples of possible patterns for children to copy.
3. Then have them glue the pasta into place.

CENTER TIP You may wish to use buttons, construction paper shapes, letters, or fabric squares as alternatives to pasta.

 **ALL CENTERS**

Day 1
AT A GLANCE

Oral Language and Vocabulary
Calendar
Message Board
Build Background

Shared Reading
Big Book *Bunny Day*
 Skill Sequence

Word Work

Phonemic Awareness
Introduce /h/
Compare and Contrast Sounds

Phonics
Connect /h/ to *Hh*
Blend Words
H/F Words *are, that, do*

Read

Group Time < Differentiated Instruction

Language Arts
Grammar: Naming Parts
Shared Writing: Use Naming Parts in Sentences
Speaking and Listening: Give Directions

Materials
- Calendar
- Talk with Me, Sing with Me Chart 19A, 19B
- Sing with Me/Background Building Audio CD
- Big Books *Bunny Day*, *The Little School Bus*
- AudioText CD
- Picture Cards: pp. 16, 19
- Alphabet Cards: *Aa, Hh, Ii, Oo, Ss, Tt*
- Decodable Reader 18
- Daily Fix-It Transparency 19

Calendar

Name the day and date
Ask a volunteer to find today's date on the calendar. Have children say the day, month, date, and year together.

Name letters in the days
- What day is today? Let's name the letters in the name for the day.
- What is the first day of the week? Name the letters.
- What is the last day of the week? Name the letters.

Message Board

Question of the week
Tell children that they will talk, sing, read, and write about the adventures of a bunny family.

Write and read the question as you track the print. Encourage children to respond in complete sentences.

> ## What adventures do you have throughout the day?

Build Background Use the Day 1 instruction on ELL Poster 19 to assess knowledge and develop concepts.

ELL Poster 19

Build Background

LET'S TALK

Build concept Display Talk with Me Chart 19A. The pictures show different things people do every day. Look at this family eating dinner. I eat dinner with my family every night. What else do you see people doing in the pictures? Do you do any of those things? Prompt children to respond in complete sentences.

Talk with Me, Sing with Me Chart

Build oral vocabulary This week we will be talking about adventures we have throughout the day. We are going to learn six new words. Listen as I say the words; you may know some of them: *chores, tidy, bustle, race, story,* and *hungry.*

LET'S LISTEN

Share Background Building Audio Play the CD that features the adventures a girl has throughout the day.

Sing with Me/Background Building Audio CD

LET'S SING/PHONOLOGICAL AWARENESS

Sing "Get Up, Get Up, It's a Beautiful Day" Display Sing with Me Chart 19B. Tell children that they are going to sing a song about things people do every day. Read the title and describe the pictures. Sing the song several times to the tune of "Row, Row, Row Your Boat." Encourage children to stand up and sing with you.

Get Up, Get Up, It's a Beautiful Day

Get up, get up, it's a beautiful day,
We have so much to do!
Let's tidy up and do our chores,
It's so much fun with you!

Talk with Me, Sing with Me Chart

Listen for /d/ Sing the first verse of the song again. Have children clap their hands each time they hear /d/. Repeat with other sounds.

Sing with Me/Background Building Audio CD

Amazing Words to build oral vocabulary

- chores
- bustle
- story
- tidy
- race
- hungry

Options Before Reading

Activate Prior Knowledge

Tell About Today Ask children to tell you about things they will do today at school.

- What will you do first?
- What will you do next?
- What will you do last?

Oral Language

What Happened? Recall something that happened to children when they arrived at school today.

- What did you do when you first arrived today?
- What did you do next?
- What did you do last?

Develop Story Concepts

Make a Story Display the cover of *Bunny Day.* Create a story about what the bunnies are doing in the picture.

OBJECTIVES

- Preview and predict.
- Listen to a story.

Materials

- Big Books *Bunny Day, The Little School Bus*

EXTEND SKILLS

Concepts of Print Guide children to identify the title, author, and illustrator.

Comprehension

MODEL READING STRATEGIES

Preview and predict

Display *Bunny Day.* Look at the cover; tell me what you see.

 I see a father rabbit and a bunny. They are lying in the grass looking at the clouds.

The title of this book is *Bunny Day.* What do you think this story will be about? Let's read to find out.

LET'S READ *Bunny Day*

Model fluent reading

Read the story with expression for enjoyment.

Big Book   **AudioText CD**

Shared Reading

ROUTINE

Day 1	Day 2	Day 3	Day 4	Day 5
Preview and make predictions about *Bunny Day.* Read the whole book for enjoyment. Introduce comprehension skill, sequence.	**Reread** *Bunny Day.* Use the Shared Reading Notes to engage children in a conversation about the story. Apply comprehension skill, sequence.	**Reread** *Bunny Day.* Develop oral vocabulary by naming objects and actions. Review comprehension skill, compare and contrast.	**Reread** *Hide, Clyde!* Apply comprehension skill, sequence.	**Read** "A Day Like Every Other Day" in the *Read Aloud Anthology.* Assess comprehension skill, sequence.

Text to World READER RESPONSE

Respond to literature

Have children sit in a circle, and hand one child a bean bag. Tell children to pass it around the circle until you say stop. Ask whoever is holding the bean bag to name one thing the bunnies do every day.

STRATEGY Predict

Check predictions

- What did you think the story would be about?
- What are some things the bunnies do during the morning, during the afternoon, or during the night?

Use the following questions to guide discussion.

- What is your favorite part of the story?
- Why do you like that part of the story?

⦿ INTRODUCE SKILL Sequence

Define Sequence

- In a story, something happens first, something happens next, and something happens last.
- The order in which these things happen is called the *sequence.*

Think Aloud First, the bunnies eat breakfast. Next, they do their chores and eat lunch. Last, the bunny children have story time and go to sleep.

Recall sequence

Display the Big Book *The Little School Bus.* Help children recall the order, or sequence, in which the animals were picked up for school.

- First, the little goat got on the bus.
- Next, the pretty pig, the sly fox, the fuzzy chick, a hairy bear, and a wiggly worm got on the bus.
- Last, the sleepy sheep got on and went back to sleep.

Relate sequence to everyday life

During the day we do things in order. Think about what you do when you arrive at school. What are three things you do when you arrive at school? Tell us what you do first, next, and last.

Text to Self

OBJECTIVES

- Respond to literature.
- Check predictions.
- Introduce sequence.

Skills Trace	
⦿ Sequence	
Introduce/Teach	TE: K.1 141, 150; K.2 327, 336; K.4 15, 24, 141, 150
Practice	TE: K.1 165, 174; K.2 287, 296; K.4 37, 46, 163, 172 PB: K.1 27, 29; K.2 47, 49; K.4 7, 9, 27, 29
Reteach/Review	TE: K.1 291, DI-47; K.2 99, 349, DI-49; K.4 DI-45, DI-47; K.5 101
Assess	TE: K.1 186, 380–382; K.2 308, 376–378; K.4 58, 184, 380–382; Unit 4 Benchmark Test

Ⓔ Ⓛ Ⓛ

Access Content Demonstrate the sequence using a flow chart or Graphic Organizer 21.

First
Eat breakfast.

⬇

Second
Do chores, eat lunch.

⬇

Third
Have story time, go to sleep.

OBJECTIVE

● Introduce /h/.

Skills Trace	
⊙ Consonant *Hh*/h/	
Introduce/Teach	TE: K.4 16–17, 30, 38
Practice	TE: K.4 30, 38, 41, 49 PB: K.4 3, 5–6, 8
Reteach/Review	TE: K.4 55, 111, DI-31
Assess	TE: K.4 56–57, 380–382; Unit 4 Benchmark Test

Materials

● Picture Cards:

doll	hat	hammer
mop	hippopotamus	hose

● Big Book *Bunny Day*
● Alphabet Cards: *Aa, Hh, Ii, Oo, Ss, Tt*
● Decodable Reader 18

ELL

Support Phonemic Awareness
English language learners may pronounce /h/ with a harsher sound that resembles the sound of the letter *j* in Spanish. Show how /h/ is pronounced by puffing air from the throat and provide extra practice with /h/ words.

Phonemic Awareness

INTRODUCE /h/

Introduce initial /h/
Today we will learn a new sound. Listen carefully as I say the sound: /h/, /h/, /h/. Say it with me: /h/, /h/, /h/. Listen to these words that begin with /h/ and say each word with me: *hat, hen, hose,* and *house.*

Compare and contrast sounds
Display the *hat* Picture Card. This is a hat. *Hat* begins with /h/; /h/, *hat.* What sound does *hat* begin with? Display the *mop* Picture Card. This is a picture of a mop. The first sound in *mop* is /m/. Do *hat* and *mop* both begin with /h/? No, *hat* and *mop* do not both begin with /h/. Which word begins with /h/, *hat* or *mop*? Continue with the following pairs of Picture Cards: *hat, hose; house, doll;* and *hammer, hippopotamus.*

Picture Cards

Name the sound
I am going to read a list of words. Tell me the first sound you hear in each word. The first word is *hill.* What is the beginning sound? (/h/) Continue with these words: *him, bed, hen, hop, mop, boy, moon,* and *hose.*

Monitor Progress | **Check Sound Fluency**

Listen for /h/ Say two words: *ham, kite.* Have children identify the word that begins with /h/. Continue with *hot, slide; hip, tent;* and *hut, soap.*

If... children cannot identify initial /h/,
then... have them say /h/ several times and ask: Can you feel the air explode when you say /h/? Practice with /h/, *hat;* /h/, *ham;* /h/, *help;* /h/, *horn.*

SUCCESS PREDICTOR

▶ **Day 1** Check Sound Fluency	**Day 2** Check Retelling/Letter-Sound Knowledge	**Day 3** Check High-Frequency Words/Word Reading	**Day 4** Check Phoneme Segmentation	**Day 5** Check Oral Vocabulary/Assess Progress

Phonics

🔄 CONNECT /h/ to *Hh*

Introduce Hh/h/

Write the word *happy* on the board. Point to the word *happy*. This is the word *happy*. The word *happy* begins with the letter *h*. The sound for *h* is /h/, /h/, /h/, *happy*.

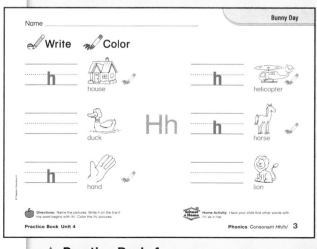

Hh
helicopter

Alphabet Card

Recognize *Hh*

Encourage children to stand up and hunt for *h*'s in the classroom.

Connect /h/ to *Hh*

Display the *Hh* Alphabet Card. Point to the helicopter. What is the name of this flying machine? *Helicopter* begins with /h/. Point to the letters on the card. What is the letter for /h/? Yes, *h* is the letter for /h/.

Point to the letters at the top of the card. The name for both of these letters is *h*. This is the uppercase *H* and this is the lowercase *h*. Guide children to draw the uppercase and lowercase letters *Hh* with their fingers.

Review letter names and sounds

What is the name of this letter? *(h)* What is the sound for this letter? *(/h/)* Continue with *Aa, Ii, Oo, Ss,* and *Tt* to prepare for the blending activity.

BLEND SOUNDS

Blend *Hh*/h/ words

Write the word *hat* on the board. This is the word *hat*. To say this word, we start with the beginning sound /h/, and then we blend the ending sounds /a/ and /t/. The word is *hat*.

Say the sounds with me: /h/ /a/ /t/. Now let's blend the sounds together: /h/ /a/ /t/, *hat*. Follow the blending practice routine with the following words: *hot, hit, sat,* and *sit*.

Word Wall HIGH-FREQUENCY WORDS

Introduce *do, are, that*

Display *do*. This is the word *do*. You cannot blend the sounds in this word. Let's say the letters together: *d, o, do*. Continue with the words *that* and *are*. Let's look in the book *Bunny Day* to find *that, are,* and *do*. Add the words to the Word Wall.

do   are   that

▲ **Practice Book 4**
Consonant *Hh*/h/, p. 3

SUCCESS PREDICTOR

Spiral REVIEW PREPARE TO READ

Review words Continue guided blending practice with these words from last week's Decodable Reader 18 *Tip the Top:*

Rod	**tip**	**top**	**Don**
did	**not**	**cot**	**Dot**

Review high-frequency words Write the word *you* on the board. This is the word *you*. What is this word? Continue the word reading routine with the words *the, is, of,* and *they.*

Group Time

On-Level

Reread Decodable Reader 18. Use the Small Group Reading **Routine.**

Strategic Intervention

Read Listen to Me Reader K.4.1. More practice with *Hh*/h/, p. DI·1.

Advanced

Reread Independent Leveled Reader K.3.6. Use the reading routine on p. DI·1. Reread to build fluency.

ELL

Group English language learners by their reading ability in English.

i Independent Activities

Self-Selected Reading See pp. TR14–15 for a bibliography of books related to the weekly concept.

Practice Book Consonant *Hh*/h/, p. 3

Centers Use the center activities on pp. 10–11 to practice this week's skills.

Journal Writing Draw and label a job you do at home every day.

Small Group Reading

DAY 1 ROUTINE

1 **Model Fluent Reading** Have children finger point as you read a page.

2 **Read Chorally** Have children finger point as they chorally read the page. Continue reading page by page, repeating steps 1 and 2.

3 **Read Individually** Have children read aloud a page in their group.

4 **Reread and Monitor Progress** As you listen to individual children reread, monitor progress and provide support.

Decodable Reader

HANDWRITING

Write uppercase *H* and lowercase *h* Words that begin with /h/ are written with either an uppercase *H* or a lowercase *h*. Remember, we use the uppercase letter at the beginning of sentences or the first letter of a person's name, such as *Harry*. Write *Harry* on the board. Follow the stroke instructions below. Now, holding your pencils in the correct position, write *H* on your paper. Repeat these instructions with lowercase *h*.

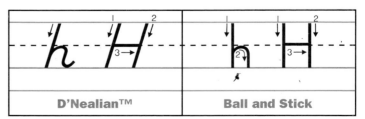

D'Nealian™	Ball and Stick

Shared Writing

GRAMMAR Naming Parts

Introduce naming parts

Show the *cat* Picture Card. Then write this sentence on the board: *The cat ran fast.* Read the sentence and have children read it with you. Every sentence has a naming part. That is the part that tells whom or what the sentence is about. What is the naming part of this sentence? *The cat ran fast.* (the cat)

Identify naming parts

Continue with sentences for the following Picture Cards: *kite—The kite was blue; man—The man had a black car; sun—The sun shone brightly.*

LET'S WRITE Connect to Grammar

Use naming parts in sentences

Let's make a list of naming parts or words that name people, animals, places, and things. Guide children to name a variety of items. Now we will use some of our naming words to write a sentence. Let's use *bunny.*

The bunny hid in the field.

Revise and edit

The first word in a sentence should begin with an uppercase letter. Did I do that? Every sentence should end with a period. Did I do that? Write three more sentences with children.

Independent writing

Have children write or dictate their own sentences using words from the list the class wrote together. Then have them illustrate their sentences. Have children read their sentences and identify the naming part of the sentence.

The boy eats dinner.

OBJECTIVES

- Introduce naming parts.
- Write sentences with naming parts.

Materials

- Picture Cards:
  cat   kite   man
  sun

DAILY FIX-IT

dan hit the ball
(Dan hit the ball.)

This week's practice sentences appear on Daily Fix-It Transparency 19.

Writing ROUTINE

Day 1 **Shared Writing** Connect to grammar.

Day 2 **Modeled Writing** Respond to literature.

Day 3 **Modeled Writing** Connect to phonics.

Day 4 **Interactive Writing** Connect to phonics.

Day 5 **Shared Writing** Write about this week's literature.

Speaking and Listening

GIVE DIRECTIONS

Introduce giving directions

When I tell you how to do a project, I am giving you directions. Directions are the information you need to do a project. When I give you directions, I try to speak loudly and clearly. I give the directions in the order that you will need to do them. **Ask children to recall a time when they have followed your directions.**

Model giving directions

I am going to give directions on how to wash your hands. I want you to follow my directions as you pretend to wash your hands. **Have children stand up as you give directions as they pretend to wash their hands.**

Practice giving directions

Give directions for making a peanut butter sandwich incorrectly. Guide children to realize that your sandwich directions would not work. Encourage children to give the sandwich directions in the correct order by using words such as *first, next, then,* and *last.*

Wrap Up Your Day!

✓ **Oral Language** Today we read about a bunny family and the things they do all day. Does your family do any of the things that the bunny family does?

✓ **Comprehension** There are things we do at school every day. What is the first thing we do when we arrive at school? What do we do after snack time? What is the last thing we do before we go home?

✓ **Grammar** Display *Bunny Day.* Point to the bunny on the cover. Let's make sentences using *bunny. Bunny slept in the woods.* What is the naming part of the sentence?

 Homework Send home this week's Family Times newsletter.

PREVIEW Day 2

Tomorrow we will read about the bunny family again.

EXTEND Your Day

TIME FOR Science

Animal Characteristics

Materials Big Book *Bunny Day;* Picture Cards: *duck* and *rabbit;* chart paper

Describe Animal Characteristics Display the *rabbit* Picture Card. Use these questions to discuss a rabbit's characteristics.

- How many legs does a rabbit have?
- Are rabbits quiet or noisy?
- What do rabbits eat?

List children's responses on chart paper.

Display the *duck* Picture Card. Ask children to describe the characteristics of a duck. Then ask children to compare and contrast the duck and the rabbit.

Write a Sentence Have each child write or dictate a sentence comparing a rabbit and a duck. Then have them illustrate their sentence. Gather children's work together to create a class book.

	Rabbit	Duck
Legs	4 legs	2 legs
Quiet	quiet	
Noisy		noisy
Food	eats vegetables and plants	plants

Grammar

Naming Parts

Illustrate Naming Parts Divide a paper into four sections for each child. Have children draw four nouns—a person, animal, place, and thing— that could be the naming part of a sentence. Then have them write or dictate a label for each picture.

Comprehension

Sequence

Dramatize *Bunny Day*
Walk through the illustrations in *Bunny Day.* Have children describe what the bunnies are doing. Small groups of children can dramatize what the bunnies are doing. For example, on pages 8 and 9 have children dramatize making beds, brushing teeth, and sweeping floors. Continue the drama activity with pages 10–11, 16–17, and 22–23.

Day 2
AT A GLANCE

Oral Language and Vocabulary
Calendar
Message Board
Build Background

Shared Reading
Big Book *Bunny Day*
Strategy Recall and Retell
⊙ **Skill** Sequence
Skill Interpret Graphic Sources:
    Illustrations

Word Work
Phonemic Awareness
Listen for /h/

Phonics
⊙ Connect /h/ to *Hh*
Blend Sounds
H/F Words *are, that, do*
Phonics Story *I Have!*

Read

Group Time < Differentiated Instruction

Language Arts
Grammar: Naming Parts
Modeled Writing: Write About
    Things We Do Every Day
Speaking and Listening:
    Expand Vocabulary

Materials
- Calendar
- Talk with Me, Sing with Me Chart, 18A, 19A, 19B
- Sing with Me/Background Building Audio CD
- Big Book *Bunny Day*
- AudioText CD
- Picture Cards: p. 32
- Phonics Songs and Rhymes Chart 19
- Phonics Songs and Rhymes Audio CD
- Alphabet Cards: *Aa, Dd, Hh, Ii, Oo, Pp, Tt,* keyboard
- Phonics Story *I Have!*

Calendar

Name the day and date
Have children find today on the calendar. Ask volunteers to name the day, month, date, and year.

Count the number of syllables
Point to the first day of the week. Say the name *Sunday.* Have children say the word and clap the number of syllables. Continue with the other days of the week.

Message Board

Question of the day
Write and read the question as you track the print. Encourage children to respond in complete sentences.

> ## What are some adventures your family has had?

Review high-frequency words
Circle the word *are* in the question. Have children say the word as you point to it. Then have them use *that* and *do* in sentences.

Build Background Use the Day 2 instruction on ELL Poster 19 to practice the Develop Vocabulary words.

ELL Poster 19

ORAL LANGUAGE

Build Background

LET'S TALK/LET'S SING

Develop oral vocabulary

Display Talk with Me Chart 19A. Point to the picture showing a child doing a *chore*.

- This child is doing a job, or a *chore*.
- Can you find a picture of a child making something neat, or *tidy*?

Sing "Get Up, Get Up, It's a Beautiful Day"

Display Sing with Me Chart 19B. The words *chores* and *tidy* are in the song. Ask children to listen for the words as you sing "Get Up, Get Up, It's a Beautiful Day."

Talk with Me, Sing with Me Chart

Get Up, Get Up, It's a Beautiful Day

Get up, get up, it's a beautiful day,
We have so much to do!
Let's tidy up and do our chores,
It's so much fun with you!

 Sing with Me/Background Building Audio CD

LET'S LEARN AMAZING WORDS

 **to build oral vocabulary**

- chores
- bustle
- story
- tidy
- race
- hungry

Oral Vocabulary   chores   tidy

DAY 2 ROUTINE

1 **Introduce** The bunnies do *chores*. *Chores* are jobs you do to make your home clean. What is our new word for jobs to make your home clean?

Demonstrate Putting toys away is a *chore*. Playing with your toys is not a *chore*. What are some *chores* you do at home?

2 **Introduce** The bunnies make their home *tidy*. *Tidy* is another word for neat or clean. What is our new word for neat or clean?

Demonstrate We put away things in our room to make it *tidy*, or neat. We fold our clothes to keep them *tidy*. What are some things in the room that we keep *tidy*?

3 **Review** We talked about two words today: *chores* and *tidy*. Which word means "jobs," *chores* or *tidy?* Which word means "to clean up," *chores* or *tidy?*

4 **Apply** Have children use *chores* and *tidy* in complete sentences. Have them act out the words.

Activate Prior Knowledge Ask children what words in their home languages are used for *tidy* and *chore*. For example, Spanish words such as *limpio* (clean, neat) and *ordinado* (ordered, neat) are used for *tidy*.

2

OBJECTIVES

- Recall story events.
- Recognize sequence of a story.
- Interpret graphic sources: illustrations.

Materials

- Big Book *Bunny Day*

Access Content If you made a graphic organizer showing sequence, refer back to it. If not, make one now and ask children what the bunnies do first, next, and last.

| **First** |
| Eat breakfast. |

| **Second** |
| Do chores, eat lunch. |

| **Third** |
| Have story time, go to sleep. |

Comprehension

MODEL READING STRATEGY
Recall and Retell

Retell the story

Using the pictures as prompts, invite children to retell the story.

Open to pages 6–7. The bunnies are coming down to breakfast. They are going to start the day. They do lots of things throughout the day. Tell me about the bunny family.

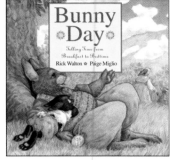

Big Book

SKILL Sequence

Model identifying sequence

Remind children that events in the story happen in order, or sequence, to help you understand what is happening. Using the illustrations in the story, model how to identify the story sequence in the morning.

 First, the bunnies eat breakfast. Next, they do some chores. Last, they have a picnic lunch.

LET'S READ *Bunny Day*

Reread the story

Ask children to listen carefully to what happens first, next, and last, or sequence, as you read. Use the Shared Reading Notes to prompt conversation about *Bunny Day*.

 AudioText CD

TEACHING TIP

Telling Time Although most children do not know how to tell time, some may know that the clocks in the pictures give clues about the time of day. Reinforce this by saying:

Yes, the clock helps us know what time it is. This clock says it is 8:00. What other things in the picture help us to know whether it is 8:00 in the morning or 8:00 in the evening?

Pages 6–7

"Bunnies, it is getting late!"
Father Rabbit says at eight.
"Time for breakfast, bunnies dear.
The sun is up and morning's here."

Shared Reading Notes

Point to the clock. It's eight o'clock. What do the bunnies do at eight? *Child may respond:* get up

- The bunnies get up and eat breakfast. Tell me about the bunnies in the picture. **open-ended**

- How many bunnies are there? *wh-* **question**

Develop Vocabulary clock, bunnies, rabbit

Pages 8–9

Faces washed until they shine,
Bunnies dress themselves at nine,
Brush their teeth, and do their chores,
Making beds and sweeping floors.

What chores do the bunnies do at nine? *Child may respond:* make beds and sweep floors

- The bunnies make their beds and sweep the floors. **Point to each bunny and ask:** What is this bunny doing? *wh-* **question**

Pages 10–11

Brooms are put away, and then,
Bunnies go outside at ten
To help their father plant some seeds,
Water flowers, pull up weeds.

How are the bunnies helping their father? *Child may respond:* planting seeds, watering flowers, pulling weeds

- The bunnies are helping their father in the garden. What are the bunnies doing? *wh-* **question**

Shared Reading Notes

Why do the bunnies get to play? *Child may respond:* Their chores are done.

• The bunnies play because their chores are done. What happens when the bunnies finish their chores?

***wh-* question**

Develop Vocabulary play

Pages 12–13

Bunnies bustle, and, thank heaven,
   All is tidy by eleven.
Chores need doing every day,
   But now the bunnies get to play.

What are the bunnies having for lunch? *Child may respond:* fruit and sandwiches

• The bunnies are having fruit and sandwiches for lunch. What do the bunnies have for lunch? ***wh-* question**

Activate Prior Knowledge Ask what kinds of food children eat for lunch at home.

Pages 14–15

Bunnies will be hungry soon.
   Picnic's spread at twelve—that's noon.
Fruit and sandwich taste so good.
   "Who would like some more?" "I would!"

What are the bunnies doing? *Child may respond:* racing

• The bunnies are having a hopping race. What are some other ways to race? **distancing**

Pages 16–17

"Ready, set? Now bunnies run!"
   Mother Rabbit says at one.
"Race and chase and bounce a bit.
   That will keep my bunnies fit."

Pages 18–19

A little rest is good for you.
It's time for bunny naps at two.
All around the house we see
Bunnies resting peacefully.

Shared Reading Notes

Why do the bunnies nap? *Child may respond:* They are tired.

- The bunnies take a nap because it is good for them. Why are the bunnies resting? **wh- question**

Develop Vocabulary nap
Expand Vocabulary peacefully

Pages 20–21

"Who will take a walk with me?"
Mother Rabbit says at three.
Lots of little bunny feet
Go out the door and down the street.

What do the bunnies do at three? *Child may respond:* take a walk

- The bunny family takes a walk at three. Let's read this page together. (Encourage children to join in as you reread the page several times.) **completion**

Pages 22–23

Pull the paper from the drawer,
Artists go to work at four.
Pens and crayons, scissors, tape—
Bunny art is taking shape.

What are the bunnies doing? *Child may respond:* cutting, painting, coloring

- The bunnies are doing different art projects. **Point to each bunny and ask: What is this bunny doing?** **wh- question**

Expand Vocabulary artist

Shared Reading Notes

What do the bunnies do at five? *Child may respond:* eat dinner

- The bunnies eat dinner at five. Let's read this page together. (Encourage children to join in as you reread the page several times.) **completion**

Pages 24–25

Hungry bunnies all arrive
In the dining room at five,
Set the table, take a seat,
Put their napkins on, and eat.

What are the bunnies doing? *Child may respond*: playing; playing games

- The bunnies are playing different games outside. Why do you think the bunnies can only play one more game? **wh- question**

Activate Prior Knowledge Ask children what games they see in the picture on pages 26–27. Use gestures to show how the games are played. Ask what games the children play at home.

Pages 26–27

Every bunny quickly picks
One last game to play at six:
Hide-and-seek or steal the flag,
Jacks or marbles, swings or tag.

How many books do the bunnies want to read? *Child may respond:* four

- The bunnies want their father to read four books. How many books do the bunnies want their father to read?
wh- question

Pages 28–29

Bunnies think that books are heaven.
Story time begins at seven.
One book, two books, three books, four.
"Please, please, Father, read some more!"

Pages 30–31

"Bunnies, it is getting late,"
Mother Rabbit says at eight.
"Into bed. Turn off the light.
Sleep well, bunnies dear. Good night!"

Page 32

Text copyright ©2002 by Rick Walton. Illustration copyright © 2002 by Paige Miglio. All rights reserved. This edition is reprinted by arrangement with Harper Collins Publishers. All Rights Reserved. Big Book version of Bunny Day published by Scott Foresman.
ISBN: 0-328-14710-9
Copyright © 2007, Pearson Education, Inc.
All Rights Reserved. Printed in the United States of America. This publication is protected by Copyright, and permission should be obtained from the publisher prior to any prohibited reproduction, storage in a retrieval system, or transmission in any form by any means, electronic, mechanical, photocopying, recording, or likewise. For information regarding permission(s), write to: Permissions Department, Scott Foresman, 1900 East Lake Avenue, Glenview, Illinois 60025.
1 2 3 4 5 6 7 8 9 10 V010 12 11 10 09 08 07 06 05

Shared Reading Notes

What do the bunnies do at eight? *Child may respond:* go to bed

- The bunnies go to bed at eight. Tell me what each bunny is doing.
  open-ended

Why are Mother and Father Bunny resting? *Child may respond:* They are tired.

- Mother and Father Bunny are tired because they were busy all day. What did Mother and Father Bunny do? **open-ended**

Monitor Progress | Check Retelling *Bunny Day*

Picture Walk and Retell Have children use the pictures in *Bunny Day* to retell the story.

If... children have difficulty retelling the story,

then... use the Retelling Cards and the Retelling Rubric to help them move toward fluent retelling.

SUCCESS PREDICTOR

Day 1
Check Sound Fluency

▶ **Day 2**
Check Retelling/ Letter-Sound Knowledge

Day 3
Check High-Frequency Words/ Word Reading

Day 4
Check Phoneme Segmentation

Day 5
Check Oral Vocabulary/ Assess Progress

Scoring Rubric | Retelling

Rubric 4 3 2 1	4	3	2	1
Setting	describes time and location	identifies time and location	omits time and location	is unable to identify time and location
Character	describes main character(s) and character development	identifies main character(s)	omits or inaccurately identifies characters	unable to identify character
Events	describes events in sequence with details	tells most events in sequence with some detail	retells first and last events but omits middle with few details	is unable to retell events

Retelling Plan

☑ **This week assess Advanced students.**

☐ Week 2 assess On-Level students.

☐ Week 3 assess Strategic Intervention students.

☐ Week 4 assess Advanced students.

☐ Week 5 assess On-Level students.

☐ Week 6 assess Strategic Intervention students.

Retelling

SUCCESS PREDICTOR

OBJECTIVES

- Listen for initial /h/.
- Connect /h/ to *Hh*.

Materials

- Phonics Songs and Rhymes Chart 19
- Alphabet Cards: *Aa, Dd, Hh, Ii, Oo, Pp, Tt*, keyboard
- Phonics Story *I Have!*

Access Content Explain that the words *Hut! Hut! Hut!* are used to mark the marching beat. Have children march in place to *Hut! Hut! Hut!*

Phonemic Awareness

PRACTICE /h/

Listen for initial /h/

Display the chart. We are going to learn a new song today. Listen carefully to the song. Play the CD or sing the song several times to the tune of "The Ants Go Marching." Encourage children to join in. Ask children to raise their hand when they hear /h/ words.

 Phonics Songs and Rhymes Audio CD

Phonics Songs and Rhymes Chart

Phonics

🎯 CONNECT /h/ to *Hh*

Recognize *H*

Ask children to identify *H* on the keyboard card.

Identify *Hh*

Display the chart. Remember we learned a new song. There were many words that began with *h*. Let's circle the words that begin with *h* on our chart. Have several children come up one at a time to circle a word that begins with *H* or *h*.

Connect /h/ to *Hh*

Write *h* on the board. What is the name of this letter? *(h)* What is the sound for this letter? *(/h/)* Repeat the routine with *H*.

Monitor Progress | Check Letter-Sound Knowledge

Connect /h/ to *Hh* Give each child a blank card. Have them write *h* on the card. I will say some words. If the word begins with /h/, hold up your card. Listen carefully: *The hippo and hen are having lunch; Harry and Holly are playing with the hose; Harold and Helen are fixing the house with hammers.*

If... children cannot connect /h/ to *Hh*,
then... have children trace the *h* Finger Tracing Card as they say the letter name.

SUCCESS PREDICTOR

Day 1	▶ Day 2	Day 3	Day 4	Day 5
Check Sound Fluency	Check Retelling/ Letter-Sound Knowledge	Check High-Frequency Words/ Word Reading	Check Phoneme Segmentation	Check Oral Vocabulary/ Assess Progress

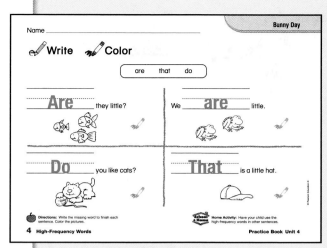

▲ Practice Book 4
High-Frequency Words, p. 4

Spiral REVIEW BLEND SOUNDS

Review letter names and sounds

Spell and blend words

PHONICS ACTIVITY MAT

Use the Alphabet Cards to review these letter names and sounds: *Aa, Dd, Hh, Ii, Oo, Pp,* and *Tt.*

Listen to the three sounds in *had:* /h/ /a/ /d/. What is the first sound in *had?* (/h/) What is the letter for that sound? *(Hh)* Write *h* on the board. Now you write *h* on your paper. Continue the routine with the remaining sounds.

Point to *had.* Help me blend the sounds together to read this word: /h/ /a/ /d/. Here is another way: /h/ -ad. The word is *had.*

Continue spell and blend practice with the following words: *hat, hop, can, hit,* and *on.*

PREPARE TO READ

Review high-frequency words

Write *are* on the board. This is the word *are.* What is this word? Continue the word reading routine with *that* and *do.*

Small Group Reading

DAY 2 ROUTINE

1 **Model Fluent Reading** Have children finger point as you read a page.

2 **Read Chorally** Have children finger point as they chorally read the page. Continue reading page by page, repeating steps 1 and 2.

3 **Read Individually** Have children read aloud a page in their group.

4 **Reread and Monitor Progress** As you listen to individual children reread, monitor progress and provide support.

Practice Book 4 Phonics Story, pp. 5–6

Group Time

On-Level
Read Phonics Story *I Have!* Use Small Group Reading **Routine.**

Strategic Intervention
Read Phonics Story *I Have!* More practice with *Hh*/h/, p. DI·2.

Advanced
Read Decodable Reader 19. Use the reading routine on p. DI·2. Apply phonics skills.

ELL
Group English language learners by their reading ability in English.

(i) Independent Activities

Self-Selected Reading See pp. TR14–15 for a bibliography of books related to the weekly concept.

Practice Book High-Frequency Words, p. 4

Centers Use the center activities on pp. 10–11 to practice this week's skills.

Journal Writing Draw and label a job you do at school every day.

Letter-Sound Knowledge
SUCCESS PREDICTOR

DAILY FIX-IT

will Heidi hear the horn
(Will Heidi hear the horn?)

Writer's Checkup

✔ The first word in a sentence begins with an uppercase letter. Did I do that?

✔ A sentence should end with a period. Did I do that?

✔ A sentence should make sense. Does my sentence make sense?

✔ A good writer uses his or her best handwriting. Did I do that?

Modeled Writing

GRAMMAR Naming Parts

Practice naming parts

Show the *hen* Picture Card and say this sentence: *The hen eats corn.* Who is this sentence about? What is the naming part? (the hen) What did the hen do? (eat corn)

Identify naming parts

Then say the following sentences and have children identify the naming part of each sentence: *The bunnies cleaned their room. Mother Rabbit made lunch. Father Rabbit planted seeds.*

Picture Card

LET'S WRITE Respond to Literature

Discuss *Bunny Day*

Display *Bunny Day.* Ask children to briefly describe what is happening in each illustration. List responses on a chart. You may wish to draw simple illustrations for each response. Then have children review their own class schedule and compare it to the bunnies' schedule.

Model writing a sentence

The bunnies do lots of the same things that we do. I make my bed before I go out in the morning. I am going to write:

I make my bed.

Independent writing

Have children write or dictate their own sentence about *Bunny Day* or copy one of the sentences the class wrote together. Then have them illustrate their sentence.

Text to Self

Bunnies like to color.

Speaking and Listening

LET'S REVIEW AMAZING WORDS

Display Talk with Me Chart 18A. Review these Amazing Words from last week.

DAY 2 ROUTINE

Oral Vocabulary   hide   scampered

1 **Introduce** If you don't want someone to find or see you, you *hide*. To *hide* means "to go where no one can see you." What is our new word for going where no one can see you?

Demonstrate When you play hide-and-go-seek, you *hide* so you cannot be seen. When are some other times you might *hide?*

2 **Introduce** Clyde scampered towards the window. *Scampered* means "ran quickly and lightly." What is our new word for running quickly and lightly?

Demonstrate When the bunnies went out to play, they might have *scampered*. Why else might they have *scampered?*

3 **Review** We talked about two words today: *hide* and *scampered.* Which word means "to go where no one can see you," *hide* or *scampered?* Which word means "ran quickly and lightly," *hide* or *scampered?*

4 **Apply** Have children use *hide* and *scampered* in complete sentences. Have them act out the words.

Wrap Up Your Day!

✓ **Oral Language** Today we read about the bunny family in *Bunny Day.* They are a busy family. What are some things your family likes to do? What words did we learn today?

✓ **Grammar** Remember the naming part of a sentence is the part that tells whom or what the sentence is about. Tell me the naming part of this sentence: Bunny Day *is a good book.*

✓ **Homework Idea** Have children take their Phonics Story home to share with their families.

PREVIEW Day 3

Tomorrow we will read about Nan and Nat and their day of playing whiffle ball. What is whiffle ball?

EXTEND Your Day

TIME FOR Science

Tools and Machines

Materials paper, drawing and writing tools

Discuss Tools and Machines Ask children to think about things they use to help them do chores.

- What are chores you and your family do around the house?
- What are things that help you do these chores?

Explain that things that help us do chores are called *tools* or *machines*. Make a chart showing two or three chores and list the tools and machines children suggest for each type of chore.

Write About Tools and Machines Ask children to help you write sentences about doing chores using these tools and machines.

> **I use a dryer to dry my clothes.**
> **I use a broom to sweep the floor.**

Invite children to help you find the naming part of each sentence and underline it. Have children write a sentence. Then ask them to act out their sentences for the class.

Clean Clothes	Clean Room	Cook
washer	mop	stove
dryer	broom	oven
iron	vacuum	microwave
	duster	mixer

Phonics

Initial Sounds

Materials large bag; objects whose names begin with *h, b, a, s, t*

Guess What Is in the Sack In a bag, put several objects whose names begin with *h, b, a, s,* or *t.* Tell children that you will give them clues about each item in your bag. It begins with /h/ and you wear it on your head. What is it? (hat)

Comprehension

Sequence/Retell

Materials 3 sentence strips

Putting a Story in Order Write one story event on each sentence strip for *Farfallina and Marcel*.

Farfallina and Marcel meet for the first time.

Farfallina and Marcel grow up.

Farfallina and Marcel meet again after they have grown up.

Have three students show the sentences out of order. Read each sentence. Have the class rearrange the children with their sentences in the correct story order and reread all three sentences.

Calendar

Name the day and date

Have a child find today's date on the calendar. Have children say the date together. Then have a volunteer name the day.

Yesterday, today, tomorrow

Point to today. Repeat the name of the day. What is the name for yesterday? Have a child point to yesterday and name the day. Repeat the procedure to name tomorrow.

Message Board

Question of the day

Write and read the question as you track the print. Encourage children to reply in complete sentences.

> ## What adventures can we find at school?

Review phonics

- What letter stands for /f/? *(Ff)*
- What word begins with /f/? *(find)*

ELL

Extend Language Use the Day 3 instruction on ELL Poster 19 to extend and enrich language.

ELL Poster 19

Oral Language and Vocabulary

Calendar
Message Board
Build Background

Shared Reading

Big Book *Bunny Day*
Skill Compare and Contrast
Skill Sequence

Word Work

Phonemic Awareness
Listen for /h/

Phonics
Connect /h/ to *Hh*
Blend and Read Words
H/F Words *are, that, do*
Kindergarten Student
Reader K.4.1

Read

Group Time < Differentiated Instruction

Language Arts

Grammar: Sentences
Modeled Writing:
Write Sentences
Speaking and Listening:
Give Directions

Materials

- Calendar
- Talk with Me, Sing with Me Chart 19A, 19B
- Sing with Me/Background Building Audio CD
- Big Book *Bunny Day*
- AudioText CD
- Alphabet Cards: *Aa, Bb, Cc, Dd, Ff, Hh, Ii, Mm, Nn, Oo, Pp, Ss, Tt*
- Picture Cards: p. 38
- Kindergarten Student Reader K.4.1
- AlphaBuddy

• •

OBJECTIVES

- Build background.
- Develop oral vocabulary.

Materials

- Talk with Me, Sing with Me Chart 19A, 19B

Amazing Words to build oral vocabulary

- chores
- bustle
- story
- tidy
- race
- hungry

E L L

Access Content Children may know the words *one, two,* and *three*. Build on this knowledge of numbers to orally introduce *first, second,* and *third*.

Build Background

LET'S TALK

Discuss things we do every day

Display Talk with Me Chart 19A. Point to photographs with children doing a chore and children racing.

Talk with Me, Sing with Me Chart

- When we clean things up, we are doing a _____. (chore) These children *bustle* to make the room tidy.

- What are these two children doing? (They are racing.) Yes, they are *racing*.

LET'S SING

Sing "Get Up, Get Up, It's a Beautiful Day"

Display Sing with Me Chart 19B. Recall that yesterday they sang "Get Up, Get Up, It's a Beautiful Day." Today ask children to clap when they hear the words *bustle* and *race*.

Sing with Me/Background Building Audio CD

LET'S LEARN AMAZING WORDS

Oral Vocabulary   bustle   race

DAY ROUTINE

1 **Introduce** The bunnies *bustle* to finish their chores. *Bustle* is another word for doing something quickly. What is our new word for doing something quickly?

Demonstrate I *bustle* to get our room ready. *Bustle* means "to do something quickly, not slowly." When do you *bustle*?

2 **Introduce** When you *race* someone, you try to finish first. *Race* means "to run very fast." What is our new word for running very fast?

Demonstrate When I walk home with my friend, we *race* to see who arrives at the door first. When do you *race*?

3 **Review** We talked about two words today: *bustle* and *race*. Which word means "to be busy and active," *bustle* or *race*? Which word means to "run very fast," *bustle* or *race*?

4 **Apply** When we *race,* we move quickly, or *bustle*. Have children use *race* and *bustle* in complete sentences.

Comprehension

REVIEW SKILL Compare and Contrast

Review compare and contrast

Remind children that we can learn by telling how things are alike and how they are different. Let's look at some pages to find out how morning and night are different and how they are alike.

Big Book

Apply compare and contrast

Pages 6–7

• What helps you know it is morning? (sunlight coming through the window, bunnies in their pajamas, hot cereal on the table)

Pages 30–31

• What helps you know it is night? (Outside the window is dark; bunny children are in their beds; one bunny is yawning.)

• How are these times different? (sunlight/dark, at the table/in bed)

• What is the same about these times? (Bunnies are in pajamas.)

LET'S READ *Bunny Day*

Develop vocabulary

Reread *Bunny Day*. Develop vocabulary by having children name objects and actions they see in the illustrations. Encourage children to relate these objects and actions to their own lives.

 AudioText CD

SKILL Sequence

Practice sequence

Remind children that events in a story happen in a certain order. Use these questions about the sequence of *Bunny Day*.

• In the story, what do the bunny children do first? (The bunnies wake up. The bunnies eat breakfast.)

• What happens just after the bunnies eat breakfast? (The bunnies do their chores.)

• What happens at the end of the story? (The bunnies read stories. The bunny children go to bed.)

• What if we change the order of the story? What if the bunnies have a picnic lunch before they eat breakfast?

OBJECTIVES

• Review compare and contrast.
• Identify story sequence.
• Put events into sequence.

Materials

• Big Book *Bunny Day*

Monitor Progress

Sequence

If... children have difficulty identifying sequence,	then ... provide choices one at a time. "Did the bunnies eat breakfast or do chores first?"

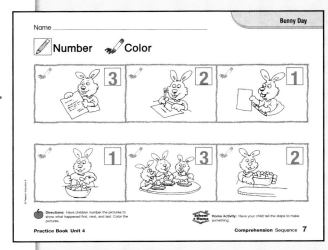

▲ **Practice Book 4** Sequence, p. 7

Phonemic Awareness

PRACTICE /h/

Discriminate /h/

I am going to say two words. Tell me which word begins with /h/. Listen carefully: *hand, foot.* Which word begins with /h/? *Hand* begins with /h/. Continue with the following pairs of words: *horse, donkey; low, high; seek, hide; happy, sad;* and *house, mouse.*

Phonics

CONNECT /h/ to *Hh*

Connect /h/ to *Hh*

Display the *Hh* Alphabet Card. What is the name of this letter? *(h)* What is the sound for this letter? (/h/) Repeat with *H*.

Initial *Hh*/h/

Display the *hat* Picture Card. This is a hat. Say it with me: /h/ /a/ /t/, *hat*. What is the first sound in *hat*? /h/ is the first sound in *hat*. Write *hat* on the board and point to the *h*.

The sound for *h* is /h/. The first sound in *hat* is /h/. Continue group practice with *hip* and *hot*.

Substitute initial and final sounds

Write *hit* on the board. Say the three sounds with me: /h/ /i/ /t/, *hit*. I can make a new word by changing the last sound. Change the *t* to *d*. Say the sounds with me: /h/ /i/ /d/, *hid*. What is the new word? The new word is *hid*.

hit   hid

Practice substituting sounds with the following words:

fat	**hip**	**dip**
cat	**him**	**tip**

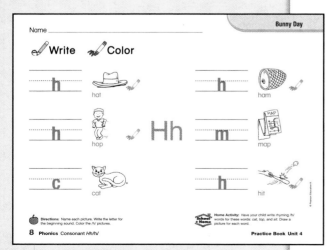

▲ **Practice Book 4**
Consonant *Hh*/h/, p. 8

Spiral REVIEW — BLEND SOUNDS

Review letter names and sounds

Display the *Hh* Alphabet Card. The name of this letter is *h*. The sound for the letter is /h/. Review the following letters: *Aa, Cc, Ii, Mm, Nn, Ss, Tt, Bb, Dd, Ff, Oo,* and *Pp.*

Blend and read words

Write *him* on the board. I am going to blend the sound of each letter together to say this word: /h/ /i/ /m/.

$$h \quad i \quad m$$

The word is *him.* Now blend the sounds with me: /h/ -im. Continue blending with *Nan, Nat, and, can, hit, top, bin, it, tin, not, sip, at, man, hot, fan,* and *nap.*

Introduce rebus words

Write *stand.* This is the word *stand.* Say the letters with me: *s, t, a, n, d, stand.*

Word Wall — HIGH-FREQUENCY WORDS

Practice high-frequency words

Write the word *are* on the board. This is the word *are.* What is this word? Repeat the routine with *that, they, do, you, see, look,* and *of.* Look for these words in the story that we read today.

Monitor Progress | High-Frequency Words/Word Reading

High-Frequency Words Write *are, that,* and *do* on the board. Have children take turns reading the words.

Blend Sounds to Read Words Write *hot* on the board. Have children blend the sound of each letter to read the word *hot.* Continue with the following words: *Nan, Nat, can, hit, top, tin, it, fan, nap, man, sip,* and *not.*

If... children cannot blend sounds to read the decodable words,
then... have them practice blending the words in chunks, /n/ -an.

If... children can successfully blend sounds to read words,
then... have them read Kindergarten Student Reader K.4.1 *All in a Day.*

If... children have difficulty reading high-frequency words,
then... write words on cards for them to practice at home.

SUCCESS PREDICTOR

Day 1	Day 2	▶ Day 3	Day 4	Day 5
Check Sound Fluency	Check Retelling/Letter-Sound Knowledge	Check High-Frequency Words/Word Reading	Check Phoneme Segmentation	Check Oral Vocabulary/Assess Progress

Group Time

On-Level

Read Kindergarten Student Reader K.4.1. Use Small Group Reading **Routine.**

Strategic Intervention

Read Kindergarten Student Reader K.4.1. More practice with *Hh* /h/, p. DI·3.

Advanced

Read Kindergarten Student Reader K.4.1. Use the reading routine on p. DI·3. Extend word reading.

ELL

Group English language learners by their reading ability in English.

(i) Independent Activities

Self-Selected Reading See pp. TR14–15 for a bibliography of books related to the weekly concept.

Practice Book Sequence, p. 7; Consonant *Hh*/h/, p. 8

Centers Use the center activities on pp. 10–11 to practice this week's skills.

Journal Writing Draw and label five words that begin with *Hh*/h/.

Spiral REVIEW

- Reviews previously taught high-frequency words.
- Reviews previously taught letters and sounds.

Word Reading

SUCCESS PREDICTOR

PREPARE TO READ

Introduce Kindergarten Student Reader K.4.1

Display the title page. We are going to read a new story. Point to the title. What is the title of the story? *All in a Day* was written by Ann Rossi. This book was illustrated by Jaime Smith.

Small Group Reading

Kindergarten Student Reader

1 **Model Fluent Reading** Have children finger point as you read a page.

2 **Read Chorally** Have children finger point as they chorally read the page. Continue reading page by page, repeating steps 1 and 2.

3 **Read Individually** Have children read aloud a page in their group.

4 **Reread and Monitor Progress** As you listen to individual children reread, monitor progress and provide support.

Do you see Nan and Nat?

Nat can hit the top of the bin.
Do you see Nat hit it?

Nan can hit the top of a tin can.
Nan can hit it.

Nat and Nan are hot, hot, hot!
They can fan, fan, fan.

Nat and Nan can nap, nap, nap.
They can see a man.

Nat and Nan are at the stand.
They can sip, sip, sip.

Look at that.
Nat and Nan are not hot.

Modeled Writing

REVIEW **GRAMMAR** Sentences

Review sentences

AlphaBuddy is going to help you write a sentence. There are different parts of a sentence. *AlphaBuddy plays with the toy.* What is the *naming part* in this sentence? What is the *action part?* In a complete sentence, we need a *naming part* and an *action part.*

Identify naming parts

Write these sentences on the board. Read each sentence and ask volunteers to circle the naming part of each sentence: *Mac ran to school; Nat walked home;* and *Pam likes the bunny.*

LET'S WRITE **Connect to Phonics**

Review letters and sounds

Display the *Hh* Alphabet Card. Review the name and sound of the letter. Point out words in *All in a Day* that begin with *h.* Continue reviewing the following letters: *Aa, Cc, Ii, Mm, Nn, Ss, Tt, Bb, Dd, Ff, Oo, Pp.*

Write sentences

I am going to write sentences using words that begin with the letter *Hh.*

I like to wear my hat.
Nat can hit the ball.

Have children read the sentences with you. Then have children point out each word that begins with /h/. Model writing more sentences that begin with /h/.

Independent writing

Have children write or dictate their own sentences using words that begin with /h/, or they may copy one of the sentences the class wrote together. Then have them illustrate their sentences.

EXTEND SKILLS

Posture for Handwriting Have children model good handwriting posture: sit tall, both feet on the floor, and arms relaxed on table.

OBJECTIVES

- Review sentences.
- Review letters and sounds.
- Write sentences.

Materials

- AlphaBuddy
- Alphabet Cards: *Aa, Bb, Cc, Dd, Ff, Hh, Ii, Mm, Nn, Oo, Pp, Ss, Tt*
- Kindergarten Student Reader K.4.1

DAILY FIX-IT

nan and Nat hit it
(Nan and Nat hit it.)

Writer's Checkup

✔ The first word in a sentence begins with an uppercase letter. Did I do that?

✔ A sentence should end with a period. Did I do that?

✔ A sentence should make sense. Does my sentence make sense?

✔ A good writer uses his or her best handwriting. Did I do that?

OBJECTIVE

● Practice giving directions.

Access Content Total physical response (TPR) helps children learn English by following directions with movements. Give children practice following AlphaBuddy's directions. Make up other directions for children to follow.

Speaking and Listening

GIVE DIRECTIONS

Practice giving directions

Have children play "AlphaBuddy Says," based on the game "Simon Says." AlphaBuddy will give directions. Listen carefully so that you can follow his directions. Have AlphaBuddy give the following directions:

• Stand up.

• Sit up.

• Put your right hand on your head.

• Put your hand on your elbow.

• Stand up and turn around.

• Sit down with your hands on your knees.

Then have children follow along as you do each action silently.

Connect giving directions

When AlphaBuddy was telling you what to do, he was giving you *directions*. *Directions* are the information you need to do a project correctly. When I give you directions, I try to speak loudly and clearly. I give the directions in the order that you will need to do them.

Wrap Up Your Day!

 Respond to Literature Today we read about Nan and Nat. The girls are twins. What did they do? They played whiffle ball, took a nap, drank lemonade, and played at the park.

 Grammar Ask children to tell you the naming part and the action part in the following sentence: *The child put on the red shirt.*

✓ **Homework Idea** Ask children to bring something or a picture of something to school that begins with /h/.

PREVIEW Day 4

Tomorrow we will read about chameleons and how they change colors.

EXTEND Your Day

Time

Materials analog and digital clocks

Reading Analog and Digital Clocks Ask children how they know what time of day it is in *Bunny Day*. Talk about how people use clocks to help them know what time it is.

Show children an analog clock and identify the long and short hands. Position the hands at 2 o'clock. Ask children what things they do at 2 o'clock in the afternoon. Repeat for 10 o'clock, 12 o'clock, and 8 o'clock.

Show children a digital clock. Using the same times as shown on the analog clock, ask children to identify the time. Compare the digital and analog clocks.

Write About Time Show children 8:00 on an analog and on a digital clock. Ask children the time shown on the clocks. Have children draw something they do at that time and write or dictate what they are doing. Encourage children to write the time at the top of their paper or write it for them.

Phonics

Making Short *o* Words

Build Words Review short *o*. Write *nod*. Say the word. Ask a volunteer to change the *n* to *s*, and then say the new word *sod*. Continue making new words by changing the initial consonant. Have children change the final consonant *d* to *t* to make new words that end with *-ot:*

nod

sod

pod

nod	cod	pod
not	cot	pot

Comprehension

Sequence

Materials Kindergarten Student Reader K.4.1; props such as a ball, cups, and sitting mats

Act Out the Sequence Reread Kindergarten Student Reader K.4.1 *All in a Day*. Have children tell you what happens first, next, and last in the story. Then have groups of three act out the story sequence.

Materials

- Calendar
- Talk with Me, Sing with Me Chart 19A, 19B
- Sing with Me/Background Building Audio CD
- Trade Book *Hide, Clyde!*
- AudioText CD
- Picture Cards: pp. 47, 49
- Alphabet Cards: *Aa, Bb, Cc, Dd, Ff, Hh, Ii, Mm, Nn, Oo, Pp, Ss, Tt*
- Decodable Reader 19

Calendar

Name the day and date
Ask a volunteer to point to and name the day. Have children repeat the day. Continue with the month, date, and year.

Last week, next week
Find today on the calendar.

- What was the date one week ago? What day of the week was it?
- What will the date be one week from today? What day of the week will it be?

Message Board

Question of the day
Write and read the question as you track the print. Encourage children to respond in complete sentences.

What do you do every night?

Review grammar
Invite a volunteer to say a sentence. Have children identify the naming part. Tell children that the naming part of the sentence is not always first.

Access Content Use the Day 4 instruction on ELL Poster 19 to support children's use of English to communicate about lesson concepts.

ELL Poster 19

Build Background

LET'S TALK

Discuss things we do every day

Display Talk with Me Chart 19A. Point to the picture at the bottom left.

- What are the children in the picture doing? Yes, they are listening to a *story*.
- These children are going to eat dinner because they are *hungry*. What do you eat when you are *hungry*?

Prompt children to respond in complete sentences.

Talk with Me, Sing with Me Chart

LET'S SING

Sing "Get Up, Get Up, It's a Beautiful Day"

Display Sing with Me Chart 19B. Sing "Get Up, Get Up, It's a Beautiful Day" and listen for the words *story* and *hungry*.

 Audio CD **Sing with Me/Background Building Audio CD**

LET'S LEARN AMAZING WORDS

Oral Vocabulary story hungry

DAY 4 ROUTINE

1 Introduce We read a *story* every day. A *story* tells us about things that happen to people, animals, or things. What is our new word for something we read?

Demonstrate *Bunny Day* is a *story*. What is another *story* we have read in class?

2 Introduce When we are *hungry,* our body is telling us we need to eat some healthful food. What is our new word for the feeling we have when we need to eat?

Demonstrate When I am *hungry*, my stomach gurgles. How do you feel when you are *hungry*?

3 Review We talked about two words today: *story* and *hungry*. Which word means "a book," *story* or *hungry*? Which word means "to need food," *story* or *hungry*?

4 Apply Have children use *story* or *hungry* in complete sentences. Have them tell a *story* that uses the word *hungry*.

OBJECTIVES

- Build background.
- Develop oral vocabulary.

 **to build oral vocabulary**

- chores
- bustle
- story
- tidy
- race
- hungry

E L L

Extend Language Tell children that there are many words that tell how people eat: *munch, chew, gobble, nibble,* and *snack*. *Munch* is another word for *chew*.

OBJECTIVE

↻ Apply sequence.

Materials

● Trade Book *Hide, Clyde!*

E L L

Extend Language As children recall the sequence of Clyde learning to hide, have them talk about the sequence using the words *first, next, then,* and *last.*

Comprehension

LET'S READ *Hide, Clyde!*

Review *Hide, Clyde!*

Display *Hide, Clyde!* In this story, Clyde learns to hide by changing colors.

● How do chameleons hide?

● Where did Clyde go in the story?

Reread *Hide, Clyde!*

Reread the book and ask children to pay attention to the places Clyde goes when learning to change colors.

Trade Book

 AudioText CD

↻ SKILL Sequence

Apply sequence to *Hide, Clyde!*

After reading ask:

● How was Clyde at changing colors in the beginning of the story? (He would always do it wrong.)

● What happened to Clyde next? (The bee flew away with him.)

● Then what happened in the house? (Clyde heard something coming and learned to hide.)

● What happened last in the story? (Clyde meets the bee again and gets a ride home.)

Practice sequence

Have children think about when Clyde learned to change colors. When was Clyde able to change colors, before or after he was stuck in the house? Have children draw pictures of Clyde hiding in a flower when he could not change colors and then when he could. Which picture happened first in the story?

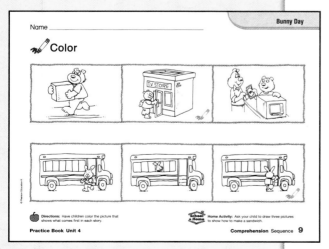

▲ **Practice Book 4** Sequence, p. 9

Phonemic Awareness

REVIEW PRACTICE /o/

Isolate /o/
Display the *olive* Picture Card. What is the first sound in *olive?* (/o/) Say it with me: /o/, /o/, /o/, *olive.* Continue with *octopus* and *otter* Picture Cards.

Segment words
I am going to say a word. I want you to tell me all of the sounds you hear in the word. Listen carefully: *hot.* What sounds do you hear in *hot?* Let's say the sounds together: /h/ /o/ /t/, *hot.* Continue with the following words: *dot, hop, mom, mop, sock, pot, top,* and *dock.*

OBJECTIVES
- Connect /o/ to *Oo.*
- Blend and read words.

Materials
- Picture Cards:

  octopus   olive   otter
- Alphabet Cards: *Aa, Bb, Cc, Dd, Ff, Hh, Ii, Mm, Nn, Oo, Pp, Ss, Tt*
- Decodable Reader 19

Monitor Progress	**Check Phoneme Segmentation**

Check Segmentation I am going to say a word. Tell me all of the sounds you hear in the word. Use the following words from Decodable Reader 19 *Hob Can Hit: Hob, can, hit, man, Dan, it, fan, Pam, Sam, did, not, hot, had, hat,* and *pop.*

If... children cannot segment sounds,
then... segment the word and have children echo you.

SUCCESS PREDICTOR

Day 1	**Day 2**	**Day 3**	▶ **Day 4**	**Day 5**
Check Sound Fluency	Check Retelling/ Letter-Sound Knowledge	Check High-Frequency Words/ Word Reading	Check Phoneme Segmentation	Check Oral Vocabulary/ Assess Progress

Phonics

Spiral REVIEW BLEND SOUNDS

Review letter names and sounds
Use Alphabet Cards to review the following letter names and their sounds: *Mm, Tt, Aa, Ss, Hh, Cc, Ii, Bb, Nn, Dd, Ff, Pp,* and *Oo.*

Blend sounds

Write *hop* on the board. I am going to blend the sound of each letter together to say this word, /h/ /o/ /p/. The word is *hop.* Say the sounds with me: /h/ /o/ /p/. Blend the sounds as I point to each letter: /h/ /o/ /p/, *hop.* The word is *hop.*

h o p

Continue blending practice with *man, Dan, Hob, can, hit, it, fan, Pam, Sam, did, not, hot, had, big, hat, pop,* and *sad.*

OBJECTIVES

- Recognize high-frequency words.
- Read decodable text.

Group Time

On-Level

Read Decodable Reader 19. Use Small Group Reading **Routine.**

Strategic Intervention

Read Decodable Reader 19. More practice with *Hh*/h/ on p. DI·4.

Advanced

Read Independent Leveled Reader K.4.1. Use Leveled Reader lesson, p. LR1. Extend word reading.

Group English language learners by their reading ability in English.

Self-Selected Reading See pp. TR14–15 for a bibliography of books related to the weekly concept.

Practice Book Sequence, p. 9; Naming Parts, p. 10

Centers Use the center activities on pp. 10–11 to practice this week's skills.

Journal Writing Draw and label three naming words.

Word Wall HIGH-FREQUENCY WORDS

Practice high-frequency words

Write the word *are* on the board. This is the word *are*. What is this word? Continue with *that, see, is, a, they,* and *do*. Look for these words in the story that we read today.

PREPARE TO READ

Introduce Decodable Reader 19

Display Decodable Reader 19 *Hob Can Hit.* Today we will read *Hob Can Hit.* Point to the title of the story. What is the title of the story? Point to the names of the author and illustrator. *Hob Can Hit* is written by Roy Kass. This story is illustrated by Ryan Bines.

Small Group Reading

DAY 4 ROUTINE

1 **Model Fluent Reading** Have children finger point as you read a page.

2 **Read Chorally** Have children finger point as they chorally read the page. Continue reading page by page, repeating steps 1 and 2.

3 **Read Individually** Have children read aloud a page in their group.

4 **Reread and Monitor Progress** As you listen to individual children reread, monitor progress and provide support.

Decodable Reader

Interactive Writing

GRAMMAR Naming Parts

Identify naming parts

I will say a sentence. Tell me which part of the sentence is the naming part. Remember the naming part tells who or what the sentence is about. Listen to the sentence: *The dog drank water.* Who drank water? Yes, the dog drank water, so *the dog* is the naming part of the sentence. **Repeat using these words instead of** *dog* in the sentence: *bear, cat, deer,* and *bunny.*

LET'S WRITE Connect to Phonics

Review letters and sounds

Display the *hen* Picture Card. This is a hen. What sound do you hear at the beginning of hen? What letter stands for /h/? **Have children dictate a list of words that begin with /h/.**

Write sentences

Write the following sentence frame on the board.

This is the way we _____. (hop)

Have children help you complete the sentence using words that begin with /h/. Have a volunteer write the word to fill in the blank. If necessary, say the word again slowly, emphasizing each sound: /h/ /o/ /p/. Then read the sentence together.

Independent writing

Have children write or dictate their own sentence by completing the sentence frame or by copying one of the sentences the class wrote together. Then have them act out their sentence.

EXTEND SKILLS

Spelling If children have difficulty spelling words with medial vowels, have them practice spelling and blending words using Letter Tiles and the Phonics Activity Mat.

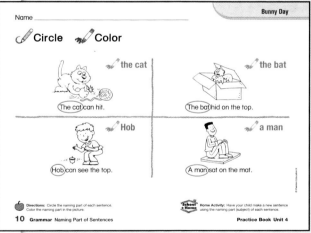

▲ **Practice Book 4**
Naming Parts, p. 10

OBJECTIVE

- Review giving directions.

Materials

- Big Book *Bunny Day*

Speaking and Listening

GIVE DIRECTIONS

Review giving directions
Remember, when we give directions, we speak loudly and clearly. We give the directions in the order that they need to be done by using the words *first, next,* and *last.*

Practice giving directions
Open *Bunny Day* to pages 8 and 9. Let's give the bunnies directions on how to make a bed. We need to use the words *first, next,* and *last* in our directions. Guide children as they give directions.

Practice giving two-step and multi-step directions, using the following pages in *Bunny Day* as the prompt:

Pages 16–17: how to hop

Pages 22–23: how to paint a picture

Pages 24–25: how to set a table

Pages 26–27: how to play hide and seek

Then have children follow along as volunteers do each action silently.

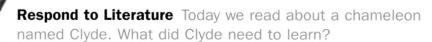

Wrap Up Your Day!

✓ **Respond to Literature** Today we read about a chameleon named Clyde. What did Clyde need to learn?

✓ **Speaking and Listening** Tell me how to write my name. Tell me how to read a book.

✓ **Homework Idea** Ask children to write a *naming part* to bring to school tomorrow.

PREVIEW Day 5

Tomorrow we will read the story "A Day Like Every Other Day." I wonder what kind of day it will be.

EXTEND Your Day

Camouflage

Materials Trade Book *Hide, Clyde!*

Discuss the Ways Chameleons Hide Display *Hide, Clyde!* Have children go through *Hide, Clyde!* Clyde is taught to change colors to match certain backgrounds. Fill in the chart with the background that Clyde was taught to change into. What color was he supposed to change into? What color did Clyde change into?

Background	Color	Clyde
leaves	green	red
stone	blue	yellow
flower	orange	purple

Connect to Writing Discuss why it would be important for animals to change colors to blend in with the background. Why does Clyde need to hide? Ask children if they know of any other animals that can change colors like Clyde. Have children draw Clyde on a background. Have them write or dictate a label with the color and name of the background.

Clyde is pink.

Drama

Dramatize the Song

Act Out "Frére Jacques" Teach children the song "Frére Jacques." Ask children whether "Frére Jacques" is a song or a story. Have children sing the song with you several times. Then ask children to pretend to sleep like Brother John as they sing. Together make up new verses for the song. Then have children draw a picture to show what they think Brother John looks like when he hears the morning bells.

Writing

Labels

Materials pattern of Clyde (chameleon) from page 9 of Patterns Book for each child

Identify Parts of a Chameleon Display page 12 of *Hide, Clyde!* Ask children to identify the chameleon's body parts. Write the following words on the board: *legs, eyes,* and *tongue.*

Give each child a chameleon pattern. Ask them to color and cut out their chameleon and then to glue it to a page. Have children label the chameleon's legs, eyes, and tongue.

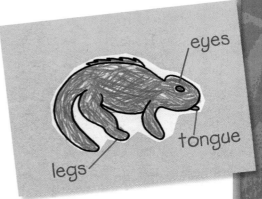

eyes

tongue

legs

Day 5
AT A GLANCE

Oral Language and Vocabulary
Calendar
Message Board
Build Background

Shared Reading
Read Aloud Anthology "A Day Like Every Other Day"
 Skill Sequence

Word Work

Phonemic Awareness
Isolate /h/

Phonics
Connect /h/ *to Hh*
H/F Words *are, that, do*
Blend and Read

Read
Group Time < Differentiated Instruction

Monitor Progress

Language Arts
Grammar: Naming Parts
Shared Writing:
    This Week We . . .
Speaking and Listening:
    Give Directions

Materials
- Calendar
- Talk with Me, Sing with Me Chart 19A, 19B
- Sing with Me/Background Building Audio CD
- *Read Aloud Anthology* "A Day Like Every Other Day"
- Alphabet Card: *Hh*
- Decodable Reader 19
- Kindergarten Student Reader K.4.1
- Phonics Story *I Have!*
- Big Book *Bunny Day*
- Picture Cards: pp. 55, 59

Calendar

Name the day and date
Recite the day, month, date, and year. Ask a volunteer to find today's date on the calendar.

Count days
Say the name of the day and the date. Count the number of Fridays there are in the month.

Message Board

Question of the week
Remind children that this week we have talked about adventures we have throughout the day.

> ## What adventures do you have throughout the day?

Review oral vocabulary
Encourage children to use oral vocabulary words *chores, tidy, bustle, race, story,* and *hungry* to discuss the question. Prompt children to respond in complete sentences.

Assess Vocabulary Use the Day 5 instruction on ELL Poster 19 to monitor children's progress with oral vocabulary.

ELL Poster 19

Build Background

LET'S TALK

Discuss things we do every day

Display Talk with Me Chart 19A. Point to the picture showing the child doing a chore.

- Is this picture showing a child doing a *chore* or reading a *story*?
- Which picture shows a dad reading a *story*?
- Which picture shows two children *racing*?
- Which picture shows what you do when you are *hungry*?

Talk with Me, Sing with Me Chart

LET'S SING

Sing "Get Up, Get Up, It's a Beautiful Day"

Display Sing with Me Chart 19B. Before singing, remind children that the words *chores, tidy, bustle, race, story,* and *hungry* are in the song.

Sing with Me/Background Building Audio CD

Get Up, Get Up, It's a Beautiful Day

Get up, get up, it's a beautiful day,
We have so much to do!
Let's tidy up and do our chores,
It's so much fun with you!

Talk with Me, Sing with Me Chart

OBJECTIVES

- Build background.
- Review oral vocabulary.

Amazing Words
to build oral vocabulary

- **chores**
- **bustle**
- **story**
- **tidy**
- **race**
- **hungry**

Monitor Progress | **Check Oral Vocabulary**

Demonstrate Word Knowledge Prompt children to use oral vocabulary words *chores, tidy, bustle, race, story,* and *hungry.* Encourage them to use complete sentences.

If... children cannot demonstrate word knowledge,
then... review oral vocabulary using Talk with Me Chart 19A and *Bunny Day.*

SUCCESS PREDICTOR

Day 1	Day 2	Day 3	Day 4	▶Day 5
Check Sound Fluency	Check Retelling/ Letter-Sound Knowledge	Check High-Frequency Words/ Word Reading	Check Phoneme Segmentation	Check Oral Vocabulary/ Assess Progress

Oral Vocabulary

SUCCESS PREDICTOR

- Practice sequence in new selection.

Materials

- *Read Aloud Anthology* "A Day Like Every Other Day"

Access Content Before reading introduce children to the characters in the story. Then use words and gestures to explain key story words.

Monitor Progress

 Sequence

If... children cannot recall the story order,	then... reteach using page DI·31.

Comprehension

READ ALOUD

Read "A Day Like Every Other Day"

Tell children that you are going to read them a story called "A Day Like Every Other Day." Ask them to listen to the order, or sequence, in which things happen in the story. Listen carefully. I am going to ask you what happened first, next, and last.

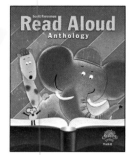

Read Aloud Anthology

CHECK SKILL Sequence

Practice sequence in "A Day Like Every Other Day"

After you read the story, ask children to tell what happened in the story by answering these questions:

- What did the child do first? (got up and got ready for school)
- What did the child do next? (His mom and dad walked him to school.)
- What did the child do then? (took the bus to the bookstore)
- What did the child do last? (took a bath and got ready for bed)

ASSESS SKILL Sequence

Assess sequence

Use the blackline master found on page 58. Copy one page for each child. Have children cut out the three scenes and glue them to another sheet of paper in the correct order.

SEQUENCE

Put these events from "A Day Like Every Other Day" in order.

Note to Teacher Have children cut out the scenes and glue them in the correct order onto another piece of paper.

▲ **Teacher's Edition 4**
Sequence, p. 58

Phonemic Awareness

REVIEW /h/

Isolate /h/

What is the first sound in *hill?* Say the word with me: *hill, /h/, /h/, /h/, hill.* Continue with the following Picture Cards: *hammer, hose, house,* and *hippopotamus.*

Identify /h/

Tell children that you will say two words. Ask them to raise their hands when you say a word that begins with /h/. Use these words: *tip, hip; pot, hot; hat, cat; mill, hill; hop, mop;* and *hen, pen.*

Phonics

⟳ REVIEW *Hh* /h/

Connect /h/ to *Hh*

Display the *Hh* Alphabet Card. What is the name of this letter? *(h)* What is the sound for this letter? *(/h/)*

Word Wall HIGH-FREQUENCY WORDS

Practice high-frequency words

Write the word *are* on the board. This is the word *are.* What is this word? Continue the routine with *that* and *do.*

Spiral REVIEW READ

Apply phonics in familiar text

Have children reread one of the readers specific to the target letter sound. You may wish to review the decodable words and high-frequency words in each reader prior to rereading.

Kindergarten Student Reader

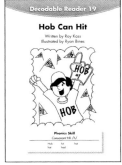

Decodable Reader

Phonics Story in Practice Book

OBJECTIVES

- Review initial /h/.
- Listen for /h/.
- Connect /h/ to *Hh*

Materials

- Alphabet Card: *Hh*
- Kindergarten Student Reader K.4.1
- Decodable Reader 19
- Phonics Story *I Have!*
- Picture Cards:

  hammer   hose   house
  hippopotamus

OBJECTIVE

⊙ Assess: connect /h/ to *Hh*.

Group Time

On-Level

Sets A and B

Strategic Intervention

Monitor Progress:
Check Phonics
Alternate Assessment, p. DI•5

Advanced

Sets B and C

ⓘ Independent Activities

Self-Selected Reading See
pp. TR14–15 for a bibliography
of books related to the weekly
concept.

Centers Use the center activities on pp. 10–11 to practice this
week's skills.

Journal Writing Draw and write
about something you will do this
weekend.

Assess Phonics For guidance in
teaching phonics to English language
learners, see the *ELL and Transition
Handbook*.

Monitor Progress

PHONICS /h/ to *Hh*

**Group
assessment**   Divide a paper into four equal sections for each child. Ask children
to draw something that begins with /h/ in each box. Then ask
children to label the picture with a word or the letter *h*.

Monitor Progress **Assess Progress**	
If... a child cannot complete the group assessment,	**then...** use the Reteach lesson on page DI•31.
If... a child draws four correct pictures but only labels them with *h*,	**then...** assess word reading Sets A and B on page 57.
If... a child draws four pictures that begin with /h/ and labels them accurately with phonetically appropriate spellings,	**then...** assess word and sentence reading with Sets B and C on page 57.

⊙ ASSESS PHONICS

**Set A: Read
the words**   Have individuals take turns reading the words. We're going to
read some words. I'll do the first one and you do the rest. The
first word is *hip,* /h/ /i/ /p/. The first word is *hip.* For each child,
record any decoding problems with initial /h/.

**Set B: Read
more words**   Have individuals take turns reading more words. We're going to
read some words. I'll do the first one and you do the rest. The
first word is *hat,* /h/ /a/ /t/. For each child, record any decoding
problems.

**Set C: Read
the sentences**   For a cumulative assessment of phonics and high-frequency words,
have each child read one or two sentences.

READ THE WORDS

 Set A

hip   hop

hot   had

READ MORE WORDS

Set B

hat   ham   hid

Hap   hot   him

READ THE SENTENCES

Set C

1. Hap can stop for it.

2. Are you at the spot?

3. That is Hob.

4. The pot had that top.

5. The pan is not hot.

Note to Teacher Set A: Children read each word. Set B: Children read each word.
Set C: Children read one or two sentences.

Bunny Day

Monitor Progress

SUCCESS PREDICTOR

SEQUENCE

Put these events from "A Day Like Every Other Day" in order.

Note to Teacher Have children cut out the scenes and glue them in the correct order onto another piece of paper.

REPRODUCIBLE PAGE • See also Assessment Handbook, p. 193

Monitor Progress

Shared Writing

GRAMMAR Naming Parts

Review naming parts

Display the *pig* Picture Card. What is the name of this animal? Listen to this sentence: *The pig lives in a pen.* Who or what is the sentence about? Have children identify the naming part of the sentence. Continue with these Picture Cards and sentences: *box—The box opens up; ant—An ant is little;* and *goat—My goat eats anything.*

Hunt for naming parts

Arrange children in pairs. Have groups walk around the room, pointing to various things. When a partner points at an object, the other must tell a sentence using that thing as the naming part.

LET'S WRITE This Week We...

Recall literature

Display the following items: *Bunny Day, Hob Can Hit, All in a Day,* Sing with Me Chart 19B, and Phonics Songs and Rhymes Chart 19. We read three new books and sang two new songs this week. Which book or song was your favorite? My favorite was the song about the ants.

Write about our favorite things

Today we will write about our favorite things.

Mr. Rob liked the ant song.

Kim liked *Bunny Day.*

Nick liked *Hob Can Hit.*

Continue the list with all children. Then have children echo read the complete list.

Independent writing

Have children copy the sentence they dictated and illustrate it.

OBJEC

- Recognize naming
- Write about our fav this week.

Materials

- Picture Cards:

  ant   box   goat   pig

- Big Book *Bunny Day*
- Kindergarten Student Reader K.4.1
- Decodable Reader 19
- Talk with Me, Sing with Me Chart 19B
- Phonics Songs and Rhymes Chart 19

D A I L Y F I X - I T

they are little bears
(They are little bears.)

ELL

Support Writing Supply English words as children write or dictate their sentence.

Access Content Encourage children to participate by following the "Hokey Pokey" directions, observing the actions of other children as needed.

Speaking and Listening

GIVE DIRECTIONS

Review giving directions

Remind children that it is important to give directions in the proper order, using a loud, clear voice. Ask them to listen for directions in this song.

The Hokey Pokey

You put your right foot in,
You take your right foot out,
You put your right foot in,
And you shake it all about.
You do the hokey pokey
And you turn yourself around.
That's what it's all about.

Connect giving directions

Check children's understanding of what they have heard. Ask children whether "The Hokey Pokey" is a song or a story. Sing the song several times. Then have children take turns singing and following two-step directions, substituting other body parts, such as knees, hands, elbows, and head. Have children follow along as you do each action silently. If time allows, have volunteers silently lead the class.

✓ **Phonics** This week we learned about the letter *Hh*. What is the sound for *Hh*? Name some words that begin with /h/.

✓ **Shared Reading** What was your favorite book or song this week?

✓ **High-Frequency Words** Write *are, that,* and *do* on the board. Read these words to me.

You've learned
006 Amazing Words
this week!

You've learned
114 Amazing Words
so far this year!

PREVIEW Next Week

Next week we will read about a little pig. What kind of adventure do you think the pig will have?

EXTEND Your Day

TIME + FOR MATH

Graphing

Materials *Bunny Day; Hide, Clyde!; Hob Can Hit; All in a Day*

Recall Favorite Stories Show each book and have children recall the story. I am going to hold up each book. Stand up when I hold up your favorite book from this week.

Graph the Results Prepare a graph with the title of each book at the bottom. Show *Bunny Day*. Count the number of children standing and record the results on the graph. Continue with the other books. Compare the results. Write a sentence about which book is the class favorite.

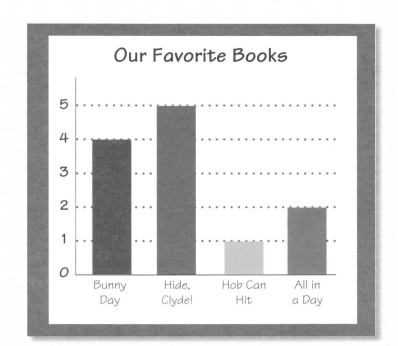

Our Favorite Books

Plant Characteristics

TIME FOR Science

Materials carrot, head of lettuce

Compare Vegetables Compare the color, shape, and texture of a carrot and a head of lettuce. Record the information on a chart such as the one shown. Help children write a sentence or two about the differences between a carrot and a head of lettuce.

Characteristic	Carrot	Lettuce
color	orange	green
shape	long cone	round
texture	hard, smooth	soft, crisp

Cooperation

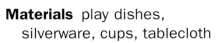

Time for SOCIAL STUDIES

Materials play dishes, silverware, cups, tablecloth

Let's Work Together Remind children that the bunny family works together throughout the day. Tell them that you will set the table for lunch. Exaggerate the difficulty of doing this alone.

What would make doing this chore easier? Encourage children to conclude that helpers would make this chore easier. Have volunteers demonstrate setting a table together.

Unit 4
Let's Explore

CONCEPT QUESTION
Where will our adventures take us?

Week 1

What adventures do you have throughout the day?

Week 2

What adventures can you have on a lucky day?

Week 3

What adventures can an animal have?

Week 4

What kind of adventure can a little girl have?

Week 5

What would it be like to take an adventure to the Antarctic?

Week 6

What kinds of adventures can you have in the city?

EXPAND THE CONCEPT
What adventures can you have on a lucky day?

Time for
SOCIAL
STUDIES

MY LUCKY DAY
Keiko Kasza

CONNECT THE CONCEPT

▶ **Build Background**

piglet	*lucky*	*cook*
fox	*filthy*	*scrubber*

It's My Lucky Day

Piglet walked through the woods one day,
Hoping to find a friend who could play,
Squirrel was scrubbing his filthy house,
"Bye, bye, Squirrel! I'll go find Mouse!"

▶ **Social Studies Content**
History

Preview Your Week

What adventures can you have on a lucky day?

Read Aloud Trade Book

Audio CD

Genre	Animal Fantasy
Phonics	Ll/l/
Comprehension Skill	Cause and Effect

Meet the Author/Illustrator

Keiko Kasza

When Keiko Kasza is writing a book, she says, "I pretend that I'm a bird looking for my mother or a pig trying to impress his girlfriend." Originally from Japan, she has published children's books in Japan and the United States. She lives in Indiana with her husband and two sons.

Read another book by Keiko Kasza.

The Wolf's Chicken Stew

Integrate Social Studies Standards

- History

Books for All Children

Listen to Me Reader

Emergent

- **Develop oral language**
- **Develop phonemic awareness**
- **Read decodable words**
- **Read high-frequency words**

✓ **Read**

Read Aloud Trade Book
My Lucky Day

Independent Leveled Reader
A Pig's Life

Kindergarten Student Reader

On-Level

- **Read connected text**
- **Apply phonics skills**
- **Read high-frequency words in context**

✓ **Build**
Concept Vocabulary
Adventures on a Lucky Day, pp. 75, 85, 100, 109, 117

✓ **Apply**
Social Studies

Chronological Time, p. 107
Cause and Effect, p. 115

Leveled Reader K.4.2

Independent

- **Practice comprehension skill: cause and effect**
- **Extend concepts**
- **Connect to Social Studies**

Independent Leveled Reader

✓ **Teach**
Science Concepts

Our Senses, p. 83
Cause and Effect with Growing Things, p. 98

Apply Phonics

Decodable Reader

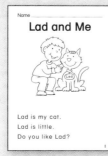

Phonics Story

Weekly Plan

READING

60–90 minutes

TARGET SKILLS OF THE WEEK

◉ **Phonics Skill**
Ll/l/

◉ **Comprehension Skill**
Cause and Effect

DAY 1 PAGES 74–83

Oral Language/Vocabulary

QUESTION OF THE WEEK, 74
What adventures can you have on a lucky day?

Build Background, 75
Talk with Me, Sing with Me Chart 20A, 20B

Amazing Words, 75
piglet, fox, lucky, filthy, cook, scrubber

Comprehension

Shared Reading, 76–77

Read Read Aloud Trade Book

Use Illustrations
Reader Response
◉ Cause and Effect

Word Work

Phonemic Awareness, 78
Introduce /l/

Phonics, 79
◉ Connect /l/ to Ll **T**

High-Frequency Words, 79
Reteach *do, are, that*

Reread Decodable Reader 19

Grouping Options 68–69

DAY 2 PAGES 84–98

Oral Language/Vocabulary

QUESTION OF THE DAY, 84
What are some things you do that are fun?

Build Background, 85
Talk with Me, Sing with Me Chart 20A, 20B

Let's Learn Amazing Words, 85
piglet, fox

Comprehension

Shared Reading, 86–93

Read Read Aloud Trade Book

Recall and Retell
◉ Cause and Effect

Word Work

Phonemic Awareness, 94
Practice /l/

Phonics, 94
◉ Connect /l/ to Ll **T**

High-Frequency Words, 95
Review *are, that, do*

Read Phonics Story

Grouping Options 68–69

LANGUAGE ARTS

20 minutes

Shared Writing, 81
Grammar: Introduce Action Parts
Connect to Grammar

Speaking and Listening, 82
Introduce Compare and Contrast

Modeled Writing, 96
Grammar: Practice Action Parts
Respond to Literature

Speaking and Listening, 97
Let's Review Amazing Words *chores, tidy*

DAILY JOURNAL WRITING

Day 1 Write or draw about one adventure the piglet had in the story.

Day 2 Dictate and draw three words that begin with /l/.

EXTEND YOUR DAY *30 minutes*

Additional Activities for Full–Day Classrooms

Day 1, 83
Time for Science: Our Senses
Grammar: Action Parts
Math: Make a Guess

Day 2, 98
Time for Science: Cause and Effect with Growing Things
Comprehension: Cause and Effect
Phonics: Connect /l/ to L

DAILY SUCCESS PREDICTORS

for Adequate Yearly Progress

Monitor Progress and Corrective Feedback

Phonemic Awareness
Check Sound Fluency, *78*
Spiral REVIEW Phonics,
High-Frequency Words

Retelling and Phonics
Check Retelling, *93*
Check Letter-Sound Knowledge, *94*
Spiral REVIEW Phonics,
High-Frequency Words

Grouping Options for Differentiated Instruction

Turn the page for the small group lesson plan.

DAY 3 — PAGES 99–107

Oral Language/Vocabulary

QUESTION OF THE DAY, 99
What things will you do on a lucky day?

Build Background, 100
Talk with Me, Sing with Me Chart 20A, 20B

Let's Learn Amazing Words, 100
lucky, filthy

Comprehension

Shared Reading, 101

Read Read Aloud
Trade Book
REVIEW Plot **T**
Cause and Effect

Word Work

Phonemic Awareness, 102
Introduce Final /l/

Phonics, 102
Connect /l/ to *Ll* **T**

High-Frequency Words, 103
Practice *we, do, that, are, the, like, you*

Read Kindergarten Student Reader K.4.2

Grouping Options 68–69

DAY 4 — PAGES 108–115

Oral Language/Vocabulary

QUESTION OF THE DAY, 108
What could happen on your lucky day?

Build Background, 109
Talk with Me, Sing with Me Chart 20A, 20B

Let's Learn Amazing Words, 109
cook, scrubber

Comprehension

Shared Reading, 110

Reread Read Aloud
Trade Book
Cause and Effect

Word Work

Phonemic Awareness, 111
REVIEW Initial /h/

Phonics, 111
Connect /l/ to *Ll* **T**

High-Frequency Words, 112
Practice *are, that, you, see, a, the, they, do*

Read Decodable Reader 20

Grouping Options 68–69

DAY 5 — PAGES 116–125

Oral Language/Vocabulary

QUESTION OF THE WEEK, 116
What adventures can you have on a lucky day?

Build Background, 117
Talk with Me, Sing with Me Chart 20A, 20B

Amazing Words, 117
Check *piglet, fox, lucky, filthy, cook, scrubber*

Comprehension

Shared Reading, 118, 122

Read *Read Aloud Anthology*
"The Three Billy Goats Gruff"

Monitor Progress
Check Cause and Effect

Word Work

Phonemic Awareness, 119
Review /l/

Phonics, 119
Connect /l/ to *Ll* **T**

High-Frequency Words, 119
Practice *are, that, do*

Grouping Options 68–69

Monitor Progress, 120–121
Read the Words
Read the Sentences

Modeled Writing, 105
Grammar: **REVIEW** Naming Parts
Connect to Phonics

Speaking and Listening, 106
Practice Compare and Contrast

Interactive Writing, 113
Grammar: Practice Action Parts
Connect to Phonics

Speaking and Listening, 114
Practice Compare and Contrast

Shared Writing, 123
Grammar: Review Action Parts
This Week We...

Speaking and Listening, 124
Review Compare and Contrast

Day 3 *Dictate and draw three words that end in -ll.*

Day 4 *Draw and label three action words.*

Day 5 *Draw or write about an adventure you had.*

Day 3, 107
Time for Social Studies: Chronological Time
Drama: Actors and Actresses
Comprehension: Cause and Effect

Day 4, 115
Time for Social Studies: Cause and Effect
Grammar: Action and Naming Parts
Math: How Much?

Day 5, 125
Time for Math: Counting Adventures
Time for Art: My Lucky Day
Time for Drama: Adventure Charades

KEY ⊙ = Target Skill **T** = Tested Skill

Word Reading
Check High-Frequency Words
and Word Reading, *103*
Spiral REVIEW Phonics,
High-Frequency Words

Phonemic Awareness
Check Phoneme Segmentation, *111*
Spiral REVIEW Phonics,
High-Frequency Words

Oral Vocabulary
Check Oral Vocabulary, *117*
Assess Phonics and
Comprehension, *120–122*

SUCCESS PREDICTOR

Small Group Plan *for Differentiated Instruction*

Daily Plan AT A GLANCE

Reading
Whole Group
- Oral Language/Vocabulary
- Comprehension
- Word Work

Group Time

Meet with small groups to provide:
- Skill Support
- Reading Support
- Skill Application

Read

This week's lessons for daily group time can be found behind the Differentiated Instruction (DI) tab on pp. DI·6–DI·10.

Language Arts
- Grammar
- Writing
- Speaking and Listening

Use *My Sidewalks on Reading Street* for early reading intervention.

DAY 1

On-Level	Strategic Intervention	Advanced
Teacher-Led *Page 80*	**Teacher-Led** *Page DI·6*	**Teacher-Led** *Page DI·6*
• Blend Sounds to Read Words • **Reread** Decodable Reader 19	• More Practice with /l/ • **Read** Listen to Me Reader K.4.2	• **Reread** Independent Leveled Reader K.4.1 • **Reread** for Fluency

ⓘ Independent Activities
While you meet with small groups, have the rest of the class…

- Read self-selected reading
- Complete Practice Book K.4 p. 13
- Visit the Literacy Centers
- Write in their journals

DAY 2

On-Level	Strategic Intervention	Advanced
Teacher-Led *Page 95*	**Teacher-Led** *Page DI·7*	**Teacher-Led** *Page DI·7*
• Practice Word Reading • **Read** Phonics Story	• More Practice with /l/ • **Read** Phonics Story	• Apply Phonics Skills • **Read** Decodable Reader 20

ⓘ Independent Activities
While you meet with small groups, have the rest of the class…

- Read self-selected reading
- Complete Practice Book K.4 p. 14
- Visit the Literacy Centers
- Write in their journals

DAY 3

On-Level	Strategic Intervention	Advanced
Teacher-Led *Pages 103–104*	**Teacher-Led** *Page DI·8*	**Teacher-Led** *Page DI·8*
• Practice Word Reading • **Read** Kindergarten Student Reader K.4.2	• Practice Reading Words with /l/ • **Read** Kindergarten Student Reader K.4.2	• Extend Word Reading • **Read** Kindergarten Student Reader K.4.2

ⓘ Independent Activities
While you meet with small groups, have the rest of the class…

- Read self-selected reading
- Complete Practice Book K.4 pp. 17, 18
- Visit the Literacy Centers
- Write in their journals

On-Level
Teacher-Led
Page 112

- Blend and Read Words with /l/
- **Read** Decodable Reader 20

Strategic Intervention
Teacher-Led
Page DI·9

- Blend and Read Words with /l/
- **Read** Decodable Reader 20

Advanced
Teacher-Led
Page LR3

- Extend Word Reading
- **Read** Independent Leveled Reader K.4.2

DAY 4

ⓘ Independent Activities

While you meet with small groups, have the rest of the class...

- Read self-selected reading
- Complete Practice Book K.4 pp. 19, 20
- Visit the Literacy Centers
- Write in their journals

On-Level
Teacher-Led
Pages 120–122

- Word Reading, Sets A and B
- Check Phonics
- Check Comprehension

Strategic Intervention
Teacher-Led
Pages 120, 122, DI·10

- Check Phonics
- Check Comprehension
- Alternate Assessment

Advanced
Teacher-Led
Pages 120–122

- Word Reading, Set B
- Sentence Reading, Set C
- Monitor Comprehension

DAY 5

ⓘ Independent Activities

While you meet with small groups, have the rest of the class...

- Read self-selected reading
- Visit the Literacy Centers
- Write in their journals

 Grouping Group English language learners by their reading ability in English.

Take It to the NET ONLINE
PearsonSuccessNet.com

Camille Blachowicz
For ideas and activities to build vocabulary, see the article "Vocabulary Instruction" by Scott Foresman author Camille Blachowicz and Peter Fisher.

TEACHER TALK

A **running record** is an assessment of a child's oral reading accuracy and fluency.

Be sure to schedule time for children to work on the theme project *"Remember When* Album." This week children should use photos, drawings, and other decorations to make scrapbook pages of family adventures.

Looking Ahead

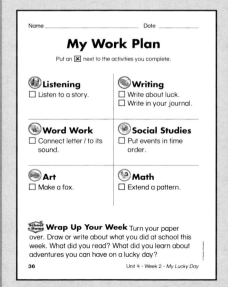

Name _____ Date _____

My Work Plan

Put an ☒ next to the activities you complete.

Listening
☐ Listen to a story.

Writing
☐ Write about luck.
☐ Write in your journal.

Word Work
☐ Connect letter *l* to its sound.

Social Studies
☐ Put events in time order.

Art
☐ Make a fox.

Math
☐ Extend a pattern.

Wrap Up Your Week Turn your paper over. Draw or write about what you did at school this week. What did you read? What did you learn about adventures you can have on a lucky day?

36   Unit 4 · Week 2 · *My Lucky Day*

▲ **Group-Time Survival Guide**
p. 36, Weekly Contract

☑ Customize Your Plan *by Strand*

ORAL LANGUAGE

Concept Development

What adventures can you have on a lucky day?

 *to build oral vocabulary* ⭐

piglet	lucky	cook
fox	filthy	scrubber

BUILD

❑ **Question of the Week** Use the Message Board to introduce and discuss the question of the week. This week children will talk, sing, read, and write about the adventure of a lucky piglet. DAY 1 *74*

❑ **Let's Talk** Use the Talk with Me Chart to introduce Amazing Words in a visual context. DAY 1 *75*

Talk with Me, Sing with Me Chart 20A

❑ **Let's Listen** Use the Sing with Me/Background Building Audio CD to build background, vocabulary, and concepts. DAY 1 *75*

❑ **Let's Sing** Use the Sing with Me Chart to sing a song about a piglet on a lucky adventure. DAY 1 *75*

Talk with Me, Sing with Me Chart 20B

DEVELOP

❑ **Question of the Day/Week** Use the questions in the Message Boards to discuss lesson concepts and how they relate to the unit theme, Let's Explore. DAY 2 *84*, DAY 3 *99*, DAY 4 *108*, DAY 5 *116*

❑ **Let's Talk** Use the Talk with Me Chart to build background, vocabulary, and concepts. DAY 2 *85*, DAY 3 *100*, DAY 4 *109*, DAY 5 *117*

❑ **Let's Sing** Use the Sing with Me Chart to sing a song about a piglet on a lucky adventure. Ask children to stand up and sing along with you, listening for the Amazing Words as they sing. DAY 2 *85*, DAY 3 *100*, DAY 4 *109*, DAY 5 *117*

CONNECT

❑ **Wrap Up Your Week!** Connect concepts and vocabulary to next week's lesson. DAY 5 *124*

CHECK

❑ **Check Oral Vocabulary** To informally assess children's oral vocabulary, have children use each word in a complete sentence. DAY 5 *117*

PHONEMIC AWARENESS

TEACH

❑ **Introduce Initial /l/** Introduce initial /l/ and identify initial sounds. DAY 1 *78*

❑ **Introduce Final /l/** Introduce and isolate final /l/. DAY 3 *102*

PRACTICE/APPLY

❑ **Listen for Sounds** Use the Phonics Songs and Rhymes Chart to listen for /l/. DAY 2 *94*

Phonics Songs and Rhymes Chart 20

RETEACH/REVIEW

❑ **Review** Review initial /h/. DAY 4 *111*

❑ **Review** Review /l/. DAY 5 *119*

❑ **Reteach Lesson** If necessary, reteach /l/. DAY 5 *DI·32*

❶ Use assessment data to determine your instructional focus.

❷ Preview this week's instruction by strand.

❸ Choose instructional activities that meet the needs of your classroom.

PHONICS

🎯 **CONNECT /l/ to Ll**

TEACH

☐ **Connect /l/ to Ll** Introduce Ll/l/. **DAY 1** 79

PRACTICE/APPLY

☐ **Connect /l/ to Ll** Practice Ll/l/. **DAY 2** 94, **DAY 3** 102

☐ **Phonics Story** Practice reading words with Ll/l/ in context. **DAY 2** 95

☐ **Kindergarten Student Reader K.4.2** Practice reading words with Ll/l/ in context. **DAY 3** 104

☐ **Decodable Reader 20** Practice reading words with Ll/l/ in context. **DAY 4** 112

☐ **Homework** Practice Book K.4, pp. 13, 18. **DAY 1** 79, **DAY 3** 102

☐ **Word Work Center** Draw pictures that begin with /l/. **ANY DAY** 72

Phonics Story

Kindergarten Student Reader K.4.2

Decodable Reader 20

RETEACH/REVIEW

☐ **Review** Review words with this week's phonics skill. **DAY 5** 119

☐ **Reteach Lesson** If necessary, reteach Ll/l/. **DAY 5** DI·32

☐ **Spiral REVIEW** Review previously taught phonics skills. **DAY 1** 80, **DAY 2** 95, **DAY 3** 103, **DAY 4** 111

ASSESS

☐ **Word and Sentence Reading** Assess children's ability to read words with Ll/l/. **DAY 5** 120-121

HIGH-FREQUENCY WORDS

HIGH-FREQUENCY WORDS
do   are   that

TEACH

☐ **Reteach** Reteach last week's high-frequency words. **DAY 1** 79

PRACTICE/APPLY

☐ **Words in Context** Read high-frequency words in the context of the Phonics Story and Decodable Reader 20. **DAY 2** 95, **DAY 4** 112

☐ **Word Wall** Use the Word Wall to review and practice high-frequency words throughout the week. **DAY 3** 103 **DAY 4** 112, **DAY 5** 119

☐ **Kindergarten Student Reader K.4.2** Practice this week's high-frequency words in context of reader. **DAY 3** 103-104, DI·8

☐ **Differentiated Text** Practice this week's high-frequency words in the context of differentiated text. **DAY 1** DI·6, **DAY 4** LR3

☐ **Homework** Practice Book K.4, p. 14 **DAY 2** 95

Phonics Story   **Decodable Reader 20**

Kindergarten Student Reader K.4.2

Listen to Me Reader K.4.2   **Independent Leveled Reader K.4.2**

RETEACH/REVIEW

☐ **Spiral REVIEW** Review previously taught high-frequency words. **DAY 2** 95, **DAY 3** 103, **DAY 4** 112, **DAY 5** 119

ASSESS

☐ **Word Reading** Assess children's ability to read this week's high-frequency words. **DAY 5** 120-121

☑ Customize Your Plan *by Strand*

COMPREHENSION

 SKILL CAUSE AND EFFECT Cause and effect is what happened and why it happened.

TEACH

❏ **Skill Lesson** Introduce and model *cause and effect*. **DAY 1** *77*

PRACTICE/APPLY

❏ **Skill in Context** Model how to identify *cause and effect*. Then read *My Lucky Day*, guiding children as they identify *cause* and *effect*. **DAY 2** *86-93*

❏ **Skill in Context** Reread *Fix-It Duck* and apply *cause* and *effect*. **DAY 4** *110*

❏ **Leveled Text** Apply *cause and effect* to leveled text. **DAY 4** *LR3*

Trade Book

Trade Book

Independent Leveled Reader K.4.2

ASSESS

❏ **Check** Read "The Three Billy Goats Gruff." Then have children identify *cause and effect*. **DAY 5** *118*

❏ **Assess** Use the blackline master on p. 122 to assess children's understanding of *cause and effect*. **DAY 5** *118, 122*

Read Aloud Anthology

RETEACH/REVIEW

❏ **Review Plot** Review definition of *plot* and apply to *My Lucky Day*. **DAY 3** *101*

❏ **Reteach Lesson** If necessary, reteach *cause and effect*. **DAY 5** *DI-32*

WRITING

TEACH

❏ **Write Together** Engage children in writing activities that develop language, grammar, and writing skills and practice phonics skills. Include independent writing as an extension of group writing activities.

Shared Writing
❏ **Connect to Grammar** **DAY 1** *81*
❏ **This Week We...** **DAY 5** *123*

Modeled Writing
❏ **Respond to Literature** **DAY 2** *96*
❏ **Connect to Phonics** **DAY 3** *105*

Interactive Writing
❏ **Connect to Phonics** **DAY 4** *113*

PRACTICE/APPLY

❏ **Daily Journal Writing** Have children write about concepts and literature in their journals. **EVERY DAY** *66-67*

❏ **Writing Center** Have children complete sentence frames. **ANY DAY** *73*

GRAMMAR

TEACH

❑ **Introduce** Introduce action parts. DAY 1 *81*

PRACTICE/APPLY

❑ **Practice** Practice action parts. DAY 2 *96*, DAY 4 *113*

❑ **Daily Fix-It** Have children find and correct errors in capitalization and punctuation. DAY 1 *81*, DAY 2 *96*, DAY 3 *105*, DAY 4 *113*, DAY 5 *123*

RETEACH/REVIEW

❑ **Review** Review last week's grammar skill, naming parts. DAY 3 *105*

❑ **Review** Review action parts. DAY 5 *123*

SPEAKING AND LISTENING

TEACH

❑ **Compare and Contrast** Introduce and model comparing and contrasting. DAY 1 *82*

PRACTICE/APPLY

❑ **Practice** Have children practice comparing and contrasting. DAY 3 *106*, DAY 4 *114*

REVIEW

❑ **Review** Review comparing and contrasting. Then have children compare and contrast food. DAY 5 *124*

INQUIRY PROJECT

TEACH

❑ **Unit Inquiry Project** Allow time for children to work on the theme project "*Remember When* Album." Have children use photos, drawings, and other decorations to make scrapbook pages of family adventures. **ANY DAY** *xxiii*

Resources for
Differentiated Instruction

Readers

Emergent

Listen to Me Reader

▶ **Oral Language**
Develop oral vocabulary.

▶ **Phonemic Awareness**
/l/ in initial and final position

◉ **Decodable Words**
Lin   Lib   lap

▶ **High-Frequency Words**
are	that	do	look
is	you	see	a

On-Level

Kindergarten Student Reader

▶ **Connected Text**
Realistic Fiction

◉ **Phonics: Ll/l/**
Lin   lid

▶ **High-Frequency Words**
are   that   do

▶ **Spiral Review:**
Decodable Words
sit	Nat	Rob	can
tap	bam	rap	on
pot	Nan	tan	pan
hit	Dad	and	pots

High-Frequency Words
a	with	me	you
we	like	to	the
look			

Independent

Leveled Reader K.4.2
Independent Leveled Reader

◉ **Comprehension:**
Cause and Effect
Identify what happens and why it happens.

▶ **Concept**
What surprises we can have on a lucky day

▶ **Social Studies**
History: events in chronological order

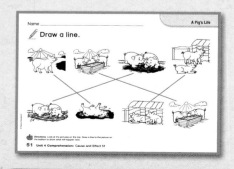

◉ **Leveled Reader,** TE, LR4

ELL

ELL Resources

- ELL Poster 20
- ELL and Transition Handbook
- ELL Notes in Teacher's Edition, pp. 74–125

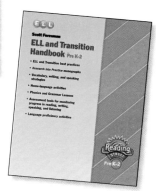

ELL Poster 20

ELL and Transition Handbook

My Sidewalks Early Reading Intervention

For students who need intensive intervention

- Effectiveness proved by scientific research
- Instruction focused on early reading success predictors
- 30 minutes of daily small-group instruction

ONLINE

PearsonSuccessNet.com

Use the Online Database of over 600 books to

- Download and print additional copies of this week's leveled readers
- Listen to the readers being read online
- Search for more titles focused on this week's skills, topic, and content

Readers' Theater Anthology

Readers' Theater Anthology

- Six scripts to build fluency
- Poetry for oral interpretation

School + Home

Homework

- Family Times Newsletter

Take-Home Books

- Kindergarten Student Readers
- Decodable Readers
- Listen to Me Readers
- Independent Leveled Readers

Literacy Centers

Listening

Let's Read
Along

- *My Lucky Day*
- *AudioText CD*

My LUCKY DAY
Keiko Kasza

Audio CD

Journal Writing

- **Day One** Write or draw about one adventure the piglet has in the story.

- **Day Two** Dictate and draw three words that begin with /l/.

- **Day Three** Dictate and draw three words that end in -*ll*.

- **Day Four** Draw and label three action words.

- **Day Five** Draw or write about an adventure you had.

Word Work

Ll
Hunt

MATERIALS
leaf Picture Card, construction paper, crayons, assorted books

Connect *Ll* to /l/

1. Show children the *leaf* Picture Card to connect /l/ to *Ll*.
2. Have children draw a very large leaf on their papers and label it *Ll*.
3. Have children look through the books and around the classroom to find pictures or objects that begin with /l/.
4. Children should then draw pictures they find on their papers within the leaf.

 This interactive CD provides additional practice.

CENTER TIP Give children examples of items they may find that begin with /l/.

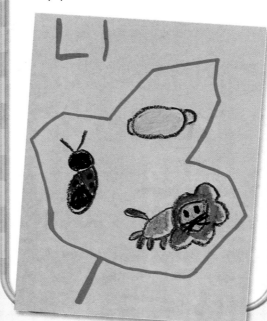

Art

Mr.
Fox

MATERIALS
brown construction paper, brown yarn, crayons

Make a Fox

1. Give children a large triangle from brown construction paper, yarn, and crayons to make a fox head.
2. Have children use crayons and construction paper for the ears, nose, eyes, and mouth.
3. Have children add yarn for the fur on the fox's head.
4. Display the yarn foxes on a bulletin board labeled *Mr. Fox*.

Scott Foresman Reading Street Centers Survival Kit

Use the *My Lucky Day* materials from the Reading Street
Centers Survival Kit to organize this week's centers.

Writing

Social Studies

Math

Lucky Me!

MATERIALS
writing paper, writing utensils, crayons

Write About Luck

1. Have the following sentence frame available for children either on the board or on paper at the center: *I was lucky when ____.* Have children copy the sentence frame on their own papers.
2. Remind children that the fox and the pig both felt lucky for different reasons.
3. Children should complete the sentence by writing, dictating, or drawing about a time they were lucky.
4. Have children draw a picture to go along with their stories.

What's Next?

MATERIALS
paper folded into three sections—label sections *First, Next,* and *Last;* writing utensils; crayons; *My Lucky Day*

Order of Events

1. Have children look through *My Lucky Day* to remind them about the story.
2. On the paper, have children draw pictures of three different events in the order they occur in the story. The first picture should reflect an event that occurred *first.*
3. The second picture should reflect an event that occurred *next.*
4. The final drawing should reflect what happened *last.*

Animal Patterns

MATERIALS
Patterns Book p. 15: *fox* and *pig,* construction paper

ABAB Patterns

1. Display a model of an ABAB pattern using the fox and pig on the table in the center.
2. Using additional fox and pig cutouts, have children work in pairs to extend the pattern.
3. Children can continue making their own patterns using the pig and fox cutouts. They can take turns extending their partner's pattern.

I was lucky when my dad gave me a bike.

First   Next   Last

ALL CENTERS

Day 1
AT A GLANCE

Oral Language and Vocabulary
Calendar
Message Board
Build Background

Shared Reading
Trade Book *My Lucky Day*
 Skill Cause and Effect

Word Work

Phonemic Awareness
Introduce /l/

Phonics
Connect /l/ to *Ll*
Blend Words
H/F Words *do, are, that*

Read

Group Time < Differentiated Instruction

Language Arts
Grammar: Action Parts
Shared Writing: Use Action
    Parts in Sentences
Speaking and Listening:
    Compare and Contrast

Materials

- Calendar
- Talk with Me, Sing with Me Chart 20A, 20B
- Sing with Me/Background Building Audio CD
- Trade Book *My Lucky Day*
- AudioText CD
- Picture Cards: pp. 78, 81
- Alphabet Cards: *Aa, Dd, Ii, Ll, Mm, Oo, Pp*
- Decodable Reader 19
- Daily Fix-It Transparency 20

Calendar

Name the day and date
Ask a volunteer to find today's date on the calendar. Have children say the day, month, date, and year together.

Last week, next week
Find today's date and read the name of the day. Then ask volunteers to point to that day last week and that day next week. Have children identify the date next Monday and last Monday.

Message Board

Question of the week
Tell children that they will have an opportunity to talk, sing, read, and write about the adventure of a lucky piglet.

Write and read the question as you track the print. Encourage children to respond in complete sentences.

> ## What adventures can you have on a lucky day?

Build Background Use the Day 1 instruction on ELL Poster 20 to assess knowledge and develop concepts.

ELL Poster 20

Build Background

LET'S TALK

Build concept
Display Talk with Me Chart 20A. Which pictures show adventures? Look at these boys laughing. What is on their faces? Why do you think they are so dirty? Prompt children to respond in complete sentences.

Build oral vocabulary
This week we will be talking about adventures you can have on a lucky day. We are going to learn six new words. Listen as I say the words: *piglet, fox, lucky, filthy, cook,* and *scrubber*.

Talk with Me, Sing with Me Chart

LET'S LISTEN

Share Background Building Audio
Play the CD that features a boy who has a lucky day.

- Why is the boy lucky?
- Does he know that he is lucky at first?

 Sing with Me/Background Building Audio CD

LET'S SING/PHONOLOGICAL AWARENESS

Sing "It's My Lucky Day"
Display Sing with Me Chart 20B. Tell children that they are going to sing a song about a piglet on a lucky adventure. Read the title and describe the pictures. Sing the song several times to the tune of "Baby Bumble Bee." Encourage children to stand up and sing with you.

Identify rhyme
Have children identify the rhyming words in each verse.

 Sing with Me/Background Building Audio CD

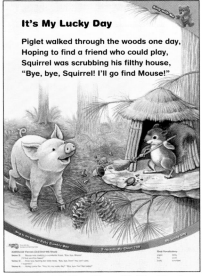

It's My Lucky Day

Piglet walked through the woods one day,
Hoping to find a friend who could play,
Squirrel was scrubbing his filthy house,
"Bye, bye, Squirrel! I'll go find Mouse!"

Talk with Me, Sing with Me Chart

Amazing Words to build oral vocabulary

- piglet
- lucky
- cook
- fox
- filthy
- scrubber

Options Before Reading

Activate Prior Knowledge

Tell About an Adventure Ask children to discuss what they think is adventurous.

- What adventure would you like to go on?
- What would make the adventure exciting?

Oral Language

Lucky Language Ask children to recall an adventure.

- Were you lucky on your adventure?
- Why was it a lucky adventure?

Develop Story Concepts

Make a Story Display the cover of *My Lucky Day*. Create a story about the fox and the piglet.

EXTEND SKILLS

Concepts of Print Point out to children how the front cover of *My Lucky Day* is different from the back cover.

Comprehension

MODEL READING STRATEGY

Use illustrations

Picture walk through *My Lucky Day.* Tell me some things you saw.

 Think Aloud I saw the pig looking scared. I saw the fox getting ready to cook the pig, but the pig got away.

The title of this book is *My Lucky Day.* What do you think this story will be about? Let's read to find out.

LET'S READ *My Lucky Day*

Model fluent reading

Read the story with expression for enjoyment.

Trade Book　　**AudioText CD**

Shared Reading

ROUTINE

Day 1	Day 2	Day 3	Day 4	Day 5
Preview and use illustrations to make predictions about *My Lucky Day.* Read the whole book for enjoyment. Introduce comprehension skill, cause and effect.	**Reread** *My Lucky Day.* Use the Shared Reading Notes to engage children in a conversation about the story. Apply comprehension skill, cause and effect.	**Reread** *My Lucky Day.* Develop oral vocabulary by naming objects and actions. Review comprehension skill, recall and retell plot.	**Reread** *Fix-It Duck.* Apply comprehension skill, cause and effect.	**Read** "The Three Billy Goats Gruff" in the *Read Aloud Anthology.* Assess comprehension skill, cause and effect.

Text to World **READER RESPONSE**

Respond to literature

Have children act out their favorite parts in the story for the class.

STRATEGY Use Illustrations

Check predictions

• What did you think the story would be about?

• What are some of the things the fox does for the piglet?

Use the following questions to guide discussion.

• Why does the fox do nice things for the piglet?

• What did the piglet do to save himself?

• Do you think the piglet was lucky, smart, or both?

INTRODUCE SKILL Cause and Effect

Define Cause and Effect

• Explain to children that things can happen because something else made it, or caused it, to happen.

• When we read what happened and figure out why it happened, we can better understand the story. This is called **cause and effect**.

Think Aloud The fox caught the pig to eat. Why didn't he eat the pig? The pig's story made the fox think he should do other things before eating the pig. Then he was too tired to eat the pig.

Recall cause and effect

Display the Trade Book *My Lucky Day*. Help children identify examples of cause and effect.

• The pig got a nice bath. Why?

• The pig had a nice dinner. Why?

• The pig got a terrific massage. Why?

Relate cause and effect to everyday life

Invite children to sit in a circle and think about why things happen. Ask a volunteer to stand and finish the thought when you say a phrase. *Because I forgot my lunch one day…*

OBJECTIVES

• Respond to literature.
• Check predictions.
• Introduce cause and effect.

Skills Trace
Cause and Effect

Introduce/Teach	TE: K.3 139, 148; K.4 77, 86; K.5 77, 86
Practice	TE: K.3 153, 161, 170, 178; K.4 93, 101, 110, 118; K.5 101, 110, 118 PB: K.3 27, 29; K.4 17, 19; K.5 17, 19
Reteach/Review	TE: K.3 DI-47; K.4 DI-46; K.5 289, DI-46; K.6 161
Assess	TE: K.3 182, 374–376; K.4 122, 380–382; K.5 122, 380–382

Access Content Demonstrate cause and effect using a graphic organizer.

> **Why did it happen?**
> The pig was dirty.

> **What happened?**
> The fox gave the pig a bath.

Text to Self

OBJECTIVE

● Introduce /l/.

Skills Trace	
🔄 **Consonant** *Ll*/l/	
Introduce/Teach	TE: K.4 78–79
Practice	TE: K.4 94, 102, 105, 113 PB: K.4 13, 15-16, 18
Reteach/Review	TE: K.4 119, 173, DI-32
Assess	TE: K.4 120-121, 380-382; Unit 4 Benchmark Test

Materials

● Picture Cards:

bag	cat	house
kite	ladybug	lake
lamp	leaf	lemon
loaf	man	map
moon	soap	tub

● Trade Book *My Lucky Day*
● Alphabet Cards: *Aa, Dd, Ii, Ll, Mm, Oo, Pp*

Support Phonemic Awareness
Speakers of Chinese, Japanese, Korean, and Vietnamese may confuse the sounds of /l/ and /r/. Give children additional practice in producing /l/ by itself and at the beginning of words.

Phonemic Awareness

INTRODUCE /l/

Introduce initial /l/

Today we will learn a new sound. Listen and watch my lips and tongue as I say the sound: /l/, /l/, /l/. Say it with me: /l/, /l/, /l/. Listen to these words that begin with /l/: *loaf, light, lemon, leaf,* and *lamp.*

Compare and contrast sounds

Display the *lake* Picture Card. This is a lake. *Lake* begins with /l/; /l/, *lake.* What sound does *lake* begin with? Display the *soap* Picture Card. This is a picture of soap. The first sound in *soap* is /s/. Say it with me: /s/, /s/, /s/, *soap.* Do *lake* and *soap* both begin with /l/? No, *lake* and *soap* do not begin with the same sound. Continue with the following pairs of Picture Cards: *ladybug, bag; kite, lamp; man, lemon;* and *loaf, moon.*

Identify initial sounds

I am going to read some words. Tell me the first sound in each word. The first word is *lap.* What is the first sound in *lap?* (/l/) Continue with these words: *leaf, moon, list, land, socks, line, lamp, ten, log, cap, leg, ladder,* and *lemon.*

Monitor Progress | Check Sound Fluency

Listen for /l/ Say two words: *lucky, fox.* Have children identify the word that begins with /l/. Continue with Picture Cards: *leaf, house; lamp, map; ladybug, cat;* and *lemon, tub.*

If... children cannot identify initial /l/,
then...say the words, emphasizing the first sound. Have them echo you.

SUCCESS PREDICTOR

▶ **Day 1** Check Sound Fluency	**Day 2** Check Retelling/ Letter-Sound Knowledge	**Day 3** Check High- Frequency Words/ Word Reading	**Day 4** Check Phoneme Segmentation	**Day 5** Check Oral Vocabulary/ Assess Progress

Phonics

CONNECT /l/ to *Ll*

Introduce *Ll*/l/

Display the cover from *My Lucky Day.* Point to the word *Lucky.* This is the word *Lucky.* The word *Lucky* begins with the uppercase letter *L.* The sound for *L* is /l/.

Trade Book

Recognize *Ll*

Encourage children to stand and point to *Ll* on the classroom alphabet chart.

Connect /l/ to *Ll*

Display the *Ll* Alphabet Card. Point to the *lemon.* What is the name of this fruit? *Lemon* begins with /l/. Point to the letters on the card. The name of the letter for /l/ is *l.* This is the uppercase *L* and this is the lowercase *l.* Invite children to write three uppercase *L*'s and three lowercase *l*'s in the air as you write the letters on the board.

Alphabet Card

Review letter names and sounds

Review the following letter names and sounds: *Ll, Oo, Aa, Ii, Mm, Pp,* and *Dd.*

BLEND SOUNDS

Blend *Ll*/l/ words

Write the word *lap* on the board. This is the word *lap.* To say this word we start with the beginning sound /l/, then we say the middle sound /a/, and the last sound /p/: /l/ /a/ /p/, *lap.*

Say all the sounds with me: /l/ /a/ /p/. Now let's blend the sounds as I point to each letter: /l/ /a/ /p/, *lap.* Repeat the blending routine with *lad, lip, pad,* and *pod.*

Word Wall HIGH-FREQUENCY WORDS

Reteach *do, are, that*

Display *do.* This is the word *do.* Let's say it together, *do.* Continue with the words *are* and *that.* Point to the words on the Word Wall.

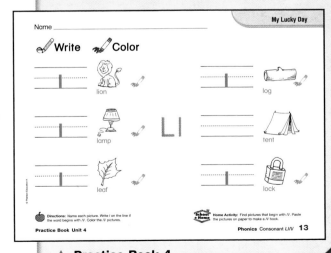

▲ **Practice Book 4**
Consonant *Ll*/l/, p. 13

SUCCESS PREDICTOR

WORD WORK

OBJECTIVES

● Review high-frequency words.
● Write uppercase and lowercase *Ll*.

Spiral REVIEW PREPARE TO READ

Review words   Continue guided blending practice with these words from last week's Decodable Reader 19 *Hob Can Hit*:

man	Dan	Hob	hit	pop
can	fan	Pam	Sam	hat
it	did	not	hot	

Review high-frequency words   Write the word *see* on the board. This is the word *see*. What is this word? Continue the word reading routine with the words *is, a,* and *they*.

Group Time

On-Level

Reread Decodable Reader 19. Use the Small Group Reading **Routine.**

Strategic Intervention

Read Listen to Me Reader K.4.2. More practice with *Ll/l/*, p. DI·6.

Advanced

Reread Independent Leveled Reader K.4.1. Use the reading routine on p. DI·6. Reread to build fluency.

E L L

Group English language learners by their reading ability in English.

i Independent Activities

Self-Selected Reading See pp. TR14–15 for a bibliography of books related to the weekly concept.

Practice Book Consonant *Ll/l/*, p. 13

Centers Use the center activities on pp. 72–73 to practice this week's skills.

Journal Writing Write or draw about one adventure the piglet has in the story.

Small Group Reading

1 **Model Fluent Reading** Have children finger point as you read a page.

2 **Read Chorally** Have children finger point as they chorally read the page. Continue reading page by page, repeating steps 1 and 2.

3 **Read Individually** Have children read aloud a page in their group.

4 **Reread and Monitor Progress** As you listen to individual children reread, monitor progress and provide support.

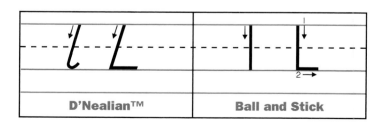

Decodable Reader

DAY 1 ROUTINE

HANDWRITING

Write *L* and *l*   Words that begin with /l/ are written with either an uppercase *L* or a lowercase *l*. Remember, we use the uppercase letter at the beginning of sentences or for the first letter of a person's name, like *Lil*. Write *Lil* on the board. Follow the stroke instructions below. Now holding your pencils in the correct position, write *L* on your paper. Repeat these instructions with lowercase *l*.

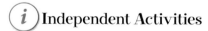	
D'Nealian™	**Ball and Stick**

Shared Writing

GRAMMAR Action Parts

Introduce action parts

Introduce the action parts of sentences by telling children: I write. Which word tells you what I am doing, or my action? Write these sentences on the board: *The cat sat; The dog ran.* Read the sentences together. Which word tells what the cat is doing? *Sat* is the action part of this sentence because it tells us what the cat is doing. Continue with the dog sentence. Repeat with other sentences the children dictate.

Identify action parts

Have children sit in a circle. Act out various actions and have the children guess the words. Have children dictate sentences about the actions you demonstrated.

LET'S WRITE Connect to Grammar

Use action parts in a sentence

Display the *man* Picture Card. Let's write a list of the action words on the board that describe something the man could do. Guide the children to name a variety of action words. Now we are going to use some of our words to write a sentence.

The man ran.

The man jumps.

Revise and edit

When we write a sentence, we use an uppercase letter for the first word. Did I write uppercase *T?* Did I end each sentence with a period?

Independent writing

Have children draw an action scene of a man doing something. Remind them to write or dictate a sentence about the man's actions and underline the action word.

OBJECTIVES

- Introduce action parts.
- Identify action parts in sentences.
- Use action parts in sentences.

Materials

- Picture Card: *man*

DAILY FIX-IT

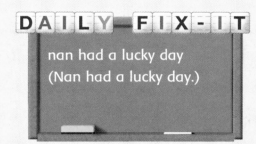

nan had a lucky day
(Nan had a lucky day.)

This week's practice sentences appear on Daily Fix-It Transparency 20.

Writing ROUTINE

Day 1 **Shared Writing**
Connect to grammar.

Day 2 **Modeled Writing**
Respond to literature.

Day 3 **Modeled Writing**
Connect to phonics.

Day 4 **Interactive Writing**
Connect to phonics.

Day 5 **Shared Writing**
Write about this week's literature.

ELL

Access Content Ask for volunteers to talk with you about what is the same and different about the names of two objects that sound similar in English and their home language.

Speaking and Listening

COMPARE AND CONTRAST

Discuss compare and contrast

Today we are going to talk about how things are alike and how they are different. For example, a piano and a radio both can be used to play music, but they look different and they are different kinds of machines. Ask children to tell how a cat and a dog are alike and how they are different.

Model compare and contrast

I want to tell how a book and a magazine are alike and how they are different. Show a book and a magazine. Describe how they are alike and different. Continue with a tree and a houseplant.

Practice compare and contrast

Instruct children to look at the cover of *My Lucky Day*. Have them tell how the fox and the pig are alike and how they are different.

Wrap Up Your Day!

✓ **Oral Language** Today we read about a piglet and a fox. They both thought it was their lucky day. Have you ever had a lucky day?

✓ **Comprehension** Things that happen in a story are made to happen, or caused by something else. What happened to the piglet and why?

✓ **Grammar** Show pages from *My Lucky Day*. What are the fox and the piglet doing? Can you name their actions?

PREVIEW Day 2

Tomorrow we will read about the piglet and the fox again.

School + Home **Homework** Send home this week's Family Times newsletter.

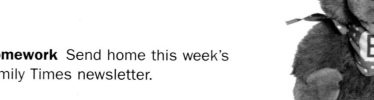

EXTEND Your Day

TIME FOR **Science**

Our Senses

Materials crayons, construction paper

Introduce the Five Senses Tell children: Every day we smell, taste, feel, see, and hear many things. The things that help us smell, taste, feel, see, and hear are called the five senses. Point to your eyes. What do you do with your eyes? How do your eyes help you? Continue with ears, nose, mouth, and hands.

Take a picture walk through the illustrations of *My Lucky Day,* pointing out the different senses that the fox and the piglet use in the story.

Ask children what senses help them experience a good meal.

Sense Pages Ask the children to name the five senses again. Write each one on the board. Have children choose a sense and write the word on their paper. Then have them draw items that the particular sense helps them to experience. Pages can be combined into class or individual sense books.

Grammar

Action Parts

Name Action Parts Write on the board: *"I _____."* Have children brainstorm a list of action words. Have them divide a paper into four sections. In each section, have them illustrate and write an action word. Extend the activity and have children act out one of their action words.

Math

Make a Guess

Materials balance; paper cups; small objects such as papers, crayons, chalk, paper clips, safety scissors, markers, pencils

Estimate Weight Display *My Lucky Day.* Remind children that the piglet kept telling the fox he needed to be bigger and fatter to make a better meal.

Show children a piece of colored chalk and a piece of white chalk. Ask them to tell which is heavier. Help children place one piece on each pan of the balance to determine which is heavier. Explain that the heavier item will make the arm of the balance go lower than the other. Continue to compare other items.

Day 2
AT A GLANCE

Oral Language and Vocabulary
Calendar
Message Board
Build Background

Shared Reading
Trade Book *My Lucky Day*
Strategy Recall and Retell
◉ **Skill** Cause and Effect

Word Work

Phonemic Awareness
Listen for /l/

Phonics
◉ Connect /l/ *to Ll*
Blend Words
H/F Words *do, are, that*
Phonics Story *Lad and Me*

Read

(Group Time) < Differentiated Instruction

Language Arts
Grammar: Action Parts
Modeled Writing: Write
  Sentences About *My Lucky
  Day*
Speaking and Listening:
  Expand Vocabulary

Materials
- Calendar
- Talk with Me, Sing with Me
  Chart 19A, 20A, 20B
- Sing with Me/Background
  Building Audio CD
- Trade Book *My Lucky Day*
- Picture Card: p. 96
- Phonics Songs and Rhymes
  Chart 20
- Phonics Songs and Rhymes
  Audio CD
- Alphabet Cards: *Aa, Dd, Ll, Pp,*
  keyboard
- Phonics Story *Lad and Me*

Calendar

Name the day and date
Ask a volunteer to find today's date on the calendar. Have children say the day, month, date, and year together.

Count days until Saturday
Remind children that there is no school on Saturday. Ask children to count the number of days until Saturday.

Message Board

Question of the day
Write and read the question as you track the print. Encourage children to respond in complete sentences.

> ## What are some things you do that are fun?

Review high-frequency words
Remind children that yesterday they learned the words *do, are,* and *that.* Circle the words in the message. Have children say the words as you point to the words.

Build Background Use the Day 2 instruction on ELL Poster 20 to practice Develop Vocabulary words.

ELL Poster 20

Build Background

LET'S TALK/LET'S SING

Develop oral vocabulary

Display Talk with Me Chart 20A. Point to the photograph of the piglet.

- This is a baby pig, or a *piglet*.
- Tell me about the picture of the *fox*.

Sing "It's My Lucky Day"

Display Sing with Me Chart 20B. Sing "It's My Lucky Day." Encourage children to join you. Ask them to clap when they hear the words *fox* and *piglet*.

Talk with Me,
Sing with Me Chart

It's My Lucky Day

Piglet walked through the woods one day,
Hoping to find a friend who could play,
Squirrel was scrubbing his filthy house,
"Bye, bye, Squirrel! I'll go find Mouse!"

Audio CD
Sing with Me/Background Building
Audio CD

LET'S LEARN AMAZING WORDS

DAY 2 ROUTINE

Oral Vocabulary   piglet   fox

1 **Introduce** In this story, the animal that has a lucky day is a *piglet*. A *piglet* is a young pig. What is the name of a young pig?

Demonstrate The *piglet* decided to visit someone and have an adventure. Whom did the *piglet* visit?

2 **Introduce** A medium-sized furry animal with a bushy tail and a pointed snout is a *fox*. A *fox* is often a character in stories.

Demonstrate Smaller or slower animals must hide from a *fox*. What did the *fox* want to eat in the story?

3 **Review** We talked about two words today: *piglet* and *fox*. Which word means "a young pig," *piglet* or *fox*? Which word is the name of a furry animal with a bushy tail and a pointed snout, *piglet* or *fox*?

4 **Apply** Have children use *piglet* and *fox* in complete sentences. Have them tell about a *piglet* or a *fox* from another story.

Amazing Words to build oral vocabulary

- piglet
- fox
- lucky
- filthy
- cook
- scrubber

ELL

Activate Prior Knowledge Ask children what words in their home languages are used for *piglet* and *fox*.

2

OBJECTIVES

- Recall story events.
- Recognize cause and effect in a story.

Materials

- Trade Book *My Lucky Day*

Access Content Have children act out something the piglet says to the fox (cause) and what the fox does as a result (effect).

Comprehension

MODEL READING STRATEGY
Recall and Retell

Retell the story

Using the pictures as prompts, invite children to retell the story.

Show the cover of the book. The fox wants to eat the piglet. The piglet doesn't want to get eaten. Tell me how the piglet is able to get the fox to do nice things for him.

Trade Book

SKILL Cause and Effect

Recognize cause and effect in a story

Remind children to think about things that happen in stories and why those things happen.

Think Aloud The piglet didn't want to get eaten, so he told the fox that he needed to be washed, fattened up, and massaged. The fox did those things and then was too tired to eat the piglet.

The piglet made the fox do many things that caused the fox to fall asleep.

TEACHING TIP

Cause and Effect Although most children may not know about cause and effect, some may have heard another story where pigs outwit a wolf. Reinforce this by saying:

In the story "The Three Little Pigs," the pigs keep the wolf from eating them by building a strong house. What other things could the pigs do to keep from being eaten?

LET'S READ *My Lucky Day*

Reread the story

Ask children to listen carefully to things that happened in the story and why those things happened as you read. Use the Shared Reading Notes to prompt conversation about *My Lucky Day*.

 **AudioText CD**

Page 3

One day, a hungry fox was preparing to hunt for his dinner. As he polished his claws, he was startled by a knock at the door.

Pages 4–5

"Hey, Rabbit!" someone yelled outside. "Are you home?"

Rabbit? thought the fox. *If there were any rabbits in here, I'd have eaten them for breakfast.*

Shared Reading Notes

What kind of animal is this? *Child may respond:* fox

- This is a fox. What is the fox doing? *wh-* **question**

Expand Vocabulary startled

What is the fox looking at? *Child may respond:* the door

- The fox is looking at the door because someone is knocking. Whom is the "someone" at the door calling for? *wh-* **question**

Develop Vocabulary rabbit

Shared Reading Notes

What was standing there when the fox opened the door? *Child may respond:* a piglet

- A piglet was standing at the door. How can you tell that the piglet was afraid when he saw the fox? **open-ended**

Expand Vocabulary delicious

Pages 6–7

When the fox opened the door, there stood a delicious-looking piglet.
"Oh, no!" screamed the piglet.
"Oh, yes!" cried the fox. "You've come to the right place."
He grabbed the piglet and hauled him inside.

What does the fox do? *Child may respond:* picks up the piglet

- The fox picked the piglet up. What is the fox going to do with the roasting pan? **wh- question**

Pages 8–9

"This must be my lucky day!" the fox shouted. "How often does dinner come knocking on the door?"
The piglet kicked and squealed, "Let me go! Let me go!"
"Sorry, pal," said the fox. "This isn't just any dinner. It's a pig roast. My favorite! Now get into this roasting pan."

What does the piglet tell the fox to do before he eats him? *Child may respond:* wash him

- The piglet tells the fox he is filthy, so he needs to be washed. Do you wash your food before you eat it? **distancing**

Pages 10–11

It was useless to struggle. "All right," sighed the piglet. "I will. But there is just one thing."
"What?" growled the fox.
"Well, I am a pig, you know. I'm filthy. Shouldn't you wash me first? Just a thought, Mr. Fox."
"Hmmm . . ." the fox said to himself, "he is filthy."

Pages 12-13

Pages 14-15

Pages 16-17

Shared Reading Notes

What is the fox doing? *Child may respond:* giving the piglet a bath

• The fox is giving the piglet a bath. What did the fox do before he could give the piglet a bath? **recall**

Develop Vocabulary bath

ELL

Access Content Tell children many years ago people did not have running water in their houses and had to do all of those things when they wanted to take a bath.

Where is the piglet now? *Child may respond:* in the pan

• The piglet is in the roasting pan. What does the piglet tell the fox to do? **recall**

What does the fox do to fatten up the piglet? *Child may respond:* makes dinner for him

• The fox makes the piglet a nice dinner to fatten him up. What is your favorite dinner? **distancing**

Develop Vocabulary dinner, cookies

Shared Reading Notes

Where is the fox going to put the piglet?
Child may respond: in the oven

- The fox is putting the piglet in the oven. What other foods is the fox going to cook when he roasts the piglet? **wh- question**

Pages 18–19

"There," said the fox. "Now you're the fattest piglet in the county. So get into the oven!"

"All right," sighed the piglet. "I will. But . . ."

"What? What? WHAT?" shouted the fox.

"Well, I am a hardworking pig, you know. My meat is awfully tough. Shouldn't you massage me first to make a more tender roast? Just a thought, Mr. Fox."

"Hmmm . . ." the fox said to himself, "I do prefer tender meat."

What does the fox do to make the piglet tender? *Child may respond:* He pushed, pulled, squeezed, and pounded on the piglet.

- The fox pushed, pulled, squeezed, and pounded to give the piglet a massage. Why does the piglet have the fox give him a bath, make dinner, and now massage him? **open-ended**

Pages 20–21

So the fox got busy.

He pushed . . .

and he pulled.

He squeezed and he pounded the piglet from head to toe.

"You give a terrific massage," said the piglet.

What does the fox look like now? *Child may respond:* tired

- The fox looks very tired. Why does the fox look tired? **open-ended**

Pages 22–23

"But," the piglet continued, "I've been working really hard lately. My back is awfully stiff. Could you push a bit harder, Mr. Fox? A little to the right, please . . . yes, yes . . . now just a little to the left . . ."

Pages 24–25

"Mr. Fox, are you there?"

Shared Reading Notes

What is the fox doing? *Child may respond:* falling down

- The fox is falling down. Why do you think the fox is falling down? Why is he so tired? **open-ended**

Pages 26–27

But Mr. Fox was no longer listening. He had passed out, exhausted. He couldn't lift a finger, let alone a roasting pan.

"Poor Mr. Fox," sighed the piglet. "He's had a busy day." Then the cleanest, fattest and softest piglet in the county picked up the rest of his cookies and headed for home.

Where is the fox? *Child may respond:* on the floor

- The fox is lying on the floor. Have you ever worked so hard that you were too tired to do anything else? **distancing**

Pages 28–29

"What a bath! What a dinner! What a massage!" cried the piglet. "This must be my lucky day!"

What is the piglet doing? *Child may respond:* running away

- The piglet is running away happy after his bath, dinner, and massage. Do you think the piglet had a lucky day? Why? **open-ended**

Shared Reading Notes

What did the piglet do when he got home? *Child may respond:* sat in a chair

• The piglet is sitting in a chair relaxing after his lucky day. Why is the piglet relaxing? **wh- question**

Pages 30–31

When he got home, the piglet relaxed before a warm fire. "Let's see," he wondered, looking at his address book. "Who shall I visit next?"

Who did the piglet visit next? *Child may respond:* the bear

• The piglet is standing at the bear's door. Do you think the piglet is surprised? **open-ended**

Page 32

Access Content Ask children if they noticed any clues that the piglet knew all along he would not be eaten by the fox. For instance, he has animals that he has already visited crossed out in his address book, and he has a map on his table to plan where to go next.

CONNECT TO SKILL Cause and Effect

Connect skill to *My Lucky Day*

Show children some pictures in the story. Ask children to tell about things that happened and why they happened.

Display page 3.

• Why was the fox polishing his claws?

Display pages 6 and 7.

• Why did the fox grab the piglet?

Display pages 12 and 13.

• Why is the piglet in the wash tub?

Display pages 26 and 27.

• Why is the fox lying on the floor?

Monitor Progress   **Check Retelling** *My Lucky Day*

Picture Walk and Retell Have children use the pictures in *My Lucky Day* to retell the story.

If... children have difficulty retelling the story,
then... use the Retelling Rubric to help them move toward fluent retelling.

SUCCESS PREDICTOR

Day 1	▶Day 2	Day 3	Day 4	Day 5
Check Sound Fluency	Check Retelling/ Letter-Sound Knowledge	Check High-Frequency Words/ Word Reading	Check Phoneme Segmentation	Check Oral Vocabulary/ Assess Progress

Scoring Rubric   Retelling

Rubric 4 3 2 1	**4**	**3**	**2**	**1**
Setting	describes time and location	identifies time and location	omits time and location	is unable to identify time and location
Character	describes main character(s) and character development	identifies main character(s)	omits or inaccurately identifies character(s)	unable to identify character
Events	describes events in sequence with details	tells most events in sequence with some detail	retells first and last events but omits middle with few details	is unable to retell events

Retelling Plan

☑ Week 1 assess Advanced students.

☑ **This week assess On-Level students.**

☐ Week 3 assess Strategic Intervention students.

☐ Week 4 assess Advanced students.

☐ Week 5 assess On-Level students.

☐ Week 6 assess Strategic Intervention students.

SUCCESS PREDICTOR

OBJECTIVES

- Listen for initial /l/.
- Connect /l/ to *Ll*.

Materials

- Phonics Songs and Rhymes Chart 20
- Alphabet Cards: *Aa, Dd, Ll, Pp,* keyboard
- Phonics Story *Lad and Me*
- Big Book *Animal ABCs*

ELL

Support Phonemic Awareness
The slang terms *crunch* and *munch* may be difficult for English language learners to understand. In Spanish, *crujido* means "crunch" and *masque* means "munch."

Phonemic Awareness

PRACTICE /l/

Listen for initial /l/

Display the chart. We are going to learn a new song today. Listen carefully to the song. Play the CD or sing the song several times to the tune of "Twinkle, Twinkle Little Star." Encourage children to join in. Then ask children to identify words that begin with /l/: *Lucy, Leopard, loves, lunch, lettuce, limes, licks, lemonade,* and *likes.*

Lucy Leopard Loves Her Lunch

Lucy Leopard loves her lunch—
Lettuce and limes to crunch and munch.
She licks up the lemonade.
She likes it best when it's homemade.
Lucy Leopard loves her lunch—
Lettuce and limes to crunch and munch.

Phonics Songs and Rhymes Chart

 **Audio CD** Phonics Songs and Rhymes Audio CD

Phonics

CONNECT /l/ to *Ll*

Recognize *Ll*

Ask children to identify *L* on the keyboard card.

Identify *Ll*

Display the chart. There were many words that began with *l* in our song. Let's circle the words that begin with *l* on our chart. Have volunteers circle one of the words that begins with *L* or *l* one at a time.

Connect /l/ to *Ll*

Write *l* on the board. What is the name of this letter? *(l)* What is the sound for this letter? *(/l/)* Repeat the routine with *L.*

Monitor Progress | **Check Letter-Sound Knowledge**

Identify *Ll* Have children write *Ll*'s on paper. The name of this letter is *l.* The sound for *l* is /l/. When I say a word that begins with /l/, hold up your paper with the *Ll*'s you wrote. Read these words: *lucky, pig, sad, lost, lemon, candy, lollipop,* and *top.*

If... children cannot connect /l/ to *Ll*,

then... use the *Ll* Alphabet Card and *Animal ABCs* to practice seeing *l*'s and saying /l/ words.

SUCCESS PREDICTOR

Day 1	**▶ Day 2**	**Day 3**	**Day 4**	**Day 5**
Check Sound Fluency	Check Retelling/ Letter-Sound Knowledge	Check High-Frequency Words/ Word Reading	Check Phoneme Segmentation	Check Oral Vocabulary/ Assess Progress

BLEND SOUNDS

Spiral Review — BLEND SOUNDS

Review letter names and sounds

Spell and blend words

PHONICS ACTIVITY MAT

Use the Alphabet Cards to review these letter names and sounds: *Ll, Aa, Dd,* and *Pp.*

Listen to the three sounds in *lap*: /l/ /a/ /p/. What is the first sound in *lap?* (/l/) What is the letter for that sound? *(l)* Write *l* on the board. Now you write *l* on your paper. Continue the routine with the remaining sounds.

l a p

Help me blend the sounds together to read this word: /l/ /a/ /p/. Here is another way: /l/ -ap. The word is *lap.*

Continue spell and blend practice with the following words: *Lad, lid, lot, hot, can, hop, on, cat, sit,* and *hit.*

PREPARE TO READ

Review high-frequency words

Write *are* on the board. This is the word *are*. What is this word? Continue the word reading routine with *that* and *do.*

Small Group Reading

DAY 2 ROUTINE

1 **Model Fluent Reading** Have children finger point as you read a page.

2 **Read Chorally** Have children finger point as they chorally read the page. Continue reading page by page, repeating steps 1 and 2.

3 **Read Individually** Have children read aloud a page in their group.

4 **Reread and Monitor Progress** As you listen to individual children reread, monitor progress and provide support.

Practice Book 4
Phonics Story, pp. 15–16

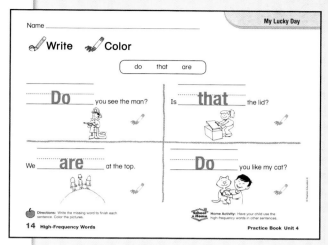

▲ **Practice Book 4**
High-Frequency Words, p. 14

Group Time

On-Level

Read Phonics Story *Lad and Me.* Use the Small Group Reading **Routine.**

Strategic Intervention

Read Phonics Story *Lad and Me.* More practice with *Ll/l/,* p. DI·7.

Advanced

Read Decodable Reader 20. Use the reading routine on p. DI·7. Apply phonics skills.

ELL

Group English language learners by their reading ability in English.

. . . .

i **Independent Activities**

Self-Selected Reading See pp. TR14–15 for books related to the weekly concept.

Practice Book High-Frequency Words, p. 14

Centers Use the center activities on pp. 72–73.

Journal Writing Dictate and draw three words that begin with /l/.

SUCCESS PREDICTOR
Letter-Sound Knowledge

OBJECTIVES

- Practice action parts.
- Write sentences about *My Lucky Day*.

Materials

- Picture Card: *lake*
- Trade Book *My Lucky Day*
- Talk with Me, Sing with Me Chart 19A

DAILY FIX-IT

will linda eat her lunch?

(Will Linda eat her lunch?)

Writer's Checkup

✔ The first word in a sentence begins with an uppercase letter. Did I do that?

✔ A sentence should end with a period. Did I do that?

✔ A sentence should make sense. Does my sentence make sense?

✔ A good writer uses his or her best handwriting. Did I do that?

Modeled Writing

GRAMMAR Action Parts

Practice action parts
Show the *lake* Picture Card. This is a lake. We can do lots of things in a lake. We can swim in a lake. We can jump in a lake. We can play in a lake. Swim, jump, and play are actions. We can do them.

Identify action parts
Display page 16 of *My Lucky Day*. Guide children to identify a variety of actions in the illustrations.

Picture Card

LET'S WRITE Respond to Literature

Discuss *My Lucky Day*
Discuss *My Lucky Day*. Ask children to briefly describe the things the fox did to prepare the piglet to be eaten. You may wish to write labels or draw simple illustrations for each response.

Model writing a sentence
The fox gave the piglet a bath so he would be clean, he cooked him a nice dinner so he would be fat, and he gave the piglet a massage so he would be tender. I am going to write:

The fox cooked piglet a big dinner.

Independent writing
Have children write or dictate their own sentences about *My Lucky Day* or copy one of the sentences the class wrote together. Then have them illustrate their sentences.

The fox fed the piglet.

Speaking and Listening

LET'S REVIEW AMAZING WORDS

Display Talk with Me Chart 19A. Review these amazing words from last week.

DAY 2 ROUTINE

Oral Vocabulary   chores   tidy

1 **Introduce** *Chores* are small jobs we have to do often. Making our beds every day is a *chore.* What is the word for jobs we do often?

Demonstrate What *chores* do we have to do to keep our classroom neat and clean?

2 **Introduce** If we want things to be neat, we want them to be *tidy.* Things are *tidy* when they are all clean.

Demonstrate We keep our class-room *tidy* when we pick up and pack away our things at the end of the day.

3 **Review** We talked about two words today: *chores* and *tidy.* Which word means "small jobs we do often," *chores* or *tidy?* Which word means "neat and clean," *chores* or *tidy?*

4 **Apply** Have children tell about *chores* they do and ways they keep things *tidy*. Assign chores to keep the classroom tidy.

Wrap Up Your Day!

✓ **Oral Language** Today we read about a piglet that outsmarts a fox in *My Lucky Day*. The piglet was able to get the fox to do lots of things for him. What things did the fox do?

✓ **Grammar** Remember, the part of the sentence that tells what someone or something is doing is the action part. Let's name some actions.

✓ **Homework Idea** Have children take their Phonics Story home to share with their families.

PREVIEW Day 3

Tomorrow we will read about some children who make music. How do you think they do it?

EXTEND Your Day

TIME FOR Science

Cause and Effect with Growing Things

Materials light-colored large construction paper, one-inch wide construction paper strips, crayons, markers, glue

Needs of Living Things Have a discussion about living things—plants, animals, or people. What do these things need to grow? Use a web graphic organizer to represent each subject. In the center circle, write or draw the living thing. Write or draw its needs in circles with lines connecting back to the center.

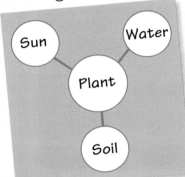

Cause and Effect Drawings

After discussing several living things, have children choose one of them to draw. Fold construction paper in half and distribute to the children. Have them draw their living thing on the right side. Then have them draw one of the things their subject needs to live on the left. If they have drawn a person, they could draw a glass of water or a plate of food on the left side. Show children how to use three paper strips to make an arrow. Glue the arrow between the left and right sides of the paper.

Comprehension
Cause and Effect

Materials Patterns Book p. 15: *fox, piglet;* craft sticks; crayons; glue

Puppet Play Discuss with children what made the fox and piglet act the way they did in the story. Then discuss how the story would have been different if the fox was not hungry or the piglet was not very clever.

Divide the children into groups of two. Have each pair make simple puppets by coloring and cutting out the fox and piglet patterns and gluing them onto craft sticks. Challenge children to create a skit about how the story would have been different if one or both of the above events occurred in the story. Have each group present the puppet play to the class.

Phonics
Connect /l/ to *L*

Materials L-shaped paper

Lucky Adventures Give each child a large piece of paper in the shape of an *L*. Tell children to imagine they have been given three wishes for a lucky adventure. They may wish for three exciting things as long as they begin with the letter *L*. Have children write the names or draw pictures of the three things on their paper *L*. Display them on a *Lucky L* bulletin board.

Calendar

Name the day and date

Point out today's date on the calendar and read the day, month, date, and year. Point to the day, month, date, and year and have children identify each.

Order of the days

Point out the order of the days in each week. Have children recite the days of the week together.

Message Board

Question of the day

Write and read the question as you track the print. Encourage children to reply in complete sentences.

> ## What things will you do on a lucky day?

Review phonics

- What letter stands for /l/? *(Ll)*

- In which words do you hear /l/? *(will, lucky)*

ELL

Extend Language Use the Day 3 instruction on ELL Poster 20 to extend and enrich language.

ELL Poster 20

Materials

● Talk with Me, Sing with Me Chart 20A, 20B

to build oral vocabulary

- • piglet
- • lucky
- • cook
- • fox
- • filthy
- • scrubber

Access Content Ask children what words are used for *lucky* and *filthy* in their home languages.

Build Background

LET'S TALK

Develop oral vocabulary

Display Talk with Me Chart 20A. Point to the photograph of the boys after playing.

- How do these boys look? **(dirty)** Another word for very dirty is *filthy*.

- How would you feel if you were given a special party and presents? You might feel *lucky*.

Talk with Me, Sing with Me Chart

LET'S SING

Sing "It's My Lucky Day"

Display Sing with Me Chart 20B. Remind the class that yesterday they sang "It's My Lucky Day" and learned the words *piglet* and *fox*. Today sing the song again. Ask children to clap when they hear the words *lucky* and *filthy*.

 Sing with Me/Background Building Audio CD

LET'S LEARN AMAZING WORDS

Oral Vocabulary   lucky   filthy

DAY 3 ROUTINE

1 **Introduce** The pig was *lucky* to have the fox do so many nice things for him. *Lucky* is when good things happen. What is our new word for having good things happen?

Demonstrate The fox thought he was *lucky* to have a pig come to his house. How have you been *lucky*?

2 **Introduce** The pig was very dirty from being outside in the mud. He told the fox that he was *filthy*. What is our new word for very dirty?

Demonstrate If you play soccer in the rain, you will probably get *filthy*. Can you think of a time when you were *filthy*?

3 **Review** We talked about two words today: *lucky* and *filthy*. Which word means "very dirty," *lucky* or *filthy*? Which word means "having good things happen," *lucky* or *filthy*?

4 **Apply** Have children talk about times they were *lucky* or *filthy* in complete sentences.

Comprehension

REVIEW SKILL Plot

Review plot

Remind children that the plot of a story is what happens in the beginning, middle, and end. When we remember these events in order, we can tell other people all about the story.

Apply recall and retell plot

- What was the first thing that happened?
- Next, the piglet got the fox to do many nice things for him. What happened to the fox?
- Then, what did the piglet do?
- What happened at the very end of the story that makes us wonder if the pig planned his whole lucky day?

LET'S READ *My Lucky Day*

Develop vocabulary

Reread *My Lucky Day*. Develop vocabulary by having children talk about the story. Encourage children to use names and describe objects and actions. Then ask children to talk about lucky adventures they have had.

 AudioText CD

SKILL Cause and Effect

Practice cause and effect

Explain to children that characters in *My Lucky Day* do or say things that cause other things to happen.

- What did the piglet say to the fox to keep the fox from cooking him?
- What caused the fox to fall down and let the piglet go free?
- What did the piglet do to try to have another lucky day?

Monitor Progress

Cause and Effect

If... children have difficulty understanding cause and effect,	then... ask a question such as "Why did the fox make dinner for the pig?" and connect question and answer in a cause and effect statement.

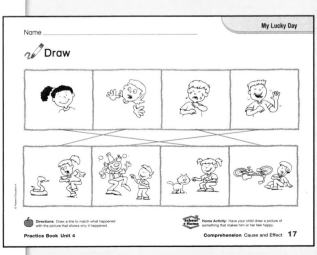

▲ **Practice Book 4**
Cause and Effect, p. 17

WORD WORK

- Isolate final /l/.
- Connect /l/ to *Ll*.
- Introduce final *-ll*.
- Substitute phonemes.
- Blend and read words.

Materials

- Picture Cards:

doll	bubble	ladybug
lake	lamp	lemon
pail	puzzle	seal

- Alphabet Cards: *Aa, Bb, Cc, Dd, Hh, Ii, Ll, Mm, Nn, Oo, Pp, Rr, Ss, Tt*
- Kindergarten Student Reader K.4.2

Phonemic Awareness

PRACTICE Final /l/

Isolate final /l/

Display the *doll* Picture Card. This is a *doll*. Do you hear /l/ in *doll*? /l/ is at the end of the word.

Practice final /l/

Display the *bubble* Picture Card. This is a *bubble*. Where do you hear /l/ in *bubble*? Yes, we hear /l/ at the end of *bubble*. Continue with the following Picture Cards: *ladybug, lake, pail, lamp, lemon, puzzle,* and *seal*.

Phonics

↻ CONNECT /l/ to *Ll*

Connect /l/ to *Ll*

Display the *Ll* Alphabet Card. What is the name of this letter? *(l)* What is the sound for this letter? *(/l/)*

Introduce final *-ll*

Write the word *dill* on the board. This is *dill*. Say it with me: /d/ /i/ /l/, *dill*. What is the last sound in *dill*? /l/ is the last sound in *dill*. What letters do you see that make /l/?

Alphabet Card

dill

Substitute phonemes

Continue group practice with *Bill* and *hill*.

I can make a new word by changing the first sound. Change the *d* to *h*. Say the sounds with me: /h/ /i/ /l/, *hill*. What is the new word? The new word is *hill*.

Bill   hill

Practice substituting sounds with the following words:

fit	fill	hill
fill	hill	hip

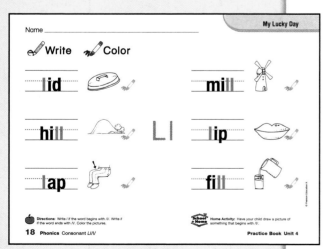

▲ **Practice Book 4**
Consonant *Ll*/l/, p. 18

Group Time

On-Level
Read Kindergarten Student Reader K.4.2. Use the Small Group Reading **Routine.**

Strategic Intervention
Read Kindergarten Student Reader K.4.2. More practice with *Ll*/l/, p. DI·8.

Advanced
Read Kindergarten Student Reader K.4.2. Use the reading routine on p. DI·8. Extend word reading.

ELL

Group English language learners by their reading ability in English.

i **Independent Activities**

Self-Selected Reading See pp. TR14–15 for a bibliography of books related to the weekly concept.

Practice Book Cause and Effect, p. 17; Consonant *Ll*/l/, p. 18

Centers Use the center activities on pp. 72–73 to practice this week's skills.

Journal Writing Dictate and draw three words that end in -*ll*.

 BLEND SOUNDS

Review letter names and sounds

Use the Alphabet Cards to review these letter names and sounds: *Mm, Tt, Aa, Ss, Pp, Cc, Ii, Bb, Nn, Rr, Dd, Oo,* and *Hh.*

Blend and read words

Write *hit* on the board. I am going to blend the sound of each letter together to say this word: /h/ /i/ /t/.

h i t

The word is *hit.* Now blend the sounds with me: /h/ /i/ /t/. The word is *hit.* Continue blending with *Nat, Lin, Rob, can, tap, bam, rap, on, pot, lid,* and *Nan.*

Word Wall HIGH-FREQUENCY WORDS

Practice high-frequency words

Write the word *we* on the board. This is the word *we.* What is this word? Repeat the routine with *do, that, are, the, like,* and *you.* Look for these words in the story that we read today.

Monitor Progress | **High-Frequency Words/Word Reading**

High-Frequency Words Write *do, are,* and *that* on the board. Have children take turns reading the words.

Blend Sounds to Read Words Write the following words on the board: *Nan, tap, rap, tan, pot, lid, bam, can, Rob, Nat, Lin,* and *hit.* I am going to point to a word. I want you to say each sound, and then blend the sounds to read the word.

If… children have difficulty reading high-frequency words,
then… write words on cards to send home for practice.

If… children have difficulty reading decodable words,
then… practice blending sounds and reading words.

If… children can successfully read words,
then… have them read Kindergarten Student Reader K.4.2 *A Musical Adventure.* **SUCCESS PREDICTOR**

 Spiral REVIEW
- Reviews previously taught high-frequency words.
- Reviews previously taught letters and sounds.

Day 1	Day 2	▶ Day 3	Day 4	Day 5
Check Sound Fluency	Check Retelling/Letter-Sound Knowledge	Check High-Frequency Words/Word Reading	Check Phoneme Segmentation	Check Oral Vocabulary/Assess Progress

ELL

Access Content Ask children to point out the naming words such as *Nan*, *Lin*, *Rob*, *pot*, *pan*, and *lid*. Have children act out the action words *see*, *hit*, *tap*, and *rap*.

PREPARE TO READ

Introduce Kindergarten Student Reader K.4.2

Display the title page. We are going to read a new story. Point to the title. The title of the story is *A Musical Adventure.* It was written by Ann Rossi.

Small Group Reading

DAY 5 ROUTINE

1 **Model Fluent Reading** Have children finger point as you read a page.

2 **Read Chorally** Have children finger point as they chorally read the page. Continue reading page by page, repeating steps 1 and 2.

3 **Read Individually** Have children read aloud a page in their group.

4 **Reread and Monitor Progress** As you listen to individual children reread, monitor progress and provide support.

Kindergarten Student Reader

Can you do it, Nat?
Can you tap, Lin?
Can you rap, Rob?

2

We can do that.
We can rap on the pot.

3

We can bam on the lid.
We can rap, tap, tap.

4

We are tops.
We can rap, tap, tap.

5

Nat can hit the lid.
Lin can bam on the can.

6

Nan can hit the pot.
Lin can tap, tap, tap.

7

Do you like that, Dad?
We can tap, tap, bam.
Dad did like it a lot!

8

Modeled Writing

REVIEW GRAMMAR Naming Parts

Review naming parts

AlphaBuddy is going to help you learn about the part of a sentence that names something. *AlphaBuddy talks.* If *talks* is the action part of the sentence, who can tell me the *naming* part?

Identify naming parts

Who else can talk? Make up some sentences for me using people and animals we have learned about in our stories. Continue to develop sentences by saying an action and having children name who or what can perform the action.

LET'S WRITE Connect to Phonics

Review letters and sounds

Display the *lamp* Picture Card. This is a lamp. What sound do you hear at the beginning of *lamp?* What letter stands for /l/? Have children dictate a list of words that begin with /l/ and a list of words that end with /l/.

Write sentences

The children in the story *A Musical Adventure* have fun tapping on pots and pans. I am going to write a sentence about a musical adventure using words that begin with the letter *Ll*.

Lil likes to tap on lids.

Have children read the sentence with you. Then have them point out each word that begins with /l/.

Independent writing

Have children write or dictate a sentence about their own musical adventures. Then have them illustrate their sentences.

OBJECTIVES

- Review naming parts.
- Review letters and sounds.
- Write about musical adventures.

Materials

- AlphaBuddy
- Picture Card: *lamp*

DAILY FIX-IT

the piglet had a lucky day
(The piglet had a lucky day.)

EXTEND SKILLS

Handwriting Remind children to place a period or question mark at the end of every sentence.

Writer's Checkup

- ✔ The first word in a sentence begins with an uppercase letter. Did I do that?
- ✔ A sentence should end with a period. Did I do that?
- ✔ A sentence should make sense. Does my sentence make sense?
- ✔ A good writer uses his or her best handwriting. Did I do that?

OBJECTIVE

● Practice compare and contrast.

ELL

Access Content To clarify this exercise, bring pictures of items to compare and contrast. Allow children to listen to others before joining in, if necessary.

Speaking and Listening

Text to World COMPARE AND CONTRAST

Practice compare and contrast

Let's play "Alike and Different." AlphaBuddy will name two things, and we will describe how they are alike and different. Have AlphaBuddy name the following pairs:

- breakfast and dinner
- a bath and a shower
- a fox and a pig

Connect compare and contrast

When we tell what is the same and what is different about two things, we learn more about both things. When we do this with things from a story, we learn more about the story.

Wrap Up Your Day!

☑ **Respond to Literature** Today we read about a musical adventure. Have you ever played a musical instrument?

☑ **Grammar** Ask children to tell you the naming part in these sentences: *The cat ran fast; The toy made noise;* and *The children played ball.*

☑ **Homework Idea** Ask children to bring in something or a picture of something that ends in *-ll.*

PREVIEW Day 4

Tomorrow we will read about an unlucky duck!

EXTEND Your Day

Chronological Time

Materials Trade Book *My Lucky Day*

Page through *My Lucky Day* and have children describe what happened in the story. Allow each child to add one or two sentences. Model correct use of words related to chronology, such as *first*, *next,* and *last*.

- When the fox decided to give the piglet a bath, what was the first thing he did? (First, he made a fire.)
- What did he do next? (Next, he carried in water.)
- What did he do last? (He gave the piglet a bath.)

Choose three children to act out the events. Have one child pretend to be the fox and show how he made a fire. Then have the second child pretend to be the fox carrying the water. Ask the third child to pretend to be the fox giving the piglet a bath. Choose other groups of three children to act out the events.

Then review your own class schedule and ask children what they do first, next, and last each day.

Time for SOCIAL STUDIES

Drama
Actors and Actresses

Dramatize the Story Divide children into groups. Assign each group a different scene from *My Lucky Day*. Ask each group to practice acting out the scene they were assigned. When each group is ready to perform, have them act out their scenes in sequential order of the story for the other children.

Comprehension
Cause and Effect

What Happened? Explain to children that you will describe a scene that could happen to the characters from *My Lucky Day*. Tell them that their job is to tell you what might have happened.

- The piglet walks out to find the ground wet and clouds in the sky. What happened?
- The piglet gets an apple to eat, but now he is crying and the fox is eating the apple. What happened?
- The piglet says he needs a massage so he won't be tough, and the fox puts him in the roasting pan instead. What happened?

Day 4
AT A GLANCE

Oral Language and Vocabulary
Calendar
Message Board
Build Background

Shared Reading
Trade Book *Fix-It Duck*
 Skill Cause and Effect

Word Work
Phonemic Awareness
Review /h/

Phonics
Blend Sounds
H/F Words *do, are, that*
Decodable Reader 20

Read
Group Time < Differentiated Instruction

Language Arts
Grammar: Action Parts
Interactive Writing:
  Write a Song
Speaking and Listening:
  Compare and Contrast

Materials
- Calendar
- Talk with Me, Sing with Me Chart 20A, 20B
- Sing with Me/Background Building Audio CD
- Trade Book *Fix-It Duck*
- AudioText CD
- Picture Cards: pp. 111, 113
- Alphabet Cards: *Aa, Bb, Cc, Dd, Ff, Hh, Ii, Kk, Ll, Nn, Oo, Pp, Ss, Tt*
- Decodable Reader 20

Calendar

Name the day and date	Ask a volunteer to find today's date on the calendar. Have children say the day, month, date, and year together.
Yesterday, today, and tomorrow	Have children point to yesterday, today, and tomorrow on the calendar. Ask what day of the week it will be tomorrow.

Message Board

Question of the day	Write and read the question as you track the print. Encourage children to respond in complete sentences.

What could happen on your lucky day?

Review grammar	Have volunteers identify the action parts of the responses.

Extend Language Use the Day 4 instruction on ELL Poster 20 to support children's use of English to communicate about lesson concepts.

ELL Poster 20

ORAL LANGUAGE

Build Background

LET'S TALK

Discuss what we are learning

Display Talk with Me Chart 20A. Point to the picture of the cooks.

• What are these people doing? (cooking) Each one of these people is a *cook*.

Point to the picture of the brush.

• What is happening in this picture? (A person is washing dishes.) We can call the person or this tool a *scrubber*.

Prompt children to respond in complete sentences.

Talk with Me, Sing with Me Chart

LET'S SING

Sing "It's My Lucky Day"

Display Sing with Me Chart 20B. Sing "It's My Lucky Day." Encourage children to listen for the words *cooking* and *scrubbing*.

 Sing with Me/Background Building Audio CD

LET'S LEARN AMAZING WORDS

OBJECTIVES
● Build background.
● Develop oral vocabulary.

• piglet   • fox
• lucky   • filthy
• cook   • scrubber

Access Content Ask children how they say *cook* and *scrubber* in their own languages.

Oral Vocabulary   cook   scrubber   DAY 4 ROUTINE

1 **Introduce** A *cook* is the person who prepares our meals. In our story, the fox is the *cook*. What's our new word for a person who prepares meals?

Demonstrate The fox is making spaghetti for the piglet. What else is the *cook* going to make?

2 **Introduce** The fox washes the filthy piglet. A *scrubber* is someone who cleans something dirty. What is our new word for a person working hard to wash?

Demonstrate When something dirty needs cleaning, we might need a *scrubber*. The piglet says the fox is a good *scrubber*.

3 **Review** We talked about two words today: *cook* and *scrubber*. Which word means "a person who prepares meals," *cook* or *scrubber*? Which word means "the person who is working hard to clean something dirty," *cook* or *scrubber*?

4 **Apply** Have children pantomime *cook* and *scrubber*.

SHARED READING

OBJECTIVE

↻ Apply cause and effect.

Materials

● Trade Book *Fix-It Duck*

ELL

Extend Language Remind English language learners that the term *fix-it* is an expression to describe someone who likes to repair things. Also point out the different sound effect words in the story, including *pop, splash, drip, bleat, quack,* and *wail.*

Comprehension

LET'S READ *Fix-It Duck*

Review *Fix-It Duck*

Display *Fix-It Duck.* Jez Alborough is the author. What does the author do?

● What do you remember about *Fix-It Duck*?

● What are some of the duck's problems?

Reread *Fix-It Duck*

Reread the book and ask children to pay attention to what causes the problems that Duck has.

Trade Book

 AudioText CD

↻ SKILL Cause and Effect

Apply cause and effect to *Fix-It Duck*

After reading, ask:

● What are some of the problems we saw Duck trying to fix? (leaks at his house and Sheep's house)

● What makes a lot of rain come into Sheep's home? (Duck breaks the window.)

● What makes Sheep's house go into the lake? (Duck uses a ladder to hook it to the truck.)

● What really makes water drip at Duck's house? (He forgets to turn off the bath water.)

Practice cause and effect

Have children talk about a problem they have, such as a broken pencil point. Then have them think about how that happened. What makes our pencils need sharpening? What other problems might we have that need fixing?

Text to Self

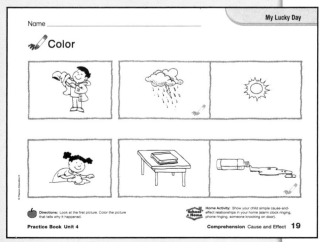

▲ **Practice Book 4**
Cause and Effect, p. 19

Phonemic Awareness

REVIEW PRACTICE Initial /h/

Isolate initial /h/
Display the *hat* Picture Card. What is the first sound in the word *hat?* (/h/) Say it with me: /h/, *hat.* Continue with *hose.*

Identify initial /h/
Display the *hen* Picture Card. The word *hen* begins with /h/. Say it with me: /h/, *hen.* Display the *hammer* Picture Card. What is the first sound in *hammer?* Continue with *pig, crab, hippopotamus,* and *bus.*

Segment words
I am going to say a word. I want you to tell me all of the sounds you hear in the word. Listen carefully: *hot.* What sounds do you hear in *hot?* Let's say the sounds together: /h/ /o/ /t/, *hot.* Continue with the following words: *lot, hop, mom, lap, luck, pot, top,* and *lock.*

Monitor Progress | **Check Phoneme Segmentation**

Check Segmentation I am going to say a word. Tell me all of the sounds you hear in the word. Use the following words from Decodable Reader 20 *Can It Fit?: Tab, bat, lid, fit, Lil, lit, doll, lap, did, not, it,* and *Kit.*

If... children cannot segment sounds,
then... segment the word and have children echo you.

SUCCESS PREDICTOR

Day 1
Check Sound Fluency

Day 2
Check Retelling/ Letter-Sound Knowledge

Day 3
Check High- Frequency Words/ Word Reading

▶ **Day 4**
Check Phoneme Segmentation

Day 5
Oral Vocabulary/ Assess Progress

Phonics

Spiral REVIEW BLEND SOUNDS

Review letter names and sounds
Use Alphabet Cards to review the following letter names and their sounds: *Tt, Aa, Ss, Pp, Cc, Ii, Bb, Nn, Dd, Kk, Ff, Oo, Ll,* and *Hh.*

Blend sounds

PHONICS ACTIVITY MAT

This word is *Lil.* Say the three sounds with me: /l/ /i/ /l/. Blend the sounds as I point to each letter: /l/ /i/ /l/, *Lil.* The word is *Lil.*

L i l
→ → →
→

Continue with the following words: *lid, bat, fit, Tab, sat, lap, did, lit, doll, can,* and *not.*

Phoneme Segmentation
SUCCESS PREDICTOR

OBJECTIVES

● Recognize high-frequency words.
● Read decodable text.

Word Wall HIGH-FREQUENCY WORDS

Practice high-frequency words

Write the word *are* on the board. This is the word *are*. What is this word? Continue with *that, you, see, a, the, they,* and *do.* Look for these words in the story that we read today.

PREPARE TO READ

Introduce Decodable Reader 20

Display Decodable Reader 20 *Can It Fit?* Today we will read *Can It Fit?* Point to the title of the story. What is the title of the story? Point to the names of the author and illustrator. *Can It Fit?* is written by Myleen Rush. This story is illustrated by Gloria Leek.

Group Time

On-Level

Read Decodable Reader 20. Use the Small Group Reading **Routine.**

Strategic Intervention

Read Decodable Reader 20. More practice with *Ll/l/*, p. DI·9.

Advanced

Read Independent Leveled Reader K.4.2. Use Leveled Reader lesson, p. LR3. Extend word reading.

Group English language learners by their reading ability in English.

- -

i Independent Activities

Self-Selected Reading See pp. TR14–15 for a bibliography of books related to the weekly concept.

Practice Book Cause and Effect, p. 19; Action Parts, p. 20

Centers Use the center activities on pp. 72–73 to practice this week's skills.

Journal Writing Draw and label three action words.

Small Group Reading

DAY 4 ROUTINE

1 **Model Fluent Reading** Have children finger point as you read a page.

2 **Read Chorally** Have children finger point as they chorally read the page. Continue reading page by page, repeating steps 1 and 2.

3 **Read Individually** Have children read aloud a page in their group.

4 **Reread and Monitor Progress** As you listen to individual children reread, monitor progress and provide support.

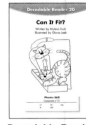

Decodable Reader

Interactive Writing

GRAMMAR Action Parts

Practice action parts
Remember that sentences have naming parts and action parts. Who can tell me the action part in the sentence *Judy dances?* What are some different actions you can do? Have children to think of different actions and use them in complete sentences. Then have them name the action part.

LET'S WRITE Connect to Phonics

Review letters and sounds
Display the *doll* Picture Card. This is a doll. What sound do you hear at the end of *doll?* What letter stands for /l/? Continue reviewing initial and final /l/ with the following Picture Cards: *lamp, leaf, lemon, pail, seal.*

Write a song
Write the following song on chart paper.

> **Lil and Lin play with _____, (dolls)**
> **play with _____, (dolls)**
> **play with _____. (dolls)**
> **Lil and Lin play with _____, (dolls)**
> **They like _____. (dolls)**

Have children suggest a word that begins or ends with /l/ to complete the song. Then sing it with children to the tune of "London Bridge." Have children continue to suggest additional /l/ words to create other verses for the class to sing.

Independent writing
After children have sung several verses, have them write a sentence and draw a picture illustrating the action.

Mary plays soccer.

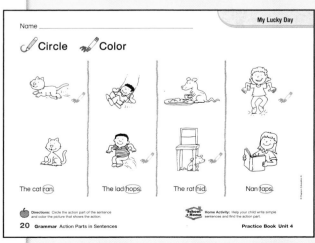

▲ **Practice Book 4** Action Parts, p. 20

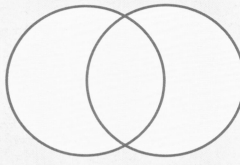

ELL

Access Content Use a Venn diagram to show differences and similarities more clearly.

Can It Fit?   **Fix-It-Duck**

Speaking and Listening

Text to Text COMPARE AND CONTRAST

Review compare and contrast

Remember that we have been talking about how things are alike and how they are different. Let's look at the two stories we read today: *Can It Fit?* and *Fix-It Duck.* Who are the characters? Are they people or animals?

Practice compare and contrast

Ask children to list characteristics of one story. After listing things about one story, do the same for the other. Prompt children to find similarities in setting, characters, and other characteristics in the stories. Then help them look for differences.

Wrap Up Your Day!

 Respond to Literature Today we read about Fix-It Duck. What did the duck do?

 Speaking and Listening Let's talk about the ways we go home from school. How are our travels alike? How are they different?

 Homework Idea Have children ask a family member what would happen if no one cooked dinner.

PREVIEW Day 5

Tomorrow we will read about three goats who trick someone to stay safe.

EXTEND Your Day

Time for
SOCIAL STUDIES

Cause and Effect

Materials Trade Book *Fix-It Duck*, construction paper, crayons

Discuss Cause and Effect Page through *Fix-It Duck* and help children create a list of things that happened (effects) and why they happened (causes). Record the items in a chart.

Putting It in Order Divide the class into small groups. Ask groups to act out cause and effect situations.

Cause	Effect
faucet is left on	ceiling drips
needs a ladder	goes to Sheep's house
tried to close window	window broken

Grammar
Action and Naming Parts

Illustrate Parts of a Sentence Give each child two small pieces of paper. On one piece, children will write their names to serve as the naming part of your sentences. On the other piece of paper, they will draw an action that is fun and easy to act out to serve as the action part of your sentences. Assist children by listing possible actions they can draw.

Put all naming papers in one basket and all action papers in a separate basket. Have children sit in a circle. Pull out one paper from each basket. The child called will act out the action selected.

Math
How Much?

Materials clear plastic pitcher, clear plastic cups, tablespoon, water, Trade Book *My Lucky Day*

How Much Water Display pages 12–13 of *My Lucky Day*. The fox carried buckets of water to fill the wash tub. How many buckets of water do you think it took to fill the washtub?

Hold up the plastic cup and the tablespoon. How many tablespoons of water will it take to fill this cup? Help me count. Count the number of table-spoons of water it takes to fill the cup. Repeat with how many cups of water are needed to fill the pitcher.

Day 5
AT A GLANCE

Oral Language and Vocabulary
Calendar
Message Board
Build Background

Shared Reading
Read Aloud Anthology "The Three Billy Goats Gruff"
◉ **Skill** Cause and Effect

Word Work
Phonemic Awareness
Review /l/

Phonics
◉ Connect /l/ *to Ll*
H/F Words *do, are, that*
Blend and Read

Read
Group Time < Differentiated Instruction

Monitor Progress

Language Arts
Grammar: Action Parts
Shared Writing: This Week We . . .
Speaking and Listening: Compare and Contrast

Materials

- Calendar
- Talk with Me, Sing with Me Chart 20A, 20B
- Sing with Me/Background Building Audio CD
- *Read Aloud Anthology* "The Three Billy Goats Gruff"
- Picture Cards: p. 119
- Decodable Reader 20
- Kindergarten Student Reader K.4.2
- Phonics Story *Lad and Me*
- Trade Book *My Lucky Day*
- Phonics Songs and Rhymes Chart 20
- Phonics Songs and Rhymes Audio CD

Calendar

Name the day and date	Ask a volunteer to find today's date on the calendar. Instruct the class to name the day and say today's date.
Name letters in the day	Ask volunteers to identify each letter in the name for today. Continue with the names of other days in the week.

Message Board

Question of the week	Remind children that this week we have talked about a very lucky piglet.

> ## What adventures can you have on a lucky day?

Review oral vocabulary	Encourage children to use oral vocabulary words *piglet, fox, lucky, filthy, cook,* and *scrubber* to discuss the question. Prompt children to respond in complete sentences.

Assess Vocabulary Use the Day 5 instruction on ELL Poster 20 to monitor children's progress with oral vocabulary.

ELL Poster 20

Build Background

LET'S TALK

Discuss the piglet and the fox

Display Talk with Me Chart 20A.

- Which pictures show the *piglet* and the *fox?* Which one do you think is a faster runner?
- Who is often *filthy*, a *piglet* or a *fox?*
- Which picture shows a *cook?*
- Which picture shows a *scrubber?*
- Which picture shows someone who is having a *lucky* day?

Talk with Me, Sing with Me Chart

Amazing Words *to build oral vocabulary*

- piglet
- lucky
- cook
- fox
- filthy
- scrubber

LET'S SING

Sing "It's My Lucky Day"

Display Sing with Me Chart 20B. Remind children that the words *piglet, filthy, cook (cooking), scrubber (scrubbing), fox,* and *lucky* are in the song.

 Sing with Me/Background Building Audio CD

It's My Lucky Day

Piglet walked through the woods one day,
Hoping to find a friend who could play,
Squirrel was scrubbing his filthy house,
"Bye, bye, Squirrel! I'll go find Mouse!"

Talk with Me, Sing with Me Chart

Monitor Progress | **Check Oral Vocabulary**

Demonstrate Word Knowledge Prompt children to use oral vocabulary words *piglet, fox, lucky, filthy, cook,* and *scrubber.* Encourage children to use complete sentences.

If… children have difficulty using oral vocabulary words,

then… review meanings with Talk with Me Chart 20A and *My Lucky Day.*

SUCCESS PREDICTOR

Day 1
Check Sound Fluency

Day 2
Check Retelling/ Letter-Sound Knowledge

Day 3
Check High-Frequency Words/ Word Reading

Day 4
Check Phoneme Segmentation

▶ **Day 5**
Check Oral Vocabulary/ Assess Progress

Oral Vocabulary

SUCCESS PREDICTOR

OBJECTIVE

- Identify cause and effect in a new selection.

Materials

- *Read Aloud Anthology* "The Three Billy Goats Gruff"

ELL

Access Content Before reading aloud, introduce children to the characters (goats, troll) in the story. Then use words and gestures to explain these key story words: *trip-trap, grunted, wrinkled, twitched,* and *gobble.*

Monitor Progress

Cause and Effect

If... children cannot identify cause and effect,	then... reteach using page DI·32.

CAUSE AND EFFECT

Color the top picture. Color the one picture at bottom that made it happen.

Note to Teacher Have children color the large scene and the one other picture that made the large scene happen.

▲ **Teacher's Edition 4**
Cause and Effect, p. 122

Comprehension

READ ALOUD

Read "The Three Billy Goats Gruff"

Tell children that you are going to read them a story about three goats who trick a troll into letting them cross his bridge. Listen carefully. I am going to read you a story, and then I will ask you to tell me some of the things that happened and why they happened.

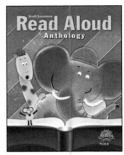
Read Aloud Anthology

CHECK SKILL Cause and Effect

Practice cause and effect in "The Three Billy Goats Gruff"

After you read the story, ask children what happened when the first goat was allowed to cross the bridge.

- Why did the troll let him cross? (The littlest goat said he could catch a bigger goat if he waited.)
- Why was the second goat allowed to cross? (He told the troll that he could catch a very large goat if he waited.)
- Why didn't the biggest goat get caught? (He was so big that he could easily butt the troll away.)

Each thing happened because of something else. We can say some things made, or caused, other things to happen.

ASSESS SKILL Cause and Effect

Assess cause and effect

Use the blackline master found on page 122. Copy one page for each child. Have children color the scene of the billy goats grazing in the fresh field and the one scene that caused that ending.

Phonemic Awareness

REVIEW /l/

Review initial /l/

Display Picture Card *lake.* What is the first sound in *lake?* Say the word with me: *lake,* /l/, /l/, /l/, *lake.* Review initial /l/ with the following Picture Cards: *loaf, ladybug, lemon, leaf,* and *lamp.*

Phonics

 REVIEW *Ll*/l/

Connect /l/ to *Ll*

Write *l* on the board. What is the name of this letter? If I add *-ab* to /l/, I make the word *lab.* What word do I make if I add *-ad* to /l/? Continue substituting with the phonograms *-id* and *-ot.* Write *-ill* on the board. If I put /m/ in front of *-ill* what word do I make? Continue substituting with the following sounds: /p/, /b/, /d/, /f/, /h/, and /w/.

Word Wall HIGH-FREQUENCY WORDS

Practice high-frequency words

Write the word *are* on the board. This is the word *are.* What is this word? Continue the routine with *that* and *do.* Have children find the high-frequency words in the following sentence: *What are we going to do with that?*

 READ

Apply phonics in familiar text

Have children reread one of the readers that applies the target letter sound. You may wish to review the decodable words and high-frequency words that appear in each reader prior to rereading.

Kindergarten Student Reader

Decodable Reader

Phonics Story in Practice Book

5

OBJECTIVE

⊙ Assess: connect /l/ to *Ll.*

Group Time

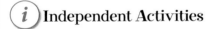

On-Level

Sets A and B

Strategic Intervention

Monitor Progress: Check Phonics Alternate Assessment, p. DI·10

Advanced

Sets B and C

i **Independent Activities**

Self-Selected Reading See pp. TR14–15 for a bibliography of books related to the weekly concept.

Centers Use the center activities on pp. 72–73 to practice this week's skills.

Journal Writing Draw or write about an adventure you had.

Support Phonics For guidance in teaching phonics to English language learners, see the *ELL and Transition Handbook.*

PHONICS /l/ to *Ll*

Group assessment

Help children fold a sheet of paper into four sections. Ask children to draw something that begins or ends with /l/ in each box. Then ask children to label the picture with the word or the letter *l.*

Monitor Progress Assess Progress	
If… a child cannot complete the group assessment,	**then…** use the Reteach lesson on page DI·32.
If… a child draws four pictures that begin or end with /l/ but labels them incorrectly,	**then…** assess word reading Sets A and B on page 121.
If… a child draws four pictures that begin or end with /l/ and labels them accurately with phonetically appropriate spellings,	**then…** assess word and sentence reading with Sets B and C on page 121.

⊙ ASSESS PHONICS

Set A: Read the words

Have individuals take turns reading the words. We're going to read some words. I'll do the first one and you do the rest. The first word is *lip:* /l/ /i/ /p/. The first word is *lip.* For each child, record any decoding problems.

Set B: Read more words

Have individuals take turns reading more words. We're going to read some words. I'll do the first one and you do the rest. The first word is *fill:* /f/ /i/ /l/. For each child, record any decoding problems.

Set C: Read the sentences

For a cumulative assessment of phonics and high-frequency words, have each child read one or two sentences.

READ THE WORDS

Set A

lip   lap

lad   lid

READ MORE WORDS

Set B

fill   lob   mill

hill   doll   Bill

READ THE SENTENCES

Set C

1. Dan is a sad lad.

2. That is my cap.

3. You are a little cat.

4. Did Bill and Lil go to see the pit?

5. Do Dan and Bill have dill?

Note to Teacher Set A: Children read each word. Set B: Children read each word.
Set C: Children read one or two sentences.

My Lucky Day

Monitor Progress

SUCCESS PREDICTOR

CAUSE AND EFFECT

Color the top picture. Color the one picture at the bottom that makes it happen.

Note to Teacher Have children color the large scene and the one other picture that makes the large scene happen.

© Scott Foresman K

Monitor Progress

Shared Writing

GRAMMAR Action Parts

Review action parts

An action part of a sentence is a word that tells what is happening. **Drop a paper on the floor.** I dropped the paper. What did I do to the paper? Right, I dropped it. *Dropped the paper* is the action part of the sentence.

Illustrate action parts

Have children write or dictate a sentence with an action word and then act out their sentence.

LET'S WRITE This Week We...

Recall literature

Display the following items: Trade Book *My Lucky Day;* Decodable Reader 20 *Can It Fit?;* Kindergarten Student Reader K.4.2 *A Musical Adventure;* Phonics Story *Lad and Me;* Talk with Me, Sing with Me Chart 20B; and Phonics Songs and Rhymes Chart 20. We read four new books and sang two new songs this week. Which story had your favorite adventure?

Write sentences

Today we will write about something we feel lucky about.

Mr. Thomas went on a trip.

Bret saw an owl.

Jade got a cat.

Continue the list with all children. Then have children echo read the complete list.

Independent writing

Have children copy the sentence they dictated and illustrate it. Ask them to read the sentence back to you as they are able.

OBJECTIVES

- Recognize action parts.
- Write about lucky things.

Materials

- Trade Book *My Lucky Day*
- Kindergarten Student Reader K.4.2
- Decodable Reader 20
- Phonics Story *Lad and Me*
- Talk with Me, Sing with Me Chart 20B
- Phonics Songs and Rhymes Chart 20

DAILY FIX-IT

i am lucky
(I am lucky.)

ELL

Support Writing Supply English words as children write or dictate their sentence.

My Lucky Day   123

OBJECTIVE

● Review compare and contrast.

ELL

Access Content Encourage children to participate by having them compare two foods: oranges and apples.

Speaking and Listening

COMPARE AND CONTRAST

Review compare and contrast

Display Phonics Songs and Rhymes Chart 20. Play "Lucy Leopard Loves Her Lunch" on the Phonics Songs and Rhymes Audio CD.

 Phonics Songs and Rhymes Audio CD

Phonics Songs and Rhymes Chart

Connect compare and contrast

Ask children to identify the food in Lucy Leopard's lunch. Make a list of the foods on chart paper. Have children tell how Lucy's lunch is like or different from their lunch.

Wrap Up Your Week!

 Phonics This week we learned about the letter *Ll*. What is the sound for *Ll*? Name some words that begin with /l/.

 Shared Reading What was your favorite book or song this week?

 High-Frequency Words Write *are*, *that*, and *do* on the board. Read these words to me.

You've learned  **Amazing Words this week!**

You've learned  **Amazing Words so far this year!**

PREVIEW Next Week

Next week we will read about a little mouse. What adventures could a mouse have?

EXTEND Your Day

TIME
+ FOR
MATH

Counting Adventures

Materials counters

Count to Fifteen Provide each child with fifteen counters. Tell a humorous adventure story. Include numbers of people or things in your story. Every time a number is mentioned the children should count it. Here is an example:

> I went on a camping trip. On the trip I saw one bear. I also saw three raccoons. I went fishing in the lake and caught two fish. When I drove home, three deer crossed the road in front of my car. How many animals did I see?

The children should have separated out one counter for the bear, three for the raccoons, two for the fish, and three for the deer. They should have counted nine counters for the animals in the story. Repeat with another scenario and other numbers.

Children can also tell stories in small groups. The child telling the story will also have to count out the counters to keep track of the correct count.

My Lucky Day

TIME FOR ART

Materials construction paper, crayons, glitter, glue

Lucky Tokens Have children think of a day when good things happened to them. Have them draw a picture of that time. After they are done, have them outline one special thing in their pictures with glue. Sprinkle glitter over their pictures to make that lucky thing stand out.

Adventure Charades

PLAYBILL TIME FOR DRAMA

Imaginary Adventures Brainstorm with children some adventures they have seen or read about that they would like to do. Make a list on the board. Assign partners and give each group an adventure to act out. Have the groups present their adventure skits. Let the class guess what their adventure was.

Unit 4
Let's Explore

CONCEPT QUESTION

Where will our adventures take us?

EXPAND THE CONCEPT
What adventures can an animal have?

CONNECT THE CONCEPT

▶ **Build Background**

woodland	vale	comfortable
nest	hollow	shadows

A New Woodland Nest

"I need a new woodland nest,"
Said the mouse, "I want the best."
Mole offered his hole, safe from the cold.
"Oh, but I really can't rest."

▶ **Science Content**
Life Science

Preview Your Week

What adventures can an animal have?

Big Book

Audio CD

Genre	Rhyming/Concept Story
Phonics	Consonant Blends
Comprehension Skill	Sequence

Meet the Illustrator

LeUyen Pham

LeUyen Pham (pronounced Le Win) was born in Vietnam and grew up in California. She worked in animation until deciding to illustrate children's books full-time. She has won many awards for her illustrations.

Read another book illustrated by LeUyen Pham.

Twenty-One Elephants

• **Kindergarten Student Readers**
• **Listen to Me Readers**
• **Independent Leveled Readers**
• **Decodable Readers**

Books for All Children

Emergent

Listen to Me Reader

• **Develop oral language**
• **Develop phonemic awareness**
• **Read decodable words**
• **Read high-frequency words**

On-Level

Kindergarten Student Reader

• **Read connected text**
• **Apply phonics skills**
• **Read high-frequency words in context**

Leveled Reader K.4.3

Independent

Independent Leveled Reader

• **Practice comprehension skill:** sequence
• **Extend concepts**
• **Connect to Science**

Apply Phonics

Decodable Reader

Phonics Story

Integrate Science Standards

• Life Science

✓ Read

Big Book *One Little Mouse*

Independent Leveled Reader *The Path to Frog's New Home*

✓ Build
Concept Vocabulary

Adventures Animals Can Have, pp. 139, 149, 162, 171, 179

✓ Apply
Science

Animal Characteristics, p. 147
Animals: Similarities and Differences, p. 160
Animal Habitats, p. 169
Similarities and Differences, p. 177
Animal Movement, p. 187

Time for SOCIAL STUDIES

✓ Teach
Social Studies Concept

Make a Map, p. 187

Weekly Plan

READING

60–90 minutes

TARGET SKILLS OF THE WEEK

- **Phonics Skill**
  Consonant Blends
- **Comprehension Skill**
  Sequence

DAY 1   PAGES 138–147

Oral Language/Vocabulary

QUESTION OF THE WEEK, 138
What adventures can an animal have?

Build Background, 139
Talk with Me, Sing with Me Chart 21A, 21B

Amazing Words, 139
woodland, nest, vale, hollow, comfortable, shadows

Comprehension

Shared Reading, 140–141

Read Big Book

Preview and Predict
Reader Response
Sequence **T**

Word Work

Phonemic Awareness, 142
Introduce Initial Blends

Phonics, 143
Consonant Blends **T**

High-Frequency Words, 143
Introduce *one, two, three, four, five*

Reread Decodable Reader 20

Grouping Options 132–133 →

DAY 2   PAGES 148–160

Oral Language/Vocabulary

QUESTION OF THE DAY, 148
What kind of adventure do you think four or five animals can have?

Build Background, 149
Talk with Me, Sing with Me Chart 21A, 21B

Let's Learn Amazing Words, 149
woodland, nest

Comprehension

Shared Reading, 150–155

Read Big Book

Recall and Retell
Sequence **T**

Word Work

Phonemic Awareness, 156
Practice Blends

Phonics, 156
Consonant Blends **T**

High-Frequency Words, 157
Review *one, two, three, four, five, have, I, is, like, you, do, see*

Read Phonics Story

Grouping Options 132–133 →

LANGUAGE ARTS

20 minutes

Shared Writing, 145
Grammar: Introduce Complete Sentences
Connect to Grammar

Speaking and Listening, 146
Introduce Retelling a Story

Modeled Writing, 158
Grammar: Practice Complete Sentences
Respond to Literature

Speaking and Listening, 159
Let's Review Amazing Words *piglet, filthy*

DAILY JOURNAL WRITING

Day 1 *Draw and label three animals the mouse tries to live with in the story.*

Day 2 *Draw a picture for one word that begins with sl- and one that begins with pl-.*

EXTEND YOUR DAY   *30 minutes*
Additional Activities for Full–Day Classrooms

Day 1, 147
Time for Science: Animal Characteristics
Grammar: Complete Sentences
Math: Macaroni Math

Day 2, 160
Time for Science: Animals: Similarities and Differences
Phonics: Initial Blends Guess
Comprehension: Sequence

DAILY SUCCESS PREDICTORS →
for Adequate Yearly Progress

Monitor Progress and Corrective Feedback

Phonemic Awareness
Check Sound Fluency, *142*
Spiral REVIEW Phonics, High-Frequency Words

Retelling and Phonics
Check Retelling, *155*
Check Letter-Sound Knowledge, *156*
Spiral REVIEW Phonics, High-Frequency Words

- Practice Book K.4, *pp. 23–30*
- Talk with Me Chart 21A
- Sing with Me Chart 21B
- Phonics Songs and Rhymes Chart 21

Grouping Options for Differentiated Instruction

Turn the page for the small group lesson plan.

DAY 3 PAGES 161–169

Oral Language/Vocabulary

QUESTION OF THE DAY, 161
Where would you try to stay in the woodland?

Build Background, 162
Talk with Me, Sing with Me Chart 21A, 21B

Let's Learn Amazing Words, 162
vale, hallow

Comprehension

Shared Reading, 163

Read Big Book
REVIEW Draw Conclusions **T**
⊙ Sequence **T**

Word Work

Phonemic Awareness, 164
Introduce Final Blends

Phonics, 164
⊙ Consonant Blends **T**

High-Frequency Words, 165
Practice *one, two, three, four, five, for, I, do, you, my, like*

Read Kindergarten Student Reader K.4.3

Grouping Options 132–133

Modeled Writing, 167
Grammar: **REVIEW** Action Parts
Connect to Phonics

Speaking and Listening, 168
Practice Retelling a Story

Day 3 *Draw a picture for one word that ends with -st and one that ends with -lk.*

Day 3, 169
Time for Science: Animal Habitats
Grammar: Action Parts
Comprehension: Sequence

DAY 4 PAGES 170–177

Oral Language/Vocabulary

QUESTION OF THE DAY, 170
What are some exciting places animals live?

Build Background, 171
Talk with Me, Sing with Me Chart 21A, 21B

Let's Learn Amazing Words, 171
comfortable, shadows

Comprehension

Shared Reading, 172

Reread Read Aloud
Trade Book
⊙ Sequence **T**

Word Work

Phonemic Awareness, 173
REVIEW /l/

Phonics, 173
⊙ Consonant Blends **T**

High-Frequency Words, 174
Practice *one, two, three, four, five, a*

Read Decodable Reader 21

Grouping Options 132–133

Interactive Writing, 175
Grammar: Practice Complete Sentences
Connect to Phonics

Speaking and Listening, 176
Practice Retelling a Story

Day 4 *Write about two little animals.*

Day 4, 177
Time for Science: Similarities and Differences
Grammar: Animal Sentences
Comprehension: Sequence

DAY 5 PAGES 178–187

Oral Language/Vocabulary

QUESTION OF THE WEEK, 178
What adventures can an animal have?

Build Background, 179
Talk with Me, Sing with Me Chart 21A, 21B

Amazing Words, 179
Check *woodland, nest, vale, hollow, comfortable, shadows*

Comprehension

Shared Reading, 180, 184

Read *Read Aloud Anthology*
"The Tale of Peter Rabbit"

Monitor Progress
⊙ Check Sequence **T**

Word Work

Phonemic Awareness, 181
Review Consonant Blends

Phonics, 181
⊙ Consonant Blends **T**

High-Frequency Words, 181
Practice *one, two, three, four, five*

Grouping Options 132–133

Monitor Progress, 182–183
Read the Words
Read the Sentences

Shared Writing, 185
Grammar: Review Complete Sentences
This Week We...

Speaking and Listening, 186
Review Retelling a Story

Day 5 *Draw or write which animal home you would choose to live in.*

Day 5, 187
Time for Science: Animal Movement
Time for Social Studies: Make a Map
Time for Math: Animal Addition

KEY ⊙ = Target Skill **T** = Tested Skill

Word Reading
Check High-Frequency Words and Word Reading, 165
Spiral REVIEW Phonics, High-Frequency Words

Phonemic Awareness
Check Phoneme Segmentation, 173
Spiral REVIEW Phonics, High-Frequency Words

Oral Vocabulary
Check Oral Vocabulary, 179
Assess Phonics and Comprehension, 182–184

SUCCESS PREDICTOR

Small Group Plan *for Differentiated Instruction*

Daily Plan AT A GLANCE

Reading
Whole Group
- Oral Language/Vocabulary
- Comprehension
- Word Work

Group Time

Meet with small groups to provide:
- Skill Support
- Reading Support
- Skill Application

Read

This week's lessons for daily group time can be found behind the Differentiated Instruction (DI) tab on pp. DI · 11–DI · 15.

Language Arts
- Grammar
- Writing
- Speaking and Listening

Use *My Sidewalks on Reading Street* for early reading intervention.

DAY 1

On-Level
Teacher-Led
Page 144
- Blend Sounds to Read Words
- **Reread** Decodable Reader 20

Strategic Intervention
Teacher-Led
Page DI · 11
- More Practice with Consonant Blends
- **Read** Listen to Me Reader K.4.3

Advanced
Teacher-Led
Page DI · 11
- **Reread** Independent Leveled Reader K.4.2
- **Reread** for Fluency

(i) Independent Activities
While you meet with small groups, have the rest of the class...
- Read self-selected reading
- Complete Practice Book K.4 p. 23
- Visit the Literacy Centers
- Write in their journals

DAY 2

On-Level
Teacher-Led
Page 157
- Practice Word Reading
- **Read** Phonics Story

Strategic Intervention
Teacher-Led
Page DI · 12
- More Practice with Consonant Blends
- **Read** Phonics Story

Advanced
Teacher-Led
Page DI · 12
- Apply Phonics Skills
- **Read** Decodable Reader 21

(i) Independent Activities
While you meet with small groups, have the rest of the class...
- Read self-selected reading
- Complete Practice Book K.4 p. 24
- Visit the Literacy Centers
- Write in their journals

DAY 3

On-Level
Teacher-Led
Pages 165–166
- Practice Word Reading
- **Read** Kindergarten Student Reader K.4.3

Strategic Intervention
Teacher-Led
Page DI · 13
- Practice Reading Words with Consonant Blends
- **Read** Kindergarten Student Reader K.4.3

Advanced
Teacher-Led
Page DI · 13
- Extend Word Reading
- **Read** Kindergarten Student Reader K.4.3

(i) Independent Activities
While you meet with small groups, have the rest of the class...
- Read self-selected reading
- Complete Practice Book K.4 pp. 27, 28
- Visit the Literacy Centers
- Write in their journals

DAY 4

On-Level
Teacher-Led
Page 174

- Blend and Read Words with Consonant Blends
- **Read** Decodable Reader 21

Strategic Intervention
Teacher-Led
Page DI · 14

- Blend and Read Words with Consonant Blends
- **Read** Decodable Reader 21

Advanced
Teacher-Led
Page LR5

- Extend Word Reading
- **Read** Independent Leveled Reader K.4.3

(i) Independent Activities

While you meet with small groups, have the rest of the class...

- Read self-selected reading
- Complete Practice Book K.4 pp. 29, 30
- Visit the Literacy Centers
- Write in their journals

DAY 5

On-Level
Teacher-Led
Pages 182–184

- Word Reading, Sets A and B
- Check Phonics
- Check Comprehension

Strategic Intervention
Teacher-Led
Pages 182, 184, DI · 15

- Check Phonics
- Check Comprehension
- Alternate Assessment

Advanced
Teacher-Led
Pages 182–184

- Word Reading, Set B
- Sentence Reading, Set C
- Monitor Comprehension

(i) Independent Activities

While you meet with small groups, have the rest of the class...

- Read self-selected reading
- Visit the Literacy Centers
- Write in their journals

 Grouping Group English language learners by their reading ability in English.

Take It to the NET™ ONLINE
PearsonSuccessNet.com

Sharon Vaughn
For ideas for ELL students, see the article "Effectiveness of Supplemental Reading Instruction..." by S. Linan-Thompson, Scott Foresman author S. Vaughn, and others.

TEACHER TALK

Differentiated instruction is instruction tailored to the needs of groups of students, such as struggling students, gifted students, or English language learners.

Be sure to schedule time for children to work on the theme project *"Remember When Album."* This week children should make album pages using cut paper, paint, or fabric to depict a future adventure.

Looking Ahead

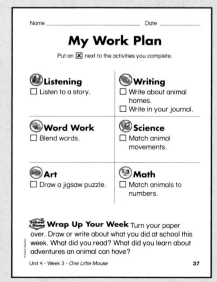

Name _____ Date _____

My Work Plan
Put an ⊠ next to the activities you complete.

Listening
☐ Listen to a story.

Writing
☐ Write about animal homes.
☐ Write in your journal.

Word Work
☐ Blend words.

Science
☐ Match animal movements.

Art
☐ Draw a jigsaw puzzle.

Math
☐ Match animals to numbers.

Wrap Up Your Week Turn your paper over. Draw or write about what you did at school this week. What did you read? What did you learn about adventures an animal can have?

Unit 4 · Week 3 · *One Little Mouse* 37

▲ **Group-Time Survival Guide** p. 37, Weekly Contract

Customize Your Plan *by Strand*

ORAL LANGUAGE

Concept Development

What adventures can an animal have?

 to build oral vocabulary

woodland	vale	comfortable
nest	hollow	shadows

BUILD

☐ **Question of the Week** Use the Message Board to introduce and discuss the question of the week. This week children will talk, sing, read, and write about adventures animals can have. DAY 1 *138*

☐ **Let's Talk** Use the Talk with Me Chart to introduce Amazing Words in a visual context. DAY 1 *139*

Talk with Me, Sing with Me Chart 21A

☐ **Let's Listen** Use the Sing with Me/Background Building Audio CD to build background, vocabulary, and concepts. DAY 1 *139*

☐ **Let's Sing** Use the Sing with Me Chart to sing a song about a mouse looking for a new house. DAY 1 *139*

Talk with Me, Sing with Me Chart 21B

DEVELOP

☐ **Question of the Day/Week** Use the questions in the Message Boards to discuss lesson concepts and how they relate to the unit theme, Let's Explore. DAY 2 *148*, DAY 3 *161*, DAY 4 *170*, DAY 5 *178*

☐ **Let's Talk** Use the Talk with Me Chart to build background, vocabulary, and concepts. DAY 2 *149*, DAY 3 *162*, DAY 4 *171*, DAY 5 *179*

☐ **Let's Sing** Use the Sing with Me Chart to sing a song about a mouse looking for a new house. Ask children to sing along with you, listening for the Amazing Words as they sing. DAY 2 *149*, DAY 3 *162*, DAY 4 *171*, DAY 5 *179*

CONNECT

☐ **Wrap Up Your Week!** Connect concepts and vocabulary to next week's lesson. DAY 5 *186*

CHECK

☐ **Check Oral Vocabulary** To informally assess children's oral vocabulary, have children use each word in a complete sentence. DAY 5 *179*

PHONEMIC AWARENESS

TEACH

☐ **Introduce Initial Blends** Introduce and isolate initial blends.
DAY 1 *142*

☐ **Introduce Final Blends** Introduce and isolate final blends.
DAY 3 *164*

PRACTICE/APPLY

☐ **Listen for Sounds** Use the Phonics Songs and Rhymes Chart to listen for initial blends. DAY 2 *156*

Phonics Songs and Rhymes Chart 21

RETEACH/REVIEW

☐ **Review** Review /l/. DAY 4 *173*

☐ **Review** Review consonant blends. DAY 5 *181*

☐ **Reteach Lesson** If necessary, reteach consonant blends.
DAY 5 *DI·33*

① Use assessment data to determine your instructional focus.

② Preview this week's instruction by strand.

③ Choose instructional activities that meet the needs of your classroom.

PHONICS

🔊 CONSONANT BLENDS

TEACH

☐ **Consonant Blends** Introduce consonant blends. DAY 1 *143*

PRACTICE/APPLY

☐ **Consonant Blends** Practice consonant blends. DAY 2 *156*, DAY 3 *164*

☐ **Phonics Story** Practice reading words with consonant blends in context. DAY 2 *157*

☐ **Kindergarten Student Reader K.4.3** Practice reading words with consonant blends in context. DAY 3 *166*

☐ **Decodable Reader 21** Practice reading words with consonant blends in context. DAY 4 *174*

☐ **Homework** Practice Book K.4, pp. 23, 28. DAY 1 *143*, DAY 3 *164*

☐ **Word Work Center** Make words using consonant blends. **ANY DAY** *136*

Phonics Story

Kindergarten Student Reader K.4.3

Decodable Reader 21

RETEACH/REVIEW

☐ **Review** Review words with this week's phonics skill. DAY 5 *181*

☐ **Reteach Lesson** If necessary, reteach consonant blends. DAY 5 *DI-33*

☐ **Spiral REVIEW** Review previously taught phonics skills. DAY 1 *144*, DAY 2 *157*, DAY 3 *165*, DAY 4 *173*

ASSESS

☐ **Word and Sentence Reading** Assess children's ability to read words with consonant blends. DAY 5 *182-183*

HIGH-FREQUENCY WORDS

HIGH-FREQUENCY WORDS
one   two   three   four   five

TEACH

☐ **Introduce** Introduce this week's high-frequency words and add them to the Word Wall. DAY 1 *143*

PRACTICE/APPLY

☐ **Words in Context** Read high-frequency words in the context of the Phonics Story and Decodable Reader 21. DAY 2 *157*, DAY 4 *174*

☐ **Word Wall** Use the Word Wall to review and practice high-frequency words throughout the week. DAY 3 *165* DAY 4 *174*, DAY 5 *181*

☐ **Kindergarten Student Reader K.4.3** Practice this week's high-frequency words in context of reader. DAY 3 *165-166*, *DI-13*

☐ **Differentiated Text** Practice this week's high-frequency words in the context of differentiated text. DAY 1 *DI-11*, DAY 4 *LR5*

☐ **Homework** Practice Book K.4, p. 24. DAY 2 *157*

Phonics Story

Decodable Reader 21

Kindergarten Student Reader K.4.3

Listen to Me Reader K.4.3

Independent Leveled Reader K.4.3

RETEACH/REVIEW

☐ **Spiral REVIEW** Review previously taught high-frequency words. DAY 2 *157*, DAY 3 *165*, DAY 4 *174*, DAY 5 *181*

ASSESS

☐ **Word Reading** Assess children's ability to read this week's high-frequency words. DAY 5 *182-183*

☑ Customize Your Plan *by Strand*

COMPREHENSION

🔵 **SKILL SEQUENCE** In a story, something happens first, something happens next, and something happens last.

TEACH

❑ **Skill Lesson** Introduce and model *sequence*. DAY 1 *141*

PRACTICE/APPLY

❑ **Skill in Context** Model how to identify *sequence*. Then read *One Little Mouse*, guiding children as they identify *sequence*. DAY 2 *150-155*

❑ **Skill in Context** Reread *Farfallina & Marcel* and apply *sequence*. DAY 4 *172*

❑ **Leveled Text** Apply *sequence* to leveled text. DAY 4 *LR5*

Big Book

Trade Book

Independent Leveled Reader K.4.3

ASSESS

❑ **Check** Read "The Tale of Peter Rabbit." Then have children identify *sequence*. DAY 5 *180*

❑ **Assess** Use the blackline master on p. 184 to assess children's understanding of *sequence*. DAY 5 *180, 184*

Read Aloud Anthology

RETEACH/REVIEW

❑ **Review Draw Conclusions** Review definition of *draw conclusions* and apply to *One Little Mouse*. DAY 3 *163*

❑ **Reteach Lesson** If necessary, reteach *sequence*. DAY 5 *DI-33*

WRITING

TEACH

❑ **Write Together** Engage children in writing activities that develop language, grammar, and writing skills and practice phonics skills. Include independent writing as an extension of group writing activities.

Shared Writing
❑ **Connect to Grammar** DAY 1 *145*
❑ **This Week We...** DAY 5 *185*

Modeled Writing
❑ **Respond to Literature** DAY 2 *158*
❑ **Connect to Phonics** DAY 3 *167*

Interactive Writing
❑ **Connect to Phonics** DAY 4 *175*

PRACTICE/APPLY

❑ **Daily Journal Writing** Have children write about concepts and literature in their journals. **EVERY DAY** *130-131*

❑ **Writing Center** Have children write about animal homes. **ANY DAY** *137*

① Use assessment data to determine your instructional focus.

② Preview this week's instruction by strand.

③ Choose instructional activities that meet the needs of your classroom.

GRAMMAR

TEACH

❑ **Introduce** Introduce complete sentences. DAY 1 *145*

PRACTICE/APPLY

❑ **Practice** Practice complete sentences. DAY 2 *158*, DAY 4 *175*

❑ **Daily Fix-It** Have children find and correct errors in capitalization and punctuation. DAY 1 *145*, DAY 2 *158*, **DAY 3** *167*, DAY 4 *175*, DAY 5 *185*

RETEACH/REVIEW

❑ **Review** Review last week's grammar skill, action parts. DAY 3 *167*

❑ **Review** Review complete sentences. DAY 5 *185*

SPEAKING AND LISTENING

TEACH

❑ **Retell a Story** Introduce and model retelling a story. DAY 1 *146*

PRACTICE/APPLY

❑ **Practice** Have children practice retelling a story. DAY 3 *168*, DAY 4 *176*

REVIEW

❑ **Review** Review retelling a story. Then have children take turns reciting lines from a rhyme. DAY 5 *186*

INQUIRY PROJECT

TEACH

❑ **Unit Inquiry Project** Allow time for children to work on the theme project "*Remember When* Album." Have children make album pages using cut paper, paint, or fabric to depict a future adventure. **ANY DAY** *xxiii*

Resources for Differentiated Instruction

Readers

Emergent

Listen to Me Reader

▶ **Oral Language**
Develop oral vocabulary.

▶ **Phonemic Awareness**
Consonant blends

🔊 **Decodable Words**
flop   spin   slam   slid
plop   land   drop   spot

▶ **High-Frequency Words**
one   two   three
four   five

On-Level

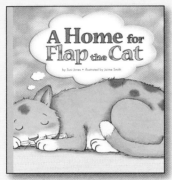

Kindergarten Student Reader

▶ **Connected Text**
Realistic Fiction

🔊 **Phonics:**
Consonant Blends
Flap   skip   stop   clap
drops spot   and

▶ **High-Frequency Words**
one   two   three
four   five

▶ **Spiral Review:**
Decodable Words
cat   Nat   Nan   hop
can   sip   dot   on
him   sit   in   lap

High-Frequency Words
for   the   I   you
likes to   my   do

Independent

Leveled Reader K.4.3
Independent Leveled Reader

🔊 **Comprehension: Sequence**
Identify beginning, middle, and end in order.

▶ **Concept**
What adventures animals can have

▶ **Science Standards**
Animal characteristics, habitat, behaviors, and movement

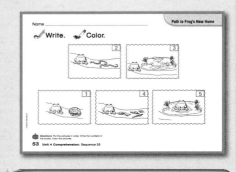

🔊 **Leveled Reader,** TE, LR6

ELL

ELL Poster 21

ELL and Transition Handbook

ELL Resources

- ELL Poster 21
- ELL and Transition Handbook
- ELL Notes in Teacher's Edition, pp. 138–187

My Sidewalks Early Reading Intervention

For students who need intensive intervention

- Effectiveness proved by scientific research
- Instruction focused on early reading success predictors
- 30 minutes of daily small-group instruction

PearsonSuccessNet.com

Use the Online Database of over 600 books to

- Download and print additional copies of this week's leveled readers
- Listen to the readers being read online
- Search for more titles focused on this week's skills, topic, and content

Readers' Theater Anthology

Readers' Theater Anthology

- Six scripts to build fluency
- Poetry for oral interpretation

Homework
- Family Times Newsletter

Take-Home Books
- Kindergarten Student Readers
- Decodable Readers
- Listen to Me Readers
- Independent Leveled Readers

Literacy Centers

Let's Read Along

- *One Little Mouse*
- AudioText CD

Audio CD

Journal Writing

- **Day One** Draw and label three animals the mouse tries to live with in the story.

- **Day Two** Draw a picture for one word that begins with *sl-* and one that begins with *pl-*.

- **Day Three** Draw a picture for one word that ends with *-st* and one that ends with *-lk*.

- **Day Four** Write about two little animals.

- **Day Five** Draw or write which animal home you would choose to live in.

Words We Know

MATERIALS
4 white index cards, 4 blue index cards, writing utensils, paper

Blend Words
1. On blue index cards, write the blends *fl-, sl-, pl-, cl-*; on white index cards, write the blends *-ap, -at, -an, -ip*.
2. Have children make words using one blue index card as a beginning blend and one white index card for the ending.
3. Children should write words on the paper.

 Phonics Activities CD This interactive CD provides additional practice.

Partner Puzzles

MATERIALS
white construction paper, crayons, scissors, envelopes or zip closure bag

Draw a Jigsaw Puzzle
1. Have children draw and color one animal from the story *One Little Mouse*.
2. After finishing their pictures, children should cut their pictures into at least four pieces.
3. After the pictures are in pieces, have children pair up and exchange pictures and try to put the pictures back together as puzzles.
4. When children are finished, they may take their puzzles home in the plastic bags.

CENTER TIP Have children write their initials on the back of each piece, so puzzles may be easily sorted and returned to the owner.

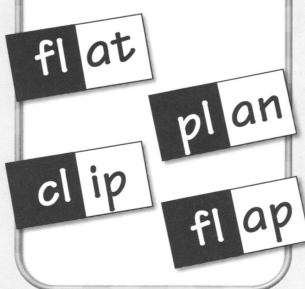

Scott Foresman Reading Street Centers Survival Kit
Use the *One Little Mouse* materials from the Reading Street
Centers Survival Kit to organize this week's centers.

Writing

Animal Adventure

MATERIALS
writing paper, writing utensils, crayons

Write About Animal Homes
1. Remind children that the mouse met many different animals on his adventure to find a new home.
2. Have children choose an animal that may or may not have been in the story.
3. Ask children to draw the animal they have chosen and its home.
4. Children should write or dictate why the mouse from the story would not like to live in their animals' homes.

CONNECT WITH SCIENCE Discuss with children various animal homes and their characteristics.

The dog house is too big for a mouse.

Science

On the Move

MATERIALS
One Little Mouse, white paper, writing utensils, crayons

Match Animal Movements
1. Remind children that the animals in the story move around in different ways. Write the words *fly, slither, hop,* and *run* on the board.
2. Have children fold their papers into four boxes and copy the words, one in each box.
3. Using the story, children should match the movement to the animal and draw the animal into the appropriate box.

fly slither
hop run

Math

A Number of Animals

MATERIALS
One Little Mouse, number words chart, white paper, crayons

Match Animals to Numbers
1. Ahead of time, make a three-column chart with the numerals 1–5 written in the first column and the corresponding number words written in the second column.
2. Using the story *One Little Mouse*, ask children to find the animals in the story that match the numbers on the chart. Write the name of the animal next to the appropriate number. Be sure to use plurals when needed.
3. Children should choose an animal set to draw and color. Label with the numeral at the top of the paper and the number word and animal name at the bottom.

CENTER TIP You may wish to remind children that the number words are now on the Word Wall.

3

three frogs

ALL CENTERS

Oral Language and Vocabulary
Calendar
Message Board
Build Background

Shared Reading
Big Book *One Little Mouse*
 Skill Sequence

Word Work

Phonemic Awareness
Introduce Initial Blends

Phonics
Consonant Blends
Blend Words
H/F Words *one, two, three, four, five*

Read

Group Time < Differentiated Instruction

Language Arts
Grammar: Complete Sentences
Shared Writing: Write Complete Sentences
Speaking and Listening: Retell a Story

Materials
- Calendar
- Talk with Me, Sing with Me Chart 21A, 21B
- Big Book *One Little Mouse*
- Trade Book *My Lucky Day*
- AudioText CD
- Alphabet Cards: *Cc, Ff, Ll, Pp, Ss*
- Decodable Reader 20
- Picture Cards: p. 142
- Daily Fix-It Transparency 21

Calendar

Name the day and date
Ask a volunteer to find today's date on the calendar. Have children say the day, month, date, and year together.

Name letters in month
Show children the name of the current month. Ask for volunteers to name each letter. Continue with other months of the year.

Message Board

Question of the week
Tell children that they will have an opportunity to talk, sing, read, and write about adventures animals can have. Write and read the question as you track the print. Encourage children to respond in complete sentences.

> ## What adventures can an animal have?

Build Background Use the Day 1 instruction on ELL Poster 21 to assess knowledge and develop concepts.

ELL Poster 21

Build Background

LET'S TALK

Build concept
Display Talk with Me Chart 21A. Ask children to look at the forest. Read the question together. Look at the pictures. What adventures could an animal have in these places? Prompt children to respond in complete sentences.

Build oral vocabulary
This week we will be talking about adventures that animals have. We are going to learn six new words. Listen as I say the words; you may know some of them: *woodland, nest, vale, hollow, comfortable,* and *shadows.*

Talk with Me, Sing with Me Chart

LET'S LISTEN

Share Background Building Audio
Play the CD that features an adventure that a small animal could have.

 Sing with Me/Background Building Audio CD

LET'S SING/PHONOLOGICAL AWARENESS

Sing "A New Woodland Nest"
Display Sing with Me Chart 21B. Tell children that they are going to sing a song about a mouse looking for a new house. Read the title and describe the pictures. Sing the song several times to the tune of "Hickory, Dickory, Dock." Encourage children to sing with you.

Recognize rhyme
Sing the first verse of the song again. Have children point out the rhyming words *nest, best,* and *rest.*

 Sing with Me/Background Building Audio CD

A New Woodland Nest

"I need a new woodland nest,"
Said the mouse, "I want the best."
Mole offered his hole, safe from the cold.
"Oh, but I really can't rest."

Talk with Me, Sing with Me Chart

- Preview and predict.
- Listen to a story.

Materials

- Big Book *One Little Mouse*
- Trade Book *My Lucky Day*

EXTEND SKILLS

Concepts of Print Guide the children to recognize the print portion of a page.

Comprehension

MODEL READING STRATEGIES

Preview and predict

Display *One Little Mouse.* Look at the cover; tell me what you see. Show me where the person who wrote the book is listed. Show me where the person who draws the pictures is listed. What are those people called?

 Think Aloud I see a little mouse sitting on a mushroom.

The title of this book is *One Little Mouse.* What do you think this story will be about? Let's read to find out.

LET'S READ *One Little Mouse*

Model fluent reading

Read the story with expression for enjoyment.

Big Book

AudioText CD

Shared Reading

ROUTINE

Day 1

Preview and make predictions about *One Little Mouse.* Read the whole book for enjoyment. Introduce comprehension skill, sequence.

Day 2

Reread *One Little Mouse.* Use the Shared Reading Notes to engage children in a conversation about the story. Apply comprehension skill, sequence.

Day 3

Reread *One Little Mouse.* Develop oral vocabulary by naming objects and actions. Review comprehension skill, draw conclusions.

Day 4

Reread *Farfallina and Marcel.* Apply comprehension skill, sequence.

Day 5

Read "The Tale of Peter Rabbit" in the *Read Aloud Anthology.* Assess comprehension skill, sequence.

Text to World **READER RESPONSE**

Respond to literature

Invite children to sit in a circle. Have them pass an object to each other. When you say stop, the child holding it should tell the first event of the story. Continue until the whole story is retold.

STRATEGY Predict

Check predictions

What did you think the story would be about?

• What are some things the mouse did in the story?

Use the following questions to guide discussion.

• What did the little mouse want to find?

• Do you think these animals are friends in real life?

 INTRODUCE SKILL Sequence

Define Sequence

• In a story, something happens first, next, and last.

• The order in which things happen is called the **sequence.**

 Think Aloud In *My Lucky Day,* we read about a piglet's adventure. What did the piglet do first, next, and last?

Recall sequence

Display the Trade Book *My Lucky Day.* Help children identify the sequence.

• First, the fox gave the piglet a bath.

• Next, the fox made a big dinner for the piglet.

• Last, the fox gave the piglet a massage.

Relate sequence to everyday life

When you get ready for school, you usually do things in a certain order. What do you do first, next, and last?

OBJECTIVES

● Respond to literature.
● Check predictions.
● Introduce sequence.
● Recognize sequential text.

Skills Trace	
 Sequence	
Introduce/Teach	TE: K.1 141, 150; K.2 327, 336; K.4 15, 24, 141, 150
Practice	TE: K.1 165, 174; K.2 287, 296; K.4 37, 46, 163, 172 PB: K.1 27, 29; K.2 47, 49; K.4 7, 9, 27, 29
Reteach/Review	TE: K.1 291, DI-47; K.2 99, 349, DI-49; K.4 DI-45, DI-47; K.5 101
Assess	TE: K.1 186, 380–382; K.2 308, 376–378; K.4 58, 184, 380–382; Unit 4 Benchmark Test

E L L

Introduce Skill Demonstrate sequence using a graphic organizer.

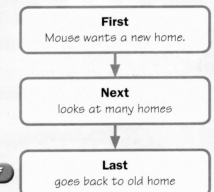

First
Mouse wants a new home.

↓

Next
looks at many homes

↓

Text to Self

Last
goes back to old home

WORD WORK

OBJECTIVE

- Introduce initial blends.

Skills Trace

↻ **Consonant Blends**

Introduce/Teach	TE: K.4 142–143, 156, 164
Practice	TE: K.4 167, 173, 175, 181 PB: K.4 23, 25–26, 28
Reteach/Review	TE: K.4 237, DI-33
Assess	TE: K.4 182–183, 380–382; Unit 4 Benchmark Test

Materials

- Big Book *One Little Mouse*
- Decodable Reader 20
- Picture Cards:

  clock   cloud   flag
  flashlight playground sled
  slide

- Alphabet Cards: *Ll, Ss, Pp, Cc, Ff*

Support Phonemic Awareness
The initial consonant blends *pl-*, *cl-*, and *fl-* exist both in English and Spanish. Help Spanish speakers discover the similarity by comparing the beginning sounds in cognates such as *planta* (plant), *clase* (class), and *flor* (flower).

Phonemic Awareness

INTRODUCE Initial Blends

Isolate initial blends

Display the *slide* Picture Card. Listen to the beginning of the word *slide*. Two sounds blend together to make the beginning sound. Say the sounds with me: /sl/, /sl/, /sl/, slide. I will say some other words. Tell me if the word begins like *slide: sled, sleep, flag, slow, clap, slip,* and *sleeve.*

Listen for *cl-*, *pl-*, *fl-*

Continue with Picture Cards to show other initial blends. Use the *cl-* in *clock* and *cloud*, the *pl-* in *playground*, and the *fl-* in *flag* and *flashlight*.

Monitor Progress   Check Sound Fluency

Discriminate Initial Blends Say two words: *slip, sip.* Have children identify the word that begins with a blend. Continue with the following words: *flip, lip; clap, cap; flap, lap;* and *crib, rib.*

If... children cannot identify initial blends,

then... have them segment the two sounds in the blend and then practice with the following words: /pl/ *plan*, /cl/ *clap*, and /fl/ *flat.*

SUCCESS PREDICTOR

▶ **Day 1**
Check Sound
Fluency

Day 2
Check Retelling/
Letter-Sound
Knowledge

Day 3
Check High-
Frequency Words/
Word Reading

Day 4
Check Phoneme
Segmentation

Day 5
Check Oral
Vocabulary/
Assess Progress

Phonics

OBJECTIVES

- ◎ Introduce consonant blends.
- Blend and read words.
- Introduce high-frequency words *one, two, three, four,* and *five.*

◎ CONSONANT BLENDS

Introduce initial blends

Display the *clock* Picture Card. What is this? What are the first two sounds in *clock*? *Clock* begins with /k/ /l/, /kl/. Say it with me: /kl/, /kl/, /kl/, *clock*. **Write *clock*.** *Clock* begins with a blend. When some consonants are together, they each say their own sound. **Point to the word *clock*.** The sound for *c* is /k/ and the sound for *l* is /l/. Put them together and we have /kl/.

Connect initial blends

Write *cl-, fl-, pl-,* and *sl-* on the board. Point to *fl-*. What are the names of these letters? What are the sounds for these letters? Say them with me: /f/ /l/, /f/ /l/, /fl/. **Continue with *cl-, pl-,* and *sl-*.**

Recognize *sl-, pl-, cl-, fl-*

Display the *cloud* Picture Card. What is this? What are the beginning sounds in *cloud*? Point to the letters for /kl/. **Continue with the following Picture Cards:** *clock, flag, flashlight, playground, sled,* and *slide.*

Review letter sounds

Review the names and sounds of the letters *Ll, Ss, Pp, Cc,* and *Ff* with Alphabet Cards.

BLEND SOUNDS

Blend words

Write the word *flap* on the board. The first two letters *f* and *l* make the blended sound /fl/. Say the blend with me: /fl/. Now, we say the last sounds of the word: /a/ /p/. Let's try to say the blend and the other two sounds one right after the other: /fl/ /a/ /p/, *flap*. **Blend the words *flat, flip, plan, plot, clap, slap,* and *slip*.**

Word Wall HIGH-FREQUENCY WORDS

Introduce high-frequency words

Display *one*. This is the word *one*. You cannot blend the sounds in this word. Let's say the letters together: *o, n, e, one*. The word is *one*. **Continue with the words *two, three, four,* and *five*.** Let's look in the book *One Little Mouse* to find *one, two, three, four,* and *five*. **Add the words to the Word Wall.**

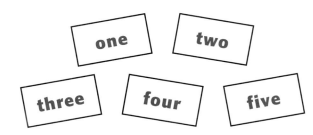

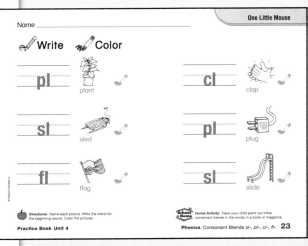

▲ **Practice Book 4**
Consonant Blends, p. 23

SUCCESS PREDICTOR

OBJECTIVES

- Review high-frequency words.
- Write uppercase and lowercase letters.

Group Time

On-Level

Reread Decodable Reader 20. Use the Small Group Reading **Routine.**

Strategic Intervention

Read Listen to Me Reader K.4.3. More practice with blends, p. DI·11.

Advanced

Reread Independent Leveled Reader K.4.2. Use the reading routine on p. DI·11. Reread to build fluency.

Group English language learners by their reading ability in English.

(i) Independent Activities

Self-Selected Reading See pp. TR14–15 for a bibliography of books related to the weekly concept.

Practice Book Consonant Blends, p. 23

Centers Use the center activities on pp. 136–137 to practice this week's skills.

Journal Writing Draw and label three animals the mouse tries to live with in the story.

Spiral REVIEW PREPARE TO READ

Review words   Continue guided blending practice with these words from last week's Decodable Reader 20 *Can It Fit?*:

on	sat	Lil	Tab
did	in	lap	not
lit	can	Kit	fit
it	lid	doll	had
bat			

Review high-frequency words   Write the word *see* on the board. This is the word *see.* What is this word? Continue the word reading routine with the words *do, the, a, that, are, you,* and *they.*

Small Group Reading

DAY 1 ROUTINE

1 **Model Fluent Reading** Have children finger point as you read a page.

2 **Read Chorally** Have children finger point as they chorally read the page. Continue reading page by page, repeating steps 1 and 2.

3 **Read Individually** Have children read aloud a page in their group.

4 **Reread and Monitor Progress** As you listen to individual children reread, monitor progress and provide support.

Decodable Reader

HANDWRITING

Write numerals   Numbers can be written with words or numerals. Numerals sometimes have a period after them, such as when we make a list. Let's practice writing the numerals and words *one, two, three, four,* and *five.* Be sure to put a period after a numeral when you write it.

Shared Writing

GRAMMAR Complete Sentences

Introduce complete sentences

A complete sentence must have a naming part and an action part. Write the following sentence on the board: *The dog ran.* Is this a complete sentence? Have children identify the parts of the sentence. A complete sentence must start with an uppercase letter. What must it end with? (a period)

Identify complete sentences

Write complete and incomplete sentences on the board. Ask children to circle the naming part, underline the action part, identify uppercase letters and punctuation marks, and fix any incomplete sentences.

LET'S WRITE Connect to Grammar

Use complete sentences

Have children dictate complete sentences about something they do to have fun. Write the sentences on the board.

Ally rides a bike.
Jamie runs in the park.

Revise and edit

Ask children to confirm that you have an uppercase letter at the beginning of the sentence and a punctuation mark at the end.

Independent writing

Have children write or dictate their own sentences. Then have volunteers act out their sentences for the class to guess.

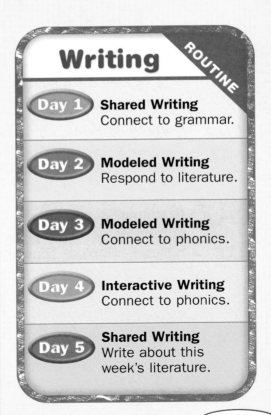

OBJECTIVES
- Introduce complete sentences.
- Write complete sentences.

DAILY FIX-IT

i sat in the car
(I sat in the car.)

This week's practice sentences appear on Daily Fix-It Transparency 21.

Writing ROUTINE

Day 1 **Shared Writing** Connect to grammar.

Day 2 **Modeled Writing** Respond to literature.

Day 3 **Modeled Writing** Connect to phonics.

Day 4 **Interactive Writing** Connect to phonics.

Day 5 **Shared Writing** Write about this week's literature.

ELL

Access Content Ask for volunteers to talk with you and retell a story they have read or heard, using book illustrations, if desired.

Speaking and Listening

RETELL A STORY

Discuss retelling a story
Today we are going to talk about retelling a story. When you are retelling a story, you have to tell what happened first, next, and last. Ask children to tell a story they know to the class.

Model retelling a story
Let's practice retelling *My Lucky Day*. I'll start. One day the hungry fox was surprised to have the piglet knock on the door. Who can tell me what happened next?

Practice retelling a story
Have children take turns finishing the story and telling the events in order. Then have volunteers retell the story of *One Little Mouse*.

Wrap Up Your Day!

✓ **Oral Language** Today we read about a little mouse who was looking for a new home. Have you ever moved to a new home?

✓ **Comprehension** In the story *One Little Mouse,* the author makes it easy to tell what happened first, next, and last because she uses numbers. At which home were the three frogs, the first, second, or third? (third)

✓ **Grammar** Today we talked about making complete sentences. Who can tell me what parts we need to make a complete sentence?

Homework Send home this week's Family Times newsletter.

PREVIEW Day 2

Tomorrow we will read *One Little Mouse* again.

EXTEND Your Day

Animal Characteristics

Materials Big Book *One Little Mouse*

Animal Differences Take a picture walk through the illustrations of *One Little Mouse.* Point out the differences in the animals by asking the following questions: What is their skin like? Where do they live? How do they move?

Write the following titles on chart paper.

Fur	Skin	Feathers	Quills

Read the titles together and ask children to think of the animals in the story. Ask which animals fit into each category.

Guess Who? Describe an animal using the categories on the chart. Have children figure out which animal from the story you are describing.

TIME FOR Science

Grammar

Complete Sentences

Materials sentence strips, paper

Sentence Strip Puzzles Write short sentences about the story *One Little Mouse* on sentence strips. Cut the sentences apart into subject and predicate parts. Show children the first part of the cut sentence strip. Ask them if it is a complete sentence. Ask them what the sentence needs to be a complete sentence. Have children create sentences by combining subjects and predicates. Have children illustrate the sentences.

Mouse   looks for a house.

Two moles   see Mouse.

Math

Macaroni Math

Materials construction paper, glue, elbow macaroni, pencil

Counting Have children write the words *one, two, three, four,* and *five* across the bottom of their papers, leaving space between each word. Then have children write the numerals 1–5 above the words. Instruct children to glue the correct number of macaroni noodles under each number.

Day 2
AT A GLANCE

Oral Language and Vocabulary
Calendar
Message Board
Build Background

Shared Reading
Big Book *One Little Mouse*
Strategy Recall and Retell
 Skill Sequence

Word Work

Phonemic Awareness
Listen for Initial Blends

Phonics
Connect Sounds to Letters in Blends
H/F Words *one, two, three, four, five*
Phonics Story *My Words*

Read

Group Time < Differentiated Instruction

Language Arts
Grammar: Complete Sentences
Modeled Writing: Write About Animals in *One Little Mouse*
Speaking and Listening: Expand Vocabulary

Materials

- Calendar
- Talk with Me, Sing with Me Chart 20A, 21A, 21B
- Sing with Me/Background Building Audio CD
- Big Book *One Little Mouse*
- AudioText CD
- Picture Card: pp. 156, 158
- Phonics Songs and Rhymes Chart 21
- Phonics Songs and Rhymes Audio CD
- Alphabet Cards: *Cc, Dd, Pp, Rr, Ss, Tt*
- Phonics Story *My Words*

Calendar

Name the day and date
Ask a volunteer to find today's date on the calendar. Have children say the day, month, date, and year together.

Identify pattern
Discuss patterns by talking about how many Saturdays are in this month. How many days are there from one Saturday to the next? Point out that there are seven days between each Saturday.

Message Board

Question of the day
Write and read the question as you track the print. Encourage children to respond in complete sentences.

> ## What kind of adventure do you think four or five animals can have?

Review high-frequency words
Have children find the words *four* and *five* in the question. Circle them and say them together.

Build Background Use the Day 2 instruction on ELL Poster 21 to practice the Develop Vocabulary words.

ELL Poster 21

Build Background

LET'S TALK/LET'S SING

Develop oral vocabulary

Display Talk with Me Chart 21A. Point to the photograph of the animal curled up in a little burrow asleep.

- What kind of *nest* does this animal have?
- What kinds of homes do other *woodland* animals have?

Sing "A New Woodland Nest"

Display Sing with Me Chart 21B. The word *nest* is what we call a home some animals build, and *woodland* is another name for a forest. Have you ever heard the words *woodland* and *nest* before? Ask children to listen for the words as you sing the song.

Talk with Me, Sing with Me Chart

A New Woodland Nest

"I need a new woodland nest,"
Said the mouse, "I want the best."
Mole offered his hole, safe from the cold.
"Oh, but I really can't rest."

Sing with Me/Background Building Audio CD

LET'S LEARN AMAZING WORDS

Amazing Words to build oral vocabulary

- woodland
- nest
- vale
- hollow
- comfortable
- shadows

Activate Prior Knowledge Ask children what words in their home languages are used for the words *woodland* and *nest.*

DAY 2 ROUTINE

Oral Vocabulary   woodland   nest

1 **Introduce** *Woodland* is another name for a forest, or a place with many trees. Many wild animals live in the *woodland.* What is our new word for a forest?

Demonstrate There are many animals that live in a *woodland.* Deer live in the *woodland.* What other animals live in a *woodland?*

2 **Introduce** The mouse in the story is looking for a new *nest,* which is a place some animals build to live. What is our new word for an animal's home?

Demonstrate Some animals, like the mouse in the story, may build a *nest.* Can you think of other animals that would build a *nest* for a home?

3 **Review** We talked about two words today: *woodland* and *nest.* Which word means "another name for a forest," *woodland* or *nest?* Which word is something animals can build to live in, *woodland* or *nest?*

4 **Apply** Have children use *woodland* and *nest* in complete sentences. Have them use the words to tell about an animal they have seen living outside.

OBJECTIVES

- Recall and retell story events.
- Identify sequence.
- Read from left to right.

Materials

- Big Book *One Little Mouse*

Access Content Emphasize the words *first, next,* and *last* as you talk about the sequence of events in the story. Then have the children repeat those words as they act out the story.

TEACHING TiP

Woodland Animals Children may not know much about moles, chickadees, or opossums. Show the pictures from the book and give background information about each, so children have a knowledge base while reading the story.

Comprehension

MODEL READING STRATEGY
Recall and Retell

Retell the story

Using the pictures as prompts, invite children to retell the story. Open to pages 6–7. We see the mouse in his nest. He thinks his nest is too small and he wants another one. He will meet many animals on his adventure.

Big Book

SKILL Sequence

Model identifying sequence

Remind children that stories have events that happen in a certain order. The things that happen first, next, and last are the order of the events in a story.

 Think Aloud Who offered the mouse their home first? Who offered next? Who offered after that? Who offered their home last?

CONCEPTS OF PRINT
Read from Left to Right

Track print

Display page 6 of *One Little Mouse.* Track print from left to right as you read the first sentence. Remind children that they should read words from left to right and from top to bottom on each page.

LET'S READ *One Little Mouse*

Reread the story

Ask children to listen as animals offer their homes first, next, and last. Use the Shared Reading Notes to prompt conversation about *One Little Mouse.*

 AudioText CD

Pages 6-7

One little mouse took a look at his house
Deep in the woodland ground.
"This nest is too small! Not roomy at all!
There must be a new one around."

Shared Reading Notes

Why did the mouse want to look for a new house? *Child may respond:* His nest was too small.

- The mouse thinks his nest is too small. **Point to the mouse's nest. What things that grow in the woodland did he use to make his nest?**
wh- question

Develop Vocabulary mouse

Pages 8-9

Two blackish moles peeked out of their holes
And called to the mouse passing by,
"We have a fine nest in which you can rest."
So little Mouse thought he would try.

But their diet was wormish,
And that made Mouse squirmish.
He very soon said, "Good-bye."

Who offered the mouse their nest first? *Child may respond:* two moles

- Two moles offered the mouse their nest. **Where did they live? wh- question**

Expand Vocabulary moles

Pages 10-11

Three meadow frogs were leaping from logs.
"You'll like sleeping here," they said.
Mouse thanked them politely, but curling up tightly
He found it too cold for a bed.

With a wheeze and a sneeze,
He was sure he would freeze.
"This never will do!" he said.

Who offered Mouse their home next? *Child may respond:* three frogs

- Three frogs offered Mouse their home in the logs. **Where do the frogs live? wh- question**

Develop Vocabulary frogs

2

Shared Reading Notes

Who offered Mouse their home next?
Child may respond: four bobwhite quail

- Four bobwhite quail with eggs in their nest offered Mouse their home. What would it feel like to sleep on eggs? **distancing**

Expand Vocabulary bobwhite quail

Pages 12–13

Four bobwhite quail ran up from the vale.
"If you're looking for someplace to rest,
We have a nice hollow, and if you will follow,
We think we have room for a guest."

But Mouse found it bumpy
And clumpy and lumpy,
Just too many eggs in the nest!

Who wanted Mouse to come home with them? *Child may respond:* five greeny snakes

- The snakes wanted Mouse to come home with them. Why didn't Mouse want to go with them? **recall**

Develop Vocabulary snakes

Activate Prior Knowledge Ask children to tell you about the animals they like best. Ask if there are any animals from their home countries that are different from what they see near school.

Pages 14–15

Five greeny snakes from meadows and lakes
Hissed, "Come home with us if you dare!"
"No, thank you," Mouse cried,
And hurried to hide.
Snakes gave him a terrible scare!

Who offered Mouse their bed on this page? *Child may respond:* six baby cottontails

- Cottontails are one kind of rabbit. How many baby rabbits are there? **recall**

Develop Vocabulary cottontails

Pages 16–17

Six baby cottontails hopped along hilly trails.
"Come, little Mouse, share our bed."
"Oh thank you," said Mouse. "I'm in need of a house."
And he happily laid down his head.

But the cottontails bunched up
And crunched up and hunched up.
"And soon I'll be scrunched up!" Mouse said.

Pages 18–19

Seven gray squirrels
Ran in circles and swirls,
Then carried Mouse up to their nest.
"You may stay here with us
If you don't make a fuss."
And Mouse said, "I will do my best."

But the nut nest was clicky
And clacky and cracky.
He left without one bit of rest.

Shared Reading Notes

Where do the squirrels make their nest?
Child may respond: in a tree

- Squirrels make their nests in trees. Do you ever see squirrels around your home? Where do squirrels like to make their nests? **distancing**

Develop Vocabulary squirrels

Pages 20–21

Eight chickadees flew in with the breeze.
"We have a fine place in the willow."
But Mouse said, "Dear me! I can't sleep in a tree!
Imagine a branch for a pillow!"

Who offers Mouse their home on this page? *Child may respond:* eight chickadees

- Eight chickadees offered their home in the willow tree. How do you think a tree branch would feel as a pillow? **open-ended**

Expand Vocabulary chickadees

Pages 22–23

Nine porcupine waddled by in a line.
They called to the mouse, "Good day!
We have a nice den, right here in the glen."
"Thank you," Mouse answered. "I'll stay."

But their sharp quills were sticking
And picking and pricking.
So Mouse quickly went on his way.

Who offers Mouse their home next? *Child may respond:* nine porcupine

- Nine porcupine want Mouse to stay with them. Why doesn't Mouse want to stay with them? **open-ended**

Expand Vocabulary porcupine, quills

Shared Reading Notes

Where did the opossums live? *Child may respond:* in a tree

- Ten opossums, who live in a tree, wanted Mouse to swing from his tail. How did Mouse feel about this? **open-ended**

Expand Vocabulary opossums

Pages 24–25

Ten small opossums were eating plum blossoms.
"Come on, sleep with us," they were singing.
They knotted his tail, and Mouse let out a wail
To find himself suddenly swinging.

"A terrible tizzy! I'm upside-down dizzy!
A mouse tail is not made for clinging."

Where does Mouse go next? *Child may respond:* back to his house

- Mouse goes back home at the end of the day. Why do you think Mouse is happy with his home now? **open-ended**

Access Content Provide background knowledge about the opossum, such as it is nocturnal and it sleeps by hanging from its tail. Tell children that many people use the nickname *possum* when talking about an opossum.

Pages 26–27

Then Mouse turned around to the darkening wood
And scampered along just as fast as he could,
Back to his own little comfortable house
(So tiny and tidy, just right for a mouse),
And when evening shadows crept over the ground
And covered the woodland, here's what was found:

What animals do we see sleeping in their beds on these pages? *Child may respond:* ten opossums, nine porcupine, eight chickadees, and seven squirrels

- The opossums, porcupine, chickadees, and squirrels are in bed. How do you get ready for bed? **distancing**

Pages 28–29

Ten small opossums asleep in the glen.
Nine porcupine nestled up in their den.
Eight chickadees roosting
High in the willows.
Seven gray squirrels using
Soft tails for pillows.

Pages 30–31

Six baby cottontails snug in their nest.
Five greeny snakes coiled up for a rest.
Four bobwhite quail very still in the vale.
Three meadow frogs sleeping on logs.
Two blackish moles deep in their holes.

30

31

Page 32

And one little mouse,
One tired little mouse,
One content little mouse,
Sound asleep in his house.

32

Shared Reading Notes

What animals do we see sleeping in their beds on these pages? *Child may respond:* six cottontails, five snakes, four bobwhite quail, three frogs, and two moles

- The cottontails, snakes, quail, frogs, and moles need their rest at the end of the day just like you do. Why do you think people and animals need to sleep at the end of the day? **distancing**

Who is asleep on this page? *Child may respond:* one mouse

- The mouse is finally asleep in his own bed. Do you think Mouse is happy to be in his own bed? **open-ended**

Retelling Plan

☑ Week 1 assess Advanced students.

☑ Week 2 assess On-Level students.

☑ **This week assess Strategic Intervention students.**

☐ Week 4 assess Advanced students.

☐ Week 5 assess On-Level students.

☐ Week 6 assess Strategic Intervention students.

Monitor Progress | Check Retelling *One Little Mouse*

Picture Walk and Retell Have children use the illustrations of *One Little Mouse* to retell the story.

If... children have difficulty retelling the story,

then... use the Retelling Cards and the Retelling Rubric to help them move toward fluent retelling.

SUCCESS PREDICTOR

Day 1
Check Sound Fluency

▶ **Day 2**
Check Retelling/ Letter-Sound Knowledge

Day 3
Check High-Frequency Words/ Word Reading

Day 4
Check Phoneme Segmentation

Day 5
Check Oral Vocabulary/ Assess Progress

Scoring Rubric | Retelling

Rubric 4 3 2 1	4	3	2	1
Setting	describes time and location	identifies time and location	omits time and location	is unable to identify time and location
Character	describes main character(s) and character development	identifies main character(s)	omits or inaccurately identifies characters	unable to identify character
Events	describes events in sequence with details	tells most events in sequence with some detail	retells first and last events but omits middle with few details	is unable to retell events

Retelling

SUCCESS PREDICTOR

- Listen for blends.
- Connect sounds to letters in blends.

Materials

- Phonics Songs and Rhymes Chart 21
- Alphabet Cards: *Cc, Dd, Pp, Rr, Ss, Tt*
- Picture Cards:

  clock   cloud   flag
  flashlight   playground
  sled   slide

- Phonics Story *My Words*

Support Phonemic Awareness
Since some languages do not have *r* and others pronounce *r* differently, help children practice the pronunciation of English words, saying the *r* first, then the blend and the word.

Phonemic Awareness

PRACTICE Blends

Listen for initial blends

Display the chart. We are going to learn a new song today. Play the CD or sing the song several times to the tune of "Jack and Jill Went Up the Hill." Ask children to join in. Have them identify initial blends: *sliding, slippery, slope, slides, slide, please, platform, clear, climbing,* and *floating*.

Sliding Down the Slippery Slope

Sliding down the slippery slope,
And floating through clear water.
The water slide's our special ride,
Please go first up the ladder.

Climbing up the platform high,
And stepping up in order.
Just ask me why I like to slide,
And I'll say it's the water!

Phonics Songs and Rhymes Chart

Phonics Songs and Rhymes Audio CD

Phonics

CONSONANT BLENDS

Identify blends

Display the chart. Remember, we learned a new song. There were many words that begin with these blends: *sl-, pl-, cl-,* and *fl-*. Let's circle the words that begin with *sl-, pl-, cl-,* and *fl-* on our chart. Have several children come up one at a time to circle a word that begins with one of these blends.

Connect sounds to letters

Write *sl-* on the board. Point to the *s.* What is the sound for this letter? Repeat with *l.* What do they sound like when they are blended together? Repeat the routine with *pl-, cl-,* and *fl-.*

Monitor Progress | **Check Letter-Sound Knowledge**

Consonant Blends Give children a sheet of paper folded in fourths. Have them write the blends *sl-, pl-, cl-,* and *fl-*, one in each section. Display Picture Cards *clock, cloud, flag, flashlight, playground, sled,* and *slide* in random order. Have children point to the correct blend on their papers when you show each card.

If... children cannot connect the sounds and letters in the blends,

then... have them practice blending the words while seeing them in writing or print.

SUCCESS PREDICTOR

Day 1	**▶ Day 2**	**Day 3**	**Day 4**	**Day 5**
Check Sound Fluency	Check Retelling/ Letter-Sound Knowledge	Check High-Frequency Words/ Word Reading	Check Phoneme Segmentation	Check Oral Vocabulary/ Assess Progress

Spiral REVIEW — BLEND SOUNDS

Review letter names and sounds

Spell and blend words

PHONICS ACTIVITY MAT

Use the Alphabet Cards to review these letter names and sounds: *Cc, Dd, Tt, Ss, Pp,* and *Rr.*

Listen to the sounds in *crib:* /kr/ /i/ /b/. What is the blended sound that starts the word *crib*? (/kr/) The letters for /kr/ are *c* and *r.*

c r i b

Point to *crib.* Help me blend the sound of each letter together to read this word: /k/ /r/ /i/ /b/. The word is *crib.*

Continue spell and blend practice with the following words: *cap, clap, can, clam, tap, trap, cab, crab, tip,* and *trip.*

PREPARE TO READ

Review high-frequency words

Write *two* on the board. This is the word *two.* What is this word? Continue the word reading routine with *one, three, four, five, have, I, is, like, you, do,* and *see.*

Small Group Reading

DAY 2 ROUTINE

1 **Model Fluent Reading** Have children finger point as you read a page.

2 **Read Chorally** Have children finger point as they chorally read the page. Continue reading page by page, repeating steps 1 and 2.

3 **Read Individually** Have children read aloud a page in their group.

4 **Reread and Monitor Progress** As you listen to individual children reread, monitor progress and provide support.

Name _____
My Words

I have one cap.
Cap is like clap.
Can you clap?

Practice Book 4
Phonics Story, pp. 25–26

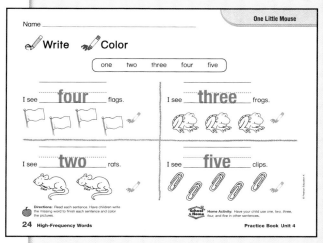

Name _____ One Little Mouse

✏ Write 🖍 Color

| one | two | three | four | five |

I see ___**four**___ flags. | I see ___**three**___ frogs.

I see ___**two**___ rats. | I see ___**five**___ clips.

Directions: Read each sentence. Have children write the missing word to finish each sentence and color the pictures.

School + Home **Home Activity:** Have your child use one, two, three, four, and five in other sentences.

24 High-Frequency Words Practice Book Unit 4

▲ **Practice Book 4**
High-Frequency Words, p. 24

Group Time

On-Level
Read Phonics Story *My Words.* Use the Small Group Reading **Routine.**

Strategic Intervention
Read Phonics Story *My Words.* More practice with initial blends, p. DI·12.

Advanced
Read Decodable Reader 21. Use the reading routine on p. DI·12. Apply phonics skills.

ELL
Group English language learners by their reading ability in English.

ⓘ Independent Activities

Self-Selected Reading See pp. TR14–15 for books related to the concept.

Practice Book High-Frequency Words, p. 24

Centers Use the center activities on pp. 136–137.

Journal Writing Draw a picture for one word that begins with *sl-* and one word that begins with *pl-.*

Letter-Sound Knowledge
SUCCESS PREDICTOR

OBJECTIVES

- Practice complete sentences.
- Write about animals in *One Little Mouse.*

Materials

- Picture Card:
  starfish
- Big Book *One Little Mouse*

DAILY FIX-IT

will he skip and spin
(Will he skip and spin?)

Writer's Checkup

✔ The first word in a sentence begins with an uppercase letter. Did I do that?

✔ A sentence should end with a period. Did I do that?

✔ A sentence should make sense. Does my sentence make sense?

✔ A good writer uses his or her best handwriting. Did I do that?

Modeled Writing

GRAMMAR Complete Sentences

Practice complete sentences

Show the *starfish* Picture Card. This is a starfish. We can make a sentence about the starfish: *The starfish swims in the ocean. The starfish* is the naming part, and *swims in the ocean* is the action part. The sentence starts with an uppercase letter and ends with a period.

Picture Card

Identify complete sentences

Write the following on the board:

> **Little Mouse ran in the woods.**
> **Little Mouse the house**
> **Little Mouse saw the moles.**

Read each item with the children and ask them to identify the sentences. Then ask why the second item is not a sentence.

LET'S WRITE Respond to Literature

Discuss *One Little Mouse*

Discuss *One Little Mouse.* Ask children to identify how many of each animal offered little Mouse their homes. List them on the board in order (for example: *two moles, three frogs,* and *four quail*).

Model writing a sentence

Many animals offered Mouse their house. Let's write complete sentences about all of them.

> **Two moles offered Mouse their house.**

Independent writing

Have children write their own sentences for an animal in the story. Then have them illustrate their sentences and make a booklet out of the pages that retell the story in sequential order.

Three frogs offered
Mouse their house.

Speaking and Listening

LET'S REVIEW AMAZING WORDS

Display Talk with Me Chart 20A. Review these Amazing Words from last week.

Oral Vocabulary   piglet   filthy

DAY 2 ROUTINE

1 **Introduce** A small pig is called a *piglet*. Who can remember the word we use when we talk about a small pig?

Demonstrate Tell me the sound a *piglet* makes.

2 **Introduce** When something is very dirty, we say it is *filthy*. What is the word we use when something is very dirty?

Demonstrate When the piglet first visited the fox, he was *filthy*. What did fox do to make him clean?

3 **Review** We talked about two words today: *piglet* and *filthy*. Which word is a name for a small pig, *piglet* or *filthy*? Which word describes something really dirty, *piglet* or *filthy*?

4 **Apply** Have children use *piglet* and *filthy* in complete sentences. Have children recall the story and tell how the words were used in the story.

Wrap Up Your Day!

 Oral Language Today we read about Mouse searching for a new home. Who were the animals that offered their homes?

 Grammar Remember, a complete sentence has a naming part and an action part, starts with an uppercase letter, and ends with a period.

 Homework Idea Have children take their Phonics Story home to share with their families.

PREVIEW Day 3

Tomorrow we will read about a cat named Flap. What do you think Flap will do in the story?

EXTEND Your Day

Animals: Similarities and Differences

Materials Big Books *Life in an Ocean*, *One Little Mouse*

Venn Diagrams Make a Venn diagram on the board or use Graphic Organizer 28. Above one circle, write *Mouse*. Above the other circle write *Fish*.

Point out the titles and explain that things that tell about the mouse are put in the *Mouse* circle, and things that tell about the fish are put in the *Fish* circle. Explain that the ways that the two animals are alike are put where the circles overlap. Have children look at the pictures and identify things to put in the diagram.

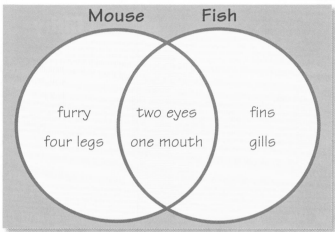

Children can also make charts to compare other animals, such as snakes and rabbits.

Phonics

Initial Blends Guess

Describe Words with Blends Make a list of words beginning with blends *cr-, dr-, tr-, st-, sp-, sl-, pl-, cl-,* or *fl-* on a piece of paper. Point to a word, showing only one volunteer. Prompt the child to give clues about the word or draw it for the class.

Comprehension

Sequence

Neighborhood Adventure With children, pretend to take an adventurous trip around the neighborhood. Have children take turns telling what they would see on the adventure. As children take turns, they are to repeat what the previous children said and then add something more, sequentially and numerically.

For example, the first child may say, "I'm going on a neighborhood adventure, and I see one school." The next child would say, "I'm going on a neighborhood adventure, and I see one school and two buses." The next child might say, "I'm going on a neighborhood adventure, and I see one school, two buses, and three trees," and so on until five children have added what they saw to the list. Then start over with a new adventure.

Calendar

Name the day and date

Ask a volunteer to find today's day and date. Have children recite the day, month, date, and year.

Count the days in the current month

Point to the calendar for the current month. Then count together from the first day of the month to the last day. Have children take turns recounting the numbers. Ask how many days are in the month.

Message Board

Question of the day

Write and read the question as you track the print.

> ## Where would you try to stay in the woodland?

Review phonics

- What letters stand for /tr/ and /st/? *(tr, st)*
- Which words begin with these blends? *(try, stay)*

Extend Language Use the Day 3 instruction on ELL Poster 21 to extend and enrich language.

ELL Poster 21

Oral Language and Vocabulary
Calendar
Message Board
Build Background

Shared Reading
Big Book *One Little Mouse*
Skill Draw Conclusions
Skill Sequence

Word Work

Phonemic Awareness
Isolate Final Blends

Phonics
Connect Sounds to Letters in Blends
H/F Words *one, two, three, four, five*
Kindergarten Student Reader K.4.3

Read

Group Time < Differentiated Instruction

Language Arts
Grammar: Review Action Parts
Modeled Writing:
   Write About Pets
Speaking and Listening:
   Retell a Story

Materials
- Calendar
- Talk with Me, Sing with Me Chart 21A, 21B
- Sing with Me/Background Building Audio CD
- Big Book *One Little Mouse*
- Trade Book *Fix-It Duck*
- AudioText CD
- Alphabet Cards: *Aa, Cc, Dd, Ff, Hh, Ii, Kk, Ll, Nn, Oo, Pp, Rr, Ss, Tt*
- Picture Cards: pp. 164, 167
- Kindergarten Student Reader K.4.3
- AlphaBuddy

Amazing Words to build oral vocabulary

- woodland
- nest
- vale
- hollow
- comfortable
- shadows

Access Content Ask children what words in their home languages are used for *vale* and *hollow.*

Build Background

LET'S TALK

Develop oral vocabulary

Display Talk with Me Chart 21A. Point to the picture of a valley. A *vale* is the grassy place at the bottom of a hill.

- What do you see in this *vale?* (river, rocks)
- When something is empty inside, we call it *hollow.* What is *hollow* in this picture? (log)

Talk with Me, Sing with Me Chart

LET'S SING

Sing "A New Woodland Nest"

Display Sing with Me Chart 21B. Recall that yesterday children sang one verse of "A New Woodland Nest" and learned the words *woodland* and *nest.* Today sing verse 2. Ask children to clap when they hear the words *vale* and *hollow.*

 Sing with Me/Background Building Audio CD

LET'S LEARN AMAZING WORDS

Oral Vocabulary   vale   hollow

DAY 3 ROUTINE

1 **Introduce** Another word for a valley is *vale.* A valley, or *vale,* is a place where the ground is lower than the hills around it. What's our new word for valley?

Demonstrate A *vale* is a good place for the bobwhite quail to live. It is quiet between the hills in the *vale.*

2 **Introduce** A *hollow* is another word for an empty spot within something, such as a tree. What is our new word for an empty place in a tree?

Demonstrate A *hollow* makes a nice home for some animals. It keeps them safe from bad weather and other animals.

3 **Review** We talked about two words today: *vale* and *hollow.* Which word means "ground between the hills," *vale* or *hollow?* Which word means "an empty space in a tree," *vale* or *hollow?*

4 **Apply** Have children use *vale* and *hollow* in complete sentences. Have children tell which animals lived in the *vale* or in a *hollow.*

Comprehension

REVIEW SKILL Draw Conclusions

Review drawing conclusions

Remind children that when they look at pictures and hear a story, they should think about what happens to the characters in a story and use what they know to decide what might happen.

Big Book

Apply drawing conclusions

- When Mouse was invited to live with the frogs, what was the problem with the cold and dampness? (The cold made Mouse sick.)

- Why did Mouse go away from the home of the cottontails? (It was too crowded and uncomfortable.)

- What would seem like a better home for Mouse? (a nest)

LET'S READ *One Little Mouse*

Develop vocabulary

Reread *One Little Mouse*. Develop vocabulary by having children identify the animals and their actions as you show the pictures from the book.

 **AudioText CD**

SKILL Sequence

Practice sequence

Remind children to think about what comes first, next, and last in a story.

- What happened first in this story? (Mouse looked for a new home.)

- After two moles invited Mouse to stay with them, what did Mouse do? (Mouse tried out many different houses.)

- At the end of the story what did Mouse and all the other animals do? (They fell asleep in their own homes.)

OBJECTIVES

- Review drawing conclusions.
- Practice sequence.

Materials

- Big Book *One Little Mouse*

Monitor Progress

Sequence

| **If...** children do not recall the sequence of events in the story, | **then...** review the story through pictures using the terms *first, next,* and *last.* |

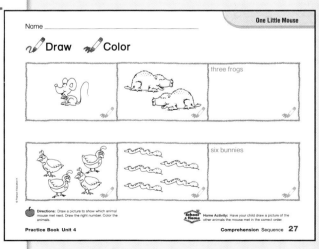

▲ **Practice Book 4** Sequence, p. 27

Phonemic Awareness

INTRODUCE Final Blends

Isolate final blends

Write *milk* on the board. Say the word with me: /m/ /i/ /l/ /k/, *milk.* Listen carefully to the end of the word. The word ends with two sounds blending together. The blended sound is /lk/. Continue with /ft/ *(lift, left, sift);* /nd/ *(land, band, sand);* /sk/ *(mask, task, ask);* and /st/ *(fast, list, past).*

Discriminate initial blends

Now say the words *snake* and *snow.* Do these words begin with the same blended sound? Say the words with me: /sn/ *-ake,* /sn/ *-ow.* Continue with the words *frog, fruit; clap, clip; and stop, step.*

Phonics

⟳ CONSONANT BLENDS

Connect sounds to letters

Display the *crab* Picture Card. Write the word on the board. What are the first sounds in *crab?* (/k/ /r/, /kr/) What are the letters for /kr/? *(c and r)* Let's say /k/ and /r/ together slowly and then faster: /kr/, /kr/, /kr/. Now, let's blend the word together: /kr/ /a/ /b/. Continue with these words: *flip, clip, drop, trap, step,* and *spin.*

Blend final sounds

Write the word *nest* on the board. This is *nest.* It has a blend at the end. What are the sounds for *s* and *t?* (/s/ /t/) Say them slowly, and then faster to make a blend: /st/, /st/. Now do the whole word: /n/ /e/ /st/, *nest.* What is the final blend in *nest?* (/st/) Continue with *rest* and *best.*

n e s t
→ → → ⟶
⟶

Practice blending sounds with the following words.

lift	**band**	**mask**	**fast**
sift	**land**	**task**	**past**

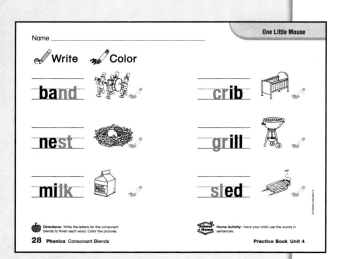

▲ **Practice Book 4**
Consonant Blends, p. 28

BLEND SOUNDS

Review letter names and sounds

Use Alphabet Cards to review the following letter names and sounds: *Aa, Cc, Dd, Ff, Hh, Ii, Kk, Ll, Nn, Oo, Pp, Rr, Ss,* and *Tt.*

Blend sounds

PHONICS ACTIVITY MAT

Write *spot* on the board. I am going to blend the sounds of this word: /sp/ /o/ /t/. The word is *spot.*

$$\text{s p o t}$$

The word is *spot.* Say the four sounds with me: /sp/ /o/ /t/. Now blend the sounds with me as I point to each letter. The word is *spot.* Continue blending practice with *sit, in, lap, Nat, and, Nan, hop, skip, stop, Flap, cat, clap, cap, sip, drops, spot, dots, on,* and *him.*

Word Wall HIGH-FREQUENCY WORDS

Practice high-frequency words

Write the word *three* on the board. This is the word *three.* What is this word? Continue the routine with *one, two, four, five, for, I, do, you, my,* and *like.*

Monitor Progress | High-Frequency Words/Word Reading

High-Frequency Words Write *one, two, three, four,* and *five* on large cards. Randomly display a card and ask a child to read it. Continue until children have several turns.

Blend Sounds to Read Words Write *drop* on the board. Let's blend the sound of each letter to read this word. Continue with the following words: *clap, spot, Nan, Nat, and, hop, cat, sit, dot,* and *lap.*

If... children have difficulty reading high-frequency words,
then... have them finger trace and name the letters in each word.

If... children cannot read words with an initial or final blend,
then... review the blending routine with them individually.

If... children can successfully read all the words,
then... have them read Kindergarten Student Reader K.4.3 *Flap the Cat.*

SUCCESS PREDICTOR

Group Time

On-Level

Read Kindergarten Student Reader K.4.3. Use the Small Group Reading **Routine.**

Strategic Intervention

Read Kindergarten Student Reader K.4.3. More practice with consonant blends, p. DI·13.

Advanced

Read Kindergarten Student Reader K.4.3. Use the reading routine on p. DI·13. Extend word reading.

ELL

Group English language learners by their reading ability in English.

....

i Independent Activities

Self-Selected Reading See pp. TR14–15 for a bibliography of books related to the weekly concept.

Practice Book Sequence, p. 27; Consonant Blends, p. 28

Centers Use the center activities on pp. 136–137 to practice this week's skills.

Journal Writing Draw a picture for one word that ends with *-st* and one that ends with *-lk.*

Spiral REVIEW

● Reviews previously taught high-frequency words.
● Reviews previously taught letters and sounds.

Day 1	Day 2	▶ Day 3	Day 4	Day 5
Check Sound Fluency	Check Retelling/ Letter-Sound Knowledge	Check High-Frequency Words/ Word Reading	Check Phoneme Segmentation	Check Oral Vocabulary/ Assess Progress

Word Reading
SUCCESS PREDICTOR

ELL

Access Content Ask children to point out the naming words, such as *Nat, Nan, Flap the Cat, I,* and *you.* Have children act out the action words *hop, skip, stop, clap, sip, spot,* and *sit.*

PREPARE TO READ

Introduce Kindergarten Student Reader K.4.3

Display the title page. We are going to read a new story. Point to the title. The title of this story is *A Home for Flap the Cat.* It was written by Susi Jones.

Small Group Reading

DAY 5 ROUTINE

1 **Model Fluent Reading** Have children finger point as you read a page.

2 **Read Chorally** Have children finger point as they chorally read the page. Continue reading page by page, repeating steps 1 and 2.

3 **Read Individually** Have children read aloud a page in their group.

4 **Reread and Monitor Progress** As you listen to individual children reread, monitor progress and provide support.

Kindergarten Student Reader

Nat and Nan hop and skip.
One hop, Nan!
One skip, Nat!

Nat and Nan stop.
Nat and Nan stop for Flap the Cat.

Two claps for Flap the Cat.
Clap, clap for Flap!

Can Flap the Cat sip three drops?
Flap the Cat can sip three drops.
Sip, sip, sip, Flap!

I spot four dots on Flap the Cat.
Dot, dot, dot, dot!
Do you spot dots on him?

I spot one, two, three, four, five!
Dot, dot, dot, dot, dot!
Five dots on Flap the Cat.

Flap the Cat likes to sit on my lap!
Sit, Flap, sit!

Modeled Writing

REVIEW **GRAMMAR** Action Parts

Review action parts

Hold up AlphaBuddy. Let's make up some sentences. Make AlphaBuddy dance. What is AlphaBuddy doing? That's right, *AlphaBuddy dances*. Who can tell me the action part of that sentence?

Identify action parts

Have AlphaBuddy walk, run, twirl, and fly. Now what is AlphaBuddy doing? Continue to ask children to identify the action part of each sentence.

LET'S WRITE Connect to Phonics

Review letters and sounds

Display the *snake* Picture Card. Write the word on the board. What are the first sounds in *snake*? What are the letters for /sn/? Continue the review using words from *A Home for Flap the Cat* that begin or end with a consonant blend.

Write sentences

Nat and Nan had a cat named Flap. Do you have a pet? I am going to write a sentence about my pet.

I have a pet frog.

Have children read the sentence with you. Point out that the word *frog* begins with /fr/. Have children identify the letters that stand for /fr/. Model writing more sentences using consonant blends.

Independent writing

Have children write or dictate their own sentences about animals, or they may copy one of the sentences the class wrote together. Then have them illustrate their sentences.

OBJECTIVE

● Practice retelling a story.

Materials

● Trade Book *Fix-It Duck*

ELL

Access Content Display Trade Book *Fix-It Duck*. As you retell the story, turn to the pages where the pictures will help children follow the story and answer the questions.

Speaking and Listening

RETELL A STORY

Practice retelling a story

Display Trade Book *Fix-It Duck*. Guide children to recall *Fix-It Duck*. Let's retell the story together.

● First, Duck sees water dripping from his ceiling and he wants to fix it.

● What happened next? (He goes to borrow a ladder from Sheep. He finds more problems at Sheep's house, and he tries to fix those too.)

● Then Duck pulls Sheep's house to another friend's house, so he can fix it.

● What happened last? (Sheep's house is ruined. The animals find out that the water leak at Duck's house happened because he forgot to turn off his bath water.)

Connect retelling a story

When we retell a story, we don't have to use exactly the same words. We say the important parts of the story in the order in which they happen.

Wrap Up Your Day!

✓ **Respond to Literature** Today we read about a cat named Flap who needed a home.

✓ **Grammar** Dictate simple sentences from the retelling of a story and ask children to circle the action parts.

✓ **Homework Idea** Have children make a list of words that end in *-nd*.

PREVIEW Day 4

Tomorrow we will read about best friends who grow up.

EXTEND Your Day

TIME FOR **Science**

Animal Habitats

Materials Big Books *One Little Mouse* and *Life in an Ocean,* large blue construction paper, crayons, green tissue paper, glue

Woodlands and Oceans Draw two charts on the board, one labeled *Woodlands* and one labeled *Ocean.* Each chart should have two columns, one labeled *Plants* and the other labeled *Animals.* We have been reading about the woodlands. What sorts of plants do we find in the woodlands? Page through *One Little Mouse* to give children ideas. List plant names on the board in the correct column.

What kinds of animals live in the woodlands? Page through *One Little Mouse* to help children name animals. List animals in the appropriate table. Repeat this process to fill in the *Ocean* table.

Woodlands		Ocean	
Plants	Animals	Plants	Animals

Who Am I? Have children choose an animal from one of the charts. Ask them to act out the animal and have other children figure out which animal they are acting out.

Grammar
Action Parts

Act Out Sentences

Sentences have naming parts and action parts. The action part of a sentence tells what a person or animal is doing. List actions on the board.

Now I'll choose a verb for the action part of a sentence. The naming part of my sentence is: [Name of a child in your class]. *[Name] hops.* Go ahead, [Name], hop! Have children make up sentences for each other to act out.

Comprehension
Sequence

The Animal Dance Today I am going to teach you an animal dance. The dance has four steps that you must follow in order, so listen and watch carefully while I show you what to do.

First, open and close your hands like duck beaks. Model each step as you go. Second, fold your arms under and flap like a chicken. Third, bend your knees like a monkey. Fourth, clap your hands four times and start all over again.

Who remembers the steps I just told you? Let's do the steps in order. Review all of the steps.

Day 4
AT A GLANCE

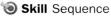

Materials

- Calendar
- Talk with Me, Sing with Me Chart 21A, 21B
- Sing with Me/Background Building Audio CD
- Trade Book *Farfallina and Marcel*
- AudioText CD
- Picture Cards: pp. 173, 175
- Decodable Reader 21

Calendar

Name the day and date
Ask a volunteer to find today's date on the calendar. Have children say the day, month, date, and year together.

"Daily" actions
Have children name the days of the week in order. What is the first sound in *Sunday?* Let's think of an action we can do on Sunday that begins with the same sound. On Sunday, we (sing). Repeat with each day of the week.

Message Board

Question of the day
Write and read the question as you track the print. Encourage children to respond in complete sentences.

> ## What are some exciting places animals live?

Review grammar
Point out naming parts and action parts of children's responses.

Access Content Use the Day 4 instruction on ELL Poster 21 to support children's use of English to communicate about lesson concepts.

ELL Poster 21

Build Background

LET'S TALK

Develop oral vocabulary

Display Talk with Me Chart 21A.

- What do you see that we could say is *comfortable?* What is something *comfortable* you have?

- Where do you see *shadows?* Will we see *shadows* outside today?

Prompt children to respond in complete sentences.

**Talk with Me,
Sing with Me Chart**

LET'S SING

Sing "A New Woodland Nest"

Display Sing with Me Chart 21B. Sing "A New Woodland Nest." Encourage children to listen for the words *comfortable* and *shadows.*

**Sing with Me/Background Building
Audio CD**

LET'S LEARN AMAZING WORDS

Oral Vocabulary comfortable shadows

DAY 4 ROUTINE

1 **Introduce** When you are *comfortable,* it means that your body is relaxed and not too cold or hot, such as when you are curled up in a blanket. What is our new word for relaxed and cozy?

Demonstrate Mouse kept looking for a home that would be *comfortable.* Why do we want our beds to be cozy and *comfortable?*

2 **Introduce** *Shadows* are made when the light is blocked. When you put your hand in front of a light, you make *shadows.* What is our new word?

Demonstrate When we go out into the sunshine, our bodies make *shadows.* Would we see *shadows* on a dark, gloomy day?

3 **Review** We talked about two words today: *comfortable* and *shadows.* Which word means "relaxed and cozy," *comfortable* or *shadows?* Which word means "the dark shapes made when light is blocked," *comfortable* or *shadows?*

4 **Apply** Have children use *comfortable* and *shadows* in complete sentences.

OBJECTIVES

- Build background.
- Develop oral vocabulary.

Amazing Words to build oral vocabulary

- woodland   • nest
- vale   • hollow
- comfortable • shadows

Extend Language Ask children how they say *comfortable* and *shadows* in their own languages.

4

ELL

Extend Language Encourage children to translate words used to tell about sequence from their native language to English. Include words such as *first, second, next,* and *last.*

Comprehension

LET'S READ *Farfallina and Marcel*

Review *Farfallina and Marcel*

Display *Farfallina and Marcel.* Tell me about what you see.

● What do you remember about Farfallina and Marcel?

● Is this story real or make-believe?

Reread *Farfallina and Marcel*

Reread the story and ask children to pay attention to the changes in Farfallina and Marcel.

Trade Book

 AudioText CD

⊙ SKILL Sequence

Apply sequence

After reading, ask:

● How did Farfallina change from the beginning of the story to the end of it?

● Did Marcel change?

Practice sequence

Write *How did Farfallina change?* on the board. Ask children to identify the three main stages of Farfallina's transformation *(caterpillar, cocoon,* and *butterfly).* Have children act out the three stages of Farfallina's transformation.

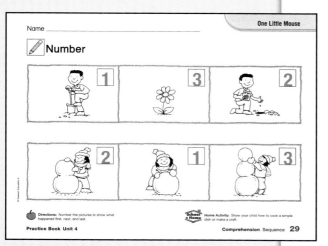

▲ **Practice Book 4** Sequence, p. 29

Phonemic Awareness

REVIEW PRACTICE /l/

Practice /l/   Display the *ladybug* Picture Card. What is the first sound in the word *ladybug*? Say it with me: /l/. Continue with *lamp* and *lemon*. Repeat the routine for final /l/ with the *seal, doll,* and *pail* Picture Cards.

Monitor Progress | **Check Phoneme Segmentation**

Check Segmentation Practice phoneme segmentation using words from Decodable Reader 21 *One to Five.* After I say a word, tell me the sounds in the word.

sat	**mat**	**flop**	**ran**	**pan**	**spin**
hid	**lid**	**slam**	**land**	**lap**	**drop**
top	**plop**	**stop**			

If… children cannot segment words into phonemes,
then… provide additional words to practice blending.

SUCCESS PREDICTOR

Day 1
Check Sound
Fluency

Day 2
Check Retelling/
Letter-Sound
Knowledge

Day 3
Check High-
Frequency Words/
Word Reading

▶ **Day 4**
Check Phoneme
Segmentation

Day 5
Check Oral
Vocabulary/
Assess Progress

Phonics

Spiral REVIEW BLEND SOUNDS

Blend sounds

Write *lap.* Let's blend the sound of each letter together to say this word: /l/ /a/ /p/, *lap.* The word is *lap.*

Now let's try it with a new word. **Write *spin* on the board.** This word begins with *sp-*. Remember, we blend the sounds of the letters together to make /sp/. Say /sp/ *-in* with me: /sp/ /i/ /n/. The word is *spin.* **Continue with** *sat, hid, on, in, jump, mat, lid, top, flop, slam, plop, ran, land, pan,* and *drop.*

OBJECTIVES
● Practice /l/.
● Blend sounds.

Materials
● Picture Cards:
  doll   ladybug   lamp
  lemon   pail   seal
● Decodable Reader 21

Phoneme Segmentation

SUCCESS
PREDICTOR

- Recognize high-frequency words.
- Read decodable text.

Word Wall HIGH-FREQUENCY WORDS

Practice high-frequency words

Write the word *four* on the board. This is the word *four.* What is this word? Continue with *one, two, three, five,* and *a.* Look for these words in the story that we read today.

PREPARE TO READ

Introduce Decodable Reader 21

Display Decodable Reader 21 *One to Five.* Point to the story. Today we will read *One to Five.* Point to the title. What is the title of this story? Point to the name of the author. *One to Five* is written by Heather Leavy. This story is illustrated by Kris Pool.

Group Time

On-Level

Read Decodable Reader 21. Use the Small Group Reading **Routine.**

Strategic Intervention

Read Decodable Reader 21. More practice with blends, p. DI·14.

Advanced

Read Independent Leveled Reader K.4.3. Use Leveled Reader lesson, p. LR5. Extend word reading.

Group English language learners by their reading ability in English.

i Independent Activities

Self-Selected Reading See pp. TR14–15 for a bibliography of books related to the weekly concept.

Practice Book Sequence, p. 29; Complete Sentences, p. 30

Centers Use the center activities on pp. 136–137 to practice this week's skills.

Journal Writing Write about two little animals.

Small Group Reading

1 **Model Fluent Reading** Have children finger point as you read a page.

2 **Read Chorally** Have children finger point as they chorally read the page. Continue reading page by page, repeating steps 1 and 2.

3 **Read Individually** Have children read aloud a page in their group.

4 **Reread and Monitor Progress** As you listen to individual children reread, monitor progress and provide support.

Decodable Reader

DAY 4 ROUTINE

Interactive Writing

GRAMMAR Complete Sentences

Identify complete sentences

When we write sentences, they need to be complete. A sentence tells us a complete idea. It must have a naming part and an action part. Listen to this sentence: *The dog barked.* What is the naming part? What is the action part?

What do I have to do to the first letter of every sentence? What do I put at the end of a sentence? **Have children give both a naming part and an action part to write a sentence as a class.**

LET'S WRITE Connect to Phonics

Review letters and sounds

Display the *crab* Picture Card. Write the word on the board. What are the first sounds in *crab*? *Crab* begins with /k/ /r/, /kr/. What are the letters for /kr/? Let's blend the sound of each letter together to say this word: /kr/ /a/ /b/. The word is *crab*.

Write sentences

Write the following sentence frames on the board.

A _____ lives in the sea. (crab)

The _____ spins a beautiful web. (spider)

Have children help you choose words to complete the sentences. Have a volunteer write the word to fill in the first blank. Repeat the word slowly if necessary. Then write the word to complete the second sentence. Have children help spell the consonant blend at the beginning of the word as you write. Then read the sentences together.

Independent writing

Have children write the name of their favorite animal or copy an animal name from the board. Have them draw the animal's home and shape the animal from modeling clay to set in its home.

EXTEND SKILLS

Spelling If children have difficulty spelling words with initial blends, use Alphabet Cards to connect letters to sounds.

OBJECTIVES

- Practice complete sentences.
- Review letters and sounds.
- Write about favorite animals.

Materials

- Picture Card: *crab*

DAILY FIX-IT

the goose was big
(The goose was big.)

ELL

Support Writing Allow children to use *One Little Mouse* to view animals and confirm their names.

▲ **Practice Book 4**
Complete Sentences, p. 30

Speaking and Listening

RETELL A STORY

Review retelling a story

Today we are going to retell a story. When we retell a story, we use words such as *first, next, then,* and *last,* so we can understand the order of the events in the story.

Practice retelling a story

Help me retell the story we read today, *Farfallina and Marcel.* Guide children to use the pictures in the story to assist in retelling. Prompt by asking children what happens next.

Break the story up into several segments to allow several children to practice retelling the story. Invite children to the front of the class to retell a small piece of the story using pictures in the book.

Wrap Up Your Day!

 Respond to Literature Today we read about five noisy animals. Who can retell the story *One to Five?*

 Speaking and Listening Ask children to tell their parents one of the stories they read this week.

Homework Idea Have children write a complete sentence about their day.

PREVIEW Day 5

Tomorrow we will read about Peter Rabbit. What adventures do you think he will have?

EXTEND Your Day

Similarities and Differences

Adventures of Farfallina and Marcel Take a picture walk through *Farfallina and Marcel*. Have children point out the different characteristics of both animals. Include color, size, where they live, how they move, and what they do.

Make a Venn Diagram Create a Venn diagram. Label one circle *Farfallina* and the other *Marcel*. Have children list things they know that are different about each animal in the circles. For example, the *Farfallina* circle could say *Farfallina can climb trees*. The *Marcel* circle could say *Marcel likes to swim*. List the things that are the same (such as *Farfallina and Marcel both like playing*) where the circles overlap.

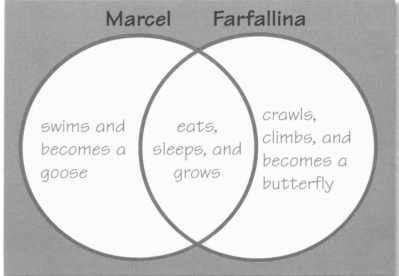

Marcel   Farfallina

swims and becomes a goose | eats, sleeps, and grows | crawls, climbs, and becomes a butterfly

Grammar
Animal Sentences

What Adventures Can Animals Have? As a class, discuss different adventures animals can have. Give children ideas: *go on a walk, climb trees,* and *fly south*. Write these phrases on the board. On a sheet of paper, have children turn the sentence parts into complete sentences. If needed, provide the supplementary sentence sections *Animals can…* and *Animals like to…* so that children can copy them from the board. Ask children to draw pictures for their sentences.

Animals climb trees.

Comprehension
Sequence

What Comes Next? Take a picture walk through the illustrations of *Farfallina and Marcel*. Have children identify the different activities the friends do. Make a list on chart paper. Number the activities. Divide the class into as many groups as you have activities. Have each group act out an activity from *Farfallina and Marcel* in sequential order.

1. Play hide and seek
2. Take rides
3. Fly places
4.
5.

Day 5
AT A GLANCE

Oral Language and Vocabulary
Calendar
Message Board
Build Background

Shared Reading
Read Aloud Anthology
"The Tale of Peter Rabbit"
⊚ **Skill** Sequence

Word Work

Phonemic Awareness
Review Blends

Phonics
⊚ Connect Sounds to Letters in Blends
H/F Words *one, two, three, four, five*

Read

Group Time < Differentiated Instruction

Monitor Progress

Language Arts
Grammar: Complete Sentences
Shared Writing:
   This Week We . . .
Speaking and Listening:
   Retell a Story

Materials

- Calendar
- Talk with Me, Sing with Me Chart 21A, 21B
- Sing with Me/Background Building Audio CD
- *Read Aloud Anthology* "The Tale of Peter Rabbit"
- Picture Cards: p. 181
- Decodable Reader 21
- Kindergarten Student Reader K.4.3
- Phonics Story *My Words*
- Big Book *One Little Mouse*
- Phonics Songs and Rhymes Chart 21

Calendar

Name the day and date
Ask a volunteer to find today's date on the calendar. Have the children say the day, month, date, and year together.

Yesterday, today, and tomorrow
Point to today on the calendar. What day of the week was it yesterday? What day will it be tomorrow?

Message Board

Question of the week
Remind children that this week we have talked about little Mouse's adventures in looking for a new home.

> ## What adventures can an animal have?

Review oral vocabulary
Encourage children to use oral vocabulary words *woodland, nest, vale, hollow, comfortable,* and *shadows* to talk about animal adventures. Remind children to respond in complete sentences.

Assess Vocabulary Use the Day 5 instruction on ELL Poster 21 to monitor children's progress with oral vocabulary.

ELL Poster 21

Build Background

LET'S TALK

Discuss animal adventures

Display Talk with Me Chart 21A. Point to the picture showing the tree in the field. Prompt children to respond in complete sentences.

- What do you see by the tree?
- Which picture shows something *comfortable?*
- Did these animals live in a *woodland* or a *vale?*

Talk with Me, Sing with Me Chart

LET'S SING

Sing "A New Woodland Nest"

Display Sing with Me Chart 21B. Remind children that the words *woodland, nest, vale, hollow, comfortable,* and *shadows* are in the song.

 Sing with Me/Background Building Audio CD

A New Woodland Nest

"I need a new woodland nest,"
Said the mouse, "I want the best."
Mole offered his hole, safe from the cold.
"Oh, but I really can't rest."

Talk with Me, Sing with Me Chart

Monitor Progress · Check Oral Vocabulary

Demonstrate Word Knowledge Prompt children to demonstrate knowledge of oral vocabulary words *woodland, nest, vale, hollow, comfortable,* and *shadows.* Encourage them to use complete sentences.

If… children have difficulty using oral vocabulary words,

then… provide additional practice with Talk with Me Chart 21A and *One Little Mouse.*

SUCCESS PREDICTOR

Day 1
Check Sound Fluency

Day 2
Check Retelling/ Letter-Sound Knowledge

Day 3
Check High- Frequency Words/ Word Reading

Day 4
Check Phoneme Segmentation

▶ **Day 5**
Check Oral Vocabulary/ Assess Progress

OBJECTIVES

- Build background.
- Review oral vocabulary.

Amazing Words to build oral vocabulary

- woodland
- vale
- comfortable
- nest
- hollow
- shadows

Oral Vocabulary

SUCCESS PREDICTOR

SEQUENCE

Put events from "The Tale of Peter Rabbit" in order.

Note to Teacher Have children cut out the scenes from the story and glue them onto another paper in sequential order. Have them label the sequence 1–4.

▲ **Teacher's Edition 4**
Sequence, p. 184

Comprehension

READ ALOUD

Read "The Tale of Peter Rabbit"

Tell children that you are going to read a story about a young rabbit who always seems to get into trouble. Ask them to listen carefully to the sequence of story events. I am going to read you a story and then ask you to tell me what happened first, next, and last.

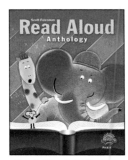

Read Aloud Anthology

CHECK SKILL Sequence

Practice sequential text in "The Tale of Peter Rabbit"

After you read the story, ask children to identify the sequence.

- What happens to Peter first?
- What does he do next?
- Then what happens in the garden?
- What does Peter do last?

ASSESS SKILL Sequence

Assess sequence

Use the blackline master found on page 184. Copy one page for each child. Have children cut out the three scenes and glue them to another sheet of paper in the correct order. Have children label the scenes *1, 2,* or *3.*

Phonemic Awareness

REVIEW Consonant Blends

Practice blends

Display the *dress* Picture Card. What is the blend at the beginning of *dress?* Say the word with me: /dr/ /e/ /s/. Review initial blends with: *slip, plan, clap, flip, crib, stop, trip,* and *spin.* Show the *desk* Picture Card. Say the word *desk,* emphasizing the final blend. The word *desk* ends with /sk/. Review final blends with *cost, lift, milk,* and *land.*

Phonics

REVIEW Consonant Blends

Connect sounds to letters

Display the *crab* Picture Card. What is the name of this animal? What is the blend at the beginning of the word *crab?* (/kr/) What letters stand for this blend? *(cr)* Write the letters *c* and *r.* Repeat with *drum, train, stamp,* and *spoon.*

Picture Card

Word Wall HIGH-FREQUENCY WORDS

Practice high-frequency words

Write the word *five* on the board. This is the word *five.* What is this word? Continue the routine with *one, two, three,* and *four.*

Spiral REVIEW READ

Apply phonics in familiar text

Have children reread one of the readers. You may wish to review the words that appear in each reader prior to rereading.

Kindergarten Student Reader

Decodable Reader

Phonics Story in Practice Book

OBJECTIVES

- Practice consonant blends.
- Connect sounds to letters in blends.

Materials

- Picture Cards:

  crab   desk   dress
  drum   spoon   stamp
  train

- Kindergarten Student Reader K.4.3
- Decodable Reader 21
- Phonics Story *My Words*

OBJECTIVE

 Assess consonant blends.

Group Time

On-Level

Sets A and B

Strategic Intervention

**Monitor Progress:
Check Phonics
Alternate Assessment, p. DI·15**

Advanced

Sets B and C

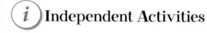 **Independent Activities**

Self-Selected Reading See pp. TR14–15 for a bibliography of books related to the weekly concept.

Cross-Curricular Centers Use center activities on pp. 136–137 to practice this week's skills.

Journal Writing Draw or write which animal home you would choose to live in.

Support Phonics For guidance in teaching phonics to English language learners, see the *ELL and Transition Handbook*.

PHONICS Consonant Blends

Group assessment

Divide a paper into fourths for each child. When I say a word, write the blend you hear in that word in one of the boxes. The blends may be at the beginning or at the end of the words, so listen carefully: *stop, crab, milk,* and *band.* Say words slowly and repeat, emphasizing blends.

Monitor Progress Assess Progress	
If… a child cannot complete the group assessment,	**then**… use the Reteach lesson on page DI·33.
If… a child writes any letters in the blends correctly,	**then**… assess word reading Sets A and B on page 183.
If… a child correctly writes all four blends,	**then**… assess word and sentence reading with Sets B and C on page 183.

ASSESS PHONICS

Set A: Read the words

Have individuals take turns reading the words. We're going to read some words. I'll do the first one and you do the rest. The first word is *spot:* /sp/ /o/ /t/. The first word is *spot.* For each child, record any decoding problems with initial blends.

Set B: Read the words

Have individuals take turns reading more words. We're going to read some words. I'll do the first one and you do the rest. The first word is *hand*: /h/ /a/ /nd/. For each child, record any decoding problems.

Set C: Read the sentences

For a cumulative assessment of phonics and high-frequency words, have each child read one or two sentences.

READ THE WORDS

Set A

spot   flat

crib   trap

READ MORE WORDS

Set B

hand   spin   clap

mask   trip   mist

READ THE SENTENCES

Set C

1. I have one fast raft.

2. We can see three drops.

3. Two kids are with me.

4. Look at the four maps.

5. Five masks are a lot.

Note to Teacher Set A: Children read each word. Set B: Children read each word.
Set C: Children read one or two sentences.

One Little Mouse

Monitor Progress

SUCCESS PREDICTOR

Put events from "The Tale of Peter Rabbit" in order.

Note to Teacher Have children cut out the scenes from the story and glue them onto another paper in sequential order. Have them label the sequence 1–3.

REPRODUCIBLE PAGE • See also Assessment Handbook, p. 197

Monitor Progress

Shared Writing

GRAMMAR Complete Sentences

Review complete sentences

A complete sentence must start with an uppercase letter and end with a punctuation mark. A complete sentence must have a naming part and an action part. It must tell about a complete idea.

Practice complete sentences

Ask a volunteer to name a person or animal. Have another child complete the sentence by giving an action part.

LET'S WRITE This Week We...

Recall literature

We read three new books and we sang two new songs about animal adventures this week. Which book or song was your favorite? My favorite was *One Little Mouse*.

Write sentences

Today we will write about our favorite animals and what they did in the stories or songs.

The mouse looked for a house.
The frog hopped.
The rabbit went to bed.

Continue the list with all children. Make sure children dictate complete sentences. Then have children read the complete list with you.

Independent writing

Have children copy the sentence they dictated and illustrate it.

The rabbit went to bed.

OBJECTIVES

- Recognize complete sentences.
- Respond to literature through writing.

Materials

- Big Book *One Little Mouse*
- Kindergarten Student Reader K.4.3
- Decodable Reader 21
- Talk with Me, Sing with Me Chart 21B
- Phonics Songs and Rhymes Chart 21

DAILY FIX-IT

the mouse fell in the hole
(The mouse fell in the hole.)

Support Writing Supply English words as children write or dictate their sentences.

OBJECTIVE

● Review retelling a story.

Access Content Explain meanings of *buckle*, *pick up*, and *shut* to help children understand and participate.

Speaking and Listening

RETELL A STORY

Review retelling a story

Today we are going to talk about retelling a story. When you are retelling a story, you tell the most important parts in the correct order.

> **One, two, buckle my shoe.**
> **Three, four, shut the door.**
> **Five, six, pick up sticks.**
> **Seven, eight, lay them straight.**
> **Nine, ten, a big fat hen.**

Connect retelling a story

Check children's understanding of what they have heard. Recite "One, Two, Buckle My Shoe" several times. Then have the children take turns reciting lines from "One, Two, Buckle My Shoe" in order and acting them out.

Wrap Up Your Week!

☑ **Shared Reading** What was your favorite book or song this week?

☑ **Phonics** This week we learned about blends. What is a blend? Name some words that begin with a blend.

☑ **High-Frequency Words** Write *one*, *two*, *three*, *four*, and *five* on the board. Read these words to me.

You've learned	You've learned
006 Amazing Words	**126** Amazing Words
this week!	so far this year!

PREVIEW Next Week

Next week we will read about the adventures of three bears and a little girl. What do you think will happen?

EXTEND Your Day

Animal Movement

Materials books showing pictures of animals, chart paper, markers

Study Animals Show pictures of a variety of animals. Explain that each animal moves in its own unique way. Tell students to look at the pictures of animals and think of other animals. Ask:

- Which animals swim?
- Which animals crawl?
- Which animals fly?
- Which animals climb?
- Which animals hop?

Make a Chart Record the answers to each question in a chart. Then ask: Which animals move in more than one way?

swim	crawl	fly	climb	hop
fish	bug	bird	cat	rabbit
shark				
whale				

Have a volunteer imitate the movement of each animal in the chart.

Make a Map

Time for **SOCIAL STUDIES**

Mouse's Travels Draw a long path on a sheet of mural paper. Sketch a mouse head at the beginning of the path on the left side of the paper. Have children mark off spaces along the path to show all the places the little mouse traveled. Then have children draw animals and locations on the map.

Animal Addition

Materials copies of small pictures of animals, paper, pencil

Addition Give children a set of animal pictures. Tell them to select two pictures and place them in front of them. Then tell children to select three more pictures and place them below the other two. Ask the children how many animal pictures they have. Continue giving other addition problems. You may wish to write the problem on the board to show children the addition fact: 2 + 3 = 5.

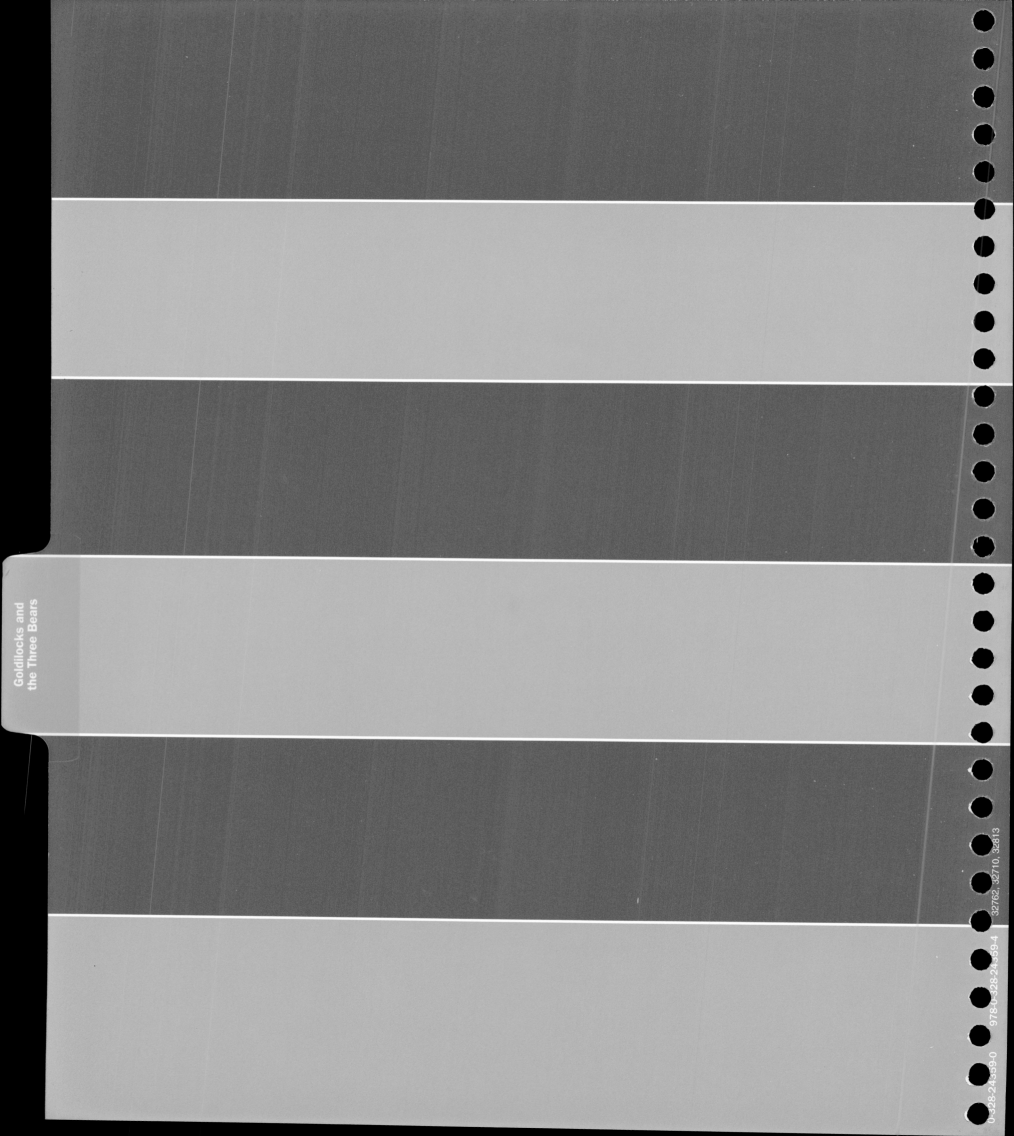

Goldilocks and
the Three Bears

Unit 4
Let's Explore

CONCEPT QUESTION
Where will our adventures take us?

EXPAND THE CONCEPT
What kind of adventure can a little girl have?

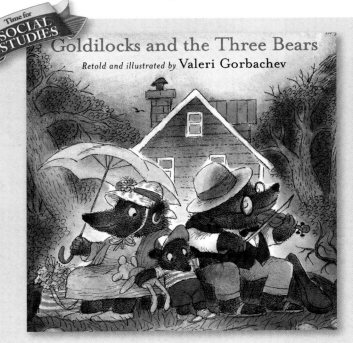

Time for SOCIAL STUDIES

Goldilocks and the Three Bears

Retold and illustrated by Valeri Gorbachev

CONNECT THE CONCEPT

▶ **Build Background**

bears	*cottage*	*middle-sized*
porridge	*big*	*small*

In a Small Cottage

In a small cottage
there lived three bears,
One big, one small,
one middle-sized bear.
They went for a walk
to get some air,
When little Goldilocks
found their lair.

▶ **Social Studies Content**
Government

Preview Your Week

What kind of adventure can a little girl have?

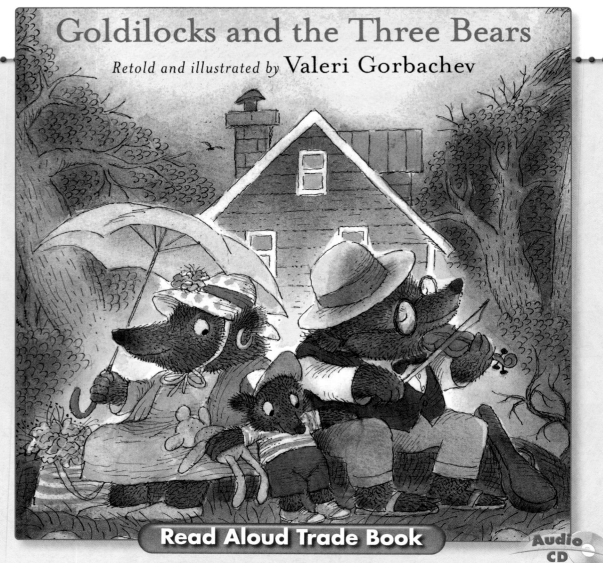

Goldilocks and the Three Bears

Retold and illustrated by **Valeri Gorbachev**

Read Aloud Trade Book

Audio CD

Genre	Classic Traditional Tale
Phonics	Gg/g/
Comprehension Skill	Character

Meet the Author/Illustrator

Valeri Gorbachev

Valeri Gorbachev moved to the United States from the Ukraine in 1991. He has illustrated over fifty children's books and was the author of over half of them. He has achieved fame in both Europe and the United States for his work, and his books have been translated into Finnish, German, and Spanish.

Read another book by Valeri Gorbachev.

One Rainy Day

Choose words to put in the sentences.

The _ _ _ _ _ _ has a _ _ _ _ _ _ .

Tim _ _ _ _ _ _ the _ _ _ _ _ _ .

Sue can _ _ _ _ _ _ with her _ _ _ _ _ _ .

Jim _ _ _ _ _ _ his _ _ _ _ _ _ .

wig   bit   sip   fig   hit   lip   pig   hip

FS-32054 Phonics Basics

Choose words to put in the sentences.

The _____ has a _____.

Tim _____ the _____.

Sue can _____ with her _____.

Jim _____ his _____.

wig   bit   sip   fig   hit   sip   lip   pig   hip

Choose words to put in the sentences.

The _ _ _ _ _ _ has a _ _ _ _ _ _ .

Tim _ _ _ _ _ _ the _ _ _ _ _ _ .

Sue can _ _ _ _ _ _ with her _ _ _ _ _ _ .

Jim _ _ _ _ _ _ his _ _ _ _ _ _ .

| wig | bit | sip | fig | hit | lip | pig | hip |

FS-32054 Phonics Basics

PHONICS Consonant Blends

Group assessment

Divide a paper into fourths for each child. When I say a word, write the blend you hear in that word in one of the boxes. The blends may be at the beginning or at the end of the words, so listen carefully: *stop, crab, milk,* and *band*. Say words slowly and repeat, emphasizing blends.

Monitor Progress Assess Progress	
If... a child cannot complete the group assessment,	**then...** use the Reteach lesson on page DI·33.
If... a child writes any letters in the blends correctly,	**then...** assess word reading Sets A and B on page 183.
If... a child correctly writes all four blends,	**then...** assess word and sentence reading with Sets B and C on page 183.

⊚ ASSESS PHONICS

Set A: Read the words

Have individuals take turns reading the words. We're going to read some words. I'll do the first one and you do the rest. The first word is *spot:* /sp/ /o/ /t/. The first word is *spot.* For each child, record any decoding problems with initial blends.

Set B: Read the words

Have individuals take turns reading more words. We're going to read some words. I'll do the first one and you do the rest. The first word is *hand:* /h/ /a/ /nd/. For each child, record any decoding problems.

Set C: Read the sentences

For a cumulative assessment of phonics and high-frequency words, have each child read one or two sentences.

Read It ONLINE
PearsonSuccessNet.com

- Kindergarten Student Readers
- Listen to Me Readers
- Independent Leveled Readers
- Decodable Readers

Books for All Children

Emergent

- **Develop oral language**
- **Develop phonemic awareness**
- **Read decodable words**
- **Read high-frequency words**

Listen to Me Reader

On-Level

- **Read connected text**
- **Apply phonics skills**
- **Read high-frequency words in context**

Kindergarten Student Reader

Leveled Reader K.4.4

Independent

- **Practice comprehension skill: character**
- **Extend concepts**
- **Connect to Social Studies**

Independent Leveled Reader

Apply Phonics

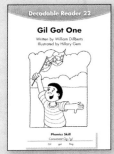

Decodable Reader

Phonics Story

Time for SOCIAL STUDIES

Integrate Social Studies Standards

- Government

 Read

Read Aloud Trade Book
Goldilocks and the Three Bears

Independent Leveled Reader
Five Bears All in a Den

 Build
Concept Vocabulary
Adventures Children Can Have, pp. 201, 211, 226, 235, 243

 Apply
Social Studies

Rules at Home, p. 209
Make a Map, p. 224
Understanding Signs, p. 233
Good Citizens Follow Rules, p. 241
School Rules, p. 251
Citizenship, p. 251

TIME FOR Science

Teach
Science Concepts

The Five Senses, p. 241

Goldilocks and the Three Bears **191**

Weekly Plan

READING

60–90 minutes

TARGET SKILLS OF THE WEEK

⊙ **Phonics Skill**
Gg/g/

⊙ **Comprehension Skill**
Character

DAY 1 — PAGES 200–209

Oral Language/Vocabulary

QUESTION OF THE WEEK, 200
What kind of adventure can a little girl have?

Build Background, 201
Talk with Me, Sing with Me Chart 22A, 22B

Amazing Words, 201
bears, porridge, cottage, big, middle-sized, small

Comprehension

Shared Reading, 202–203

Read Read Aloud Trade Book

Preview and Predict
Reader Response
⊙ Character **T**

Word Work

Phonemic Awareness, 204
Introduce /g/

Phonics, 205
⊙ Connect /g/ to *Gg* **T**

High-Frequency Words, 205
Reteach *one, two, three, four, five*

Reread Decodable Reader 21

Grouping Options 194–195

DAY 2 — PAGES 210–224

Oral Language/Vocabulary

QUESTION OF THE DAY, 210
Are there one, two, three, four, or five bears in this story?

Build Background, 211
Talk with Me, Sing with Me Chart 22A, 22B

Let's Learn Amazing Words, 211
bears, porridge

Comprehension

Shared Reading, 212–219

Read Read Aloud Trade Book

Recall and Retell
⊙ Character **T**

Word Work

Phonemic Awareness, 220
Practice /g/

Phonics, 220
⊙ Connect /g/ to *Gg* **T**

High-Frequency Words, 221
Review *one, two, three, four, five, you*

Read Phonics Story

Grouping Options 194–195

LANGUAGE ARTS

20 minutes

DAY 1

Shared Writing, 207
Grammar: Introduce Telling Sentences
Connect to Grammar

Speaking and Listening, 208
Introduce Discussions

DAY 2

Modeled Writing, 222
Grammar: Practice Telling Sentences
Respond to Literature

Speaking and Listening, 223
Let's Review Amazing Words *woodland, nest*

DAILY JOURNAL WRITING

Day 1 *Draw or label one adventure Goldilocks had at the bears' home.*

Day 2 *Draw and label your favorite bear.*

EXTEND YOUR DAY *30 minutes*
Additional Activities for Full–Day Classrooms

Day 1, 209
Time for Social Studies: Rules at Home
Comprehension: Class Character Book
High-Frequency Words and Math: Math Words

Day 2, 224
Time for Social Studies: Make a Map
Grammar: Telling Sentences
Phonics: Connect /g/ to *Gg*

DAILY SUCCESS PREDICTORS
for Adequate Yearly Progress

Monitor Progress and Corrective Feedback

Phonemic Awareness
Check Sound Fluency, *204*
Spiral REVIEW Phonics,
High-Frequency Words

Retelling and Phonics
Check Retelling, *219*
Check Letter-Sound Knowledge, *220*
Spiral REVIEW Phonics,
High-Frequency Words

Grouping Options for Differentiated Instruction

Turn the page for the small group lesson plan.

DAY 3 PAGES 225–233

Oral Language/Vocabulary

QUESTION OF THE DAY, 225
Why is Goldilocks visiting the bears?

Build Background, 226
Talk with Me, Sing with Me Chart 22A, 22B

Let's Learn Amazing Words, 226
cottage, big

Comprehension

Shared Reading, 227

Read Read Aloud
Trade Book
REVIEW Setting **T**
🎯 Character **T**

Word Work

Phonemic Awareness, 228
Introduce Final /g/

Phonics, 228
🎯 Connect /g/ to Gg **T**

High-Frequency Words, 229
Practice *one, two, three, four, five, for, little, they, of, the, to*

Read Kindergarten Student Reader K.4.4

Grouping Options 194–195

Modeled Writing, 231
Grammar: **REVIEW** Complete Sentences
Connect to Phonics

Speaking and Listening, 232
Practice Discussing Authors and Illustrators

Day 3 *Draw and label three words that begin with /g/.*

Day 3, 233
Time for Social Studies: Understanding Signs
Math: How Many?
Grammar: Sentences

DAY 4 PAGES 234–241

Oral Language/Vocabulary

QUESTION OF THE DAY, 234
What adventure have you had?

Build Background, 235
Talk with Me, Sing with Me Chart 22A, 22B

Let's Learn Amazing Words, 235
middle-sized, small

Comprehension

Shared Reading, 236

Reread Read Aloud
Trade Book
🎯 Character **T**

Word Work

Phonemic Awareness, 237
REVIEW Consonant Blends

Phonics, 237
🎯 Connect /g/ to Gg **T**

High-Frequency Words, 238
Practice *is, one, two, three, four, five, a*

Read Decodable Reader 22

Grouping Options 194–195

Interactive Writing, 239
Grammar: Practice Telling Sentences
Connect to Phonics

Speaking and Listening, 240
Practice Discussions

Day 4 *Dictate or write one sentence that tells about porridge.*

Day 4, 241
Time for Social Studies: Good Citizens Follow Rules
Grammar: Telling Sentences
Science: The Five Senses

DAY 5 PAGES 242–251

Oral Language/Vocabulary

QUESTION OF THE WEEK, 242
What kind of adventure can a little girl have?

Build Background, 243
Talk with Me, Sing with Me Chart 22A, 22B

Amazing Words, 243
Check *bears, porridge, cottage, big, middle-sized, small*

Comprehension

Shared Reading, 244, 248

Read *Read Aloud Anthology* "A Canary's Song"

Monitor Progress
🎯 Check Character **T**

Word Work

Phonemic Awareness, 245
Review /g/

Phonics, 245
🎯 Connect /g/ to Gg **T**

High-Frequency Words, 245
Practice *one, two, three, four, five*

Grouping Options 194–195

Monitor Progress, 246–247
Read the Words
Read the Sentences

Shared Writing, 249
Grammar: Review Telling Sentences
This Week We...

Speaking and Listening, 250
Review Discussions

Day 5 *Draw or write about what you would have done if the bears found you in their home.*

Day 5, 251
Time for Social Studies: School Rules
Time for Math: Words and Numbers
Time for Social Studies: Citizenship

KEY 🎯 = Target Skill **T** = Tested Skill

Word Reading Check High-Frequency Words and Word Reading, *229*
Spiral REVIEW Phonics, High-Frequency Words

Phonemic Awareness Check Phoneme Segmentation, *237*
Spiral REVIEW Phonics, High-Frequency Words

Oral Vocabulary Check Oral Vocabulary, *243*
Assess Phonics and Comprehension, *246–248*

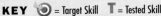

SUCCESS PREDICTOR

Small Group Plan *for Differentiated Instruction*

Daily Plan
AT A GLANCE

Reading
Whole Group
- Oral Language/Vocabulary
- Comprehension
- Word Work

Group Time

Meet with small groups to provide:
- Skill Support
- Reading Support
- Skill Application

Read

This week's lessons for daily group time can be found behind the Differentiated Instruction (DI) tab on pp. DI·16–DI·20.

Language Arts
- Grammar
- Writing
- Speaking and Listening

Use *My Sidewalks on Reading Street* for early reading intervention.

DAY 1

On-Level	Strategic Intervention	Advanced
Teacher-Led *Page 206*	**Teacher-Led** *Page DI·16*	**Teacher-Led** *Page DI·16*
• Blend Sounds to Read Words • **Reread** Decodable Reader 21	• More Practice with g/g/ • **Read** Listen to Me Reader K.4.4	• **Reread** Independent Leveled Reader K.4.3 • **Reread** for Fluency

(i) Independent Activities

While you meet with small groups, have the rest of the class...

- Read self-selected reading
- Complete Practice Book K.4 p. 33
- Visit the Literacy Centers
- Write in their journals

DAY 2

On-Level	Strategic Intervention	Advanced
Teacher-Led *Page 221*	**Teacher-Led** *Page DI·17*	**Teacher-Led** *Page DI·17*
• Practice Word Reading • **Read** Phonics Story	• More Practice with g/g/ • **Read** Phonics Story	• Apply Phonics Skills • **Read** Decodable Reader 22

(i) Independent Activities

While you meet with small groups, have the rest of the class...

- Read self-selected reading
- Complete Practice Book K.4 p. 34
- Visit the Literacy Centers
- Write in their journals

DAY 3

On-Level	Strategic Intervention	Advanced
Teacher-Led *Pages 229–230*	**Teacher-Led** *Page DI·18*	**Teacher-Led** *Page DI·18*
• Practice Word Reading • **Read** Kindergarten Student Reader K.4.4	• Practice Reading Words with g/g/ • **Read** Kindergarten Student Reader K.4.4	• Extend Word Reading • **Read** Kindergarten Student Reader K.4.4

(i) Independent Activities

While you meet with small groups, have the rest of the class...

- Read self-selected reading
- Complete Practice Book K.4 pp. 37, 38
- Visit the Literacy Centers
- Write in their journals

---

① Begin with whole class skill and strategy instruction.
② Meet with small groups to provide differentiated instruction.
③ Gather the whole class back together for language arts.

DAY 4

On-Level
Teacher-Led
Page 238
- Blend and Read Words with g/g/
- **Read** Decodable Reader 22

Strategic Intervention
Teacher-Led
Page DI · 19
- Blend and Read Words with g/g/
- **Read** Decodable Reader 22

Advanced
Teacher-Led
Page LR7
- Extend Word Reading
- **Read** Independent Leveled Reader K.4.4

ⓘ Independent Activities

While you meet with small groups, have the rest of the class…

- Read self-selected reading
- Complete Practice Book K.4 pp. 39, 40
- Visit the Literacy Centers
- Write in their journals

DAY 5

On-Level
Teacher-Led
Pages 246–248
- Word Reading, Sets A and B
- Check Phonics
- Check Comprehension

Strategic Intervention
Teacher-Led
Pages 246, 248, DI · 20
- Check Phonics
- Check Comprehension
- Alternate Assessment

Advanced
Teacher-Led
Pages 246–248
- Word Reading, Set B
- Sentence Reading, Set C
- Monitor Comprehension

ⓘ Independent Activities

While you meet with small groups, have the rest of the class…

- Read self-selected reading
- Visit the Literacy Centers
- Write in their journals

Ⓔ Ⓛ Ⓛ **Grouping** Group English language learners by their reading ability in English.

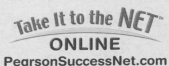

Take It to the NET™ ONLINE
PearsonSuccessNet.com

Deborah Simmons
For research on word recognition and diverse learners, see the article "Understanding the Primary Role of Word Recognition …" by D. Chard, and Scott Foresman authors D. Simmons and E. Kame'enui.

TEACHER TALK

Shared reading is teacher-led reading of a big book or chart. The teacher points to each word while reading aloud, and children join in on the second or third reading.

Be sure to schedule time for children to work on the theme project *"Remember When* Album." This week children should mark places they have been on an outline map to include in the album.

Looking Ahead

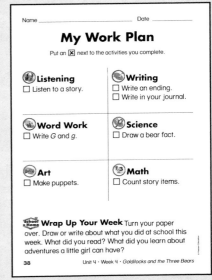

Name _____ Date _____

My Work Plan

Put an ☒ next to the activities you complete.

Listening
☐ Listen to a story.

Writing
☐ Write an ending.
☐ Write in your journal.

Word Work
☐ Write *G* and *g*.

Science
☐ Draw a bear fact.

Art
☐ Make puppets.

Math
☐ Count story items.

Wrap Up Your Week Turn your paper over. Draw or write about what you did at school this week. What did you read? What did you learn about adventures a little girl can have?

38   Unit 4 · Week 4 · *Goldilocks and the Three Bears*

▲ **Group-Time Survival Guide**
p. 38, Weekly Contract

☑ Customize Your Plan *by Strand*

ORAL LANGUAGE

Concept Development

What kind of adventure can a little girl have?

 *Amazing Words* to build oral vocabulary

bears	cottage	middle-sized
porridge	big	small

BUILD

☐ **Question of the Week** Use the Message Board to introduce and discuss the question of the week. This week children will talk, sing, read, and write about a little girl and her adventure. **DAY 1** *200*

☐ **Let's Talk** Use the Talk with Me Chart to introduce Amazing Words in a visual context. **DAY 1** *201*

Talk with Me, Sing with Me Chart 22A

☐ **Let's Listen** Use the Sing with Me/Background Building Audio CD to build background, vocabulary, and concepts. **DAY 1** *201*

☐ **Let's Sing** Use the Sing with Me Chart to sing a song about things in the small cottage home of a family of bears. **DAY 1** *201*

Talk with Me, Sing with Me Chart 22B

DEVELOP

☐ **Question of the Day/Week** Use the questions in the Message Boards to discuss lesson concepts and how they relate to the unit theme, Let's Explore. **DAY 2** *210*, **DAY 3** *225*, **DAY 4** *234*, **DAY 5** *242*

☐ **Let's Talk** Use the Talk with Me Chart to build background, vocabulary, and concepts. **DAY 2** *211*, **DAY 3** *226*, **DAY 4** *235*, **DAY 5** *243*

☐ **Let's Sing** Use the Sing with Me Chart to sing a song about things in the small cottage home of a family of bears. Ask children to sing along with you, listening for the Amazing Words as they sing. **DAY 2** *211*, **DAY 3** *226*, **DAY 4** *235*, **DAY 5** *243*

CONNECT

☐ **Wrap Up Your Week!** Connect concepts and vocabulary to next week's lesson. **DAY 5** *250*

CHECK

☐ **Check Oral Vocabulary** To informally assess children's oral vocabulary, have children use each word in a complete sentence. **DAY 5** *243*

PHONEMIC AWARENESS

TEACH

☐ **Introduce Initial /g/** Introduce and discriminate initial /g/. **DAY 1** *204*

☐ **Introduce Final /g/** Introduce final /g/. **DAY 3** *228*

PRACTICE/APPLY

☐ **Listen for Sounds** Use the Phonics Songs and Rhymes Chart to listen for /g/. **DAY 2** *220*

Phonics Songs and Rhymes Chart 22

RETEACH/REVIEW

☐ **Review** Review consonant blends. **DAY 4** *237*

☐ **Review** Review /g/. **DAY 5** *245*

☐ **Reteach Lesson** If necessary, reteach /g/. **DAY 5** *DI·34*

① Use assessment data to determine your instructional focus. ② Preview this week's instruction by strand. ③ Choose instructional activities that meet the needs of your classroom.

PHONICS

⟳ **CONNECT /g/ to Gg**

TEACH

- [ ] **Connect /g/ to Gg** Introduce Gg/g/. **DAY 1** 205

PRACTICE/APPLY

- [ ] **Connect /g/ to Gg** Practice Gg/g/. **DAY 2** 220, **DAY 3** 228

- [ ] **Phonics Story** Practice reading words with Gg/g/ in context. **DAY 2** 221

- [ ] **Kindergarten Student Reader K.4.4** Practice reading words with Gg/g/ in context. **DAY 3** 230

- [ ] **Decodable Reader 22** Practice reading words with Gg/g/ in context. **DAY 4** 238

- [ ] **Homework** Practice Book K.4, pp. 33, 38. **DAY 1** 205, **DAY 3** 228

- [ ] **Word Work Center** Write Gg. **ANY DAY** 198

Phonics Story

Kindergarten Student Reader K.4.4

Decodable Reader 22

RETEACH/REVIEW

- [ ] **Review** Review words with this week's phonics skill. **DAY 5** 245

- [ ] **Reteach Lesson** If necessary, reteach Gg/g/. **DAY 5** DI-34

- [ ] **Spiral REVIEW** Review previously taught phonics skills. **DAY 1** 206, **DAY 2** 221, **DAY 3** 229, **DAY 4** 237

ASSESS

- [ ] **Word and Sentence Reading** Assess children's ability to read words with Gg/g/. **DAY 5** 246–247

HIGH-FREQUENCY WORDS

HIGH-FREQUENCY WORDS

| one | two | three | four | five |

TEACH

- [ ] **Reteach** Reteach last week's high-frequency words. **DAY 1** 205

PRACTICE/APPLY

- [ ] **Words in Context** Read high-frequency words in the context of the Phonics Story and Decodable Reader 22. **DAY 2** 221, **DAY 4** 238

- [ ] **Word Wall** Use the Word Wall to review and practice high-frequency words throughout the week. **DAY 3** 229, **DAY 4** 238, **DAY 5** 245

- [ ] **Kindergarten Student Reader K.4.4** Practice this week's high-frequency words in context of reader. **DAY 3** 229–230, DI-18

- [ ] **Differentiated Text** Practice this week's high-frequency words in the context of differentiated text. **DAY 1** DI-16, **DAY 4** LR7

- [ ] **Homework** Practice Book K.4, p. 34. **DAY 2** 221

Phonics Story

Decodable Reader 22

Kindergarten Student Reader K.4.4

Listen to Me Reader K.4.4

Independent Leveled Reader K.4.4

RETEACH/REVIEW

- [ ] **Spiral REVIEW** Review previously taught high-frequency words. **DAY 2** 221, **DAY 3** 229, **DAY 4** 238, **DAY 5** 245

ASSESS

- [ ] **Word Reading** Assess children's ability to read this week's high-frequency words. **DAY 5** 246–247

COMPREHENSION

 SKILL CHARACTER A character is a person or an animal in a story.

TEACH

❏ **Skill Lesson** Introduce and model *character*. DAY 1 *203*

PRACTICE/APPLY

❏ **Skill in Context** Model how to identify *character*. Then read *Goldilocks and the Three Bears*, guiding children as they practice *character*. DAY 2 *212-219*

❏ **Skill in Context** Reread *My Lucky Day* and apply *character*. DAY 4 *236*

❏ **Leveled Text** Apply *character* to leveled text. DAY 4 *LR7*

Trade Book

Trade Book

Independent Leveled Reader K.4.4

ASSESS

❏ **Check** Read "A Canary's Song." Then have children practice *character*. DAY 5 *244*

❏ **Assess** Use the blackline master on p. 248 to assess children's understanding of *character*. DAY 5 *244, 248*

Read Aloud Anthology

RETEACH/REVIEW

❏ **Review Character** Review definition of *setting* and apply to *Goldilocks and the Three Bears*. DAY 3 *227*

❏ **Reteach Lesson** If necessary, reteach *character*. DAY 5 *DI-34*

WRITING

TEACH

❏ **Write Together** Engage children in writing activities that develop language, grammar, and writing skills and practice phonics skills. Include independent writing as an extension of group writing activities.

Shared Writing
❏ **Connect to Grammar** DAY 1 *207*
❏ **This Week We...** DAY 5 *249*

Modeled Writing
❏ **Respond to Literature** DAY 2 *222*
❏ **Connect to Phonics** DAY 3 *231*

Interactive Writing
❏ **Connect to Phonics** DAY 4 *239*

PRACTICE/APPLY

❏ **Daily Journal Writing** Have children write about concepts and literature in their journals. **EVERY DAY** *192-193*

❏ **Writing Center** Write an ending to the story. **ANY DAY** *199*

① Use assessment data to determine your instructional focus.

② Preview this week's instruction by strand.

③ Choose instructional activities that meet the needs of your classroom.

GRAMMAR

TEACH

☐ **Introduce** Introduce telling sentences. DAY 1 *207*

PRACTICE/APPLY

☐ **Practice** Practice telling sentences. DAY 2 *222*, DAY 4 *239*

☐ **Daily Fix-It** Have children find and correct errors in capitalization and punctuation. DAY 1 *207*, DAY 2 *222*, **DAY 3** *231*, DAY 4 *239*, DAY 5 *249*

RETEACH/REVIEW

☐ **Review** Review last week's grammar skill, complete sentences. DAY 3 *231*

☐ **Review** Review telling sentences. DAY 5 *249*

SPEAKING AND LISTENING

TEACH

☐ **Discussions** Introduce and model discussions. DAY 1 *208*

PRACTICE/APPLY

☐ **Practice** Have children practice discussions. DAY 3 *232*, DAY 4 *240*

REVIEW

☐ **Review** Review discussions. Then have children discuss authors and illustrators. DAY 5 *250*

INQUIRY PROJECT

TEACH

☐ **Unit Inquiry Project** Allow time for children to work on the theme project "*Remember When* Album." Have children mark places they have been on an outline map to include in the album. **ANY DAY** *xxiii*

Resources for
Differentiated Instruction

Emergent

Listen to Me Reader

▶ **Oral Language**
Develop oral vocabulary.

▶ **Phonemic Awareness**
/g/ in initial and final position

◉ **Decodable Words**
Gib   got   Gil

▶ **High-Frequency Words**
one   two   three
four   five   it

On-Level

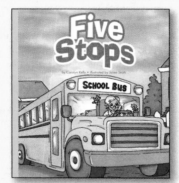

Kindergarten Student Reader

▶ **Connected Text**
Realistic Fiction

◉ **Phonics: Gg/g/**
big   Gil   Gab
got   flag

▶ **High-Frequency Words**
one   two   three
four   five

▶ **Spiral Review:**
Decodable Words
and   Sam   stop   Nat
Nan   hop   Lin   skips
Dad   Sal   Ann   Kim
Tim   lots   dots   Kip
sits   drop   kids   bus

High-Frequency Words
I   am   with   my
for   little they   he
of   the

Independent

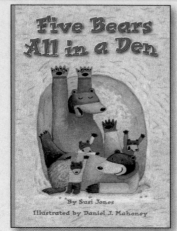

Leveled Reader K.4.4
Independent Leveled Reader

◉ **Comprehension: Character**
Identify and describe characters.

▶ **Concept**
What adventures children can have

▶ **Social Studies Standards**
Rules and laws

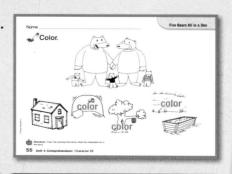

Leveled Reader, TE, LR8

ELL Poster 22

ELL and Transition Handbook

ELL Resources
- ELL Poster 22
- ELL and Transition Handbook
- ELL Notes in Teacher's Edition, pp. 200–251

For students who need intensive intervention
- Effectiveness proved by scientific research
- Instruction focused on early reading success predictors
- 30 minutes of daily small-group instruction

PearsonSuccessNet.com

Use the Online Database of over 600 books to

- Download and print additional copies of this week's leveled readers
- Listen to the readers being read online
- Search for more titles focused on this week's skills, topic, and content

Readers' Theater Anthology

Readers' Theater Anthology
- Six scripts to build fluency
- Poetry for oral interpretation

Homework
- Family Times Newsletter

Take-Home Books
- Kindergarten Student Readers
- Decodable Readers
- Listen to Me Readers
- Independent Leveled Readers

Literacy Centers

Listening

Word Work

Art

Let's Read
Along

- *Goldilocks and the Three Bears*
- **AudioText CD**

Journal Writing

- **Day One** Draw and label one adventure Goldilocks had at the bears' home.

- **Day Two** Draw and label your favorite bear.

- **Day Three** Draw and label three words that begin with /g/.

- **Day Four** Dictate or write one sentence that tells about porridge.

- **Day Five** Draw or write about what you would have done if the bears found you in their home.

The Giant
Gg

MATERIALS
construction paper, crayons, glitter, glue, shoe box top

Match Gg to /g/
1. Have children write a large upper-case *G* and a lowercase *g* on construction paper.
2. Have children use their fingers to spread the glue completely over both letters.
3. Children should then spread the glitter on the glue. Shake the extra glitter into the shoe box top.

CENTER TIP Have wipes available for children to clean the glue off their fingers.

 This interactive CD provides additional practice.

Story
Puppets

MATERIALS
brown paper lunch bags; variety of art materials such as yarn, buttons, and fabric; construction paper; crayons; scissors; glue

Create Puppets
1. Have children create a brown paper-bag puppet of one of the characters from the story, either a bear or Goldilocks.
2. Children should use the materials to make eyes, a nose, mouth, hair, and other decorations for their puppets.

CENTER TIP After the center time is completed, you may wish to have children use their puppets to act out the story.

Scott Foresman Reading Street Centers Survival Kit

Use the *Goldilocks and the Three Bears* materials
from the Reading Street Centers Survival Kit
to organize this week's centers.

 Writing

What If?

MATERIALS
writing paper, writing utensils,
crayons

Create an Ending

1. Write the following sentence on the board: *What if the bears had not come back home?*
2. Have children write or dictate what they think would have happened if the bears had not come back from their walk at the end of the story.
3. Children should illustrate a picture to go along with their new ending.

If the bears didn't come home, Goldilocks would have played ball.

 Science

Bear Facts

MATERIALS
nonfiction books about bears,
drawing paper, writing utensils,
crayons

Picture the Fact

1. Share the bear books with children. Make a list of bear facts on the board. Facts you might include are:
   • Bears sleep through much of the winter.
   • Bears eat fish.
   • Bears eat berries.
   • Bears can stand up on their hind feet.
2. Have children choose and copy one of the facts onto their own papers.
3. Children should then draw a picture illustrating the bear fact.

Bears eat fish.

 Math

Counting Up

MATERIALS
Goldilocks and the Three Bears, white paper, writing utensils, crayons

Count

1. Have the following words available for children at the center: ___ bears, ___ girl, ___ bowls of porridge, ___ broken chair.
2. Have children fold their papers into four boxes and copy each phrase into a box.
3. Children should count items in the story to finish the statements and fill in the appropriate number.
4. Children should draw a picture of each object in the boxes to illustrate the statements.

3 bears

1 girl

3 bowls of porridge.

1 broken chair

 **ALL CENTERS**

Oral Language and Vocabulary

Calendar
Message Board
Build Background

Shared Reading

Trade Book *Goldilocks and the Three Bears*
◉ **Skill** Character

Word Work

Phonemic Awareness
Introduce /g/
Listen for /g/
Segment and Blend Words

Phonics
◉ Connect /g/ to *Gg*
Blend Words
H/F Words *one, two, three, four, five*

Read

Group Time < Differentiated Instruction

Language Arts

Grammar: Telling Sentences
Shared Writing: Write Telling Sentences
Speaking and Listening: Discuss Authors and Illustrators

Materials

- Calendar
- Talk with Me, Sing with Me Chart 22A, 22B
- Sing with Me/Background Building Audio CD
- Trade Book *Goldilocks and the Three Bears*
- AudioText CD
- Picture Cards: p. 204
- Alphabet Cards: *Aa, Dd, Gg, Ii, Ll, Nn, Oo, Pp*
- Decodable Reader 21
- Daily Fix-It Transparency 22

Calendar

Name the day and date

Ask a volunteer to find today's date on the calendar. Have children say the month, day, date, and year together.

Yesterday, today, and tomorrow

Point to the calendar as you ask these questions:

- Who can remember yesterday's date?
- Who can tell me what tomorrow's date will be?
- What day is it today?

Message Board

Question of the week

Tell children that they will have an opportunity to talk, sing, read, and write about a little girl and her adventure.

Write and read the question as you track the print. Encourage children to respond in complete sentences.

> ## What kind of adventure can a little girl have?

Build Background Use the Day 1 instruction on ELL Poster 22 to assess knowledge and develop concepts.

ELL Poster 22

Build Background

LET'S TALK

Build concept

Display Talk with Me Chart 22A. Prompt children to respond in complete sentences. Point to the picture of the cottage.

This is someone's home. Who usually lives in a home like this? Sometimes in make-believe stories, animals act like people. In the story we will read, three bears will live in a home like this. Point to the girl in the chairs. Which chair looks like it is the right size for her?

Talk with Me, Sing with Me Chart

Build oral vocabulary

This week we will be talking about what people see, feel, smell, and hear on an adventure. We are going to learn six new words. Listen as I say the words; you may know some of them: *bears, porridge, cottage, big, middle-sized,* and *small.*

LET'S LISTEN

Share Background Building Audio

Play the CD that features a poem about bears.

 Sing with Me/Background Building Audio CD

LET'S SING/PHONOLOGICAL AWARENESS

Sing "In a Small Cottage"

Display Sing with Me Chart 22B. Tell children that they are going to sing a song about things in the small cottage home of a family of three bears. Read the title and describe the pictures. Sing the song several times to the tune of "Rock-a-Bye Baby." Encourage children to sing with you.

In a Small Cottage

In a small cottage
   there lived three bears,
One big, one small,
   one middle-sized bear.
They went for a walk
   to get some air,
When little Goldilocks
   found their lair.

Count sounds

Say the word *in.* Have children count the sounds they hear: /i/ /n/. Repeat with the words *big* and *small.*

 Sing with Me/Background Building Audio CD

Talk with Me, Sing with Me Chart

Amazing Words to build oral vocabulary

- bears
- cottage
- middle-sized
- porridge
- big
- small

Options Before Reading

Activate Prior Knowledge

What Is a Family? Ask children to discuss what makes a family.

- What are some things you would see in a family?
- What does a family do together?
- What does a family need to do to get along?

Oral Language

Family Homes Ask children to identify what makes a house feel like a home.

- Where do families live?
- What homes can be seen on your way to school?
- How do neighbors show they care about families?

Develop Story Concepts

Make a Story Display the cover of *Goldilocks and the Three Bears.* Create a story about what families do together.

OBJECTIVES

- Preview and predict.
- Listen to a story.

Materials

- Trade Book *Goldilocks and the Three Bears*

EXTEND SKILLS

Concepts of Print Guide the children to identify the author, illustrator, and title of the book. Show them several other versions of *Goldilocks and the Three Bears*. Help children notice differences in the illustrations of the same story.

Comprehension

MODEL READING STRATEGIES

Preview and predict

Display *Goldilocks and the Three Bears.* Look at the cover and tell me what you see.

 I see a family of three bears sitting in their yard. The father bear is playing the violin.

The title of this book is *Goldilocks and the Three Bears.* Who do you think Goldilocks is? Her name is Goldilocks, so I think her hair may be gold. Let's read to find out.

LET'S READ
Goldilocks and the Three Bears

Model fluent reading

Read the story with expression for enjoyment.

Trade Book **AudioText CD**

Shared Reading
ROUTINE

Day 1

Preview and make predictions about *Goldilocks and the Three Bears.* Read the book for enjoyment. Introduce comprehension skill, character, and describe actions and traits.

Day 2

Reread *Goldilocks and the Three Bears.* Use the Shared Reading Notes to engage children in a conversation about the story. Apply comprehension skill, character similarities and differences.

Day 3

Reread *Goldilocks and the Three Bears.* Develop oral vocabulary by naming objects and actions. Review comprehension skill, setting.

Day 4

Reread *My Lucky Day.* Apply comprehension skill, character analysis—why two characters see the same event differently.

Day 5

Read "A Canary's Song" in the *Read Aloud Anthology.* Assess comprehension skill, character similarities and differences.

Text to World READER RESPONSE

Respond to literature

Divide the class into four groups based on the characters from *Goldilocks and the Three Bears:* Goldilocks, the father bear, the mother bear, and the baby bear. Have each group tell whether their character is big or small, an animal or a person, and happy or sad.

STRATEGY Predict

Check predictions

- What did you think the story would be about?
- Who is in the story?

Use the following questions to guide discussion.

- Was it right for Goldilocks to enter the bears' house?
- What do you think happened to Goldilocks after she ran away?
- What is your favorite part of the story?

INTRODUCE SKILL Character

Define Character

- *Characters* are the people or animals in stories. They can be real or make-believe.
- Are the characters in *Goldilocks and the Three Bears* make-believe or real?

Think Aloud Goldilocks entered the bears' home while they were out. She ate their food, sat in their chairs, and slept in Baby Bear's bed.

Recall character actions and traits

Display *Little Quack.* Help children describe the actions and traits of the characters.

- Mama Duck brings her ducklings to the pond. She wants them to go into the water.
- The ducklings are scared to go into the pond, but one by one they learn how to paddle.

Relate character to everyday life

Goldilocks is a make-believe girl who does things that real children would never do. What are some of those things? (goes into a strange house by herself; eat strangers' food) What do the bears do that real bears wouldn't do? (live in a house; sleep in beds)

OBJECTIVES

- Respond to literature.
- Check predictions.
- Introduce character: describe actions and traits.

Skills Trace	
Character	
Introduce/Teach	TE: K.1 15, 24, 269, 278; K.4 203, 212; K.6 77, 86
Practice	TE: K.1 31, 39, 48, 56, 291, 300, 308; K.4 219, 227, 236, 244; K.6 91, 99, 108, 116 PB: K.1 7, 9, 47, 49; K.4 37, 39; K.6 17, 19
Reteach/Review	TE: K.1 101, DI-45, DI-49; K.3 223; K.4 DI-48; K.5 227; K.6 DI-46
Assess	TE: K.1 60, 312, 380–382, K.4 248, 380–382; K.6 120, 378–380; Unit 1 Benchmark Test;

E L L

Access Content Review other books you have read as a class and describe the characters' traits and what their actions show.

OBJECTIVES

- Introduce /g/.
- Segment and blend words.

Skills Trace

 Gg/g/

Introduce/Teach	TE: K.4 204–205
Practice	TE: K.4 220, 228, 231, 237, 239, 245 PB: K.4 33, 35–36, 38
Reteach/Review	TE: K.4 299, 363, DI-34
Test	TE: K.4 246–247, 380–382; Unit 4 Benchmark Test

Materials

- Picture Cards:

  garden   glove   goat
  goose   gum

- Trade Book *Goldilocks and the Three Bears*
- Alphabet Cards: *Aa, Dd, Gg, Ii, Ll, Nn, Oo, Pp*
- Decodable Reader 21

 **ELL**

Support Phonemic Awareness
Speakers of Hmong, Khmer, Korean, and Vietnamese may confuse a hard g with /k/. Help children practice distinguishing the sounds in word pairs such as *gold, cold; got, cot;* and *game, came.*

Phonemic Awareness

INTRODUCE /g/

Listen for initial /g/

Today we will learn a new sound. Listen carefully: /g/, /g/, /g/. Say it with me: /g/, /g/, /g/.

Display the *gum* Picture Card. *Gum* begins with /g/; /g/, *gum*. What sound does *gum* begin with? Continue with *goat, goose,* and *garden.*

Picture Card

Discriminate initial /g/

I am going to say two words. Listen carefully to the first sound in each word. Tell me which word begins with /g/. Say these words aloud: *bird, good; give, saw; girl, walk.*

Segment and blend words

Display the *glove* Picture Card. This is a glove. The first sounds in *glove* are /g/ and /l/. /g/ and /l/ blended together make /gl/. Say it with me: /gl/, /gl/, *glove.* What are the first sounds in *glove?* Continue with the following words: *glass, grab, grin, crab, clock, black,* and *snap.*

Monitor Progress | Check Sound Fluency

Listen for /g/ Say two words: *gobble, wobble.* Have children identify the word that begins with /g/. Continue with *go, duck; game, cat; garden, leaf;* and *heat, girl.*

If… children cannot identify initial /g/,

then… have them say /g/ several times and ask: Is your mouth open and your tongue humped at the back of your mouth? Put your hand on your throat and see if your voice box is on. Your throat moves when you say /g/ when your voice box is on. Can you feel your throat move? Practice with /g/ go, /g/ gas, /g/ gate, and /g/ girl.

SUCCESS PREDICTOR

▶ Day 1	Day 2	Day 3	Day 4	Day 5
Check Sound Fluency	Check Retelling/Letter-Sound Knowledge	Check High-Frequency Words/Word Reading	Check Phoneme Segmentation	Check Oral Vocabulary/Assess Progress

Phonics

 ## CONNECT /g/ to *Gg*

OBJECTIVES

- Connect /g/ to *Gg*.
- Blend and read words.
- Review letter names and sounds.
- Reteach high-frequency words *one, two, three, four, five*.

Introduce *Gg*/g/

Display the cover of *Goldilocks and the Three Bears.* Point to the word *Goldilocks.* This is the name *Goldilocks. Goldilocks* begins with an uppercase *G.* The sound for *G* is /g/, /g/, /g/, *Goldilocks.*

Trade Book

Recognize *Gg*

Point to Father Bear's glasses. People wear glasses to help them see better. The word *glasses* begins with /g/. Let's put our glasses on. Now look around our room. Do you see any *Gg*'s?

Connect /g/ to *Gg*

Display the *Gg* Alphabet Card. Point to *G.* The name of this letter is *G.* The sound for this letter is /g/. Point to the goose. What is the name of this animal? *Goose* begins with /g/. Repeat for lowercase *g.* Have children write *G* and *g* in the air.

Alphabet Card

Review letter names and sounds

Use Alphabet Cards to review the names and sounds of the letters *Aa, Dd, Ii, Ll, Nn, Oo,* and *Pp.*

BLEND SOUNDS

Blend words

Write *got* on the board. *Got* has three sounds. I am going to blend the sound of each letter together to say this word: /g/, /o/, /t/, *got.*

Say the sounds with me: /g/ /o/ /t/. Now blend the sounds to say the word: /g/ /o/ /t/, *got.* Continue blending practice with *gap, glad,* and *grin.*

Word Wall HIGH-FREQUENCY WORDS

Reteach *one, two, three, four, five*

Display *five.* This is the word *five.* Continue with *one, two, three,* and *four.* Have children find the words on the Word Wall.

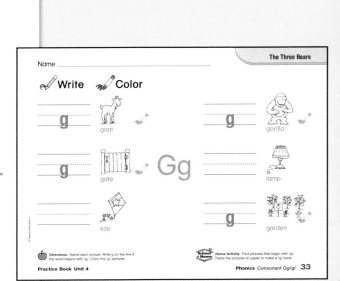

▲ **Practice Book 4**
Consonant *Gg*/g/, p. 33

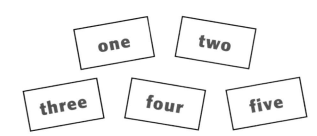

one

two

three

four

five

SUCCESS PREDICTOR

OBJECTIVES

- Review high-frequency words.
- Write *Gg*.

Group Time

On-Level

Reread Decodable Reader 21. Use the Small Group Reading **Routine.**

Strategic Intervention

Read Listen to Me Reader K.4.4. More practice with *Gg/g/*, p. DI·16.

Advanced

Reread Independent Leveled Reader K.4.4. Use the reading routine on p. DI·16. Reread to build fluency.

ELL

Group English language learners by their reading ability in English.

i **Independent Activities**

Self-Selected Reading See pp. TR14–15 for a bibliography of books related to the weekly concept.

Practice Book Consonant *Gg/g/*, p. 33

Centers Use the center activities on pp. 198–199 to practice this week's skills.

Journal Writing Draw and label one adventure Goldilocks had at the bears' home.

Spiral REVIEW **PREPARE TO READ**

Review words Continue guided blending practice with these words from last week's Decodable Reader 21 *One to Five:*

flop	spin	slam	drop
plop	stop	land	jump

Review high-frequency words Write the word *one* on the board. This is the word *one.* What is this word? Continue the word reading routine with *two, three, four,* and *five.*

Small Group Reading

DAY 1 ROUTINE

1 **Model Fluent Reading** Have children finger point as you read a page.

2 **Read Chorally** Have children finger point as they chorally read the page. Continue reading page by page, repeating steps 1 and 2.

3 **Read Individually** Have children read aloud a page in their group.

4 **Reread and Monitor Progress** As you listen to individual children reread, monitor progress and provide support.

Decodable Reader

HANDWRITING

Write *Gg* Words that begin with /g/ are written with either an uppercase *G* or a lowercase *g.* Remember, we use the uppercase letter at the beginning of sentences or for the first letter of a person's name, such as *Goldilocks.* Write *Goldilocks* on the board following the stroke instructions below. Repeat the routine with lowercase *g.*

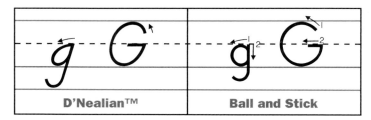

D'Nealian™	Ball and Stick

Shared Writing

GRAMMAR Telling Sentences

Introduce telling sentences

A *telling sentence* is a statement about something. It begins with an uppercase letter and ends with a period. It must have a naming part and an action part. **Display Talk with Me Chart 22A. Write on the board:** *The little girl is sitting.* *The little girl is sitting.* What is the naming word in this sentence? *(girl)* What describing word tells about the girl? *(little)* What is she doing? (sitting) *The little girl is sitting* is a telling sentence.

Identify telling sentences

Write the sentence fragment *I apple* on the board. Is this a telling sentence? How can we change it to make it a telling sentence?

LET'S WRITE Connect to Grammar

Write a telling sentence

Let's write a telling sentence about the adventure a little girl could have.

The girl took a walk in the woods.

Does it have an action part and a naming part? Does it start with an uppercase letter and end with a period? Do we need to add anything to make this a complete sentence?

Revise and edit

Write two sentence fragments and have children help you edit them to make complete telling sentences.

Independent writing

Have children copy one of the sentences the class wrote together or write their own telling sentence. Then have them illustrate their sentences.

OBJECTIVES

● Introduce telling sentences.
● Write a telling sentence.

Materials

● Talk with Me, Sing with Me Chart 22A

DAILY FIX-IT

the three bears live in a cottage

(The three bears live in a cottage.)

This week's practice sentences appear on Daily Fix-It Transparency 22.

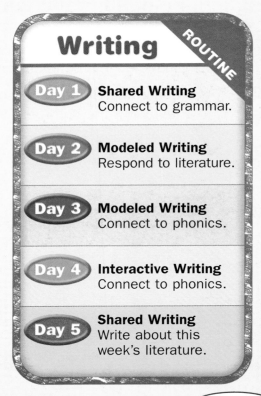

Writing ROUTINE

Day 1 Shared Writing
Connect to grammar.

Day 2 Modeled Writing
Respond to literature.

Day 3 Modeled Writing
Connect to phonics.

Day 4 Interactive Writing
Connect to phonics.

Day 5 Shared Writing
Write about this week's literature.

OBJECTIVE

- Discuss the role of authors and illustrators.

Access Content Ask for volunteers to show and talk with you about illustrations they think are interesting from some of the books in the class library.

Speaking and Listening

DISCUSSIONS

Have a discussion

Today we are going to talk about the authors and illustrators of books. What does the author of a book do? What does the illustrator do? Display *Goldilocks and the Three Bears.* Tell children who the author/illustrator is.

Model having a discussion

Take a picture walk through *Goldilocks and the Three Bears.* Ask the children how the illustrations show the bear family is a friendly, happy family. How do the illustrations help us understand the story?

Practice having a discussion

Ask a volunteer to come to the front of the room. Ask the child which illustration is his or her favorite. Prompt the child to discuss why he or she likes the illustration.

Wrap Up Your Day!

 Oral Language Today we read about the adventures of a little girl. Tell me about one adventure from the book.

 Comprehension Every story that we read has characters. Tell about the baby bear in this story.

 Grammar Show *Goldilocks and the Three Bears.* Point to the bear family on the cover. Make a telling sentence about the family.

 Homework Send home this week's Family Times newsletter.

PREVIEW Day 2

Tomorrow we will read about the adventures of Goldilocks and the bears again.

EXTEND Your Day

Time for
SOCIAL
STUDIES

Rules at Home

Materials construction paper, crayons

Discuss Safety in the Home Have the class tell what safety rules they have at school and at home. Make two lists of rules on the board—one for school and one for home. List the children's suggestions on the board.

Have children create an illustration for one of the rules. Arrange the pictures on a bulletin board display. Label the display *Safety*.

Comprehension

Class Character Book

Materials construction paper, crayons, stapler

Character Actions and Traits Divide children into small groups. Assign each group one of the following scenes:

- Goldilocks finds the cottage.
- Goldilocks tastes the porridge.
- Goldilocks sits in a chair.
- Goldilocks runs away.

Have children draw what Goldilocks thinks or feels in the scene and label the drawing.

Staple the pages together. Create a book cover, title page, and an author and illustrator page for all the children's names. Have children read the Goldilocks book together.

High-Frequency Words and Math

Math Words

Illustrate Mathematical Words Give each child a sheet of construction paper with the words *one, two, three, four,* and *five* written across the top. Have children read the words together. Draw pictures to show how many for each of these words. Under the word *one,* draw a picture of *one* thing from the story. Under *two,* draw *two* objects. Draw pictures showing the correct number of items from the story under *three, four,* and *five.*

Oral Language and Vocabulary

Calendar
Message Board
Build Background

Shared Reading

Trade Book *Goldilocks and the Three Bears*
Strategy Recall and Retell
Skill Character

Word Work

Phonemic Awareness
Listen for /g/

Phonics
Connect /g/ to *Gg*
Blend Sounds
H/F Words *one, two, three, four, five*
Phonics Story *How Many?*

Read

 Group Time < Differentiated Instruction

Language Arts

Grammar: Telling Sentences
Modeled Writing: Sentences About Goldilocks
Speaking and Listening: Expand Vocabulary

Materials

- Calendar
- Talk with Me, Sing with Me Chart 21A, 22A, 22B
- Sing with Me/Background Building Audio CD
- Trade Book *Goldilocks and the Three Bears*
- AudioText CD
- Picture Card: p. 222
- Phonics Songs and Rhymes Chart 22
- Phonics Songs and Rhymes Audio CD
- Alphabet Cards: *Aa, Cc, Dd, Ee, Gg, Ii, Kk, Nn, Oo, Pp, Ss,* keyboard
- Phonics Story *How Many?*

Calendar

Name the day and date
Ask a volunteer to find today's date on the calendar. Have children say the month, day, date, and year together.

Count how many days until Sunday
Point to today's date on the calendar. What day is today? Have a volunteer find Sunday on the calendar. Let's count the number of days between now and Sunday.

Message Board

Question of the day
Write and read the question as you track the print. Encourage children to respond in complete sentences.

> ## Are there one, two, three, four, or five bears in this story?

Review high-frequency words
Have children find *one, two, three, four,* and *five* in today's question. Circle the words and say them together.

Build Background Use the Day 2 instruction on ELL Poster 22 to practice the Develop Vocabulary words.

ELL Poster 22

Build Background

- Build background.
- Develop oral vocabulary.

LET'S TALK/LET'S SING

Develop oral vocabulary

Display Talk with Me Chart 22A. Point to the picture of the real bears and then the porridge.

- What kind of animals are these? (bears) Are the *bears* in this picture real or make-believe? (real) Are the bears in our story real or make-believe? (make-believe)

- What do you see in this picture? (porridge) *Porridge is another word for oatmeal. Have you ever eaten porridge?*

Talk with Me,
Sing with Me Chart

In a Small Cottage

In a small cottage
there lived three bears,
One big, one small,
one middle-sized bear.
They went for a walk
to get some air,
When little Goldilocks
found their lair.

Sing "In a Small Cottage"

Display Sing with Me Chart 22B. The words *bears* and *porridge* are in the song "In a Small Cottage." Ask children to listen for the words as you sing the song.

 Sing with Me/Background Building Audio CD

Amazing Words to build oral vocabulary

- bears
- cottage
- middle-sized
- porridge
- big
- small

LET'S LEARN AMAZING WORDS

Oral Vocabulary bears porridge

DAY 2 ROUTINE

1 **Introduce** *Bears* are large animals. *Bears* have shaggy fur and small tails. What is our new word for large animals with shaggy fur and small tails?

Demonstrate The *bears* in this story are make-believe. Where do real *bears* live?

2 **Introduce** In our story, Goldilocks eats *porridge,* which is another word for oatmeal. You eat *porridge* with a spoon while it is still warm. What is our new word for a thick, hot cereal?

Demonstrate Eating cereal, hot or cold, for breakfast is a healthy food choice. *Porridge* is an old-fashioned name for hot cereal. What does *porridge* look like?

3 **Review** We talked about two words today: *bears* and *porridge*. Which word means "large animals with shaggy fur and small tails," *bears* or *porridge?* Which word names "a thick, hot cereal," *bears* or *porridge?*

4 **Apply** Have children use *bears* and *porridge* in complete sentences. Have them tell about Goldilocks's visit.

ELL

Activate Prior Knowledge Invite children to share how they say *bears* and *porridge* in their home languages.

Access Content As you model the skill, invite children to act out the events in the story and how the characters reacted to them.

EXTEND SKILLS

Respond to Literature After reading the story, have children act out the things Goldilocks does when she is at the bears' house. Have children show how the author might feel about Goldilocks eating all of the baby bear's porridge. Then have children draw a picture to show what they think is the author's favorite part.

Comprehension

MODEL READING STRATEGY
Recall and Retell

Retell the story

Using the pictures as prompts, invite children to retell the story.

Open to pages 6–7. We see the bears going for a walk and Goldilocks coming to the house. What does Goldilocks do when she is inside the house? What do the bears do when they get home?

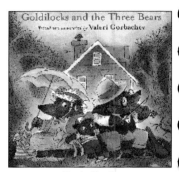

Trade Book

 SKILL *Character*

Model identifying character

Remind children that characters are the people or animals in a story. They can be real or make-believe and alike or different.

 Think Aloud The four characters in the story are Goldilocks and the three bears. How are the three bears alike? How are they different from each other? How is Goldilocks like the bears? How is she different?

CONCEPTS OF PRINT
Print Conveys Meaning

Recognize that print conveys meaning

Display the cover of *Goldilocks and the Three Bears*. Explain to children that words tell us things. When we read words, we learn things. Point to the title of the book and the name of the author. This tells us that the name of the book is *Goldilocks and the Three Bears* and the name of the author, or the person who wrote the book, is Valeri Gorbachev.

LET'S READ *Goldilocks and the Three Bears*

Reread the story

Ask children to listen for how the characters Goldilocks and the bears are the same and different. Use the Shared Reading Notes to prompt conversation about *Goldilocks and the Three Bears*.

 **AudioText CD**

Shared Reading Notes

Pages 2–3

How many bears lived together in the cottage in the woods? *Child may respond:* three

- There were three bears living in a cottage in the woods. Tell me about the big, middle-sized, and small bears. **open-ended**

Develop Vocabulary woods

Pages 4–5

What did the father, mother, and baby bears decide to do one morning? *Child may respond:* go for a walk

- The bears were going for a walk while their porridge cooled. Have you ever eaten porridge? **distancing**

Develop Vocabulary father

Shared Reading Notes

While the bears were gone, who wandered by their cottage? *Child may respond:* Goldilocks

- Goldilocks wandered by the bears' cottage. Tell me about Goldilocks. **open-ended**

Expand Vocabulary wandered

Pages 6–7

While they were gone, a little girl named Goldilocks came past their cottage.

What did Goldilocks do before she went inside? *Child may respond:* She peeked in the window.

- Goldilocks peeked in the window and saw that no one was home, so she went inside. What did she see once she was inside the cottage? *wh-* **question**

Expand Vocabulary delicious

Pages 8–9

She peeked in the window, and when she saw that no one was at home, she went inside.

There on the table sat the three bowls of porridge. The porridge smelled so delicious that Goldilocks just had to have some.

Whose porridge did Goldilocks try first? *Child may respond:* the father bear's

- First, Goldilocks tried the father bear's porridge. How do you think porridge would taste? **open-ended**

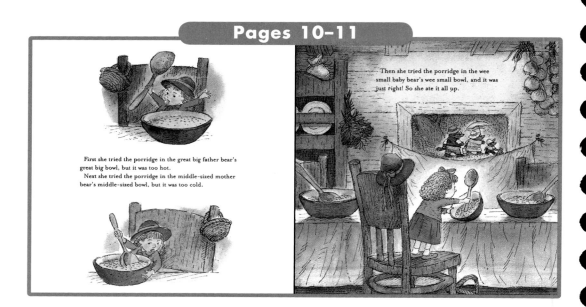

Pages 10–11

First she tried the porridge in the great big father bear's great big bowl, but it was too hot.
Next she tried the porridge in the middle-sized mother bear's middle-sized bowl, but it was too cold.

Then she tried the porridge in the wee small baby bear's wee small bowl, and it was just right! So she ate it all up.

Pages 12-13

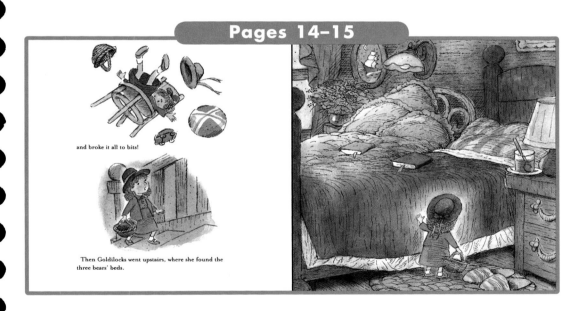

When she had finished the porridge, Goldilocks wandered into the sitting room where she found the three bears' chairs. First she tried the great big father bear's great big chair, but it was too hard.
Next she tried the middle-sized mother bear's middle-sized chair, but it was too soft.

Then she tried the wee small baby bear's wee small chair, and it was just right! So Goldilocks sat down in the chair . . .

Pages 14-15

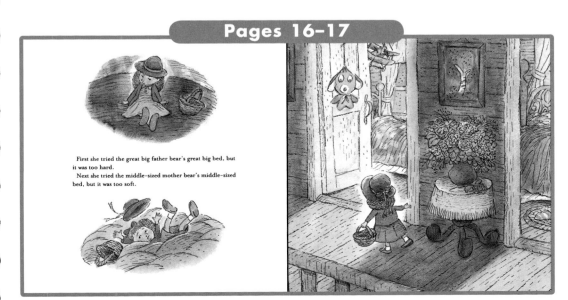

and broke it all to bits!

Then Goldilocks went upstairs, where she found the three bears' beds.

Pages 16-17

First she tried the great big father bear's great big bed, but it was too hard.
Next she tried the middle-sized mother bear's middle-sized bed, but it was too soft.

Shared Reading Notes

Which chair did Goldilocks like best?
Child may respond: the baby bear's chair

- Goldilocks tried all three chairs but she liked the baby bear's best. Do Goldilocks and the three bears seem to notice each other? How can you tell? **open-ended**

Develop Vocabulary mother

Activate Prior Knowledge Explain that the phrase *just right* means "the way she likes it," and *sitting room* is another name for family room, living room, or den.

What happened when Goldilocks sat in the baby bear's chair? *Child may respond:* She broke it all to bits.

- Goldilocks broke the chair. How do you think the baby bear will feel about his chair? **open-ended**

What did Goldilocks try next? *Child may respond:* the beds

Next Goldilocks tried the bears' beds. Have children complete the following sentences as you read them aloud: First she tried the great big father bear's great big bed, but it was _____. Next she tried the middle-sized mother bear's middle-sized bed, but it was _____.
completion

Goldilocks and the Three Bears 215

Shared Reading Notes

What happened when Goldilocks tried the baby bear's bed? *Child may respond:* She fell asleep.

- Goldilocks fell asleep in baby bear's bed. Who returned home? **wh- question**

Develop Vocabulary baby

Access Content Ask children if they have a special chair at home that they like to sit in. Ask them to tell why they like the chair.

Pages 18–19

Then she tried the wee small baby bear's wee small bed, and it was just right! So Goldilocks lay down and fell fast asleep.

No sooner had Goldilocks fallen asleep than the three bears returned home. Their walk had made them very hungry, so they hurried right into the kitchen.

What did Goldilocks leave in the father bear's and mother bear's porridge? *Child may respond:* the spoon

- The mother bear and father bear knew someone had been eating their porridge because the spoon had been left in it. How did the baby bear know someone had been eating his porridge? **recall**

Pages 20–21

Goldilocks had left the spoon in the great big father bear's porridge.
"Someone has been eating my porridge!" said the great big father bear in his great big voice.
The middle-sized mother bear saw that the spoon had been left in her bowl of porridge, too. "Someone has been eating my porridge!" said the middle-sized mother bear in her middle-sized voice.
Then the wee small baby bear looked at his bowl of porridge. "Someone has been eating my porridge!" cried the wee small baby bear in his wee small voice. "And they've eaten it all up!"
The three bears hurried into the sitting room.

How did the mother bear and father bear know that someone had been sitting in their chairs? *Child may respond:* The pillows had been moved.

- The mother bear and father bear knew someone had been sitting in their chairs because the pillows had been moved. How does the baby bear know someone had been sitting in his chair? **recall**

Pages 22–23

Goldilocks had knocked the pillow off the great big father bear's chair. "Someone has been sitting in my chair!" said the great big father bear in his great big voice.
The pillow on the middle-sized mother bear's chair had been moved, too. "Someone has been sitting in my chair!" said the middle-sized mother bear in her middle-sized voice.
Then the wee small baby bear looked at his chair.

"Someone has been sitting in my chair," cried the wee small baby bear in his wee small voice, "and they've broken it to bits!"

Pages 24–25

Shared Reading Notes

Where did the three bears go next? *Child may respond:* upstairs

• The three bears went upstairs next. What do you think they are looking for upstairs? **open-ended**

Pages 26–27

How did the mother bear and father bear know someone had been sleeping in their beds? *Child may respond:* The covers were messed up.

• The mother bear and father bear knew someone had been in their beds because the covers were messed up. What did the mother bear and father bear say when they saw that their beds had been messed up? **completion**

Pages 28–29

Who did baby bear find in his bed? *Child may respond:* Goldilocks

• The baby bear finds Goldilocks in his bed. What is Goldilocks doing? ***wh-* question**

Shared Reading Notes

What did Goldilocks do when she saw the bears? *Child may respond:* She leaped out of bed, jumped through the window, climbed down the roof, and ran away.

- Goldilocks ran away when she saw the bears. Why do you think she ran away? **open-ended**

Pages 30-31

She leaped out of bed, jumped through the window, clambered down from the roof, and ran away just as fast as she could go.

What happened to Goldilocks afterwards? *Child may respond:* No one knows.

- We don't know what happened to Goldilocks. What do you think would have happened if Goldilocks had stayed to talk to the bears? **open-ended**

Page 32

What happened to Goldilocks afterwards, no one knows. The three bears never saw her again, and they lived happily ever after in their cottage in the woods.

CONNECT TO SKILL Character

Connect *Goldilocks and the Three Bears* to character

This book told about the adventures of a girl named Goldilocks and a family of bears.

- Why do you think Goldilocks went inside the bears' house when she saw that no one was home?
- What would you have done if you were Goldilocks?
- Why do you think the bears were surprised to find someone in their house?
- What would you have done if you were one of the three bears?
- Why do you think Goldilocks ran away?
- What do you think would have happened if she had stayed?

Monitor Progress | Check Retelling *The Three Bears*

Picture Walk and Retell Help children use the pictures in *Goldilocks and the Three Bears* to retell the story.

If... children have difficulty retelling the story,
then... use the Retelling Rubric to help them move toward fluent retelling.

SUCCESS PREDICTOR

Day 1	▶ Day 2	Day 3	Day 4	Day 5
Check Sound Fluency	Check Retelling/ Letter-Sound Knowledge	Check High-Frequency Words, Word Reading	Check Phoneme Segmentation	Check Oral Vocabulary/ Assess Progress

Scoring Rubric | Retelling

Rubric 4 3 2 1	**4**	**3**	**2**	**1**
Setting	describes time and location	identifies time and location	omits time and location	is unable to identify time and location
Character	describes main character(s) and character development	identifies main character(s)	omits or inaccurately identifies character(s)	unable to identify character
Events	describes events in sequence with details	tells most events in sequence with some detail	retells first and last events but omits middle with few details	is unable to retell events

Retelling Plan

- ☑ Week 1 assess Advanced students.
- ☑ Week 2 assess On-Level students.
- ☑ Week 3 assess Strategic Intervention students.
- ☑ **This week assess Advanced students.**
- ☐ Week 5 assess On-Level students.
- ☐ Week 6 assess Strategic Intervention students.

Retelling

SUCCESS PREDICTOR

OBJECTIVES

- Listen for /g/.
- Connect /g/ to *Gg*.

Materials

- Phonics Songs and Rhymes Chart 22
- Alphabet Cards: *Aa, Cc, Dd, Ee, Gg, Ii, Kk, Nn, Oo, Pp, Ss,* keyboard
- Phonics Story *How Many?*

ELL

Support Phonemic Awareness
Clarify meanings in the song by explaining that *shakes a leg* means "hurries" or "moves quickly," and *gaggle of geese* means "a group of geese."

Phonemic Awareness

PRACTICE /g/

Listen for /g/   Display the chart. We are going to learn a new song today. Listen carefully for words that begin with /g/. Play the CD or sing the song to the tune of "Row, Row, Row Your Boat" several times.

Discriminate /g/   Replay the song. Raise your hand each time you hear a word that begins with /g/. Identify *Gertie, Gopher, Gary, giggled, Galloping, gaggle,* and *geese.*

Phonics Songs and Rhymes Audio CD

Phonics Songs and Rhymes Chart

Phonics

⟳ CONNECT /g/ to *Gg*

Recognize G   Ask children to identify *G* on the keyboard card.

Identify Gg   Display the chart. There were many words with *G* and *g* in the song. Let's circle the *Gg* words on our chart. Have children circle a word that begins with *G* or *g*.

Connect /g/ to Gg   Write *g* on the board. What is the name of this letter? *(g)* What is the sound for this letter? *(/g/)* Repeat the routine with *G.*

Monitor Progress | Check Letter-Sound Knowledge

Connect /g/ to Gg Have each child write *G* and *g* on an index card. Tell them you will read some words. If they hear /g/, they should hold up their *Gg* card. Read the following sentences:

> **The girls can get the geese.**
> **The goats galloped out of the gate.**
> **Give Gary a gift.**

If... children cannot recognize initial *G* or *g*,
then... have children trace the *g* Finger Tracing Card as they say /g/.

SUCCESS PREDICTOR

Day 1	▶ Day 2	Day 3	Day 4	Day 5
Check Sound Fluency	Check Retelling/ Letter-Sound Knowledge	Check High-Frequency Words/ Word Reading	Check Phoneme Segmentation	Check Oral Vocabulary/ Assess Progress

▲ **Practice Book 4**
High-Frequency Words, p. 34

 BLEND SOUNDS

Review letter names and sounds

Spell and blend words

PHONICS ACTIVITY MAT

Use the Alphabet Cards to review these letter names and sounds: *Aa, Nn, Dd, Cc, Ss, Ee, Oo, Gg, Kk, Ii,* and *Pp.*

Listen to the three sounds in *dog:* /d/ /o/ /g/. What is the first sound in *dog?* (/d/) What is the letter for that sound? (d) Write *d* on the board. Now you write *d* on your paper. Continue the routine with the remaining sounds.

d o g
→ → →
→

Point to *dog.* Help me blend the sound of each letter together to read this word: /d/ /o/ /g/. The word is *dog.*

Continue spell and blend practice with the following words: *and, can, Lin, Hap, send, kids, pig,* and *frog.*

PREPARE TO READ

Review high-frequency words

Write *four* on the board. This is the word *four.* What is this word? Continue the routine with *one, two, three, five,* and *you.*

Small Group Reading

DAY 2 ROUTINE

1 **Model Fluent Reading** Have children finger point as you read a page.

2 **Read Chorally** Have children finger point as they chorally read the page. Continue reading page by page, repeating steps 1 and 2.

3 **Read Individually** Have children read aloud a page in their group.

4 **Reread and Monitor Progress** As you listen to individual children reread, monitor progress and provide support.

Name _____
How Many?

Lin and Hap can see one dog.

1

Practice Book 1
Phonics Story, pp. 35–36

Group Time

On-Level

Read Phonics Story *How Many?* Use the Small Group Reading **Routine.**

Strategic Intervention

Read Phonics Story *How Many?* More practice with *Gg*/g/, p. DI·17.

Advanced

Read Decodable Reader 22. Use the reading routine on p. DI·17. Apply phonics skills.

ELL

Group English language learners by their reading ability in English.

i **Independent Activities**

Self-Selected Reading See pp. TR14–15 for books related to the weekly concept.

Practice Book High-Frequency Words, p. 34

Centers Use the center activities on pp. 198–199.

Journal Writing Draw and label your favorite bear.

Letter-Sound Knowledge

SUCCESS PREDICTOR

OBJECTIVES

- Practice telling sentences.
- Write sentences about Goldilocks.

Materials

- Picture Card: *glove*
- Trade Book *Goldilocks and the Three Bears*
- Talk with Me, Sing with Me Chart 21A

DAILY FIX-IT

gus can get the gum

(Gus can get the gum.)

Writer's Checkup

✔ The first word in a sentence begins with an uppercase letter. Did I do that?

✔ A sentence should end with a period. Did I do that?

✔ A sentence should make sense. Does my sentence make sense?

✔ A good writer uses his or her best handwriting. Did I do that?

Modeled Writing

GRAMMAR Telling Sentences

Practice telling sentences

Display the *glove* Picture Card. This is a picture of a glove. We can tell something about the glove. We can say, "Gary lost his glove at school." Sentences that tell something about someone or something are called *telling sentences*.

Picture Card

Identify telling sentences

I am going to read groups of words. Tell me if each group is a telling sentence. Read the following groups of words:

sunny day on Monday

Goldilocks went in the cottage.

The bed was just right.

in his wee small voice

LET'S WRITE Respond to Literature

Discuss *Goldilocks and the Three Bears*

Display *Goldilocks and the Three Bears.* Ask children to make up telling sentences by using the words and illustrations from the story.

Model writing a sentence

Goldilocks runs away when the bears come home. Where do you think she went? She may have gone home. I'm going to write:

Goldilocks ran home.

She told her parents about the bears.

Independent writing

Have children write or dictate their own telling sentences about *Goldilocks and the Three Bears,* or copy one of the sentences the class wrote together. Then have them illustrate their sentences.

Goldilocks went home and took another nap.

Speaking and Listening

LET'S REVIEW AMAZING WORDS

Display Talk with Me Chart 21A. Review these Amazing Words from last week.

DAY 2 ROUTINE

Oral Vocabulary   woodland   nest

1 **Introduce** Many animals live in the forest. Another name for a place with many trees and animals is *woodland*. What's our new word for a forest area with many trees?

Demonstrate Remember, the *woodland* has many trees. Animals in the *woodland* make their homes there. Can you think of any animals that would live in the *woodland*?

2 **Introduce** Point to the picture of the mouse's home. This is a *nest*. Some animals build *nests* for their homes.

Demonstrate A *nest* is a place that some animals build to live in. Can you name an animal that lives in a *nest*?

3 **Review** We talked about two words today: *woodland* and *nest.* Which word is another word for "forest," *woodland* or *nest?* Which word names a place some animals build to live, *woodland* or *nest*?

4 **Apply** Have children use *woodland* and *nest* in complete sentences. Have them draw a picture of a *woodland* with a *nest*.

Wrap Up Your Day!

PREVIEW Day 3

☑ **Oral Language** Today we read about Goldilocks and her adventures when she was in the three bears' home. Goldilocks ate the bears' porridge. What else did Goldilocks do?

☑ **Grammar** Telling sentences tell us what someone or something does. Can you give me a telling sentence about one of the bears in the story?

☑ **Homework Idea** Have children take their Phonics Story home to share with their families.

Tomorrow we will read about Goldilocks and the three bears again. Which character is your favorite?

EXTEND Your Day

Make a Map

Materials chart paper, mural paper, crayons or paints

Map an Adventure Ask children to tell where Goldilocks went on her adventure through the woods in *Goldilocks and the Three Bears.* Ask children to name other places they think she could visit. What places might Goldilocks want to see? Where would you go if you went out in your neighborhood? Record the list on chart paper, ending at the three bears' house.

> 1. store
> 2. park
> 3. playground
> 4. friend's home
> 5. the three bears' house

Time for SOCIAL STUDIES

After children have compiled the list, make a map of the places Goldilocks would visit by drawing a path across the mural paper and putting numbers at each location. Then have groups of children work together to paint or color pictures of their location. When the pictures are done, have children "read" the map by locating places on the map and telling where it is. Use questions that make comparisons such as: Is the bears' house closer to the park or the store? If you left the park and went to the right, would you go to the store or the playground? Children may enjoy creating an "adventure" map of their neighborhood using a similar format.

Grammar
Telling Sentences

Talk About Safety Invite a police officer, crossing guard, or other person who works in the safety industry to talk to the children about the importance and purpose of having rules.

Then have children write the beginning of this telling sentence at the top of their papers:

We have rules because . . .

Have children write or dictate how they would complete the telling sentence and then illustrate their sentences.

Phonics
Connect /g/ to *Gg*

Good Goats Give each child a sheet of construction paper cut into the shape of a goat.

Have children write or draw /g/ words on their goat cutouts. If they have trouble thinking of a word, let them look through the Picture Cards and choose one that begins with /g/. Hang the *Good Goats* to a bulletin board. Add grass and trees to make it resemble a farm pasture.

Calendar

Name the day and date

Ask a volunteer to find today's date on the calendar. Have children recite the day, month, date, and year.

Count school days in the month

Look at this month's page on the calendar. Remind children that Saturdays, Sundays, and holidays are not school days. Then count together from the first school day to the last school day of the month to find out how many school days there are.

Message Board

Question of the day

Write and read the question as you track the print. Remind children to respond in complete sentences.

Why is Goldilocks visiting the bears?

Review phonics

- What letter does *Goldilocks* begin with? *(G)*
- What is the sound for *G?* (/g/)

Extend Language Use the Day 3 instruction on ELL Poster 22 to extend and enrich language.

ELL Poster 22

Oral Language and Vocabulary
Calendar
Message Board
Build Background

Shared Reading
Trade Book *Goldilocks and the Three Bears*
Skill Setting
Skill Character

Word Work
Phonemic Awareness
Introduce Final /g/

Phonics
Connect /g/ to *Gg*
H/F Words *one, two, three, four, five*
Kindergarten Student Reader K.4.4

Read

Group Time < Differentiated Instruction

Language Arts
Grammar: Complete Sentences
Modeled Writing: Write About Riding on a Bus
Speaking and Listening: Discuss Authors and Illustrators

Materials
- Calendar
- Talk with Me, Sing with Me Chart 22A, 22B
- Sing with Me/Background Building Audio CD
- Trade Book *Goldilocks and the Three Bears*
- AudioText CD
- Alphabet Cards: *Aa, Bb, Cc, Dd, Ee, Ff, Gg, Hh, Ii, Kk, Ll, Mm, Nn, Oo, Pp, Rr, Ss, Tt, Ww, Yy*
- Picture Cards: p. 228
- Kindergarten Student Reader K.4.4
- AlphaBuddy
- Big Book *Animal ABCs*

Amazing Words to build oral vocabulary

- bears
- cottage
- middle-sized
- porridge
- big
- small

Access Content Ask children what words in their home languages are used for *cottage* and *big*.

Build Background

LET'S TALK

Develop oral vocabulary

Display Talk with Me Chart 22A. Point to the cottage and the father bear.

- Where did the three bears live? (in a cottage) They lived in a *cottage* in the woods. What is a *cottage?*
- What did the father bear look like? Everything about him was *big.* His porridge bowl, his chair, and his bed were all *big.*

Talk with Me, Sing with Me Chart

LET'S SING

Sing "In a Small Cottage"

Display Sing with Me Chart 22B. Sing the song "In a Small Cottage." Ask children to clap when they hear the words *cottage* and *big.*

 Sing with Me/Background Building Audio CD

LET'S LEARN AMAZING WORDS

Oral Vocabulary   cottage   big

DAY 5 ROUTINE

1 **Introduce** A little house in the woods is called a *cottage.* A *cottage* is where the three bears lived. What's our new word for a little house in the woods?

Demonstrate In real life, people, not bears, might live in a *cottage* in the woods. Did you ever see a *cottage* in the woods?

2 **Introduce** When something takes up a lot of space, we say it is *big.* What's our new word for something that takes up a lot of space?

Demonstrate Father bear was *big* next to the mother bear and the baby bear. A *big* person is usually taller than others. Who is *big* in your family?

3 **Review** We talked about two words today: *cottage* and *big.* Which word means "a little house in the woods," *cottage* or *big?* Which word means "something that takes up a lot of space," *cottage* or *big?*

4 **Apply** Have children use *cottage* and *big* in complete sentences. Ask them to show something that is *big* and to make the shape of a *cottage.*

Comprehension

REVIEW SKILL Setting

Review setting

Remind children to think about when and where a story takes place.

Goldilocks and the Three Bears
Retold and illustrated by Valeri Gorbachev

Trade Book

Apply setting

- Where did the three bears live? (in a cottage)

- Where did the three bears go for a walk? (in the woods)

- Does this story happen in a place that is real or make-believe? (make-believe)

- The story starts with the words "Once upon a time." Do you think the story happened recently, or a long time ago? (a long time ago)

LET'S READ
Goldilocks and the Three Bears

Develop vocabulary

Reread *Goldilocks and the Three Bears*. Develop vocabulary by having children talk about this adventure story and imagine being there themselves.

 AudioText CD

SKILL Character

Practice character

Ask children to list the characters in *Goldilocks and the Three Bears*. Tell them that each character is different from the others, but they also are alike.

- How are Goldilocks and the baby bear different? (Goldilocks is a girl and the baby bear is a bear.)

- How are Goldilocks and the baby bear the same? (They are both young. They are about the same size.)

- How are Goldilocks and the mama bear alike? (They are both female.)

OBJECTIVES

- Review setting.
- Character: identify similarities and differences.

Materials

- Trade Book *Goldilocks and the Three Bears*

Monitor Progress

Character

If... children cannot identify similarities and differences among characters,	then... ask comparative questions: "Which character in the story was bigger?"

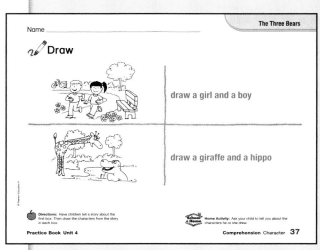

Name _____

The Three Bears

✏ **Draw**

draw a girl and a boy

draw a giraffe and a hippo

Directions: Have children tell a story about the first box. Then draw the characters from the story in each box.

Home Activity: Ask your child to tell you about the characters he or she drew.

Practice Book Unit 4

Comprehension Character **37**

▲ **Practice Book 4** Character, p. 37

Phonemic Awareness

INTRODUCE Final /g/

Practice initial /g/

Display the *gum* Picture Card. What is the first sound in *gum?* Say the word with me: /g/ /u/ /m/, *gum.* The first sound is /g/. Continue with *got* and *gap.*

Introduce final /g/

Display the *bag* Picture Card. Listen as I say this word: *bag,* /b/ /a/ /g/, *bag.* What is the last sound in *bag?* Say the word with me and listen carefully: /b/ /a/ /g/, *bag.* The last sound is /g/. Continue with Picture Cards *pig* and *jug.*

Discriminate final /g/

I am going to say two words. Listen carefully to the last sound in each word. Tell me which word ends with /g/ like *bag.* Read these words aloud: *bit, sag; dog, doll; bug, mud; crab, rug;* and *goat, tag.*

Phonics

🔄 CONNECT /g/ to *Gg*

Connect /g/ to *Gg*

Display the *Gg* Alphabet Card. What is the name of this letter? *(Gg)* What is the sound for this letter? (/g/) Point to the *goose.* What is this? What is the first sound in *goose?*

Substitute final sounds

Write *mug* on the board. This word has three sounds. Say them with me: /m/ /u/ /g/. The word is *mug.* We can make a new word by changing the last sound. Change the *g* to *d.* Say the sounds with me: /m/ /u/ /d/, *mud.* The new word is *mud.* Continue substituting final sounds with the following words: *bat, bag; tag, tap; pig, pit; rag, rat.*

Alphabet Card

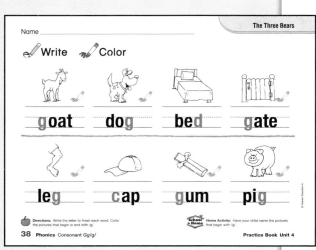

▲ **Practice Book 4**
Consonant *Gg*/g/, p. 38

Spiral REVIEW · BLEND SOUNDS

Review letter names and sounds

Display the *Gg* Alphabet Card. What is the name of this letter? What is the sound for this letter? Review the following letters: *Ll, Tt, Ss, Nn, Bb, Aa, Cc, Dd, Ee, Ff, Hh, Ii, Kk, Mm, Oo, Pp, Rr, Ww,* and *Yy.*

Blend sounds

Write *Gil* on the board. I am going to blend the sound of each letter together to say this word: /g/ /i/ /l/.

G i l
→ → →
→

The word is *Gil.* Say the three sounds with me: /g/ /i/ /l/, *Gil.* Continue the routine with *stop, at, stops, big, Nat, Nan, hop, on, Gab, Sal, can, not, Ann, Dan, Kim, skips, Tim, has, lots, dots, Kip, sits, Lin, drop, kids,* and *flag.*

Word Wall HIGH-FREQUENCY WORDS

Practice high-frequency words

Write the word *three* on the board. This is the word *three.* What is this word? Continue the routine with *one, two, four, five, for, little, they, of, the,* and *to.*

Introduce rebus words

Display *bus.* This is the word *bus.* What word is this? Repeat with *school.*

Monitor Progress — High-Frequency Words/Word Reading

High-Frequency Words Write *one, two, three, four,* and *five* on the board. Have children take turns reading the words.

Blend Sounds to Read Words Write *stop* on the board. Have children blend the sounds of each letter to read this word. Continue with the following words: *Nat, Nan, hop, kids, drop, skips, lots, dots, flag, Sam, at, Lin, Gab, Sal,* and *can.*

If... children cannot read the high-frequency words,
then... write the words on cards for them to practice at home.

If... children cannot blend sounds to read words,
then... provide practice blending the words in chunks, /g/ -il.

If... children can blend sounds to read the words,
then... have them read Kindergarten Student Reader K.4.4 *Five Stops.*

SUCCESS PREDICTOR

Group Time

On-Level
Read Kindergarten Student Reader K.4.4. Use the Small Group Reading Routine.

Strategic Intervention
Read Kindergarten Student Reader K.4.4. More practice with *Gg/g/,* p. DI·18.

Advanced
Read Kindergarten Student Reader K.4.4. Use reading routine on p. DI·18. Extend word reading.

ELL
Group English language learners by their reading ability in English.

(i) Independent Activities

Self-Selected Reading See pp. TR14–15 for a bibliography of books related to the weekly concept.

Practice Book Character, p. 37; Consonant *Gg/g/,* p. 38

Centers Use the center activities on pp. 198–199 to practice this week's skills.

Journal Writing Draw and label three words that begin with /g/.

Spiral REVIEW
● Reviews previously taught high-frequency words.
● Reviews previously taught letters and sounds.

SUCCESS PREDICTOR

3

PREPARE TO READ

ELL

Access Content Ask children to point out the naming words, such as *Nan, Nat, Sam,* and *Lin.* Have children act out the action words *stop, hop, drop,* and *skip.*

Introduce Kindergarten Student Reader K.4.4

Display the title page. We are going to read a new story. **Point to the title.** What is the title of the story? *Five Stops* was written by Carolyn Kelly. This story was illustrated by Jaime Smith.

Small Group Reading

1 Model Fluent Reading Have children finger point as you read a page.

2 Read Chorally Have children finger point as they chorally read the page. Continue reading page by page, repeating steps 1 and 2.

3 Read Individually Have children read aloud a page in their group.

4 Reread and Monitor Progress As you listen to individual children reread, monitor progress and provide support.

Kindergarten Student Reader

I am Sam.
I stop at five stops with my big bus.

2

Nat and Nan stop.
Nat and Nan stop for Flap the Cat.

3

At stop two, Gil and Gab hop on the big bus.
Dad and little Sal can not.

4

I stop for Ann and Dan.
They hop on at stop three.

5

Kim skips on at stop four.
Not Tim. He has lots of dots.

6

The last one is Kip.
He got on at stop five.
He sits with Lin.

7

I drop the kids at the flag.
Nat, Nan, Lin, Gil, Gab, Ann, Dan, Kim, and Kip hop and skip.

8

Modeled Writing

REVIEW GRAMMAR Complete Sentences

Review complete sentences

AlphaBuddy is going to act out something. We will tell what he is doing in complete sentences.

Have AlphaBuddy clap his paws. *AlphaBuddy is clapping.* Say the sentence with me: *AlphaBuddy is clapping.* Is that a complete sentence? Yes, it is. Have AlphaBuddy act out things such as writing, twirling, and hopping. Have children take turns saying a complete sentence. Write the sentences on the board. Have children remind you to use the correct punctuation.

LET'S WRITE Connect to Phonics

Review letters and sounds

Display page 7 of *Animal ABCs.* What is the name of this picture? (gorilla) What sound does *gorilla* begin with? What letter stands for /g/? Point out the words in *Five Stops* that begin or end with /g/.

Write sentences

In our story, Nan and Nat ride a big bus to school. Let's write sentences about where we could go on a big bus.

We ride the big bus to the zoo.

Have children read the sentence with you. Point out that the word *big* ends with /g/. Have children identify the letter that stands for /g/. Model writing more sentences using words that begin or end with /g/.

Independent writing

Have children write a short story about their own adventures on a big bus, or they may copy one of the sentences the class wrote together. Remind children to write words the way they sound. Then have them illustrate their sentences.

EXTEND SKILLS

Handwriting Before you write the first sentence on the board, ask children whether you should begin at the left or right side of the board. Walk to the right side of the board and ask, "Should I begin writing here?" Let children correct you.

Classroom Resources Remind children that they can use classroom resources, such as a dictionary or their classmates, to help them as they write. Also remind them that they may ask you for help if necessary.

OBJECTIVES

- Review complete sentences.
- Review letters and sounds.
- Write about riding on a bus.

Materials

- AlphaBuddy
- Big Book *Animal ABCs*
- Kindergarten Student Reader K.4.4

DAILY FIX-IT

a baby bear is very small
(A baby bear is very small.)

Writer's Checkup

- ✔ The first word in a sentence begins with an uppercase letter. Did I do that?
- ✔ A sentence should end with a period. Did I do that?
- ✔ A sentence should make sense. Does my sentence make sense?
- ✔ A good writer uses his or her best handwriting. Did I do that?

ELL

Access Content If children have difficulty understanding what you are discussing, open a book with separate author and illustrator and point to the words and pictures as you explain what each of them does.

Speaking and Listening

DISCUSS AUTHORS AND ILLUSTRATORS

Identify authors and illustrators

Did you ever notice that there are names of one or two people on the front covers of most books? The person who writes the words in a book is called the *author*. The person who draws or paints the pictures in a book is called the *illustrator*. Those are the names shown on the covers of most books.

Connect author and illustrator to print

Sometimes one person is both the author and illustrator because he or she writes the words and draws the pictures. Display *Goldilocks and the Three Bears.* For this book, one person is both the author and illustrator.

- Who writes the words, the author or the illustrator?
- Who draws the pictures, the author or the illustrator?

Wrap Up Your Day!

 Respond to Literature Today we read about Goldilocks and the three bears. Why did she like the baby bear's things?

 Grammar Remember, the four parts of a complete sentence are a naming part, an action part, a period at the end, and an uppercase letter at the beginning.

Homework Idea Have children draw a picture of something they find at home that begins or ends with *g*.

PREVIEW Day 4

Tomorrow we will read about a lucky animal!

EXTEND Your Day

Understanding Signs

Materials drawing paper; pictures of signs: stop, school or pedestrian crossing, danger, no littering, no food or drinks

Discuss Why We Have Rules Hold up the stop sign and ask the following:

• What does this sign say?

• What are people supposed to do when they see this sign?

• Why is it there?

• What might happen if someone didn't obey this rule?

Time for SOCIAL STUDIES

Explain Why We Have Rules Every sign has a rule that goes with it. Why do you think people have rules?

Discuss the significance of the other signs, including where they might be found, what rules they indicate, and why these rules exist.

Indicate a sign in your classroom and ask children to tell you what it says. Pass out paper and ask children to draw a picture of a sign and someone either following or not following the rule.

Math

How Many?

Materials chart paper, glue, 15 pieces of macaroni

Macaroni Numbers Divide the chart into five sections. Label the sections *One, Two, Three, Four,* and *Five.*

Point to the word *one.* What is this word? (one) What comes after *one?* (two) *Two* comes after *one.* This word next to *one* is *two.* What word comes after *one* and *two?* Continue through the number five.

Give each child a piece of paper divided into five sections and fifteen pieces of macaroni. Instruct children to write the words *one* through *five* in the sections and glue the appropriate number of pieces of macaroni under each word. Have children write the numeral next to the number word.

One	Two	Three	Four	Five

Grammar

Sentences

The Sounds of Punctuation Review the end punctuation in *Goldilocks and the Three Bears.* When we see a period, a question mark, or an exclamation point, it means we are at the end of a sentence.

Ask children what each punctuation mark might sound like. Decide on a different sound to represent each mark. For example, a period can be a lip-smacking sound, a question mark sounds like a beep, and an exclamation point is a clap. As you read the story, encourage children to make the appropriate sound effects to indicate the end of a sentence.

Day 4
AT A GLANCE

Oral Language and Vocabulary
Calendar
Message Board
Build Background

Shared Reading
Trade Book *My Lucky Day*
 Skill Character

Word Work

Phonemic Awareness
Review Consonant Blends

Phonics
Blend Sounds
H/F Words *one, two, three, four, five*
Decodable Reader 22

Read
 Group Time < Differentiated Instruction

Language Arts
Grammar: Telling Sentences
Interactive Writing: Write a Newsletter
Speaking and Listening: Discuss Authors and Illustrators

Materials
- Calendar
- Talk with Me, Sing with Me Chart 22A, 22B
- Sing with Me/Background Building Audio CD
- Trade Books *My Lucky Day, Goldilocks and the Three Bears*
- AudioText CD
- Decodable Reader 22
- Alphabet Cards: *Aa, Dd, Ff, Gg, Hh, Ii, Ll, Mm, Nn, Oo, Pp, Rr, Ss, Tt, Vv*
- Picture Cards: p. 239

Calendar

Name the day and date
Ask a volunteer to find today's date on the calendar. Have children say the day, month, date, and year together.

Name letters in the month
Point to the name of the month at the top of the cal-endar. What is this month's name? What letter does it begin with? Let's spell the name of this month together. Continue spelling the names of the other months.

Message Board

Question of the day
Write and read the question as you track the print. Encourage children to respond in complete sentences.

> ## What adventure have you had?

Review grammar
Have children answer the question using a telling sentence.

Access Content Use the Day 4 instruction on ELL Poster 22 to support children's use of English to communicate about lesson concepts.

ELL Poster 22

Build Background

LET'S TALK

Develop oral vocabulary

Display Talk with Me Chart 22A. Point to the girl sitting in the chairs.

Which of the three chairs is small? Which of the three chairs is big? Which of the three chairs is middle-sized?

Encourage children to respond in complete sentences.

Talk with Me, Sing with Me Chart

LET'S SING

Sing "In a Small Cottage"

Display Sing with Me Chart 22B. Remind children that yesterday they sang "In a Small Cottage." Encourage children to listen for the words *middle-sized* and *small* as you sing verses 1 and 2.

Sing with Me/Background Building Audio CD

LET'S LEARN AMAZING WORDS

Oral Vocabulary   middle-sized   small

DAY 4 ROUTINE

1 **Introduce** *Middle-sized* tells about the size of something that is not too big and not too small. What is our new word?

Demonstrate Another word for *middle-sized* is medium. A car is *middle-sized,* or medium, when you see it next to a dump truck and a bicycle. What else is *middle-sized?*

2 **Introduce** *Small* means something is tiny. A cat is *small* compared to a person. What is our new word for something that is tiny?

Demonstrate People are *small* when they are babies, but they grow up to be adults. What else can you think of that is *small?*

3 **Review** We talked about two words today: *middle-sized* and *small.* Which word means the same thing as "little," *middle-sized* or *small?* Which word describes something that is "medium," *middle-sized* or *small?*

4 **Apply** Have children use *middle-sized* and *small* in complete sentences.

OBJECTIVES
- Build background.
- Develop oral vocabulary.

Amazing Words to build oral vocabulary

- bears
- cottage
- middle-sized

- porridge
- big
- small

ELL

Access Content Ask children how they say *middle-sized* and *small* in their home languages. Ask a volunteer to name something middle-sized and something small in the home language.

OBJECTIVE

⊙ Apply character analysis.

Materials

● Trade Book *My Lucky Day*

Extend Language Encourage children to label characters in the book with both Spanish and English words for *fox (el zorro)*, *pig (el cochinillo)*, and *bear (el oso)*.

Comprehension

LET'S READ *My Lucky Day*

Review *My Lucky Day*

Display the cover of *My Lucky Day.* Read the title and the names of the author and the illustrator. Ask children to explain the role of the author and the illustrator.

Trade Book

AudioText CD

● What are some things you remember about this book?

● Why is it called *My Lucky Day?*

Reread *My Lucky Day*

Reread *My Lucky Day* and ask children to pay attention to what each character wants.

SKILL Character

Apply character analysis to *My Lucky Day*

After reading, ask:

● What does the fox in this story want to do? **(eat the piglet)** What does the piglet want? **(an adventure)**

● The title of this story is *My Lucky Day.* Why do both characters think it's their lucky day?

● When the fox wakes up, will he still think it's his lucky day?

● What would have happened in the story if it were really the fox's lucky day?

Practice character analysis

Ask children to describe the similarities and differences between the fox and the piglet.

● What words could you use to describe the piglet? **(tricky, smart)**

● The piglet is smart and tricky. Is the fox smart and tricky too?

▲ **Practice Book 4** Character, p. 39

Phonemic Awareness

REVIEW PRACTICE Consonant Blends

Discriminate blends

I am going to say three words. Two of the words begin with the same sounds; one word begins with different sounds. I want you to tell me which words begin with the same sounds. Listen carefully: *glove, glad, crab.* Which words begin with the same sounds? *Glove* and *glad* begin with /gl/. *Crab* begins with /kr/. Let's do some more. Continue initial blend discrimination with the following word sets: *black, blue, green; clap, clock, frog; snug, truck, snail;* and *glue, spot, spill.*

Monitor Progress	**Check Phoneme Segmentation**

Check Segmentation I am going to say a word. Please tell me all of the sounds you hear in the word. Use the following words: *got, pop, sad, had, mom, flag, not, plan.*

If... children cannot identify each sound,
then... use the blending routine to practice each sound.

SUCCESS PREDICTOR

Day 1	**Day 2**	**Day 3**	▶ **Day 4**	**Day 5**
Check Sound Fluency	Check Retelling/ Letter-Sound Knowledge	Check High-Frequency Words/ Word Reading	Check Phoneme Segmentation	Check Oral Vocabulary/ Assess Progress

Phonics

Spiral REVIEW BLEND SOUNDS

Review letter names and sounds

Use Alphabet Cards to review the following letter names and sounds: *Gg, Ii, Ll, Oo, Tt, Pp, Ss, Aa, Dd, Mm, Hh, Nn, Ff, Vv,* and *Rr.*

Blend sounds

PHONICS ACTIVITY MAT

Write *Gil* on the board. I am going to blend the sound of each letter to say a word. Say the three sounds with me: /g/ /i/ /l/. Blend the sounds as I point to each letter: /g/ /i/ /i/, *Gil.*

G i l

Continue the routine with the following words: *got, pop, sad, Mom, had, plan, flag,* and *not.*

OBJECTIVES

- Review consonant blends.
- Blend and read words.

Materials

- Alphabet Cards: *Aa, Dd, Ff, Gg, Hh, Ii, Ll, Mm, Nn, Oo, Pp, Rr, Ss, Tt, Vv*
- Decodable Reader 22

ELL

Support Phonics In Spanish, the letter *g* does not appear at the end of words, so Spanish speakers may add a vowel sound after final /g/. Provide additional practice with words that end with /g/.

Phoneme Segmentation
SUCCESS PREDICTOR

OBJECTIVES

- Recognize high-frequency words.
- Read decodable text.

Group Time

On-Level

Read Decodable Reader 22. Use the Small Group Reading **Routine.**

Strategic Intervention

Read Decodable Reader 22. More practice with *Gg/g/*, p. DI·19.

Advanced

Read Independent Leveled Reader K.4.4. Use Leveled Reader lesson, p. LR7. Extend word reading.

Group English language learners by their reading ability in English.

(*i*) Independent Activities

Self-Selected Reading See pp. TR14–15 for a bibliography of books related to the weekly concept.

Practice Book Character, p. 39; Telling Sentences, p. 40

Centers Use the center activities on pp. 198–199 to practice this week's skills.

Journal Writing Dictate or write one sentence that tells about porridge.

Word Wall HIGH-FREQUENCY WORDS

Practice high-frequency words

Write the word *is* on the board. This is the word *is*. What is this word? Continue with *one, two, three, four, five,* and *a.* Look for these words in the story that we read today.

PREPARE TO READ

Introduce Decodable Reader 22

Display Decodable Reader 22 *Gil Got One.* Today we will read a new story: *Gil Got One.* Point to the title of the story. What is the title of this story? Point to the names of the author and the illustrator. *Gil Got One* is written by William Dillberts. The story is illustrated by Hillary Gem.

Small Group Reading

1 **Model Fluent Reading** Have children finger point as you read a page.

2 **Read Chorally** Have children finger point as they chorally read the page. Continue reading page by page, repeating steps 1 and 2.

3 **Read Individually** Have children read aloud a page in their group.

4 **Reread and Monitor Progress** As you listen to individual children reread, monitor progress and provide support.

Decodable Reader

Interactive Writing

GRAMMAR Telling Sentences

Identify telling sentences

Some sentences are telling sentences and some are questions. Write and read the following sentences:

What is your favorite color?

We read a book.

Which is a telling sentence? Tell me another telling sentence.

Telling sentences end with periods. What do we see at the end of the telling sentence?

LET'S WRITE Connect to Phonics

Review letters and sounds

Display the *goat* Picture Card. What is the name of this picture? What letter does *goat* begin with? What is the sound for *Gg*? Continue the review with the following Picture Cards: *goose, grapes, green*.

Write a newsletter

Let's pretend that once a year we write a newsletter to tell our friends about the adventures we have had. Today we're going to write a newsletter using words that begin or end with /g/.

Write the following text on chart paper.

> **Dear Friends,**
> **We've had many adventures this year.**
> **In June, we got a _____. (dog)**
> **In October, we ate many _____. (grapes)**
> **Tomorrow we are going to play in**
> **   the _____. (garden)**

Have children suggest words to complete the newsletter. Have a volunteer write the word to fill in the first blank. Repeat the word slowly if necessary. Then write the words to complete the remaining sentences. Read the newsletter together.

Independent writing

Have children write a letter to a friend telling what they did this week. Remind them to write words the way they sound. Also remind children to start their letters with the word *Dear*.

OBJECTIVES

- Practice telling sentences.
- Review letters and sounds.
- Write a class newsletter.

Materials

- Picture Cards:
  goat   goose   grapes   green

DAILY FIX-IT

goldilocks ate the porridge
(Goldilocks ate the porridge.)

ELL

Support Writing Observe whether children's writing shows word boundaries. Reinforce beginning and ending sounds of one or two words from their writing.

EXTEND SKILLS

Spelling If children have difficulty spelling words with medial vowels, have them practice spelling and blending words using Letter Tiles.

Name _____

✎ Draw   ✎ Color

| The dog can nab it. | The pig is big. | The cat had one hat. | The log is little. |

Directions: Draw a line from the sentence to the picture it tells about. Color the pictures.

Home Activity: Ask your child to tell you another sentence about each picture.

40 Grammar Telling Sentences   Practice Book Unit 4

The Three Bears

▲ **Practice Book 4**
Telling Sentences, p. 40

OBJECTIVE

● Practice discussions.

Access Content Allow English language learners to join in the activity when they are ready, or let them discuss the question in their home languages and then help them express their answers in English.

Speaking and Listening

DISCUSSIONS

Review discussions

We have been talking about authors and illustrators this week. We have been having a *discussion* about them. When you discuss something, you share what you know and you listen to what others have to say. What are some of the things we've said this week about authors and illustrators?

Practice discussions

Divide the children into small groups. In your groups, I would like each of you to tell the others if you think it would be better to be an author or an illustrator. Which job would be more fun? Tell the other children in your group why you think so.

Allow children a few minutes to practice in their groups, and then come back together as a class. Raise your hand if you think being an author would be more fun. Raise your hand if you think being an illustrator would be more fun.

✓ **Respond to Literature** Today we read about Gil's broken balloons. How many did he have?

✓ **Grammar** Make up a telling sentence about five balloons.

✓ **Homework Idea** Ask children to have a discussion about family adventures with a family member.

PREVIEW Day 5

Tomorrow we will read "A Canary's Song." What is a canary?

EXTEND Your Day

Good Citizens Follow Rules

Materials construction paper, paint, paintbrushes

Discuss Why We Have Rules Because people live in groups, we have rules and laws to help keep us safe and to help us live and work together.

- A good citizen follows rules and laws.
- A good citizen is respectful of other people's property.
- Do you think Goldilocks is a good citizen? Why or why not?

I'm going to tell you a story, and I want you to tell me what a good citizen might do next: It is time for lunch. Teacher has told everyone to line up. What does a good citizen do?

Work Together to Develop Rules Continue with other scenarios, such as finding something, wanting a toy at the store, and seeing a friend throw a food wrapper on the ground. Have children paint pictures of things that good citizens do and arrange the pictures in a display.

Grammar
Telling Sentences

Play a Game Have children sit in a circle. I will give you the title of a story and the first sentence. Then we will go around the circle, and each one of you can add one telling sentence. The title of the story we're going to tell first is *Goldilocks and the Three Bears.* Once upon a time, a great big father bear, a middle-sized mother bear, and a wee small baby bear lived together in a cottage in the woods.

Move around the circle, encouraging children to follow the storyline, to use their Amazing Words, and to add one telling sentence at a time. Pause to ask what makes a telling sentence. (It tells something, it begins with an uppercase letter, and it ends with a period.)

Science
The Five Senses

Good and Bad Remind children that people experience the world through their senses. Discuss sight, sound, smell, taste, and touch. What are some good sounds and bad sounds, good smells and bad smells?

Goldilocks' Adventure Make a chart with five sections labeled *She Saw, She Heard, She Smelled, She Tasted,* and *She Touched.* Ask children to list what Goldilocks experienced with her five senses and write the details in the appropriate column.

Day 5
AT A GLANCE

Oral Language and Vocabulary
Calendar
Message Board
Build Background

Shared Reading
Read Aloud Anthology
"A Canary's Song"
🔘 **Skill** Character

Word Work

Phonemic Awareness
Review Initial and Final /g/

Phonics
🔘 Connect /g/ to *Gg*
H/F Words *one, two, three, four, five*
Blend and Read Words

Read

Group Time ‹ Differentiated Instruction

Monitor Progress

Language Arts
Grammar: Telling Sentences
Shared Writing: This Week We . . .
Speaking and Listening: Discuss Authors and Illustrators

Materials

- Calendar
- Talk with Me, Sing with Me Chart 22A, 22B
- Sing with Me/Background Building Audio CD
- *Read Aloud Anthology* "A Canary's Song"
- Alphabet Card: *Gg*
- Decodable Reader 22
- Kindergarten Student Reader K.4.4
- Phonics Story *How Many?*
- Trade Book *Goldilocks and the Three Bears*
- Picture Cards: p. 245

Calendar

Name the day and date
Ask a volunteer to find today's date on the calendar. Have children say the day, month, date, and year.

Message Board

Question of the week
Remind children that this week we have talked about what people see, feel, smell, taste, and hear on an adventure.

> ## What kind of adventure can a little girl have?

Review oral vocabulary
Encourage children to use the oral vocabulary words *bears, porridge, cottage, big, middle-sized,* and *small* to discuss the question. Prompt children to respond in complete sentences.

Assess Vocabulary Use the Day 5 instruction on ELL Poster 22 to monitor children's progress with oral vocabulary.

ELL Poster 22

Build Background

LET'S TALK

Discuss characters

Display Talk with Me Chart 22A. Point to the picture of the bears.

- Do these bears look like the ones in our story?
- How are they alike and different?

Talk with Me,
Sing with Me Chart

Amazing Words to build oral vocabulary

- bears
- cottage
- middle-sized
- porridge
- big
- small

LET'S SING

Sing "In a Small Cottage"

Display Sing with Me Chart 22B. Remind children that the words *bears, porridge, cottage, big, middle-sized,* and *small* are in the song "In a Small Cottage."

Audio CD Sing with Me/Background Building Audio CD

In a Small Cottage

In a small cottage
there lived three bears,
One big, one small,
one middle-sized bear.
They went for a walk
to get some air,
When little Goldilocks
found their lair.

Talk with Me,
Sing with Me Chart

Monitor Progress | **Check Oral Vocabulary**

Demonstrate Word Knowledge Prompt children to use *bears, porridge, cottage, big, middle-sized,* and *small* in complete sentences. You may want to use Talk with Me Chart 22A to help with prompts.

If... children cannot use oral vocabulary words,

then... review definitions with Talk with Me Chart 22A and Trade Book *Goldilocks and the Three Bears.*

SUCCESS PREDICTOR

Day 1	Day 2	Day 3	Day 4	▶ Day 5
Check Sound Fluency	Check Retelling/ Letter-Sound Knowledge	Check High-Frequency Words/ Word Reading	Check Phoneme Segmentation	Check Oral Vocabulary/ Assess Progress

Oral Vocabulary

SUCCESS PREDICTOR

Comprehension

READ ALOUD

Read "A Canary's Song" Tell children that you are going to read them a story about a little boy and his bird. Ask them to listen for how the characters are alike and different from those in *Goldilocks and the Three Bears*. Listen carefully as I read the story. I am going to ask you how the characters are alike and different.

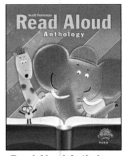
Read Aloud Anthology

CHECK SKILL Character

Identify character in "A Canary's Song" After you read the story, ask children:

- Who are the characters in this story? (Huey and his canary)
- How are Huey and the canary alike? How are they different? (They both are trying to sleep. Huey is a boy and the canary is a bird.)
- Can you see any ways in which they are like Goldilocks or the bear family? (Huey and Goldilocks are both people. The canary and the bear family are all animals that talk.)
- How are the characters in "A Canary's Song" different from the characters in *Goldilocks and the Three Bears*? (Huey is a friend to the canary. Goldilocks doesn't know the bear family.)

ASSESS SKILL Character

Assess character Use the blackline master found on page 248. Copy one page for each child. Have children draw the two characters from "A Canary's Song" in the appropriate squares.

CHARACTER
Draw the characters from "A Canary's Song."

Huey

The Canary

Note to Teacher: Have children draw the two characters from "A Canary's Song" in the appropriate boxes.

▲ **Teacher's Edition 4** Character, p. 248

Phonemic Awareness

REVIEW /g/

Practice initial and final /g/

What is the first sound in *gum?* Say the word with me: /g/ /u/ /m/, *gum.* The first sound is /g/.

What is the last sound in *big?* Say the word with me: *big,* /b/ /i/ /g/, *big.* The last sound in *big* is /g/. Review initial and final /g/ with the following words: *bag, jug, mug, goat, goose,* and *garden.*

Phonics

REVIEW *Gg/g/*

Connect /g/ to *Gg*

Display the *Gg* Alphabet Card. Point to the lowercase *g.* What is the name of this letter? *(g)* What is the sound for this letter? (/g/) Repeat the routine with uppercase *G.*

Word Wall HIGH-FREQUENCY WORDS

Practice high-frequency words

Write the word *two* on the board. This is the word *two.* What is this word? Continue the routine with *one, three, four,* and *five.*

Spiral REVIEW READ

Apply phonics in familiar text

Have children reread one of the readers specific to the target letter sound. You may wish to review the decodable words and high-frequency words that appear in each reader prior to rereading.

Kindergarten Student Reader

Decodable Reader

Phonics Story in Practice Book

OBJECTIVES

- Review initial and final /g/.
- Connect /g/ to *Gg.*

Materials

- Alphabet Card: *Gg*
- Picture Cards:

cap	cat	egg
flag	garden	goose
gum	moon	

- Kindergarten Student Reader K.4.4
- Decodable Reader 22
- Phonics Story *How Many?*

OBJECTIVE

⊙ Assess: connect /g/ to *Gg*.

Group Time

On-Level
Sets A and B

Strategic Intervention
Monitor Progress:
Check Phonics
Alternate Assessment, p. DI•20

Advanced
Sets B and C

i **Independent Activities**

Self-Selected Reading See pp. TR14–15 for a bibliography of books related to the weekly concept.

Cross-Curricular Centers Use the center activities on pp. 198–199 to practice this week's skills.

Journal Writing Draw or write about what you would have done if the bears found you in their home.

Support Phonics For guidance in teaching phonics to English language learners, see the *ELL and Transition Handbook*.

PHONICS /g/ to *Gg*

Group assessment

Divide a paper into four equal sections for each child. Display the *gum, moon, goose,* and *cat* Picture Cards. Ask children to draw pictures of the words that begin with /g/ in the top two sections. Then display the *egg, cap, garden,* and *flag* Picture Cards. Ask children to draw pictures of the words that end with /g/ in the lower two sections. Have children label their pictures.

Monitor Progress	**Assess Progress**
If... a child cannot complete the group assessment,	**then...** use the Reteach lesson on page DI•34.
If... a child correctly identifies several pictures with initial or final /g/,	**then...** assess word reading with Sets A and B on page 247.
If... a child correctly draws all four pictures of initial and final /g/ words,	**then...** assess word and sentence reading with Sets B and C on page 247.

⊙ ASSESS PHONICS

Set A: Read the words

Have individuals take turns reading the words. We're going to read some words. I'll do the first one and you do the rest. The first word is *got:* /g/ /o/ /t/. The word is *got.* For each child, record any decoding problems.

Set B: Read more words

Have individuals take turns reading the words. We're going to read some words. I'll do the first one and you do the rest. The first word is *dog:* /d/ /o/ /g/. The word is *dog.* For each child, record any decoding problems.

Set C: Read the sentences

For a cumulative assessment of phonics and high-frequency words, have each child read one or two sentences.

READ THE WORDS

got   dig

gas   log

READ MORE WORDS

Set B

dog   glad   grab

grin   pig   flag

READ THE SENTENCES

Set C

1. I see a grin on the pig.

2. The big dog can dig.

3. The dog is with me.

4. I got a little flag.

5. Can you tag me?

Note to Teacher Set A: Children read each word. Set B: Children read each word.
Set C: Children read one or two sentences.

Goldilocks and the Three Bears

SUCCESS
PREDICTOR

Draw the characters from "A Canary's Song."

Huey

The Canary

Note to Teacher Have children draw the two characters from "A Canary's Song" in the appropriate boxes.

REPRODUCIBLE PAGE • See also Assessment Handbook, p. 199

Monitor Progress

Shared Writing

GRAMMAR Telling Sentences

Review telling sentences

Review with children the definition of a telling sentence. *A telling sentence tells about something. It begins with an uppercase letter and ends with a period.* **Display the cover of *Goldilocks and the Three Bears**. What is the father bear doing? A telling sentence is *Father Bear is playing a violin.*

Illustrate telling sentences

Ask each child to draw a picture of one character from today's story. Encourage children to write or dictate a telling sentence for the picture.

LET'S WRITE This Week We...

Recall literature

This week we read three new books and we sang two new songs. Which book or song was your favorite? My favorite was the song "In a Small Cottage."

Write telling sentences

Let's write a telling sentence about some of the adventures a little girl had.

Goldilocks ate the small bear's porridge.

Goldilocks broke the small bear's chair.

Goldilocks slept in the small bear's bed.

Continue the list with the children. Then have children read the complete list with you.

Independent writing

Have children write a telling sentence or copy a sentence they dictated. Then have them illustrate their sentences.

OBJECTIVES
- Practice telling sentences.
- Write about our favorite things this week.

Materials
- Trade Book *Goldilocks and the Three Bears*

DAILY FIX-IT

i like a small cottage?

(I like a small cottage.)

ELL

Support Writing Supply English words as children write or dictate their sentences.

OBJECTIVE
● Discuss authors and illustrators.

Speaking and Listening

DISCUSSIONS

Review authors and illustrators

Remind children that the names of the author and illustrator are on the front cover of books. Many people have favorite authors and illustrators. Perhaps you have a book that you love to have read to you, or one whose pictures you look at over and over again. Have children select a favorite book and a page with their favorite illustration.

Discuss authors and illustrators

With a partner, have children tell and show the name of the author and the illustrator of the book. Then ask them to tell why it's their favorite. Have children share with the class something they learned from their partner about a book.

Wrap Up Your Week!

 Phonics This week we learned about the letter *Gg*. What is the sound for *Gg*? Name some words that begin with /g/.

 Shared Reading What was your favorite book or song this week?

 High-Frequency Words Write *three* and *four* on the board. Read these words to me.

 You've learned
006 Amazing Words
this week!

 You've learned
132 Amazing Words
so far this year!

PREVIEW Next Week

Next week we will read about an adventure to Antarctica. What do you think we will find there?

EXTEND Your Day

School Rules

Materials large mural-size paper, drawing tools, construction paper cut into 3 × 4-inch pieces, glue, sentence strips

Discuss Rules Remind children that a rule tells people what they should and should not do. Review rules that have already been set up for the classroom. Have children discuss how rules help keep order in the classroom and help keep us all safe.

Discuss safety rules for crossing the street. Ask children to suggest other rules for school and neighborhood safety. Write the rules on sentence strips.

A Safety Mural

A Safety Mural Glue the sentence strips onto a large mural paper. Divide children into groups. Give each child a 3 × 4-inch piece of construction paper. Have each group select a rule to illustrate and write words or complete sentences about the rule. Have each group glue their pictures and words or sentences on the mural paper near the rule.

Time for **SOCIAL STUDIES**

Words and Numbers

TIME + FOR MATH

Materials construction paper, crayons

Preparation Number a chart from 1 to 5 on the board.

Building Word and Number Awareness Have children look around the classroom. Ask a child to name an object of which there is only one, such as a door. Write the numeral *1* and the words *one* and *door.* Illustrate them on the chart. Read the chart aloud, and have children read it to you. Continue adding and reading quantities until the chart is completed.

Give children construction paper to construct their own chart of numerals, words, and illustrations.

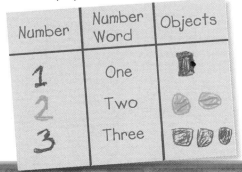

Number	Number Word	Objects
1	One	
2	Two	
3	Three	

Citizenship

Time for **SOCIAL STUDIES**

Be a Good Citizen Use the following questions to guide a discussion of character traits that include good citizenship:

- How do you think the bears felt when they found someone in their house?
- Should Goldilocks have apologized to them for going in without permission?
- What does it mean to forgive someone? Do you think the bears would forgive Goldilocks? What makes you think that?
- Have you ever forgiven someone for hurting you or taking your things?

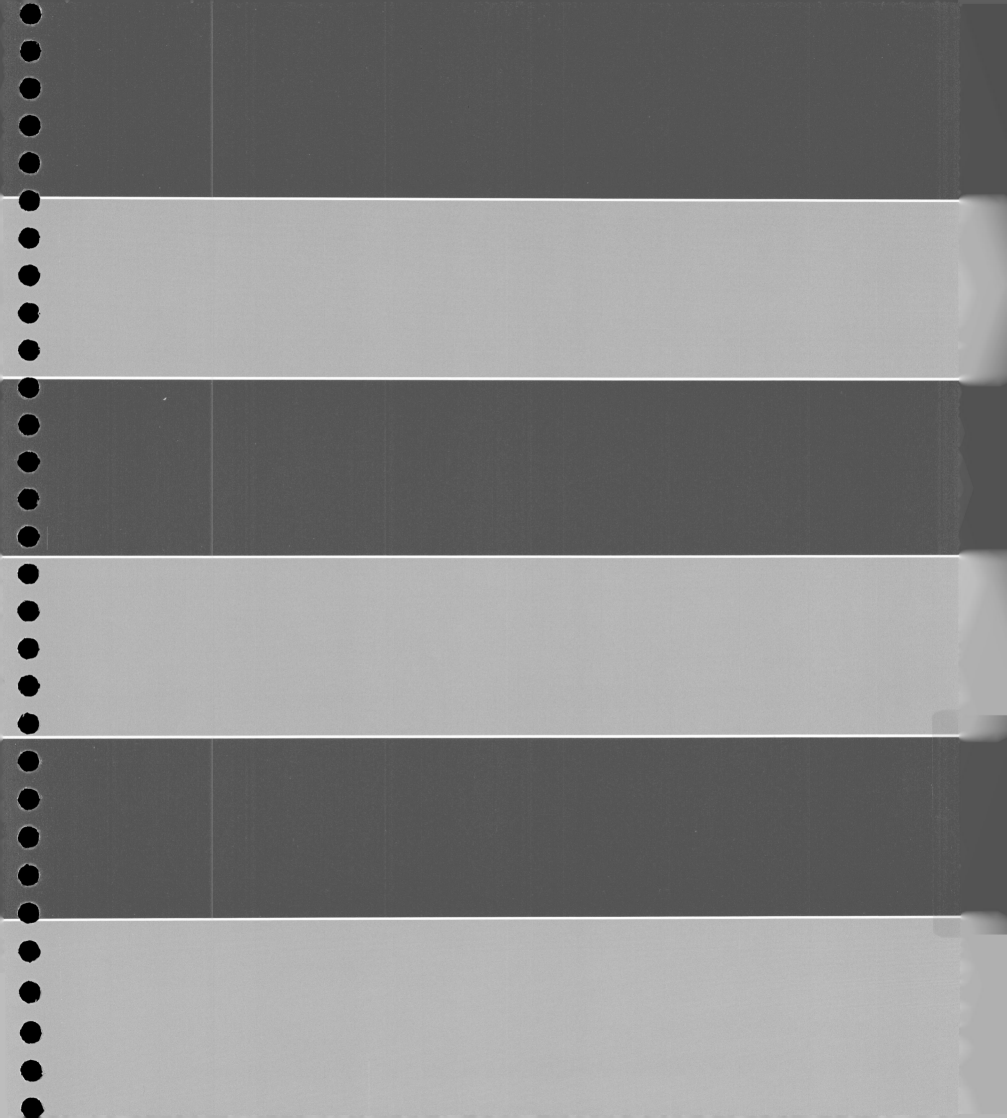

Unit 4
Let's Explore

CONCEPT QUESTION
Where will our adventures take us?

EXPAND THE CONCEPT
What would it be like to take an adventure to the Antarctic?

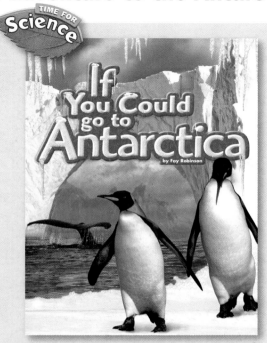

TIME FOR Science

If You Could go to Antarctica
by Fay Robinson

CONNECT THE CONCEPT

▶ **Build Background**

Antarctica	icebergs	seals
continent	penguins	whales

It's a Continent

It's a continent that's really very cold,
I don't think you'd like it when you're old.
It's a continent that's cold,
  it's a continent that's cold,
It's Antarctica, and it's really very cold!

▶ **Science Content**
Earth Science

Preview Your Week

What would it be like to take an adventure to the Antarctic?

Big Book

Audio CD

Genre	Informational Text
Phonics	Ee/e/
Comprehension Skill	Classify and Categorize

Meet the Author

Fay Robinson

Fay Robinson started out wanting to be an illustrator and ended up writing nonfiction for children. She tries to have fun while writing so that the reader will have fun reading. Formerly an elementary teacher, she now writes full-time.

Read another book by Fay Robinson.

Who Needs Birds When Dogs Can Fly?

Read It
ONLINE
PearsonSuccessNet.com

- Kindergarten Student Readers
- Listen to Me Readers
- Independent Leveled Readers
- Decodable Readers

Books for All Children

Listen to Me Reader

Emergent

- Develop oral language
- Develop phonemic awareness
- Read decodable words
- Read high-frequency words

Kindergarten Student Reader

On-Level

- Read connected text
- Apply phonics skills
- Read high-frequency words in context

Leveled Reader K.4.5

By David Erkam
Illustrated by Diana Kislauskas

Independent Leveled Reader

Independent

- Practice comprehension skill: classify and categorize
- Extend concepts
- Connect to Science

Apply Phonics

Decodable Reader

Phonics Story

TIME FOR Science

Integrate Science Standards

- Earth Science

✓ Read

Big Book *If You Could Go to Antarctica*

Independent Leveled Reader *A Walk in Antarctica*

✓ Build
Concept Vocabulary
Taking an Adventure to Antarctica, pp. 265, 275, 288, 297, 305

✓ Apply
Science

Weather, p. 273
Dressing for the Day, p. 273
Icy Cold, p. 286
A Trip to Antarctica, p. 295
Temperature, p. 313

Time for SOCIAL STUDIES

✓ Teach
Social Studies Concepts

Physical Characteristics of Places, p. 286
Landforms, p. 303

Weekly Plan

My Lesson Planner
ONLINE
PearsonSuccessNet.com

READING

60–90 minutes

TARGET SKILLS OF THE WEEK

- **Phonics Skill**
  Ee/e/

- **Comprehension Skill**
  Classify and Categorize

LANGUAGE ARTS

20 minutes

DAILY JOURNAL WRITING

EXTEND YOUR DAY *30 minutes*
Additional Activities for Full–Day Classrooms

DAILY SUCCESS PREDICTORS
for Adequate Yearly Progress

DAY 1 PAGES 264-273

Oral Language/Vocabulary

QUESTION OF THE WEEK, 264
What would it be like to take an adventure to the Antarctic?

Build Background, 265
Talk with Me, Sing with Me Chart 23A, 23B

Amazing Words, 265
Antarctica, continent, icebergs, penguins, seals, whales

Comprehension

Shared Reading, 266–267

Read Big Book

Use Text Features to Predict
Reader Response
Classify and Categorize

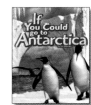

Word Work

Phonemic Awareness, 268
Introduce /e/

Phonics, 269
Connect /e/ to *Ee* **T**

High-Frequency Words, 269
Introduce *here, go, from*

Reread Decodable Reader 22

Grouping Options 258–259

Shared Writing, 271
Grammar: Introduce Uppercase Letters and Periods
Connect to Grammar

Speaking and Listening, 272
Introduce Listening for Story Elements—Character

Day 1 *Draw and label three different animals.*

Day 1, 273
Time for Science: Weather
Comprehension: Antarctic Scenes
Science/Art: Dressing for the Day

DAY 2 PAGES 274-286

Oral Language/Vocabulary

QUESTION OF THE DAY, 274
How can you go from Antarctica to here?

Build Background, 275
Talk with Me, Sing with Me Chart 23A, 23B

Let's Learn Amazing Words, 275
Antarctica, continent

Comprehension

Shared Reading, 276–281

Read Big Book

Recall and Retell
Classify and Categorize

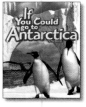

Word Work

Phonemic Awareness, 282
Practice /e/

Phonics, 282
Connect /e/ to *Ee* **T**

High-Frequency Words, 283
Review *see, have, do, my, a, you, I*

Read Phonics Story

Grouping Options 258–259

Modeled Writing, 284
Grammar: Practice Uppercase Letters and Periods
Respond to Literature

Speaking and Listening, 285
Let's Review Amazing Words *bears, porridge*

Day 2 *Dictate or write five words that rhyme with* pet.

Day 2, 286
Time for Science: Icy Cold
Phonics: Penguin Food
Geography: Physical Characteristics of Places

Monitor Progress and Corrective Feedback

Phonemic Awareness
Check Sound Fluency, *268*
Spiral REVIEW Phonics,
High-Frequency Words

Retelling and Phonics
Check Retelling, *281*
Check Letter-Sound Knowledge, *282*
Spiral REVIEW Phonics,
High-Frequency Words

Grouping Options for Differentiated Instruction

Turn the page for the small group lesson plan.

DAY 3 PAGES 287–295

Oral Language/Vocabulary

QUESTION OF THE DAY, 287
Do you want to sled in Antarctica?

Build Background, 288
Talk with Me, Sing with Me Chart 23A, 23B

Let's Learn Amazing Words, 288
icebergs, penguins

Comprehension

Shared Reading, 289

Read Big Book
REVIEW Main Idea **T**
 Classify and Categorize

Word Work

Phonemic Awareness, 290
Practice /e/

Phonics, 290
 Connect /e/ to *Ee* **T**

High-Frequency Words, 291
Practice *look, to, the, a, little, go, here, have, we, from*

Read Kindergarten Student Reader K.4.5

Grouping Options 258–259

Modeled Writing, 293
Grammar: **REVIEW** Telling Sentences
Connect to Phonics

Speaking and Listening, 294
Practice Listening for Story Elements—Character

Day 3 *Write and illustrate three adjectives that describe Antarctica.*

Day 3, 295
Time for Science: A Trip to Antarctica
Language Arts: Postcard from Antarctica
Comprehension: Classify and Categorize

DAY 4 PAGES 296–303

Oral Language/Vocabulary

QUESTION OF THE DAY, 296
What adventures can you have in the winter?

Build Background, 297
Talk with Me, Sing with Me Chart 23A, 23B

Let's Learn Amazing Words, 297
seals, whales

Comprehension

Shared Reading, 298

Reread Big Book
 Classify and Categorize

Word Work

Phonemic Awareness, 299
REVIEW /g/

Phonics, 299
 Connect /e/ to *Ee* **T**

High-Frequency Words, 300
Practice *here, go, from, the*

Read Decodable Reader 23

Grouping Options 258–259

Interactive Writing, 301
Grammar: Practice Uppercase Letters and Periods
Connect to Phonics

Speaking and Listening, 302
Practice Listening for Story Elements—Character

Day 4 *Draw and label three different things you would see in Antarctica.*

Day 4, 303
Time for Social Studies: Landforms
Math: Most and Fewest
Phonics: Matching Sounds

DAY 5 PAGES 304–313

Oral Language/Vocabulary

QUESTION OF THE WEEK, 304
What would it be like to take an adventure to the Antarctic?

Build Background, 305
Talk with Me, Sing with Me Chart 23A, 23B

Amazing Words, 305
Check *Antarctica, continent, icebergs, penguins, seals, whales*

Comprehension

Shared Reading, 306, 310

Read *Read Aloud Anthology "Peggy Penguin Goes to the Ocean"*

Monitor Progress
 Check Classify and Categorize

Word Work

Phonemic Awareness, 307
Review /e/

Phonics, 307
 Connect /e/ to *Ee* **T**

High-Frequency Words, 307
Practice *from, here, go*

Grouping Options 258–259

Monitor Progress, 308–309
Read the Words
Read the Sentences

Shared Writing, 311
Grammar: Review Uppercase Letters and Periods
This Week We...

Speaking and Listening, 312
Review Listening for Story Elements—Character

Day 5 *Draw or write about what you would wear in Antarctica.*

Day 5, 313
Time for Science: Temperature
Time for Math: Whale Math
Time for Drama: Hot or Cold?

KEY = Target Skill **T** = Tested Skill

Word Reading
Check High-Frequency Words and Word Reading, *291*
Spiral REVIEW Phonics, High-Frequency Words

Phonemic Awareness
Check Phoneme Segmentation, *299*
Spiral REVIEW Phonics, High-Frequency Words

Oral Vocabulary
Check Oral Vocabulary, *305*
Assess Phonics and Comprehension, *308–310*

SUCCESS PREDICTOR

Small Group Plan *for Differentiated Instruction*

Daily Plan
AT A GLANCE

Reading
Whole Group
- Oral Language/Vocabulary
- Comprehension
- Word Work

Group Time

Meet with small groups to provide:
- Skill Support
- Reading Support
- Skill Application

Read

This week's lessons for daily group time can be found behind the Differentiated Instruction (DI) tab on pp. DI·21–DI·25.

Language Arts
- Grammar
- Writing
- Speaking and Listening

Use *My Sidewalks on Reading Street* for early reading intervention.

DAY 1

On-Level	Strategic Intervention	Advanced
Teacher-Led *Page 270*	**Teacher-Led** *Page DI·21*	**Teacher-Led** *Page DI·21*
• Blend Sounds to Read Words • **Reread** Decodable Reader 22	• More Practice with e/e/ • **Read** Listen to Me Reader K.4.5	• **Reread** Independent Leveled Reader K.4.4 • **Reread** for Fluency

ⓘ Independent Activities
While you meet with small groups, have the rest of the class...
- Read self-selected reading
- Complete Practice Book K.4 p. 43
- Visit the Literacy Centers
- Write in their journals

DAY 2

On-Level	Strategic Intervention	Advanced
Teacher-Led *Page 283*	**Teacher-Led** *Page DI·22*	**Teacher-Led** *Page DI·22*
• Practice Word Reading • **Read** Phonics Story	• More Practice with e/e/ • **Read** Phonics Story	• Apply Phonics Skills • **Read** Decodable Reader 23

ⓘ Independent Activities
While you meet with small groups, have the rest of the class...
- Read self-selected reading
- Complete Practice Book K.4 p. 44
- Visit the Literacy Centers
- Write in their journals

DAY 3

On-Level	Strategic Intervention	Advanced
Teacher-Led *Pages 291–292*	**Teacher-Led** *Page DI·23*	**Teacher-Led** *Page DI·23*
• Practice Word Reading • **Read** Kindergarten Student Reader K.4.5	• Practice Reading Words with e/e/ • **Read** Kindergarten Student Reader K.4.5	• Extend Word Reading • **Read** Kindergarten Student Reader K.4.5

ⓘ Independent Activities
While you meet with small groups, have the rest of the class...
- Read self-selected reading
- Complete Practice Book K.4 pp. 47, 48
- Visit the Literacy Centers
- Write in their journals

On-Level

Teacher-Led
Page 300

- Blend and Read Words with e/e/
- **Read** Decodable Reader 23

Strategic Intervention

Teacher-Led
Page DI · 24

- Blend and Read Words with e/e/
- **Read** Decodable Reader 23

Advanced

Teacher-Led
Page LR9

- Extend Word Reading
- **Read** Independent Leveled Reader K.4.5

DAY 4

ⓘ Independent Activities

While you meet with small groups, have the rest of the class...

- Read self-selected reading
- Complete Practice Book K.4 pp. 49, 50
- Visit the Literacy Centers
- Write in their journals

On-Level

Teacher-Led
Pages 308–310

- Word Reading, Sets A and B
- Check Phonics
- Check Comprehension

Strategic Intervention

Teacher-Led
Pages 308, 310, DI · 25

- Check Phonics
- Check Comprehension
- Alternate Assessment

Advanced

Teacher-Led
Pages 308–310

- Word Reading, Set B
- Sentence Reading, Set C
- Monitor Comprehension

DAY 5

ⓘ Independent Activities

While you meet with small groups, have the rest of the class...

- Read self-selected reading
- Visit the Literacy Centers
- Write in their journals

 Grouping Group English language learners by their reading ability in English.

Take It to the NET™ ONLINE
PearsonSuccessNet.com

Connie Juel
For research on word identification, see the article "The Role of Orthographic Redundancy..." by Scott Foresman author Connie Juel and R. L. Solso.

TEACHER TALK

Choral reading is reading aloud together as a group.

Be sure to schedule time for children to work on the theme project *"Remember When* Album." This week children should make covers for their albums, making pouches for the passports on the inside cover.

Looking Ahead

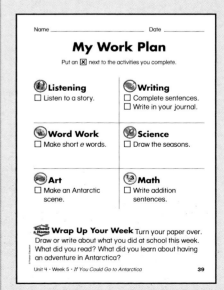

Name _____ Date _____
My Work Plan
Put an ☒ next to the activities you complete.

Listening
☐ Listen to a story.

Writing
☐ Complete sentences.
☐ Write in your journal.

Word Work
☐ Make short *e* words.

Science
☐ Draw the seasons.

Art
☐ Make an Antarctic scene.

Math
☐ Write addition sentences.

Wrap Up Your Week Turn your paper over. Draw or write about what you did at school this week. What did you read? What did you learn about having an adventure in Antarctica?

Unit 4 · Week 5 · *If You Could Go to Antarctica*   39

▲ **Group-Time Survival Guide** p. 39, Weekly Contract

ORAL LANGUAGE

Concept Development

What would it be like to take an adventure to the Antarctic?

 *to build oral vocabulary*

Antarctica	*icebergs*	*seals*
continent	*penguins*	*whales*

BUILD

- ☐ **Question of the Week** Use the Message Board to introduce and discuss the question of the week. This week children will talk, sing, read, and write about adventures in the Antarctic. DAY 1 264

Talk with Me, Sing with Me Chart 23A

- ☐ **Let's Talk** Use the Talk with Me Chart to introduce Amazing Words in a visual context. DAY 1 265

- ☐ **Let's Listen** Use the Sing with Me/Background Building Audio CD to build background, vocabulary, and concepts. DAY 1 265

- ☐ **Let's Sing** Use the Sing with Me Chart to sing a song about a very cold continent. DAY 1 265

Talk with Me, Sing with Me Chart 23B

DEVELOP

- ☐ **Question of the Day/Week** Use the questions in the Message Boards to discuss lesson concepts and how they relate to the unit theme, Let's Explore. DAY 2 274, DAY 3 287, DAY 4 296, DAY 5 304

- ☐ **Let's Talk** Use the Talk with Me Chart to build background, vocabulary, and concepts. DAY 2 275, DAY 3 288, DAY 4 297, DAY 5 305

- ☐ **Let's Sing** Use the Sing with Me Chart to sing a song about a very cold continent. Ask children to sing along with you, listening for the Amazing Words as they sing. DAY 2 275, DAY 3 288, DAY 4 297, DAY 5 305

CONNECT

- ☐ **Wrap Up Your Week!** Connect concepts and vocabulary to next week's lesson. DAY 5 312

CHECK

- ☐ **Check Oral Vocabulary** To informally assess children's oral vocabulary, have children use each word in a complete sentence. DAY 5 305

PHONEMIC AWARENESS

TEACH

- ☐ **Introduce** /e/ Introduce and listen for /e/. DAY 1 268

PRACTICE/APPLY

- ☐ **Listen for Sounds** Use the Phonics Songs and Rhymes Chart to listen for /e/. DAY 2 282

- ☐ **Practice** /e/ Isolate and discriminate /e/. DAY 3 290

Phonics Songs and Rhymes Chart 23

RETEACH/REVIEW

- ☐ **Review** Review /g/. DAY 4 299

- ☐ **Review** Review /e/. DAY 5 307

- ☐ **Reteach Lesson** If necessary, reteach /e/. DAY 5 *DI·35*

① Use assessment data to determine your instructional focus.

② Preview this week's instruction by strand.

③ Choose instructional activities that meet the needs of your classroom.

PHONICS

↻ **CONNECT /e/ to Ee**

TEACH

☐ **Connect /e/ to Ee** Introduce Ee/e/. DAY 1 269

PRACTICE/APPLY

☐ **Connect /e/ to Ee** Practice Ee/e/.
DAY 2 282, DAY 3 290

☐ **Phonics Story** Practice reading words with Ee/e/ in context. DAY 2 283

☐ **Kindergarten Student Reader K.4.5** Practice reading words with Ee/e/ in context. DAY 3 292

☐ **Decodable Reader 23** Practice reading words with Ee/e/ in context. DAY 4 300

☐ **Homework** Practice Book K.4, pp. 43, 48.
DAY 1 269, DAY 3 290

☐ **Word Work Center** Make /e/ words.
ANY DAY 262

Phonics Story

Kindergarten Student Reader K.4.5

Decodable Reader 23

RETEACH/REVIEW

☐ **Review** Review words with this week's phonics skill. DAY 5 307

☐ **Reteach Lesson** If necessary, reteach Ee/e/. DAY 5 DI-35

☐ **Spiral REVIEW** Review previously taught phonics skills.
DAY 1 270, DAY 2 283, DAY 3 291, DAY 4 299

ASSESS

☐ **Word and Sentence Reading** Assess children's ability to read words with Ee/e/. DAY 5 308–309

HIGH-FREQUENCY WORDS

HIGH-FREQUENCY WORDS
here   go   from

TEACH

☐ **Introduce** Introduce this week's high-frequency words and add them to the Word Wall. DAY 1 269

PRACTICE/APPLY

☐ **Words in Context** Read high-frequency words in the context of the Phonics Story and Decodable Reader 23.
DAY 2 283, DAY 4 300

☐ **Word Wall** Use the Word Wall to review and practice high-frequency words throughout the week. DAY 3 291, DAY 4 300, DAY 5 307

☐ **Kindergarten Student Reader K.4.5** Practice this week's high-frequency words in context of reader.
DAY 3 291–292, DI-23

☐ **Differentiated Text** Practice this week's high-frequency words in the context of differentiated text. DAY 1 DI-21, DAY 4 LR9

☐ **Homework** Practice Book K.4, p. 44.
DAY 2 283

Phonics Story

Decodable Reader 23

Kindergarten Student Reader K.4.5

Listen to Me Reader K.4.5

Independent Leveled Reader K.4.5

RETEACH/REVIEW

☐ **Spiral REVIEW** Review previously taught high-frequency words.
DAY 2 283, DAY 3 291, DAY 4 300, DAY 5 307

ASSESS

☐ **Word Reading** Assess children's ability to read this week's high-frequency words. DAY 5 308–309

☑ Customize Your Plan *by Strand*

COMPREHENSION

SKILL CLASSIFY AND CATEGORIZE Classify and categorize means to put things that are alike into groups.

TEACH

❑ **Skill Lesson** Introduce and model *classify* and *categorize*. DAY 1 267

PRACTICE/APPLY

❑ **Skill in Context** Model how to *classify* and *categorize*. Then read *If You Could Go to Antarctica*, guiding children as they *classify* and *categorize*. DAY 2 276-281

❑ **Skill in Context** Reread *See How We Grow* and apply *classify* and *categorize*. DAY 4 298

❑ **Leveled Text** Apply *classify* and *categorize* to leveled text. DAY 4 LR9

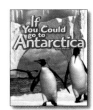
Big Book

Big Book

Independent Leveled Reader K.4.5

ASSESS

❑ **Check** Read "Peggy Penguin Goes to the Ocean." Then have children practice *classifying* and *categorizing*. DAY 5 306

❑ **Assess** Use the blackline master on p. 310 to assess children's understanding of *classify* and *categorize*. DAY 5 306, 310

Read Aloud Anthology

RETEACH/REVIEW

❑ **Review Main Idea** Review definition of *main idea* and apply to *If You Could Go to Antarctica*. DAY 3 289

❑ **Reteach Lesson** If necessary, reteach *classify* and *categorize*. DAY 5 DI-35

WRITING

TEACH

❑ **Write Together** Engage children in writing activities that develop language, grammar, and writing skills and practice phonics skills. Include independent writing as an extension of group writing activities.

Shared Writing
❑ **Connect to Grammar** DAY 1 271
❑ **This Week We...** DAY 5 311

Modeled Writing
❑ **Respond to Literature** DAY 2 284
❑ **Connect to Phonics** DAY 3 293

Interactive Writing
❑ **Connect to Phonics** DAY 4 301

PRACTICE/APPLY

❑ **Daily Journal Writing** Have children write about concepts and literature in their journals. **EVERY DAY** 256-257

❑ **Writing Center** Complete sentences. **ANY DAY** 263

GRAMMAR

TEACH

❑ **Introduce** Introduce uppercase letters and periods. DAY 1 *271*

PRACTICE/APPLY

❑ **Practice** Practice uppercase letters and periods. DAY 2 *284*, DAY 4 *301*

❑ **Daily Fix-It** Have children find and correct errors in capitalization and punctuation. DAY 1 *271*, DAY 2 *284*, DAY 3 *293*, DAY 4 *301*, DAY 5 *311*

RETEACH/REVIEW

❑ **Review** Review last week's grammar skill, telling sentences. DAY 3 *293*

❑ **Review** Review uppercase letters and periods. DAY 5 *311*

SPEAKING AND LISTENING

TEACH

❑ **Listen for Story Elements—Character** Introduce and model listening for story elements—character. DAY 1 *272*

PRACTICE/APPLY

❑ **Practice** Have children practice listening for story elements—character. DAY 3 *294*, DAY 4 *302*

REVIEW

❑ **Review** Review listening for story elements—character. Then have children identify the characters in a rhyme and act it out. DAY 5 *312*

INQUIRY PROJECT

TEACH

❑ **Unit Inquiry Project** Allow time for children to work on the theme project "*Remember When* Album." Have children make covers for their albums, making pouches for the passports on the inside cover. **ANY DAY** *xxiii*

Resources for Differentiated Instruction

Readers

Emergent

Listen to Me Reader

▶ **Oral Language**
Develop oral vocabulary.

▶ **Phonemic Awareness**
/e/ in initial and medial positions

🔁 **Decodable Words**
red   hen   pen   get
Ken

▶ **High-Frequency Words**
here   go   from   a
is   she   he   to

On-Level

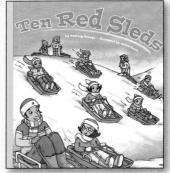

Kindergarten Student Reader

▶ **Connected Text**
Realistic Fiction

🔁 **Phonics: *Ee*/e/**
ten   red   sleds
get   Ben   tell   Ken
sled   Ted   end

▶ **High-Frequency Words**
here   go   from

▶ **Spiral Review: Decodable Words**
Nan   Nat   Dad   Sam
Bill   Don   Dan   at
and

High-Frequency Words
look   the   have   to
a   for   little   we

Independent

Leveled Reader K.4.5 Independent Leveled Reader

🔁 **Comprehension: Classify and Categorize**
Group like items together.

▶ **Concept**
What kinds of adventures you can have in Antarctica

▶ **Science Standards**
Weather: precipitation, wind, and temperature

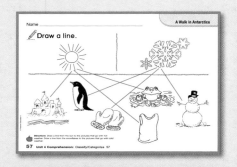

🔁 **Leveled Reader,** TE, LR10

My Sidewalks
Early Reading Intervention

ELL Resources

- ELL Poster 23
- ELL and Transition Handbook
- ELL Notes in Teacher's Edition, pp. 264–313

ELL Poster 23

ELL and Transition Handbook

For students who need intensive intervention

- Effectiveness proved by scientific research
- Instruction focused on early reading success predictors
- 30 minutes of daily small-group instruction

PearsonSuccessNet.com

Use the Online Database of over 600 books to

- Download and print additional copies of this week's leveled readers
- Listen to the readers being read online
- Search for more titles focused on this week's skills, topic, and content

Readers' Theater Anthology

Readers' Theater Anthology

- Six scripts to build fluency
- Poetry for oral interpretation

Homework

- Family Times Newsletter

Take-Home Books

- Kindergarten Student Readers
- Decodable Readers
- Listen to Me Readers
- Independent Leveled Readers

Literacy Centers

 Listening

Let's Read
along

 Word Work

Mystery
Match-Up

Art

Scenes from
Antarctica

- *If You Could Go to Antarctica*
- AudioText CD

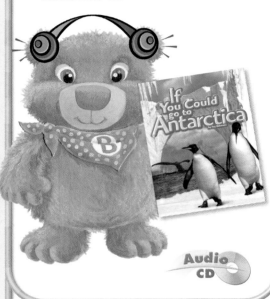

Audio CD

MATERIALS
index cards or squares of paper, paper, pencil, 2 brown paper bags

Make /e/ Words
1. Write *et, en,* and *eg* on the index cards or squares of paper. Place in a brown paper bag. Write the letters *b, d, g, h, j, k, l, m, n, p, s, t, w,* and *y* and place these in another brown paper bag.
2. Have children choose a card from each bag and put the cards together.
3. If the cards make a word that children recognize, have them write it on paper.
4. Have children place the cards back into the correct bags and draw again. Children may draw several times for this activity.

 Phonics Activities CD — This interactive CD provides additional practice.

MATERIALS
Patterns Book, p. 22: *penguins, seals;* dark blue construction paper, sponges, white paint, crayons, scissors, glue

Cut, Color, Paint
1. Have children color and cut out an Antarctic animal. Then glue the animal to the dark blue construction paper.
2. Have children add background and details to their picture with crayons.
3. Last, have children sponge paint "snow" with white paint.

Journal Writing

- **Day One** Draw and label three different animals.

- **Day Two** Dictate or write five words that rhyme with pet.

- **Day Three** Write and illustrate three adjectives that describe Antarctica.

- **Day Four** Draw and label three different things you would see in Antarctica.

- **Day Five** Draw or write about what you would wear in Antarctica.

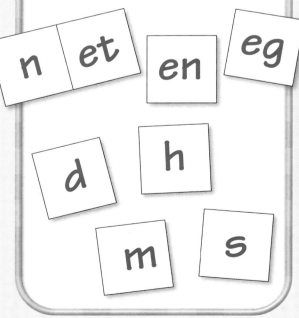

Writing

In
Antarctica

MATERIALS
a variety of writing paper and utensils

Complete Sentences

1. Write the following sentences on the board: *If I lived in Antarctica, I would see...* and *If I lived in Antarctica, I would need...*
2. Have children fold their paper in half. Have them write a sentence on each side of the paper.
3. Children can either draw a picture that completes each sentence or write the completed sentence in each box.

CENTER TIP If time allows, have children identify more than one object for each sentence.

If I lived in Antarctica, I would see a penguin.

If I lived in Antarctica, I would need a warm coat.

 Science

As the
Seasons Change

MATERIALS
construction paper, crayons

Show the Seasons

1. Make a sample paper for the center that has been folded into four boxes. Write the name of one season in each box.
2. Have children fold their papers to make four boxes, and copy the season names at the top of the boxes.
3. Ask children to draw and color a picture of what they wear and something they do in each season.
4. Circle the picture that is closest to what you would wear and do in Antarctica all year long.

1 2 3 Math

Illustrate
Addition

MATERIALS
paper, crayons, index cards

Addition Sentences

1. Write ten addition sentences whose sums are less than 12 on index cards.
2. Have children fold their paper into four sections.
3. Have children pick four index cards. Then copy the addition sentences into the four sections on their paper.
4. Have children correctly illustrate each addition sentence and write the answer.

$5+5=10$ $3+2=5$

$1+2=3$ $1+1=2$

ALL CENTERS

Oral Language and Vocabulary
Calendar
Message Board
Build Background

Shared Reading
Big Book *If You Could Go to Antarctica*
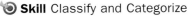 **Skill** Classify and Categorize

Word Work
Phonemic Awareness
Introduce /e/

Phonics
 Connect /e/ to *Ee*
Blend Words
H/F Words *here, go, from*

Read
 Group Time < Differentiated Instruction

Language Arts
Grammar: Uppercase Letters and Periods
Shared Writing: Use Uppercase Letters and Periods
Speaking and Listening: Story Elements—Character

Materials
- Calendar
- Talk with Me, Sing with Me Chart 23A, 23B
- Sing with Me/Background Building Audio CD
- Big Books *If You Could Go to Antarctica, One Little Mouse*
- AudioText CD
- Picture Cards: p. 268
- Alphabet Cards: *Bb, Ee, Gg, Ll, Mm, Nn, Ss, Tt*
- Decodable Reader 22
- Daily Fix-It Transparency 23

Calendar

Name the day and date
Point to today's date on the calendar and say the day, month, date, and year. Have the children echo you.

Spell the day of the week
Ask a volunteer to find today's date on the calendar. All the days of the week end in the word *day*. Who can spell the word *day?* Today is *Monday*. Look at the letters that spell it. Say them with me: *M, o, n, d, a, y*. We spelled *Monday*.

Message Board

Question of the week
Tell children that they will have an opportunity to talk, sing, read, and write about adventures in the Antarctic. Write and read the question as you track the print. Encourage children to respond in complete sentences.

> **What would it be like to take an adventure to the Antarctic?**

Build Background Use the Day 1 instruction on ELL Poster 23 to assess knowledge and develop concepts.

ELL Poster 23

Build Background

LET'S TALK

Build concept Display Talk with Me Chart 23A. Antarctica is the continent at the South Pole. The boy is pointing to Antarctica at the very bottom of the globe. These pictures show the land, water, and animals you might find in Antarctica. What do you see in the pictures? Prompt children to respond in complete sentences.

Build oral vocabulary This week we will be talking about adventures in Antarctica. We are going to learn six new words. Listen as I say the words; you may know some of them: *Antarctica, continent, icebergs, penguins, seals,* and *whales.*

Talk with Me, Sing with Me Chart

LET'S LISTEN

Share Background Building Audio Play the CD that features an interview with an explorer.

 Sing with Me/Background Building Audio CD

LET'S SING/PHONOLOGICAL AWARENESS

Sing "It's a Continent" Display Sing with Me Chart 23B. Tell children that they are going to sing a song about a very cold continent. Read the title and describe the pictures. Sing the song several times to the tune of "She'll Be Coming 'Round the Mountain." Encourage children to sing with you.

Identify repetition Have children name the repeated words in each verse.

 Sing with Me/Background Building Audio CD

It's a Continent

It's a continent that's really very cold,
I don't think you'd like it when you're old.
It's a continent that's cold,
it's a continent that's cold,
It's Antarctica, and it's really very cold!

Talk with Me, Sing with Me Chart

Amazing Words to build oral vocabulary

- Antarctica
- icebergs
- seals
- continent
- penguins
- whales

Options Before Reading

Activate Prior Knowledge

What Can You See in Antarctica? Ask children to discuss what they might see in Antarctica.

- What would Antarctica look like?
- What do you think the temperature is like?
- What would you need to wear?
- What types of animals might you find in Antarctica?

Oral Language

What Happened? Ask children to recall a time they went someplace new.

- Where did you go that was someplace different from your home?
- What was it like?
- Were the people the same or different?
- What was the weather like?

Develop Story Concepts

Make a Story Display the cover of *If You Could Go to Antarctica.* Tell a story about the water and land animals that live in Antarctica.

OBJECTIVES

- Use text features to predict a selection.
- Listen to a selection.

Materials

- Big Book *If You Could Go to Antarctica*

EXTEND SKILLS

Concepts of Print Remind children that sentences are made up of words, and words are separated by spaces to make them easier to read.

Comprehension

MODEL READING STRATEGIES

Use text features to predict

Display Big Book *If You Could Go to Antarctica.* Take a picture walk through the book and tell me what you see. This book is about a real place and real animals.

 Think Aloud It looks really cold there. Interesting animals live there.

The title of this book is *If You Could Go to Antarctica.* What do you think this selection will be about? Let's read to find out.

LET'S READ
If You Could Go to Antarctica

Model fluent reading

Read the selection with expression for enjoyment.

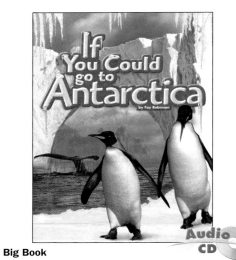

Big Book   **AudioText CD**

Shared Reading

ROUTINE

Day 1	Day 2	Day 3	Day 4	Day 5
Preview and make predictions about *If You Could Go to Antarctica.* Read the whole book for enjoyment. Introduce comprehension skill, classify and categorize.	**Reread** *If You Could Go to Antarctica.* Use the Shared Reading Notes to engage children in a conversation about the selection. Apply comprehension skill, classify and categorize.	**Reread** *If You Could Go to Antarctica.* Develop oral vocabulary by learning about new places and things. Review comprehension skill, main idea.	**Reread** *See How We Grow.* Apply comprehension skill, classify and categorize.	**Read** "Peggy Penguin Goes to the Ocean" in the *Read Aloud Anthology.* Assess comprehension skill, classify and categorize.

READER RESPONSE

Respond to literature

Have children describe the photographs in this selection. Remind them that the photographs are of a real place that is far away.

STRATEGY Predict

Check predictions

- What did you think the selection would be about?
- Which animal did you find the most interesting?

Use the following questions to guide discussion.

- Where is Antarctica?
- Is Antarctica anything like our town?

🔄 INTRODUCE SKILL
Classify and Categorize

Define Classify and Categorize

- In the story, there are many animals. Some live only in the water, some live on the land, and some live in both.
- We can remember information about the animals if we remember the ways they are the same. We can put animals that are alike together. This is called *classify and categorize.*

 Think Aloud In the book, all the animals live in a cold climate, but not all of the animals can go onto the land. Penguins and seals can go on land and in water. Why would whales not belong in that group?

Recall classify and categorize

Display *One Little Mouse.* Help children classify and categorize animals by the number of legs each animal has.

- What is the same about porcupine, opossums, squirrels, rabbits, frogs, moles, and mice? We can put them together in one group. We can call this group Animals with Four Legs.
- Snakes have no legs. Quail and chickadees have two legs. Snakes, quail, and chickadees do not belong in the group Animals with Four Legs.

Relate classify and categorize to everyday life

There are many ways we are alike. We are all people, but some of us are boys and some are girls. We can think of ourselves as two groups of people, boys and girls.

OBJECTIVES

- Respond to literature.
- Check predictions.
- 🔄 Introduce classify and categorize.

Skills Trace

🔄 **Classify and Categorize**

Introduce/Teach	TE: K.1 205, 214, 331, 340; K.4 267, 276
Practice	TE: K.1 229, 238, 246, 345, 353, 362, 370; K.4 281, 289, 298, 306
Reteach/Review	TE: K.1 DI-48, DI-50; K.2 37, 287; K.4 DI-49
Assess	TE: K.1 250, 374, 380–382; K.4 310, 380–382

Introduce Skill Review other nonfiction books about nature you have read as a class. Classify and categorize some of the animals using a T-chart.

OBJECTIVES

- Introduce /e/.
- Listen for /e/.

Skills Trace

Short e

Introduce/Teach	TE: K.4 268–269
Practice	TE: K.4 282, 290, 293, 301, 346, 354, 357, 365; K.6 154, 162, 165, 173 PB: K.4 43, 45–46, 48, 53, 55–56, 58
Reteach/Review	TE: K.4 307, 330–331, 346, 354, 371, DI-35, DI-36; K.5 47; K.6 140–141, 179, 235, DI-33
Assess	TE: K.4 308–309, 372–373, 380–382; K.6 180–181, 378–380; Unit 4 Benchmark Test

Materials

- Picture Cards:
  egg   elbow
  elephant   elevator
- Alphabet Cards: *Bb, Ee, Gg, Ll, Mm, Nn, Ss, Tt*
- Decodable Reader 22

Support Phonemic Awareness
In many languages, short vowel sounds may not exist or may only have approximations. English language learners may have a hard time hearing the differences in these sounds. Provide additional phonemic awareness activities to help children hear and pronounce words with short vowel sounds.

Phonemic Awareness

INTRODUCE /e/

Introduce /e/ Listen to our new sound: /e/, /e/, /e/. Say it with me: /e/, /e/, /e/. Display the *egg* Picture Card. This is an egg. *Egg* begins with our new sound. Listen for it: /e/ /g/, *egg*. Continue with *elbow, elephant,* and *elevator.*

Discriminate /e/ I am going to say two words. Tell me which word begins with /e/. Listen carefully: *elbow, foot.* Say the words with me: *elbow, foot.* Which word begins with /e/? *Elbow* begins with /e/. *Foot* begins with /f/. Continue with *elevator, down; monkey, elephant; escalator, up;* and *toast, egg.*

Listen for /e/ Teach children the following rhyme:

Picture Cards

Five Little Elephants

Five little elephants are at the water pool.
Evelyn said, "The water is cool."
Elbert said, "The water is deep."
Ellen said, "I want to sleep."
Eldon said, "I'll just put my trunk in."
Ester yelled, "Watch out! Ed's going to jump in."
Ed came running along the path.
Splash! Five little elephants took a shower and bath!

Have the children repeat the rhyme several times. When children are familiar with the rhyme, ask them to clap for the /e/ words.

Monitor Progress | Check Sound Fluency

Identify /e/ Words Tell children you will say these words, and they should clap for the /e/ words. Listen carefully: *Ed the elephant embarrassed Ellen; Elbert likes scrambled eggs; Eldon and Ester took the escalator up and down.*

If... children cannot identify /e/ words,

then... have them say /e/ several times. When you say /e/, your mouth is open and your tongue is behind your bottom teeth. Try it with me.

SUCCESS PREDICTOR

▶ Day 1	Day 2	Day 3	Day 4	Day 5
Check Sound Fluency	Check Retelling/ Letter-Sound Knowledge	Check High-Frequency Words/ Word Reading	Check Phoneme Segmentation	Check Oral Vocabulary/ Assess Progress

Phonics

CONNECT /e/ to *Ee*

Introduce Ee/e/

Display the *elephant* Picture Card. *This is an elephant. Elephant begins with /e/.*

Recognize Ee

Encourage children to find the letter *Ee* in your classroom. *Let's explore around our room for e's.*

Connect Ee/e/

Write the word *Ed*. *What is this word? Ed begins with /e/. What is the letter for /e/? Yes, E is the letter for /e/. Ed is a name so it begins with uppercase E.* Invite children to write the letters *E* and *e* on the board.

Picture Card

Review letter names and sounds

Display Alphabet Card *Ee*. *What is the name of this letter? (Ee) What is the sound of this letter? (/e/)* Continue with *Bb, Gg, Ll, Mm, Nn, Ss,* and *Tt* to prepare for the blending activity.

Alphabet Cards

BLEND SOUNDS

Blend words

Write the word *pet* on the board. *Pet has three sounds. I am going to blend the sound of each letter to say this word: /p/ /e/ /t/. The word is pet.*

p e t

Continue the blending practice with the following words: *met, set, bet, net, let,* and *get.*

Word Wall HIGH-FREQUENCY WORDS

Introduce here, go, from

Display *go*. *This is the word go. Say the letters with me: g, o. Let's read it together: go.* Continue with the words *here* and *from*. *You cannot blend the sounds in these words. Let's look in the book* If You Could Go to Antarctica *to find go, here, and from.* Add the words to the Word Wall.

go   here   from

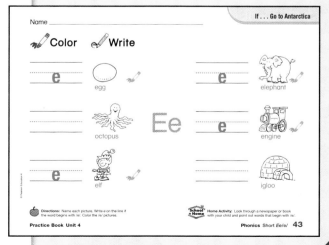

▲ **Practice Book 4**
Short *Ee*/e/, p. 43

SUCCESS PREDICTOR

OBJECTIVES

- Review decodable words.
- Write uppercase and lowercase *Ee*.

Group Time

On-Level

Reread Decodable Reader 22. Use the Small Group Reading **Routine**.

Strategic Intervention

Read Listen to Me Reader K.4.5. More practice with *Ee*/e/, p. DI·21.

Advanced

Reread Independent Leveled Reader K.4.4. Use the reading routine on p. DI·21. Reread to build fluency.

ELL

Group English language learners by their reading ability in English.

(i) Independent Activities

Self-Selected Reading See pp. TR14–15 for a bibliography of books related to the weekly concept.

Practice Book Short Vowel *Ee*/e/, p. 43

Centers Use the center activities on pp. 262–263 to practice this week's skills.

Journal Writing Draw and label three different animals.

Spiral REVIEW PREPARE TO READ

Review words Review these words from last week's Decodable Reader 22 *Gil Got One:*

Gil	got	sad	pop
Mom	had	plan	flag
not			

Review high-frequency words Write the word *a* on the board. This is the word *a.* What is this word? Continue the word reading routine with the words *is, one, two, three, four,* and *five.*

Small Group Reading

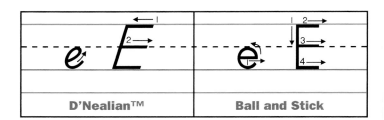

DAY 1 ROUTINE

1 **Model Fluent Reading** Have children finger point as you read a page.

2 **Read Chorally** Have children finger point as they chorally read the page. Continue reading page by page, repeating steps 1 and 2.

3 **Read Individually** Have children read aloud a page in their group.

4 **Reread and Monitor Progress** As you listen to individual children reread, monitor progress and provide support.

Decodable Reader

HANDWRITING

Write *E* and *e* Write *Ed* on the board. This is the uppercase *E*. We use uppercase letters at the beginning of sentences and for the first letter in a person's name. *Ed* begins with *E*. Watch as I trace the uppercase *E* with my finger. Follow the stroke instructions pictured below. Now you trace the *E* on your paper. Repeat the routine to write lowercase *e*.

e *E*	*e* *E*
D'Nealian™	**Ball and Stick**

Shared Writing

GRAMMAR
Uppercase Letters and Periods

OBJECTIVES
- Introduce uppercase letters and periods.
- Write sentences with uppercase letters and periods.

Introduce uppercase letters and periods

A complete sentence must start with an uppercase letter and end with a period. Show children what an uppercase letter looks like and what a period looks like in some simple sentences.

Identify uppercase letters and periods

Write: *i sat in my seat* and *I sat in my seat.* on the board. Ask children to find the differences between the two sentences.

LET'S WRITE Connect to Grammar

Use uppercase letters and periods

Have children dictate a sentence about cold weather. Write it on the board, but do not use uppercase letters or periods.

it is cold in the winter

i like snow

Revise and edit

Ask children to identify what the sentences are missing.

Independent writing

Have children copy the sentence they dictated and circle the uppercase letter and period. Then have them illustrate the sentence.

DAILY FIX-IT

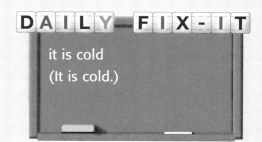

it is cold
(It is cold.)

This week's practice sentences appear on Daily Fix-It Transparency 23.

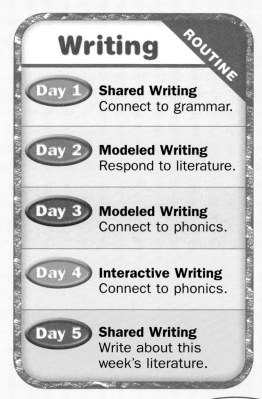

Writing ROUTINE

Day 1 **Shared Writing**
Connect to grammar.

Day 2 **Modeled Writing**
Respond to literature.

Day 3 **Modeled Writing**
Connect to phonics.

Day 4 **Interactive Writing**
Connect to phonics.

Day 5 **Shared Writing**
Write about this week's literature.

OBJECTIVES

- Introduce listen for story elements—character.

Materials

- *Read Aloud Anthology* "Peggy Penguin Goes to the Ocean"

Access Content Ask for volunteers to talk with you about characters they have read about in a story.

Speaking and Listening

LISTEN FOR STORY ELEMENTS— CHARACTER

Discuss listen for story elements— character

Characters are the people or animals in a story. They can be real or make-believe. If you listen carefully to the story, you can learn a lot about the characters.

Model listen for story elements— character

Last week we read *Goldilocks and the Three Bears.* Goldilocks is a character in the story. What other people or animals are in *Goldilocks and the Three Bears?* Would you want Goldilocks to be your friend? Would you like to live near the three bears?

Practice listen for story elements— character

Read "Peggy Penguin Goes to the Ocean" from the *Read Aloud Anthology.* Tell children you are going to read a story they have not heard before. Encourage children to listen carefully to learn about characters in the new story.

Wrap Up Your Day!

 Oral Language Today we read about a new continent. Did you learn something new about Antarctica?

 Comprehension Which animals live in the water around Antarctica? Which animals live on land there?

 Grammar Today we talked about two things you need to make a complete sentence. Can you remember them both?

Tomorrow we will read about Antarctica again.

 Homework Send home this week's Family Times newsletter.

EXTEND Your Day

Weather

Materials weather section from the newspaper, writing and drawing tools

Weather Report Ask children to describe the weather outside. Read the weather forecast for your local city. Point out the temperature. Explain to children that if the temperature number goes up, it is hotter; if the temperature number goes down, it is colder. Read the weather forecast for a city that has a different temperature than yours.

- Which city has a hotter temperature?
- What do you think they are wearing today?

Instruct children to fold their papers in half and illustrate a picture of what the weather looks like in their city. On the other side, they are to draw a picture of what the weather looks like in the other city. Write or dictate a label for each city.

TIME FOR Science

Comprehension

Antarctic Scenes

Materials shoe (or similar) boxes, modeling clay, construction paper, scissors, glue, Big Book *If You Could Go to Antarctica*

Make a Model of Antarctica Ask children to think of the land and animals in Antarctica. Distribute clay for making animals. Features may be added by sticking small pieces of construction paper into the clay. Have children cut land or water shapes out of paper and glue them into the box. Place animals in appropriate areas in the box. Display scenes around the room.

Science/Art

Dressing for the Day

Materials construction paper, drawing tools, various books about weather

Illustrate Weather Have children look at various books and discuss the weather. Ask children what they would wear in different types of weather. Write the names of the four seasons on the board and review seasonal changes with them.

Have children fold a piece of construction paper to make four sections. Ask the children to label each of the four sections with the name of a season. Then have them illustrate pictures of what they would wear outside in each season.

Day 2
AT A GLANCE

Oral Language and Vocabulary
Calendar
Message Board
Build Background

Shared Reading
Big Book *If You Could Go to Antarctica*
Strategy Recall and Retell
Skill Classify and Categorize

Word Work

Phonemic Awareness
Practice /e/

Phonics
Connect /e/ to *Ee*
Blend Sounds
H/F Words *here, go, from*
Phonics Story *Ten, Ten, Ten!*

Read

 Group Time < Differentiated Instruction

Language Arts
Grammar: Uppercase Letters and Periods
Modeled Writing: Write Sentences About Antarctica
Speaking and Listening: Expand Vocabulary

Materials

- Calendar
- Talk with Me, Sing with Me Chart 22A, 23A, 23B
- Sing with Me/Background Building Audio CD
- Big Book *If You Could Go to Antarctica*
- AudioText CD
- Picture Card: p. 284
- Phonics Songs and Rhymes Chart 23
- Phonics Songs and Rhymes Audio CD
- Alphabet Cards: *Aa, Bd, Cc, Dd, Ee, Ff, Hh, Ll, Nn, Pp, Rr, Tt,* keyboard
- Phonics Story *Ten, Ten, Ten!*

Calendar

Name the day and date
Ask a volunteer to find today's date on the calendar. Have children read the day, month, date, and year together.

Yesterday, today, and tomorrow
Circle yesterday and tomorrow on the calendar. One of these two days is tomorrow. One is yesterday. Who can tell us which is which?

Message Board

Question of the day
Write and read the question as you track the print. Encourage children to respond in complete sentences.

> ## How can you go from Antarctica to here?

Review high-frequency words
Remind children they learned the words *here, go,* and *from* yesterday. Have children find the words *here, go,* and *from* in the question of the day. Circle them and say them together.

Build Background Use the Day 2 instruction on ELL Poster 23 to practice the Develop Vocabulary words.

ELL Poster 23

Build Background

LET'S TALK/LET'S SING

Develop oral vocabulary

Display Talk with Me Chart 23A. Point to the photographs of the animals.

- What makes *Antarctica* so interesting?
- What animals live on the *continent* of Antarctica?

Sing "It's a Continent"

Display Sing with Me Chart 23B. Antarctica is a continent, or piece of land, that is very cold. Have you ever heard the words *Antarctica* and *continent* before? Ask children to listen for the words as you sing the song.

Sing with Me/Background Building Audio CD

Talk with Me, Sing with Me Chart

It's a Continent

It's a continent that's really very cold,
I don't think you'd like it when you're old.
It's a continent that's cold,
it's a continent that's cold,
It's Antarctica, and it's really very cold!

LET'S LEARN AMAZING WORDS

Oral Vocabulary Antarctica continent

DAY 2 ROUTINE

1 **Introduce** *Antarctica* is a big area of cold, ice-covered land around the South Pole. What is our new word for a large area of land near the South Pole?

Demonstrate Even though *Antarctica* is very cold, many animals live there. Penguins live there. What other animals live on the continent of *Antarctica*?

2 **Introduce** Antarctica is the name of a *continent*. A *continent* is a big area of land. What is our new word for a big area of land?

Demonstrate Antarctica is the name of one *continent*. There are seven *continents*. Does anyone know the name of any of the other *continents*?

3 **Review** We talked about two words today: *Antarctica* and *continent*. Which word is "a cold land with ice near the South Pole," *Antarctica* or *continent*? Which word is "a big area of land," *Antarctica* or *continent*?

4 **Apply** Have children use *Antarctica* and *continent* in complete sentences. Have them explain how cold they think it is in *Antarctica*.

Amazing Words to build oral vocabulary

- Antarctica
- continent
- icebergs
- penguins
- seals
- whales

Activate Prior Knowledge Ask children what words in their home languages are used for the words *Antarctica* and *continent*.

Access Content Encourage children to use the English words for items that are put into a category. For instance, encourage them to say the words *penguins*, *seals*, and *whales* and the category *Animals*.

Comprehension

MODEL READING STRATEGY
Recall and Retell

Retell the selection

Using the pictures as prompts, invite children to retell the selection.

Display the cover. Here we see one animal we might find in Antarctica. It is a penguin. What do you remember about penguins? What else might you see if you went to Antarctica?

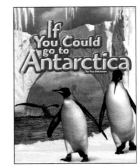

Big Book

Text to Self **SKILL**
Classify and Categorize

Model classify and categorize

Remind children that some of the things mentioned in the selection could be put together in a group because they are alike in some way. For instance, the book talks about penguins, seals, and whales. They are alike because they are all animals that live in Antarctica.

Think Aloud We could make a group out of these things because they are all alike. What could we call this group?

CONCEPTS OF PRINT Parts of a Book

Identify parts of a book

Display *If You Could Go to Antarctica*. Have children help you identify the parts of the book, such as the front cover, back cover, title page, and inside pages.

LET'S READ
If You Could Go to Antarctica

Reread the selection

Ask children to listen for things we would see in Antarctica and how they are alike as you read. Use the Shared Reading Notes to prompt conversation about *If You Could Go to Antarctica*.

 **AudioText CD**

TEACHING Tip

Antarctica You may want to show children more maps and give more information about the continents of the world.

Pages 2-3

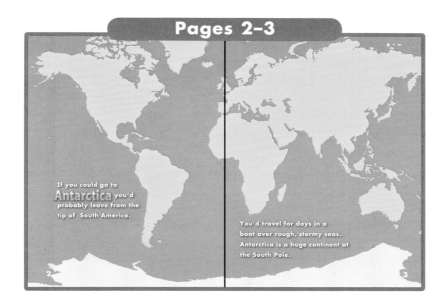

If you could go to **Antarctica** you'd probably leave from the tip of South America.

You'd travel for days in a boat over rough, stormy seas. Antarctica is a huge continent at the South Pole.

2   3

Shared Reading Notes

Point to the tip of South America on page 2. *If you could go to Antarctica, you would probably leave from here. What is the name of this continent? Child may respond:* South America

- You would leave from South America. From South America how would you get to Antarctica? **recall**

- Where is Antarctica on this map? ***wh-* question**

Pages 4–5

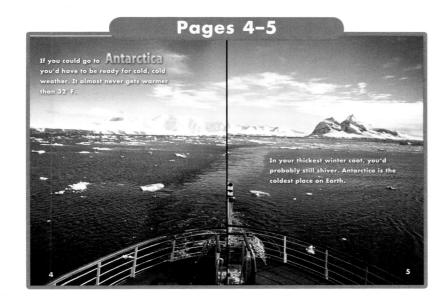

If you could go to **Antarctica** you'd have to be ready for cold, cold weather. It almost never gets warmer than 32° F.

In your thickest winter coat, you'd probably still shiver. Antarctica is the coldest place on Earth.

4   5

What is the weather like in Antarctica? Child may respond: It is very cold.

- It is very cold in Antarctica. How can you tell from the pictures that it is very cold there? **open-ended**

Expand Vocabulary thickest

How do you think the author feels about the weather in Antarctica? Why do you think that? Child may respond: She does not like it because you'd still shiver in your thickest coat.

Pages 6-7

If you could go to **Antarctica** you would find snow and ice that almost never melts.

On the shore near the sea, the wind can blow 50 miles per hour for weeks at a time.

6   7

What is special about the snow and ice in Antarctica? Child may respond: They almost never melt.

- The snow and ice almost never melt because it is so cold in Antarctica. What else makes it feel cold there? ***wh-* question**

Shared Reading Notes

What sometimes breaks off and falls into the sea? *Child may respond:* chunks of snowy ice

• Chunks of snowy ice break off and float in the sea. What are these floating shapes called? ***wh-* question**

Develop Vocabulary thunder

What animal do we see on this page? *Child may respond:* penguins

• Penguins live in Antarctica. Why do penguins gather in large groups? **recall**

Activate Prior Knowledge Ask children to tell you about what they know about penguins. Ask them if they have ever seen penguins at the zoo.

How are penguins different from most other birds? *Child may respond:* They don't fly.

• Penguins don't fly, but they can travel very quickly in the water. How do penguins move quickly on the ice? **recall**

Shared Reading Notes

Pages 14-15

If you could go to **Antarctica**, you might see seals. Seals live in the ice-cold waters. A thick layer of fat, called blubber, keeps them warm.

Seals come to land or solid ice to have their pups. Mothers must teach their pups to swim.

14   15

What other animal might you see in Antarctica? *Child may respond:* seals

- Seals live in the ice-cold water and have their babies on land. What helps keep them warm? **recall**

Pages 16-17

Humpback whales are huge but acrobatic animals. They can be 50 feet long—as long as a tractor-trailer—but they can throw their bodies completely out of the water.

If you could go to **Antarctica**, you might see whales lunging up from the water. Many whales visit the Antarctic in the summer.

16   17

What other animal might you see in Antarctica? *Child may respond:* whales

- Many whales come to Antarctica in the summer. Tell me about this whale. **open-ended**

Pages 18-19

If you could go to **Antarctica**, you might not see any plants. Most plants can't grow in the snow.

In some places along the coast where the snow melts, green mats of moss and grass sprout from the rocks.

18   19

Why might you not see any plants in Antarctica? *Child may respond:* Most plants can't grow in the snow.

- Most plants can't grow in Antarctica. How is that different from where you live? **open-ended**

Expand Vocabulary coast

Shared Reading Notes

Who are the only people you might see in Antarctica? *Child may respond:* scientists

- Scientists work in Antarctica. What are they studying there? **recall**

Expand Vocabulary scientists

If you could go to Antarctica, what would you see? *Child may respond:* icebergs, snow, and water; penguins, seals, and whales

- Antarctica is full of ice and snow, penguins, seals, and whales. Let's answer the question from the book: Would you visit if you could? Why or why not? **distancing**

Access Content Some children may not understand some of the figures of speech on page 22. Explain that "icebergs as big as forests" means very large icebergs; "white fields of snow" means that the snow covers miles and miles; and "sheets of ice" means large walls of ice.

Pages 20–21

If you could go to Antarctica, you might see scientists at work. They are the only people in Antarctica. They are studying the unusual plants, animals, and weather.

THE UNITED STATES OF AMERICA
AMUNDSEN – SCOTT SOUTH POLE STATION

20   21

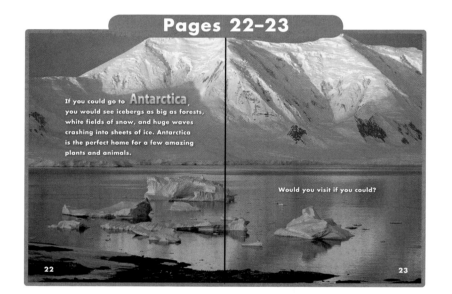

Pages 22–23

If you could go to Antarctica, you would see icebergs as big as forests, white fields of snow, and huge waves crashing into sheets of ice. Antarctica is the perfect home for a few amazing plants and animals.

Would you visit if you could?

22   23

CONNECT TO SKILL
Classify and Categorize

Connect *If You Could Go to Antarctica* to classify and categorize

This book told about what it is like on the coldest place on Earth, Antarctica.

- Which animals live in Antarctica?
- What is the land like in Antarctica?
- Who are the only people living in Antarctica?

If we made a group of *Things in Antarctica,* we could write whales, penguins, seals, icebergs, ice, ocean, and scientists.

- Could trees be a part of that group?
- Could cows and horses be a part of that group?

Trees, cows, and horses do not belong in the group *Things in Antarctica* because they cannot live in Antarctica.

Monitor Progress | Check Retelling/Summarizing

Picture Walk and Retell Help children use the pictures in *If You Could Go to Antarctica* to summarize the selection.

If... children have difficulty summarizing the selection,

then... use the Retelling Cards and the Retelling Rubric to help them move toward fluent retelling.

SUCCESS PREDICTOR

Day 1	▶ Day 2	Day 3	Day 4	Day 5
Check Sound Fluency	Check Retelling/ Letter-Sound Knowledge	Check High-Frequency Words/ Word Reading	Check Phoneme Segmentation	Check Oral Vocabulary/ Assess Progress

Retelling Plan

- ☑ Week 1 assess Advanced students.
- ☑ Week 2 assess On-Level students.
- ☑ Week 3 assess Strategic Intervention students.
- ☑ Week 4 assess Advanced students.
- ☑ **This week assess On-Level students.**
- ☐ Week 6 assess Strategic Intervention students.

Scoring Rubric | Expository Retelling

Rubric 4 3 2 1	4	3	2	1
Topic	describes main topic	identifies main topic with some details early in retelling	identifies main topic but does not include details	is unable to identify main topic
Important Ideas	gives accurate information about ideas using key vocabulary	gives accurate information about ideas with some key vocabulary	gives limited or inaccurate information about ideas	gives no information about ideas
Conclusions	draws conclusions to generalize beyond the text	draws conclusions about the text	is able to tell some learnings about the text	is unable to tell learnings about the text

Retelling

SUCCESS PREDICTOR

WORD WORK

OBJECTIVES

- Practice /e/.
- Connect /e/ to *Ee*.
- Review letter names and sounds.
- Blend words.

Materials

- Phonics Songs and Rhymes Chart 23
- Alphabet Cards: *Aa, Bd, Cc, Dd, Ee, Ff, Hh, Ll, Nn, Pp, Rr, Tt,* keyboard
- Phonics Story *Ten, Ten, Ten!*

Support Phonemic Awareness
Ask children about words in their own language that start with or include /e/.

Phonemic Awareness

PRACTICE /e/

Listen for /e/   Display the chart. We are going to learn a new song today. Listen carefully to the song. Play the CD or sing the song several times to the tune of "Polly, Put the Kettle On." Encourage children to join in. Have children identify words that contain /e/: *Ellen, sent, red, sled, Eddie, pet, wet, when, went,* and *next.*

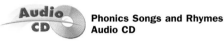 **Phonics Songs and Rhymes Audio CD**

Phonics Songs and Rhymes Chart

Phonics

 CONNECT /e/ to *Ee*

Recognize E   Ask children to identify *E* on the keyboard card.

Identify Ee   Remember we learned a new song with many *e* words. Let's circle the *e* words on our chart. Have several children circle a word that begins with or has *e* in the middle.

Connect /e/ to Ee   Display the *Ee* Alphabet Card. What is the name of this letter? *(e)* What is the sound for this letter? *(/e/)* Repeat the routine with *E.*

Monitor Progress | Check Letter-Sound Knowledge

Connect /e/ to Ee Have children write *E* on a piece of paper. The name of this letter is *E.* The sound for *E* is /e/. I am going to say a word. If you hear /e/ in the word, hold up your *E.* Use the following words: *egg, Ed, Sam, red, mop, jet, elf,* and *dog.*

If... children cannot connect /e/ to *Ee,*
then... have them trace the *e* on the Finger Tracing Card as they say *Ee/e/.*

SUCCESS PREDICTOR

Day 1	▶ Day 2	Day 3	Day 4	Day 5
Check Sound Fluency	Check Retelling/ Letter-Sound Knowledge	Check High-Frequency Words/ Word Reading	Check Phoneme Segmentation	Check Oral Vocabulary/ Assess Progress

 BLEND SOUNDS

Review letter names and sounds

Use the Alphabet Cards to review these letter names and sounds: *Aa, Bb, Cc, Dd, Ee, Ff, Hh, Ll, Nn, Pp, Rr,* and *Tt.*

Spell and blend words

PHONICS ACTIVITY MAT

Listen to the three sounds in *ten:* /t/ /e/ /n/. What is the first sound in *ten?* (/t/) What is the letter for that sound? *(t)* Write *t* on the board. Write *t* on your paper. Continue the routine with the remaining sounds.

Alphabet Card

Point to the word *ten.* Help me blend the sound of each letter together to read this word: /t/ /e/ /n/. The word is *ten.* Continue with: *pen, hen, pet, bell, can, fat,* and *red.*

PREPARE TO READ

Review high-frequency words

Write *see* on the board. This is the word *see.* What is this word? Continue the word reading routine with *have, do, my, a, you,* and *I.*

Small Group Reading

DAY 2 ROUTINE

1 **Model Fluent Reading** Have children finger point as you read a page.

2 **Read Chorally** Have children finger point as they chorally read the page. Continue reading page by page, repeating steps 1 and 2.

3 **Read Individually** Have children read aloud a page in their group.

4 **Reread and Monitor Progress** As you listen to individual children reread, monitor progress and provide support.

**Practice Book 4
Phonics Story, pp. 45–46**

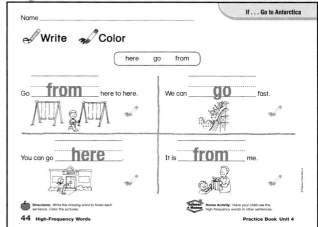

▲ **Practice Book 4**
High-Frequency Words, p. 44

Group Time

On-Level

Read Phonics Story *Ten, Ten, Ten!* Use the Small Group Reading Routine.

Strategic Intervention

Read Phonics Story *Ten, Ten, Ten!* More practice with *Ee*/e/, p. DI·22.

Advanced

Read Decodable Reader 23. Use the reading routine on p. DI·22. Apply phonics skills.

E L L

Group English language learners by their reading ability in English.

_i_ **Independent Activities**

Self-Selected Reading See pp. TR14–15 for books related to the weekly concept.

Practice Book High-Frequency Words, p. 44

Centers Use the center activities on pp. 262–263.

Journal Writing Dictate or write five words that rhyme with *pet.*

Letter-Sound Knowledge
SUCCESS PREDICTOR

OBJECTIVES

- Practice uppercase letters and periods.
- Write sentences about Antarctica.

Materials

- Picture Card: *lemon*
- Big Book *If You Could Go to Antarctica*
- Talk with Me, Sing with Me Chart 22A

DAILY FIX-IT

ken can get a pet

(Ken can get a pet.)

Writer's Checkup

- ✔ The first word in a sentence begins with an uppercase letter. Did I do that?
- ✔ A sentence should end with a period. Did I do that?
- ✔ A sentence should make sense. Does my sentence make sense?
- ✔ A good writer uses his or her best handwriting. Did I do that?

Modeled Writing

GRAMMAR
Uppercase Letters and Periods

Practice uppercase letters and periods

Display the *lemon* Picture Card. This is a picture of a lemon. Let's write a sentence about it. *A lemon is yellow.* When we have a telling sentence, we have to make the first letter uppercase and put a period at the end.

Picture Card

Identify uppercase letters and periods

Display pages 8 and 9 of *If You Could Go to Antarctica*. Guide children to identify sentences that begin with a uppercase letter and end with a period. Tell them that the word *Antarctica* begins with an uppercase letter every time it is written because it is the name of a specific place.

LET'S WRITE Respond to Literature

Discuss *If You Could Go to Antarctica*

Display *If You Could Go to Antarctica*. Ask children to tell about things they would see there. Encourage them to point out the uppercase letters and periods in the text.

Model writing a sentence

If I could go to Antarctica, I would see many things. I would see different kinds of animals and a lot of ice. I might also see a few people. I would like to see penguins the most. For my sentence I am going to write:

I would see a penguin.

Independent writing

Have children draw a picture of what they might see in Antarctica. Then have them write or dictate a label for their pictures. Gather children's papers to make a class book.

Speaking and Listening

LET'S REVIEW AMAZING WORDS

Display Talk with Me Chart 22A. Review these Amazing Words from last week.

DAY 2 ROUTINE

Oral Vocabulary   bears   porridge

1 **Introduce** *Bears* are large animals with long, shaggy fur. What is our new word for these animals?

Demonstrate Tell me about when *bears* hibernate.

2 **Introduce** The bears in the story made a hot cereal like oatmeal called *porridge*. What is the name of the hot cereal?

Demonstrate What is your favorite kind of cereal? Have you ever had *porridge?*

3 **Review** We talked about two words today: *bears* and *porridge.* Which word names large furry animals, *bears* or *porridge?* Which word names a hot cereal, *bears* or *porridge?*

4 **Apply** Have children use *bears* and *porridge* in complete sentences. Have them act like *bears* eating *porridge.*

Wrap Up Your Day!

✓ **Oral Language** Today we read about Antarctica. What were some of the things you might see in Antarctica? What do you remember about them?

✓ **Grammar** Remember, we use uppercase letters in special names and to start a sentence. What do we use at the end of a sentence?

✓ **Homework Idea** Have children take their Phonics Story home to share with their families.

PREVIEW Day 3

Tomorrow we will read about Antarctica again. Which animal would you like to learn more about?

EXTEND Your Day

Icy Cold

Materials two bowls, ice cubes, water, two thermometers

How Cold Is Ice? Fill two identical bowls, one with water (room temperature) and one with ice cubes. Explain to children how to read the thermometer. (Read on the Fahrenheit scale.) Place one thermometer in the ice bowl and one in the water bowl. Help children read the thermometers. Write the temperatures of each bowl on the board with the appropriate label *Ice* or *Water*.

• Which bowl is colder?

• Which temperature is colder?

Tell children that the lower number means a colder temperature. What will happen if I leave the bowl of ice here until tomorrow?

Confirm tomorrow that the ice has melted and measure the temperatures in the bowls again.

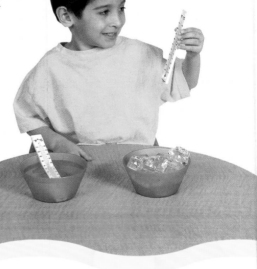

Phonics

Penguin Food

Materials construction-paper squares, penguin outline on large sheet of paper

Feed the Penguin Attach the penguin outline to a bulletin board. Give each child a construction-paper square. Have children draw a picture of an /e/ word on the square. Then have them label the picture. Ask a child to show his or her picture. If the picture has /e/, attach it to the bulletin board by the penguin. Continue until everyone has had a turn to feed the penguin.

Geography

Physical Characteristics of Places

Icebergs Have children look at photographs of icebergs. Then ask them to think of describing words to tell about icebergs.

Preparation Freeze water in a small bowl or container to make a mini-iceberg. In a large bowl of very cold water, float the iceberg and observe its properties. Does it get smaller? Does it move around?

Remind children that icebergs float in the ocean in much the same way their "iceberg" is floating. Ask them to describe the iceberg you made. In what ways is it the same description they used for the large icebergs they saw in the photographs? In what ways is it different?

Calendar

Name the day and date
Ask a volunteer to find today's date on the calendar. Have children recite the day, month, date, and year.

Count days
Display this month's calendar page and point to each day as you count together the days in a week. Point out that it is seven days, or one week, from Wednesday (counting starts on Thursday) to Wednesday.

Message Board

Question of the day
Write and read the question as you track the print. Encourage children to respond in complete sentences.

> ## Do you want to sled in Antarctica?

Review phonics
Read the question and ask a volunteer to find the word with /e/. Then have children name other *-ed* words, such as *red, bed, fed, led, Ned, Ted, wed, sped,* and *Fred.*

Extend Language Use the Day 3 instruction on ELL Poster 23 to extend and enrich language.

ELL Poster

Oral Language and Vocabulary
Calendar
Message Board
Build Background

Shared Reading
Big Book *If You Could Go to Antarctica*
Skill Main idea
Skill Classify and Categorize

Word Work
Phonemic Awareness
Practice /e/

Phonics
Connect /e/ to *Ee*
Blend Onset and Rime
H/F Words *here, go, from*
Kindergarten Student Reader K.4.5

Read
Group Time < Differentiated Instruction

Language Arts
Grammar: Telling Sentences
Modeled Writing: Write About Winter Adventures
Speaking and Listening: Listen for Story Elements—Character

Materials
- Calendar
- Talk with Me, Sing with Me Chart 23A, 23B
- Sing with Me/Background Building Audio CD
- Big Books *If You Could Go to Antarctica, Animal ABCs*
- AudioText CD
- Picture Cards: pp. 290, 293
- Kindergarten Student Reader K.4.5
- AlphaBuddy
- Alphabet Cards: *Bb, Dd, Ee, Gg, Ii, Kk, Ll, Nn, Oo, Rr, Ss, Tt*

- Build background.
- Develop oral vocabulary.

Materials

- Talk with Me, Sing with Me Chart 23A, 23B

to build oral vocabulary

- Antarctica
- continent
- icebergs
- penguins
- seals
- whales

E L L

Access Content Ask children what words in their home languages are used for *icebergs* and *penguins*.

Build Background

LET'S TALK

Discuss Antarctica

Display Talk with Me Chart 23A.

- What do we call these pieces of floating ice? *(icebergs)* Icebergs float in the water all around Antarctica and other cold continents.

- What are these animals called? *(penguins)* Penguins are birds, but they cannot fly.

Talk with Me, Sing with Me Chart

LET'S SING

Sing "It's a Continent"

Display Sing with Me Chart 23B. Sing "It's a Continent." Today sing both verses. Ask children to clap when they hear the words *icebergs* and *penguins*.

 **Sing with Me/Background Building Audio CD**

LET'S LEARN AMAZING WORDS

Oral Vocabulary icebergs penguins

DAY 3 ROUTINE

1 **Introduce** Huge chunks of ice that float in the ocean are called *icebergs.* What's our new word for the huge chunks of ice floating near Antarctica? **Demonstrate** Did you know that *icebergs* can be as tall as buildings?

2 **Introduce** *Penguins* are sea birds with flippers that live in Antarctica. *Penguins* can swim and walk but cannot fly. What's our new word for these birds? **Demonstrate** Have you ever seen *penguins* at the zoo diving into the cold water?

3 **Review** We talked about two words today: *icebergs* and *penguins.* Which word means "huge chunks of floating ice," *icebergs* or *penguins?* Which word means "sea birds of Antarctica," *icebergs* or *penguins?*

4 **Apply** Have children use *icebergs* and *penguins* in complete sentences. Have them pretend to be *penguins* walking on *icebergs.*

Comprehension

REVIEW SKILL Main Idea

Review main idea

Remind children that when they hear a selection, they can think about what the book is all about.

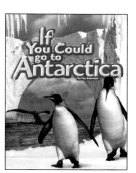

Big Book

Apply main idea

- What was *If You Could Go to Antarctica* all about? (the continent of Antarctica and what it is like)

- Antarctica is icy and cold. Antarctica has penguins, whales, and seals, but very few plants. There are few plants because it almost never gets warm enough for them to grow. This is what the selection is all about.

LET'S READ
If You Could Go to Antarctica

Develop vocabulary

Reread *If You Could Go to Antarctica.* Develop vocabulary by having children talk about the various animals mentioned in the book. Encourage them to use words such as *Antarctica, continent, icebergs, penguins, seals,* and *whales.*

 **AudioText CD**

SKILL Classify and Categorize

Practice classify and categorize

Remind children that the animals in *If You Could Go to Antarctica* all swim, so in that way they are the same. But in other ways they are each different.

- What kind of animal are penguins? (birds)
- Which animal in the book can lunge high out of the ocean and then dive deep underwater? (the whale)
- Who wears coats, boots, scarves, and gloves to keep warm in Antarctica? (people)

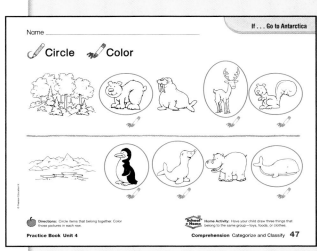

▲ **Practice Book 4**
Classify and Categorize, p. 47

Big Book

OBJECTIVES

- Practice /e/.
- Connect /e/ to *Ee*.
- Blend onset and rime.

Materials

- Picture Card:
  egg
- Big Book *Animal ABCs*
- Kindergarten Student Reader K.4.5
- Alphabet Cards: *Bb, Dd, Ee, Gg, Ii, Kk, Ll, Nn, Oo, Rr, Ss, Tt*

Phonemic Awareness

PRACTICE /e/

Isolate initial /e/

Show children the *egg* Picture Card. What is the first sound in *egg?* Say the word with me: /e/ /g/, *egg.* The first sound in *egg* is /e/. Continue practice with *Ed* and *elf.*

Discriminate medial /e/

Listen to the three sounds in this word, red /r/ /e/ /d/, red. What is the middle sound in *red?* I am going to say two words, and I want you to tell me which word has middle /e/. Listen carefully: *big bed.* Which word has middle /e/? *Bed* has middle /e/. The middle sound in *big* is /i/. Continue with the following word pairs: *pink dress; blue bell; one hen; six men; wet cows; pig pen;* and *green sled.*

Picture Card

Phonics

CONNECT /e/ to *Ee*

Connect /e/ to *Ee*

Display page 5 of *Animal ABCs.* What animal is this? (elephant) What is the name of the first letter in *elephant? (e)* What is the sound for *e?* (/e/)

Blend onset and rime

Write the word *pet* on the board. This is the word *pet.* Say it with me: /p/ -et, *pet.* What is the middle sound in the word *pet?* Point to the *e.* /e/ is the middle sound in *pet.* Repeat with *set, let, met, bet, net, men, pen, den, hen, Len, Meg, peg,* and *beg.*

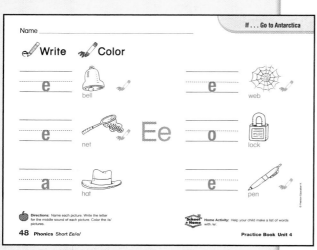

▲ **Practice Book 4**
Consonant *Ee*/e/, p. 48

Spiral REVIEW — BLEND SOUNDS

Review letter names and sounds

Display the *Ee* Alphabet Card. The name of this letter is *e*. What is the name of this letter? The sound for this letter is /e/. What is the sound for this letter? Review the following letters: *Bb, Dd, Gg, Ii, Kk, Ll, Nn, Oo, Rr, Ss,* and *Tt*.

Blend sounds

PHONICS ACTIVITY MAT

Write *Nan* on the board. I am going to blend the sound of each letter together to say this word: /n/ /a/ /n/.

N a n

This word is *Nan*. Say the sounds with me: /n/ /a/ /n/. Now blend the sounds with me as I point to each letter. The word is *Nan*. Continue blending practice with: *Nat, Dad, gets, red, sleds, get, Ben, Sam, and, tell, at, end, ten, Ken, Bill, Don, Dan,* and *Ted*.

Word Wall — HIGH-FREQUENCY WORDS

Practice high-frequency words

Write the word *look* on the board. This is the word *look*. What is this word? Repeat with *to, the, a, little, go, here, have, we,* and *from*. Look for these words in the story we read today.

Monitor Progress | High-Frequency Words/Word Reading

High-Frequency Words Write *here, go,* and *from* on the board. Have children take turns reading the words.

Blend Sounds to Read Words Write the following words on the board: *Nat, Ted, end, Ben, sled, Sam, Don, Dad, tell, Bill, ten, Ken, red, Dan,* and *get*. Have children blend the sound of each letter together to read the word.

If... children cannot read high-frequency words,
then... write missed words on cards for practice at home.

If... children cannot read decodable words,
then... provide additional blending practice.

If... children successfully read words,
then... have them read Kindergarten Student Reader K.4.5 *Ten Red Sleds*.

SUCCESS PREDICTOR

Day 1	Day 2	▶ Day 3	Day 4	Day 5
Check Sound Fluency	Check Retelling/ Letter-Sound Knowledge	Check High-Frequency Words/ Word Reading	Check Phoneme Segmentation	Check Oral Vocabulary/ Assess Progress

Group Time

On-Level

Read Kindergarten Student Reader K.4.5. Use the Small Group Reading **Routine.**

Strategic Intervention

Read Kindergarten Student Reader K.4.5. More practice with *Ee*/e/, p. DI·23.

Advanced

Read Kindergarten Student Reader K.4.5. Use the reading routine on p. DI·23. Extend word reading.

ELL

Group English language learners by their reading ability in English.

(i) Independent Activities

Self-Selected Reading See pp. TR14–15 for a bibliography of books related to the weekly concept.

Practice Book Classify and Categorize, p. 47; Short *Ee*/e/, p. 48

Centers Use the center activities on pp. 262–263 to practice this week's skills.

Journal Writing Write and illustrate three adjectives that describe Antarctica.

Spiral REVIEW

- Reviews previously taught high-frequency words.
- Reviews previously taught letters and sounds.

Word Reading

SUCCESS PREDICTOR

PREPARE TO READ

Access Content Ask children to point out the naming words, such as *Nat, Nan, Ben,* and *Dad.* Have children act out the way you sit on a sled. Demonstrate the concept *end to end.*

Introduce Kindergarten Student Reader K.4.5

Display the title page. We are going to read a new story. Point to the title. What is the title of this story? *Ten Red Sleds* was written by Padraig George.

DAY 3 ROUTINE

Small Group Reading

1 **Model Fluent Reading** Have children finger point as you read a page.

2 **Read Chorally** Have children finger point as they chorally read the page. Continue reading page by page, repeating steps 1 and 2.

3 **Read Individually** Have children read aloud a page in their group.

4 **Reread and Monitor Progress** As you listen to individual children reread, monitor progress and provide support.

Kindergarten Student Reader

Look, Nan! Look, Nat!
Dad, get the red sleds.

Get Ben! Get Sam!
Ben and Sam have red sleds.

Ben, tell Ken to get a sled.
Ken, get a red sled.

Bill, get Don and Dan.
Don and Dan, get a sled from Bill.

Dad, get a sled for little Ted.
We have sleds. Here we go!

Look at ten red sleds go!
Ten red sleds go from end to end.

We get to the end.
Ten red sleds, here we go.

Modeled Writing

REVIEW **GRAMMAR** Telling Sentences

Identify telling sentences

AlphaBuddy is going to help us remember what telling sentences are. Remember that a telling sentence tells us something; it does not ask a question. It ends with a period.

Review telling sentences

First, AlphaBuddy will say a sentence. Then we will decide if it is a telling sentence or not.

- My name is AlphaBuddy. (telling sentence)
- I bear (not a telling sentence)
- I live in a house. (telling sentence)
- Do you like my bandanna? (not a telling sentence)

LET'S WRITE Connect to Phonics

Review letters and sounds

Display the *egg* Picture Card. What is the name of this picture? What letter does *egg* begin with? What is the sound for *Ee*? (/e/) Continue using Picture Cards to review the following letters: *Bb, Nn, Rr, Dd, Kk, Ff, Oo, Hh, Ll, Gg*.

Write sentences

In the story *Ten Red Sleds*, Nan and Nat go sledding with Dad. Have you ever gone sledding in the winter? Let's write a sentence about things we can do in winter.

We can ride in a red sled.

Have children read the sentence with you. Ask them to find the words that have /e/. Have them identify the letter that stands for /e/. Remind children that a sentence should begin with an upper-case letter and end with a period.

Independent writing

Have children write or dictate a sentence about winter activities, or they may copy one of the sentences the class wrote together. Have them illustrate their sentences.

EXTEND SKILLS

Handwriting Remind children to put spaces between words as they write their sentences. If needed, have them place a finger between two words so that they leave enough space.

OBJECTIVES

- Review telling sentences.
- Review letters and sounds.
- Write about winter adventures.

Materials

- AlphaBuddy
- Picture Cards for *Bb, Dd, Ee, Ff, Gg, Hh, Kk, Ll, Nn, Oo, Rr*

DAILY FIX-IT

i have a red sled
(I have a red sled.)

Writer's Checkup

- ✔ The first word in a sentence begins with an uppercase letter. Did I do that?
- ✔ A sentence should end with a period. Did I do that?
- ✔ A sentence should make sense. Does my sentence make sense?
- ✔ A good writer uses his or her best handwriting. Did I do that?

ELL

Access Content If children have difficulty identifying the characters in a story, have them listen carefully for names of animals or people.

Speaking and Listening

LISTEN FOR STORY ELEMENTS– CHARACTER

Practice listening for character

Let's play "Who Is the Character?" AlphaBuddy will tell you some stories. Tell me who the characters are.

- Once, there was a little cottage in the woods. In this cottage, there lived three bears: a papa bear, a mama bear, and a baby bear. Who are the characters? **(three bears: papa, mama, and baby bears)**

- There were two animals that both thought it was their lucky day. Who are the characters? **(the fox and the piglet)**

Practice listening for character

It's important to know the characters in a story so you can find out what happens to them and understand why they do things.

Wrap Up Your Day!

 Respond to Literature Today we read about ten sleds. Have you ever been on a sled? What was it like?

 Grammar Ask children to make up telling sentences about some of their favorite characters.

 Homework Idea Have children find three /e/ objects in their homes.

PREVIEW Day 4

Tomorrow we will read about two characters that grow and change.

EXTEND Your Day

A Trip to Antarctica

Materials large brown construction paper, scissors, crayons, stapler

What Is the Weather Like in Antarctica?
Prompt children to consider the temperature, wind, and precipitation in Antarctica. Explain that precipitation is rain, snow, sleet, or hail. Record the information on a chart. Talk about how to dress in extremely cold weather and what the sky looks like in a snowstorm. Describe hail, snow, and gale force winds.

Weather and People What people live in Antarctica? (**scientists**) Why are they the only people who live there? Where do the scientists get fruits and vegetables to eat if it is too cold to grow plants?

TIME FOR Science

Have children draw pictures of things they would bring with them for a trip to Antarctica. Remind them to include food and warm clothing. Have them cut out their drawings. Prepare "suitcases" by folding brown paper in half. Staple strips of paper at edges opposite the fold for handles. Have children "pack" their items in their suitcases.

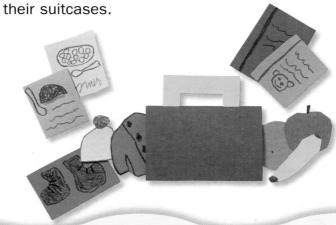

Language Arts
Postcard from Antarctica

Wish You Were Here If you took a trip to Antarctica, you might send a postcard home to tell your family about your adventure. What could you tell your family about Antarctica? Write children's responses on the board.

Distribute paper postcards. Have children illustrate one side and write a message about Antarctica and a family member's name and location on the other side.

To Mom
It is cold and it
snows a lot.
123 Main St.

Comprehension
Classify and Categorize

Animals on Land and in Water Remind children that you have read about many different animals. Display *If You Could Go to Antarctica, One Little Mouse,* and *Life in an Ocean.* Ask them to name animals from the books. Write the names of the animals on the board. Draw a T-chart next to the list of animals. Label one column *Land Animals* and one column *Water Animals.* Ask children to help you sort the animals according to where they live. When you come to an animal that lives both on land and in the water, explain that you will put that animal in the place where it lives most of the time.

Land Animals	Water Animals
rabbit	fish
mouse	whales

Day 4
AT A GLANCE

Oral Language and Vocabulary
Calendar
Message Board
Build Background

Shared Reading
Big Book *See How We Grow*
Skill Classify and Categorize

Word Work

Phonemic Awareness
Review /g/

Phonics
Blend Sounds
H/F Words *here, go, from*
Decodable Reader 23

Read

Group Time < Differentiated Instruction

Language Arts
Grammar: Uppercase Letters and Periods
Interactive Writing:
   Write Sentences Using /e/
Speaking and Listening:
   Story Elements—Character

Materials

- Calendar
- Talk with Me, Sing with Me Chart 23A, 23B
- Sing with Me/Background Building Audio CD
- Big Books *See How We Grow, Animal ABCs*
- AudioText CD
- Picture Cards: p. 299
- Decodable Reader 23

Calendar

Name the day and date
Point to today's date on the calendar and read the day, month, date, and year. Have children echo you.

Count syllables in months
Name the month. Remind children that you can count the number of syllables in a word by clapping.

- How many syllables are in the name of this month? next month?

Message Board

Question of the day
Write and read the question as you track the print. Encourage children to respond in complete sentences.

> ## What adventures can you have in the winter?

Review grammar
Encourage children to use telling sentences to answer the question.

Access Content Use the Day 4 instruction on ELL Poster 23 to support children's use of English to communicate about lesson concepts.

ELL Poster 23

Build Background

LET'S TALK

Develop oral vocabulary

Display Talk with Me Chart 23A.

- Point to the *seals.* What are these animals called? Where do *seals* live?
- Point to the *whales.* What are these animals called? Where do *whales* live?

LET'S SING

Sing "It's a Continent"

Display Sing with Me Chart 23. Sing "It's a Continent." Encourage children to listen for the words *seals* and *whales* as you sing.

Sing with Me/Background Building Audio CD

Talk with Me, Sing with Me Chart

Amazing Words to build oral vocabulary

- Antarctica
- icebergs
- seals
- continent
- penguins
- whales

ELL

Access Content Invite children to act out how the *seals* in the selection walk on land and how they swim in the water. Encourage them to move like *whales* and to pretend to blow water from their blowholes.

LET'S LEARN AMAZING WORDS

Oral Vocabulary seals whales

DAY 4 ROUTINE

1 **Introduce** *Seals* are animals that can live on land and in cold ocean waters. They have thick fur, a layer of fat to keep them warm, and whiskers. What is the name of these animals?

Demonstrate Baby *seals* are called pups. They can't swim when they are born. Who do you think teaches them to swim?

2 **Introduce** *Whales* are large animals that live in ocean waters. *Whales* breathe air through holes on the tops of their heads. *Whales* have flippers and wide, flat tails. What is the name for these large animals?

Demonstrate Blue *whales* are the largest animals in the world. *Whales* do not live in the same place all year but move around the ocean to find food. What do you think *whales* might eat?

3 **Review** We talked about two words today: *seals* and *whales.* Which word means "large animals that live in the ocean," *seals* or *whales?* Which word means "furry animals with flippers and whiskers that live on land and in water," *seals* or *whales?*

4 **Apply** Have children use *whales* and *seals* in complete sentences. Have them use the words to tell about Antarctica.

Extend Language Recalling *See How We Grow,* have children pantomime a baby taking its first wobbly steps.

Comprehension

LET'S READ *See How We Grow*

Review *See How We Grow*

Display *See How We Grow.* Point out how the photographs show the changes in the twins.

● Why do you think this book is called *See How We Grow?*

● How do we know the twins grew? What changes did you see?

Big Book

AudioText CD

Reread *See How We Grow*

Reread the book and ask children to pay attention to what is alike and different between the twins as babies and as older children.

↻ SKILL Classify and Categorize

Apply classify and categorize

After reading, ask:

● What are some things Samantha and Serena did when they were babies? (drank milk, liked to be cuddled)

● What are some things Samantha and Serena do now that they are older children? (use a spoon, talk, walk)

Practice classify and categorize

Using a T-chart, classify babies and children. Ask children to help you name things babies do and things older children do. Show children the pages of the book for help.

● Does "goes to school" belong in the baby column? No, only older children go to school.

● Does "drinks milk from bottle" belong in the baby column? Yes, only babies drink milk from a bottle.

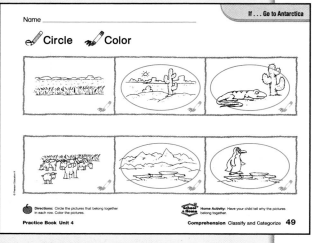

▲ **Practice Book 4**
Classify and Categorize, p. 49

Phonemic Awareness

REVIEW PRACTICE /g/

OBJECTIVES

- Review /g/.
- Substitute phonemes.
- Blend and read.

Materials

- Picture Cards:

dog	egg	flag
garden	goat	goose
gum	jug	pig

- Decodable Reader 23 *Red Hen*
- Big Book *Animal ABCs*

Review /g/

Display the *dog* Picture Card. What is this? Say it with me: /d/ /o/ /g/, *dog*. What is the ending sound in *dog*? The ending sound is /g/. Use the *goat* Picture Card to identify an initial sound. Show a Picture Card; have children tell you if the word begins or ends with /g/. Use the following cards: *goose, gum, garden, jug, flag,* and *pig*.

Substitute phonemes

Display the *egg* Picture Card. What word can we make if we add /b/ to -eg? /b/ -eg, beg. Continue substituting initial sounds with /l/, /m/, and /p/.

Monitor Progress | **Check Phoneme Segmentation**

Check Segmentation Practice phoneme segmentation using words from Decodable Reader 23 *Red Hen*. After I say a word, you tell me all the sounds in the word. Tell me the three sounds in *red*.

pen	**Ben**	**Ken**	**hen**	**get**	**can**
ran	**hid**	**did**	**not**	**got**	**Len**

If... children cannot break words into individual sounds,
then... provide additional decodable words to practice phoneme segmentation.

 SUCCESS PREDICTOR

Day 1	**Day 2**	**Day 3**	**▶ Day 4**	**Day 5**
Check Sound Fluency	Check Retelling/ Letter-Sound Knowledge	Check High-Frequency Words/ Word Reading	Check Phoneme Segmentation	Check Oral Vocabulary/ Assess Progress

Phonics

Spiral REVIEW BLEND SOUNDS

Review letter names and sounds

Use *Animal ABCs* to review the following letter names and sounds: *Aa, Bb, Cc, Dd, Ee, Gg, Hh, Ii, Kk, Ll, Nn, Oo, Pp,* and *Rr*.

Blend sounds

PHONICS ACTIVITY MAT

Write *get* on the board. I am going to blend the sound of each letter together to say this word: /g/ /e/ /t/.

g e t
→ → →
─────→

The word is *get*. We can also blend sounds this way: /g/ -et, /g/ -et, get. What word can I make when I change the first letter *g* to *m*?

OBJECTIVES

- Recognize high-frequency words.
- Read decodable text.

Group Time

On-Level

Read Decodable Reader 23. Use the Small Group Reading **Routine.**

Strategic Intervention

Read Decodable Reader 23. More practice with *Ee*/e/, p. DI·24.

Advanced

Read Independent Leveled Reader K.4.5. Use Leveled Reader lesson, p. LR9. Extend word reading.

ELL

Group English language learners by their reading ability in English.

(*i*) Independent Activities

Self-Selected Reading See pp. TR14–15 for a bibliography of books related to the weekly concept.

Practice Book Classify and Categorize, p. 49; Uppercase Letters and Periods, p. 50

Centers Use the center activities on pp. 262–263 to practice this week's skills.

Journal Writing Draw and label three different things you would see in Antarctica.

Word Wall HIGH-FREQUENCY WORDS

Practice high-frequency words

Write the word *here* on the board. This is the word *here*. What is this word? Continue with *go, from,* and *the.* Look for these words in the story that we read today.

PREPARE TO READ

Introduce Decodable Reader 23

Display Decodable Reader 23 *Red Hen*. Today we will read a new story, *Red Hen*. Point to the title of the story. What is the title of this story? What do you see on the cover of this story? What do you think this story will be about?

Small Group Reading

DAY 4 ROUTINE

1 **Model Fluent Reading** Have children finger point as you read a page.

2 **Read Chorally** Have children finger point as they chorally read the page. Continue reading page by page, repeating steps 1 and 2.

3 **Read Individually** Have children read aloud a page in their group.

4 **Reread and Monitor Progress** As you listen to individual children reread, monitor progress and provide support.

Decodable Reader

Interactive Writing

GRAMMAR
Uppercase Letters and Periods

Identify uppercase letters and periods

We have learned that all sentences start with an uppercase letter. Telling sentences always have periods at the end. **Allow volunteers to add uppercase letters and periods to sentences you write on the board.**

LET'S WRITE Connect to Phonics

Review letters and sounds

Display page 5 of *Animal ABCs*. What is the name of this picture? (elephant) What sound does elephant begin with? What letter stands for /e/?

Write sentences

Write the following sentence frames on the board.

We saw a _____ at the farm. (hen)

Do you like to see the _____ at the zoo? (elephants)

Have children help you complete the sentences. Ask a volunteer to write the word to fill in the first blank. Then have children name the beginning sound in the word *elephant* as you write the word on the board. Read the sentences together.

Independent writing

Have children write or dictate their own sentences using words with /e/, or they may copy one of the sentences the class wrote together. Then have them illustrate their sentences.

EXTEND SKILLS

Spelling If children spell words with /el/ as the letter *l*, they may not be hearing /e/. Review connecting /e/ to *Ee*. Then review blending /e/ and /l/.

TEACHING TIP

Use Technology You may wish to have children use a graphic arts program on the computer to illustrate their stories.

OBJECTIVES

- Practice uppercase letters and periods.
- Review letters and sounds.
- Write sentences using /e/.

Materials

- Big Book *Animal ABCs*

it is cold here
(It is cold here.)

Support Writing Allow children with the same home language to share their ideas in that language and discuss how to express them in English before writing.

If . . . Go to Antarctica

Name _____

✏ Write ✏ Draw

the pet sat in a tent

The pet sat in a tent.

Directions: Write the sentence using an uppercase letter and a period. Draw a picture for the sentence.

Home Activity: Write sentences without uppercase letters and periods. Have your child write the sentences correctly.

50 Grammar Uppercase Letters and Periods

Practice Book Unit 4

▲ **Practice Book 4**
Uppercase Letters and Periods, p. 50

Access Content Allow the English language learners to join in the activity when they are ready, or let them discuss the questions in their home languages and then help them express them in English.

Speaking and Listening

LISTEN FOR STORY ELEMENTS— CHARACTER

Review character

The *characters* in a story are the people or animals in it. We can find out what the characters are like by listening carefully. In *Goldilocks and the Three Bears*, what is Goldilocks like? Is she shy or adventurous? Is she a child or a grown-up? What does she look like?

Practice listening for character

I'm going to tell you a story and I want you to listen carefully. Afterward, I'm going to ask you two questions: What does this character do? And, would you want this character as a friend? Retell familiar stories, such as *My Lucky Day* and "The Tale of Peter Rabbit."

Wrap Up Your Day!

✓ **Respond to Literature** Today we read about two babies growing up. Do you remember being a baby?

✓ **Speaking and Listening** Ask children to tell about the characters in *Goldilocks and the Three Bears.*

✓ **Homework Idea** Ask children to bring in three words that need to begin with an uppercase letter.

PREVIEW Day 5

Tomorrow we will read about another adventure.

EXTEND Your Day

Landforms

Materials pictures of landforms, Big Book *If You Could Go to Antarctica,* paper, drawing tools

Antarctic Landforms Page through *If You Could Go to Antarctica* and ask children to identify what the land looks like.

Encourage children to identify both similarities and differences between Antarctica and their neighborhood. Are there mountains where we live? Are there icebergs? Is the land flat?

Explain that when we travel to different parts of the world there are differences in the land. Show the landform photographs. Are there hills or mountains? Is the ground covered with rocks or sand? Is there water nearby in a river, lake, or ocean?

Illustrate a Landform Distribute drawing paper and ask children to draw themselves at a landform they would like to see.

Time for
SOCIAL STUDIES

Math
Most and Fewest

Counting Animals Page through *If You Could Go to Antarctica.* Ask children which page has the most animals on it. Ask which pages have just a few animals. Help the children count the number of penguins on pages 12–13, seals on pages 14–15, and whales on pages 16–17. Record the numbers in tallies on a chart.

Animals	How Many?
penguin	
seals	
whales	

Writing Telling Sentences Have children write a telling sentence about one of the animals they counted. Remind them to use uppercase letters and a period.

Phonics
Matching Sounds

Going to... Tell children to think of words that begin with /g/ and that could be used in this sentence: *I am going to _____.* Begin the game by saying: *I am going to the garden.* Ask a volunteer to tell which words begin with /g/. Have children take turns telling where they are going and completing the sentence with words that begin with /g/.

The activity can be modified for c/k/ by using this sentence: *I am coming to see a _____.* Give this example: *I am coming to see a cub.* Have children take turns by completing the sentence with words that begin with c/k/.

Day 5
AT A GLANCE

Oral Language and Vocabulary
Calendar
Message Board
Build Background

Shared Reading
Read Aloud Anthology "Peggy Penguin Goes to the Ocean"
Skill Classify and Categorize

Word Work
Phonemic Awareness
Practice /e/

Phonics
Connect /e/ to Ee
H/F Words *here, go, from*

Read
Group Time < Differentiated Instruction

Monitor Progress

Language Arts
Grammar: Uppercase Letters and Periods
Shared Writing: This Week We...
Speaking and Listening: Character

Materials

- Calendar
- Talk with Me, Sing with Me Chart 23A, 23B
- Sing with Me/Background Building Audio CD
- Read Aloud Anthology "Peggy Penguin Goes to the Ocean"
- Decodable Reader 23
- Kindergarten Student Reader K.4.5
- Phonics Story *Ten, Ten, Ten!*
- Big Book *If You Could Go to Antarctica*

Calendar

Name the day and date Point to today's date on the calendar. Have the children say the day, month, date, and year together.

Last week, next week Review the dates from one week ago and from next week with children. Remind them that each week has the same number of days in the same order.

Message Board

Question of the week Remind the children that this week we have talked about what it is like in Antarctica.

> ## What would it be like to take an adventure to the Antarctic?

Review oral vocabulary Encourage children to use oral vocabulary words *Antarctica, continent, icebergs, penguins, seals,* and *whales* in their responses. Prompt them to respond in complete sentences.

Assess Vocabulary Use the Day 5 instruction on ELL Poster 23 to monitor children's progress with oral vocabulary.

ELL Poster 23

Build Background

LET'S TALK

Discuss adventures in Antarctica

Display Talk with Me Chart 23A. Point to the picture of the whales.

- Is this a picture of *penguins* or *whales?*
- Which picture shows *seals?*
- Which picture shows *icebergs* in *Antarctica?*

Talk with Me, Sing with Me Chart

LET'S SING

Sing "It's a Continent"

Display Sing with Me Chart 23B. Remind children that the words *Antarctica, continent, icebergs, penguins, seals,* and *whales* are in the song.

 Sing with Me/Background Building Audio CD

It's a Continent

It's a continent that's really very cold,
I don't think you'd like it when you're old.
It's a continent that's cold,
   it's a continent that's cold,
It's Antarctica, and it's really very cold!

Talk with Me, Sing with Me Chart

Monitor Progress | **Check Oral Vocabulary**

Demonstrate Word Knowledge Prompt children to demonstrate knowledge of oral vocabulary words *Antarctica, continent, icebergs, penguins, seals, whales.* Encourage them to use the words in complete sentences.

If... children cannot demonstrate knowledge of oral vocabulary words,

then... review words and meanings using Talk with Me Chart 23A and *If You Could Go to Antarctica.*

SUCCESS PREDICTOR

Day 1	Day 2	Day 3	Day 4	▶ Day 5
Check Sound Fluency	Check Retelling/ Letter-Sound Knowledge	Check High-Frequency Words/ Word Reading	Check Phoneme Segmentation	Check Oral Vocabulary/ Assess Progress

Oral Vocabulary
SUCCESS PREDICTOR

OBJECTIVE

- Classify and categorize in new selection.

Materials

- *Read Aloud Anthology* "Peggy Penguin Goes to the Ocean"

Monitor Progress

Classify and Categorize

| If... children cannot classify and categorize, | then... reteach using page DI·35. |

Comprehension

READ ALOUD

Read "Peggy Penguin Goes to the Ocean"

Tell children that you are going to read them a story about a penguin's first trip to the ocean. Ask them to listen carefully to the story. Listen carefully. I am going to read you a story and then we will talk about the penguins at the snow hill and the ocean.

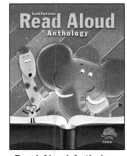

Read Aloud Anthology

CHECK SKILL
Classify and Categorize

Practice classify and categorize in "Peggy Penguin Goes to the Ocean"

After you read the story, ask children to think about what happens at the snow hill and what happens at the ocean.

- How does Peggy slide down the hill of snow? (beak first)
- Who does Peggy cuddle with? (the grown-up penguins)
- Who does Peggy meet on the ocean shore? (a seal)
- Why does Peggy lose track of her penguin friends while swimming? (She chases a small fish.)

ASSESS SKILL
Classify and Categorize

Assess classify and categorize

Use the blackline master found on page 310. Copy one page for each child. Have children cut out pictures and glue them in the appropriate column on the T-chart.

CLASSIFY AND CATEGORIZE

Cut out pictures and glue them on the correct side of the chart.

| At Snow Hill | At the Ocean |
| | |

Note to Teacher Have children cut out pictures and glue them on the appropriate side of the T-chart.

▲ **Teacher's Edition 4**
Classify and Categorize, p. 310

Phonemic Awareness

REVIEW /e/

Isolate /e/

What is the first sound in *egg*? Say the word with me: /e/, /e/, /e/, *egg*. Review initial /e/ with the words *Ed* and *elf*.

What is the middle sound in *ten*? Say *ten* with me: /t/ /e/ /n/, *ten*. Review medial /e/ with the words *men*, *bet*, *get*, *bed*, and *peg*.

Phonics

REVIEW *Ee*/e/

Connect /e/ to *Ee*

Display Alphabet Card *Ee*. What is the name of this letter? *(e)* What is the sound for this letter? *(/e/)* This is an *escalator*. What is the first sound in *escalator*? Repeat the routine with *E*.

Word Wall HIGH-FREQUENCY WORDS

Practice high-frequency words

Write the word *from* on the board. This is the word *from*. What is this word? Continue the routine with *here* and *go*.

Spiral REVIEW READ

Apply phonics in familiar text

Have children reread one of the readers that applies the target letter sound. You may wish to review the decodable words and the high-frequency words that appear in each reader prior to rereading.

Kindergarten Student Reader

Decodable Reader

Phonics Story in Practice Book

OBJECTIVES

- Review initial and medial /e/.
- Connect /e/ to *Ee*.

Materials

- Kindergarten Student Reader K.4.5
- Decodable Reader 23
- Phonics Story *Ten, Ten, Ten!*
- Alphabet Card: *Ee*

5

Monitor Progress

OBJECTIVE

 Assess: connect /e/ to *Ee*.

Group Time

On-Level

Sets A and B

Strategic Intervention

Monitor Progress:
Check Phonics
Alternate Assessment, p. DI·25

Advanced

Sets B and C

(*i*) **Independent Activities**

Self-Selected Reading See pp. TR14–15 for a bibliography of books related to the weekly concept.

Centers Use the center activities on pp. 262–263 to practice this week's skills.

Journal Writing Draw or write about what you would wear in Antarctica.

Support Phonics For guidance in teaching phonics to English language learners, see the *ELL and Transition Handbook*.

PHONICS /e/ to *Ee*

Group assessment	Give children a sheet of paper divided into four sections. Have children draw a picture of a word containing /e/ in each box and label it with the word or the letter *e*.

Monitor Progress — Assess Progress	
If... a child cannot complete the group assessment,	**then**... use the Reteach lesson on page DI·35.
If... a child correctly draws four words with /e/,	**then**... assess word reading Sets A and B on page 309.
If... a child correctly draws and labels four /e/ words,	**then**... assess word and sentence reading with Sets B and C on page 309.

ASSESS PHONICS

Set A: Read the words	Have individuals read the words. We're going to read some words. I'll do the first one and you do the rest. The first word is *hen*, /h/ /e/ /n/. For each child, record any decoding problems.
Set B: Read more words	Have individuals take turns reading the words. We're going to read some words. I'll do the first one and you do the rest. The first word is *pet*, /p/ /e/ /t/. The word is *pet*. For each child, record any decoding problems.
Set C: Read the sentences	For a cumulative assessment of phonics and high-frequency words, have each child read one or two sentences.

READ THE WORDS

Set A

hen   pen

left   egg

✂ - ✂

READ MORE WORDS

Set B

pet   dress   lend

beg   sent   mend

✂ - ✂

READ THE SENTENCES

Set C

1. Ben is here in the den.

2. The red net is on top of the well.

3. Len and Ken go to the pen.

4. Meg is my little hen.

5. The men went to get a pet.

Note to Teacher Set A: Children read each word. Set B: Children read each word.
Set C: Children read one or two sentences.

If You Could Go to Antarctica

Monitor Progress

SUCCESS PREDICTOR

CLASSIFY AND CATEGORIZE

Cut out the pictures and glue them on the correct side of the chart.

At Snow Hill	At the Ocean

Note to Teacher Have children cut out pictures and glue them on the appropriate side of the T-chart.

© Scott Foresman K

REPRODUCIBLE PAGE • See also Assessment Handbook, p. 201

Monitor Progress

Shared Writing

GRAMMAR
Uppercase Letters and Periods

Review uppercase letters and periods

A complete sentence must start with an uppercase letter and end with a period. Some letters look almost the same when they are uppercase or lowercase letters and some look very different. Who can show me an uppercase letter that looks almost the same as the lowercase letter? (for example, *Cc, Ff,* or *Oo*) Who can write a period?

Illustrate uppercase letters and periods

Ask for volunteers to write uppercase letters and periods on the board. Where do you find uppercase letters? Where do you find periods?

LET'S WRITE This Week We...

Recall literature

We read and sang about a new place this week. Antarctica is different from everywhere else in the world. It is very cold and almost no people live there. What animals do you remember from *If You Could Go to Antarctica?*

Write sentences

Today we will write about the animals in the book.

Ms. Woody saw a penguin.
Chase likes the whale.
Erica saw a seal.

Continue the list with children using their names. Then have children echo read a sentence. Encourage children to use complete sentences. Check for uppercase letters and periods.

Independent writing

Have children copy the sentence they dictated and illustrate it with an animal from the book.

Chase likes the whale.

OBJECTIVES

● Recognize uppercase letters and periods.
● Respond to literature through writing.

Materials

● Big Book *If You Could Go to Antarctica*

DAILY FIX-IT

the sled is red
(The sled is red.)

ELL

Support Writing Supply English words as children write or dictate their sentences.

E L L

Access Content Encourage children to participate by having them select a familiar book and identify the characters in the story.

Speaking and Listening

LISTEN FOR STORY ELEMENTS— CHARACTER

Review listening for story elements— character

Today we are going to talk about characters in a story. When you are listening to a story, the characters are the people or animals that the story is about.

> **Jack and Jill**
> **went up the hill**
> **to fetch a pail of water.**
> **Jack fell down**
> **and broke his crown**
> **and Jill came tumbling after.**

Connect listening for story elements— character

To check that children understand what they have heard, read or sing "Jack and Jill" several times. Have the children identify the characters in the rhyme and carefully act it out.

Wrap Up Your Week!

✓ **Phonics** This week we learned about the letter *Ee*. What is the sound for *Ee?* Name some words that contain /e/.

✓ **Shared Reading** What was your favorite book or song this week?

✓ **High-Frequency Words** Write *here, to,* and *from* on the board. Read these words to me.

You've learned **006 Amazing Words** this week!

You've learned **138 Amazing Words** so far this year!

PREVIEW Next Week

Next week we will read about a little girl and her abuela. Does anyone know what the word *abuela* means?

EXTEND Your Day

Temperature

Materials thermometer

Reading a Thermometer Discuss with children how a thermometer works. Show them that when the numbers on the thermometer are lower, it is cooler, and when the numbers on the thermometer are higher, it is warmer. Tell children 32 degrees Fahrenheit means it is freezing and 90 degrees Fahrenheit or more means it is really hot.

- How does your body feel when it is hot?
- How does your skin feel when it is very cold?
- What do you think happens to the red line on the thermometer on a hot day? On a cold day?

Guess the Temperature

Have children guess the temperature of Antarctica. Show them the lowest number on your thermometer. Tell them the temperature in the middle of Antarctica is about -70 degrees Fahrenheit. The lowest temperature ever in Antarctica was -128.6 degrees and the highest ever, near the sea, was 59 degrees.

Whale Math

TIME + FOR MATH

Materials fish or whale crackers, photocopies of two circles side by side, pencils

Addition Give children 7 crackers each and a circle paper. Tell them to select 4 fish or whales and place them in one circle. Tell children to select 3 more and place them in the other circle. Ask the children how many fish and whales they have all together. Demonstrate 4 + 3 = 7 on the board. Tell children to write their math problem on their paper. Continue giving addition problems with the sum of 7. Have children write a problem on their papers. After eating their crackers, children should place fish or whale shapes in the circles to illustrate the math problem.

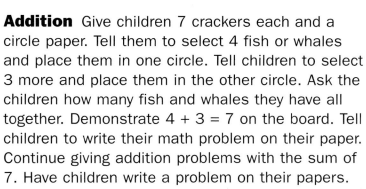

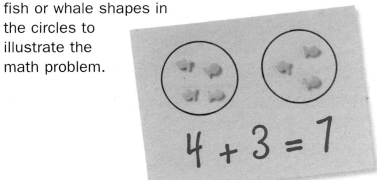

Hot or Cold?

Act It Out Discuss with children things you do when you are hot and things you do when you are cold. Prepare 6–8 slips of paper with the words *cold* or *hot* written on them and place them in a bowl or other container. Have a child come forward and choose a paper. The child should act out one thing he or she would do in that kind of weather. Remaining children can guess what the weather is like, *hot* or *cold*.

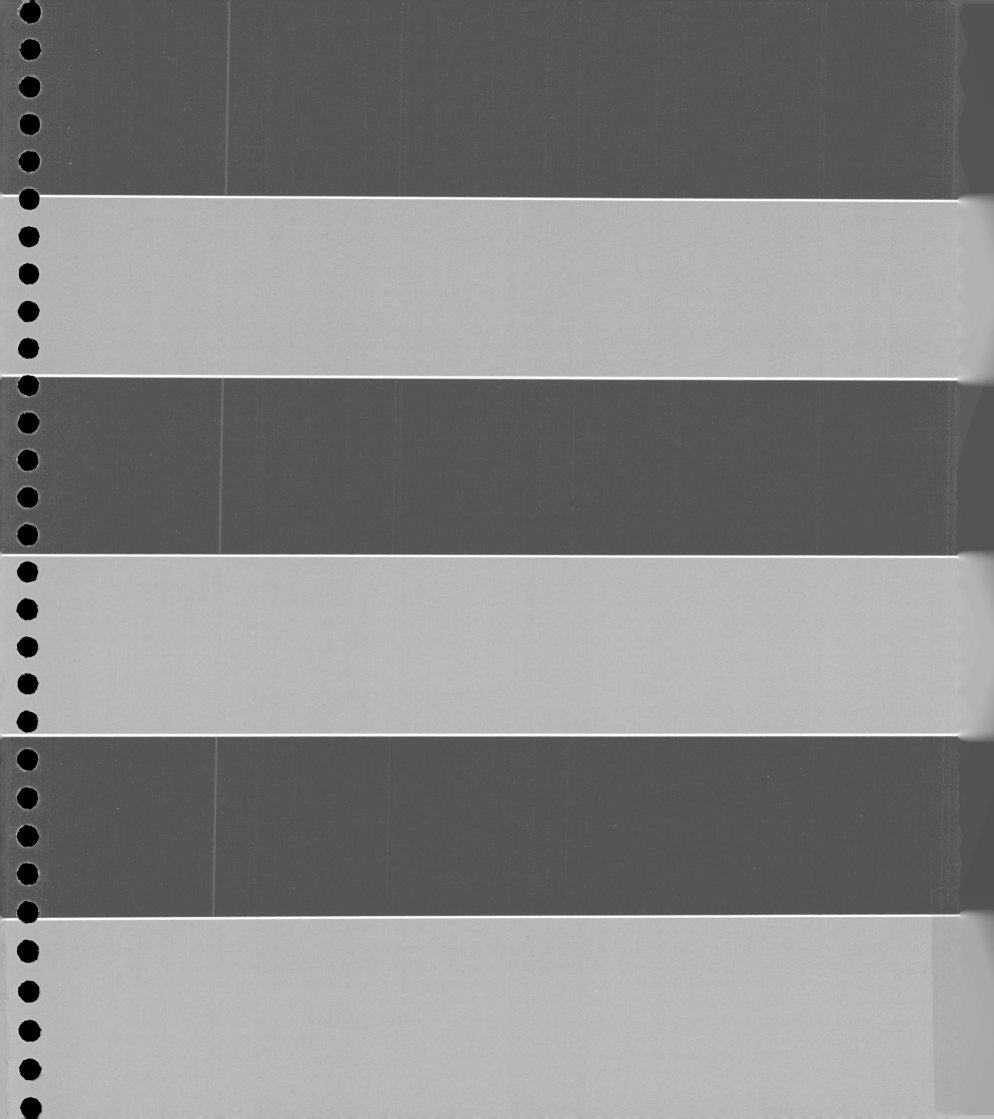

Unit 4
Let's Explore

Week 6

EXPAND THE CONCEPT
What kinds of adventures can you have in the city?

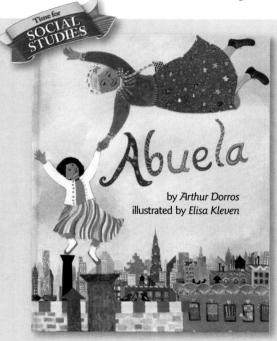

Time for SOCIAL STUDIES

Abuela
by *Arthur Dorros*
illustrated by *Elisa Kleven*

CONCEPT QUESTION
Where will our adventures take us?

Week 1

What adventures do you have throughout the day?

Week 2

What adventures can you have on a lucky day?

Week 3

What adventures can an animal have?

Week 4

What kind of adventure can a little girl have?

Week 5

What would it be like to take an adventure to the Antarctic?

Week 6

What kinds of adventures can you have in the city?

CONNECT THE CONCEPT

▶ **Build Background**

abuela	flock	airport
adventure	city	harbor

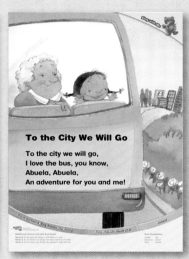

To the City We Will Go

To the city we will go,
I love the bus, you know,
Abuela, Abuela,
An adventure for you and me!

▶ **Social Studies Content**
Transportation, Culture

Preview Your Week

What kind of adventures can you have in the city?

by *Arthur Dorros*
illustrated by *Elisa Kleven*

Read Aloud Trade Book

Audio CD

Genre Fiction

Phonics Ee/e/

Comprehension Skill Setting

Meet the Author

Arthur Dorros

Arthur Dorros has had over twenty children's books published. He says, "Part of writing and illustrating is like being a detective, with sense as alert as possible, always on the lookout for new ideas and pieces that help put the whole story together."

Read another book by Arthur Dorros.

This Is My House

Read It
ONLINE
PearsonSuccessNet.com

- Kindergarten Student Readers
- Listen to Me Readers
- Independent Leveled Readers
- Decodable Readers

Time for
SOCIAL STUDIES

Books for All Children

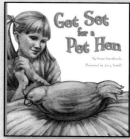

Listen to Me Reader

Emergent

- **Develop oral language**
- **Develop phonemic awareness**
- **Read decodable words**
- **Read high-frequency words**

Kindergarten Student Reader

On-Level

- **Read connected text**
- **Apply phonics skills**
- **Read high-frequency words in context**

Leveled Reader K.4.6

Independent Leveled Reader

Independent

- **Practice comprehension skill:** setting
- **Extend concepts**
- **Connect to Social Studies**

Apply Phonics

Decodable Reader

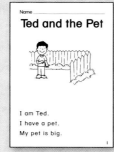

Phonics Story

Integrate Social Studies Standards

- Transportation
- Culture

✓ Read

Read Aloud Trade Book *Abuela*

Independent Leveled Reader *Washington, D.C.*

✓ Build
Concept Vocabulary

Adventures You Can Have in the City, pp. 327, 337, 352, 361, 369

✓ Apply
Social Studies

Scenes from Our City, p. 335
Traveling, p. 350
Ways to Travel, p. 359
National Symbols, p. 367
American Flag, p. 377
Transportation Collage, p. 377

Weekly Plan

READING

60–90 minutes

TARGET SKILLS OF THE WEEK

◎ **Phonics Skill**
Ee/e/

◎ **Comprehension Skill**
Setting

DAY 1   PAGES 326–335

Oral Language/Vocabulary

QUESTION OF THE WEEK, 326
What kind of adventures can you have in the city?

Build Background, 327
Talk with Me, Sing with Me Chart 24A, 24B

Amazing Words, 327
abuela, adventure, flock, city, airport, harbor

Comprehension

Shared Reading, 328–329

Read Read Aloud
Trade Book

Preview and Predict
Reader Response
◎ Setting **T**

Word Work

Phonemic Awareness, 330
Reteach /e/

Phonics, 331
◎ Connect /e/ to *Ee* **T**

High-Frequency Words, 331
Reteach *here, go, from*

Reread Decodable Reader 23

Grouping Options 320–321

DAY 2   PAGES 336–350

Oral Language/Vocabulary

QUESTION OF THE DAY, 336
How is the city the same as or different from here?

Build Background, 337
Talk with Me, Sing with Me Chart 24A, 24B

Let's Learn Amazing Words, 337
abuela, adventure

Comprehension

Shared Reading, 338–345

Read Read Aloud
Trade Book

Recall and Retell
◎ Setting **T**

Word Work

Phonemic Awareness, 346
Practice /e/

Phonics, 346
◎ Connect /e/ to *Ee* **T**

High-Frequency Words, 347
Review *here, go, I, have, is, a, my, the, to, has, see, do*

Read Phonics Story

Grouping Options 320–321

LANGUAGE ARTS

20 minutes

Shared Writing, 333
Grammar: Introduce Pronoun *I*
Connect to Grammar

Speaking and Listening, 334
Introduce Listening to Poems

Modeled Writing, 348
Grammar: Practice Pronoun *I*
Respond to Literature

Speaking and Listening, 349
Let's Review Amazing Words *Antarctica, continent*

DAILY JOURNAL WRITING

Day 1   *Draw or write about something you might see in a city.*

Day 2   *Dictate, illustrate, or write three words that rhyme with bed.*

EXTEND YOUR DAY   *30 minutes*
Additional Activities for Full–Day Classrooms

Day 1, 335
Time for Social Studies: Scenes from Our City
Grammar: Write a Poem
Literature: Poetry

Day 2, 350
Time for Social Studies: Traveling
Comprehension: Settings
Grammar: Pronoun *I*

DAILY SUCCESS PREDICTORS ➤

for Adequate Yearly Progress

Monitor Progress and Corrective Feedback

Phonemic Awareness
Check Sound Fluency, *330*
Spiral REVIEW Phonics,
High-Frequency Words

Retelling and Phonics
Check Retelling, *345*
Check Letter-Sound Knowledge, *346*
Spiral REVIEW Phonics,
High-Frequency Words

Grouping Options for Differentiated Instruction

Turn the page for the small group lesson plan.

DAY 3 — PAGES 351–359

Oral Language/Vocabulary

QUESTION OF THE DAY, 351
Did you ever go on a city adventure?

Build Background, 352
Talk with Me, Sing with Me Chart 24A, 24B

Let's Learn Amazing Words, 352
flock, city

Comprehension

Shared Reading, 353

Read Read Aloud
Trade Book
REVIEW Realism and Fantasy **T**
Setting **T**

Word Work

Phonemic Awareness, 354
Practice /e/

Phonics, 354
Connect /e/ to *Ee* **T**

High-Frequency Words, 355
Practice *go, here, to, they, the, see, we, you, look, one, from*

Read Kindergarten Student Reader K.4.6

Grouping Options 320–321

Modeled Writing, 357
Grammar: **REVIEW** Uppercase Letters and Periods
Connect to Phonics

Speaking and Listening, 358
Practice Listening to Poems

Day 3 *Dictate or write four words that rhyme with bell. Draw a picture of one of them.*

Day 3, 359
Time for Social Studies: Ways to Travel
Comprehension: Real or Imaginary
Phonics: Organize Words

DAY 4 — PAGES 360–367

Oral Language/Vocabulary

QUESTION OF THE DAY, 360
How can you get to the city?

Build Background, 361
Talk with Me, Sing with Me Chart 24A, 24B

Let's Learn Amazing Words, 361
airport, harbor

Comprehension

Shared Reading, 362

Reread Big Book
Setting **T**

Word Work

Phonemic Awareness, 363
REVIEW /g/

Phonics, 363
Connect /e/ to *Ee* **T**

High-Frequency Words, 364
Practice *go, here, from, a, is, have*

Read Decodable Reader 24

Grouping Options 320–321

Interactive Writing, 365
Grammar: Practice Pronoun *I*
Connect to Phonics

Speaking and Listening, 366
Practice Listening to Poems

Day 4 *Dictate or write three short e words.*

Day 4, 367
Time for Social Studies: National Symbols
Phonics: Initial and Final *Gg*
Comprehension: Settings

DAY 5 — PAGES 368–377

Oral Language/Vocabulary

QUESTION OF THE WEEK, 368
What kind of adventures can you have in the city?

Build Background, 369
Talk with Me, Sing with Me Chart 24A, 24B

Amazing Words, 369
Check *abuela, adventure, flock, city, airport, harbor*

Comprehension

Shared Reading, 370, 374

Read *Read Aloud Anthology*
"Apple Juice Tea"

Monitor Progress
Check Setting **T**

Word Work

Phonemic Awareness, 371
Review /e/

Phonics, 371
Connect /e/ to *Ee* **T**

High-Frequency Words, 371
Practice *here, go, from*

Grouping Options 320–321

Monitor Progress, 372–373
Read the Words
Read the Sentences

Shared Writing, 375
Grammar: Review Pronoun *I*
This Week We...

Speaking and Listening, 376
Review Listening to Poems

Day 5 *Draw or write about an adventure you have had with a family member.*

Day 5, 377
Time for Math: Graphing
Time for Social Studies: American Flag
Time for Social Studies: Transportation Collage

KEY = Target Skill **T** = Tested Skill

Word Reading
Check High-Frequency Words
and Word Reading, *355*
Spiral REVIEW Phonics,
High-Frequency Words

Phonemic Awareness
Check Phoneme Segmentation, *363*
Spiral REVIEW Phonics,
High-Frequency Words

Oral Vocabulary
Check Oral Vocabulary, *369*
Assess Phonics and
Comprehension, *372–374*

SUCCESS PREDICTOR

Small Group Plan *for Differentiated Instruction*

Daily Plan AT A GLANCE

Reading
Whole Group
- Oral Language/Vocabulary
- Comprehension
- Word Work

Group Time

Meet with small groups to provide:
- Skill Support
- Reading Support
- Skill Application

Read

This week's lessons for daily group time can be found behind the Differentiated Instruction (DI) tab on pp. DI·26–DI·30.

Language Arts
- Grammar
- Writing
- Speaking and Listening

Use *My Sidewalks on Reading Street* for early reading intervention.

DAY 1

On-Level
Teacher-Led
Page 332
- Blend Sounds to Read Words
- **Reread** Decodable Reader 23

Strategic Intervention
Teacher-Led
Page DI·26
- More Practice with e/e/
- **Read** Listen to Me Reader K.4.6

Advanced
Teacher-Led
Page DI·26
- **Reread** Independent Leveled Reader K.4.5
- **Reread** for Fluency

ⓘ Independent Activities
While you meet with small groups, have the rest of the class...
- Read self-selected reading
- Complete Practice Book K.4 p. 53
- Visit the Literacy Centers
- Write in their journals

DAY 2

On-Level
Teacher-Led
Page 347
- Practice Word Reading
- **Read** Phonics Story

Strategic Intervention
Teacher-Led
Page DI·27
- More Practice with e/e/
- **Read** Phonics Story

Advanced
Teacher-Led
Page DI·27
- Apply Phonics Skills
- **Read** Decodable Reader 24

ⓘ Independent Activities
While you meet with small groups, have the rest of the class...
- Read self-selected reading
- Complete Practice Book K.4 p. 54
- Visit the Literacy Centers
- Write in their journals

DAY 3

On-Level
Teacher-Led
Pages 355–356
- Practice Word Reading
- **Read** Kindergarten Student Reader K.4.6

Strategic Intervention
Teacher-Led
Page DI·28
- Practice Reading Words with e/e/
- **Read** Kindergarten Student Reader K.4.6

Advanced
Teacher-Led
Page DI·28
- Extend Word Reading
- **Read** Kindergarten Student Reader K.4.6

ⓘ Independent Activities
While you meet with small groups, have the rest of the class...
- Read self-selected reading
- Complete Practice Book K.4 pp. 57, 58
- Visit the Literacy Centers
- Write in their journals

DAY 4

On-Level

Teacher-Led
Page 364

- Blend and Read Words with e/e/
- **Read** Decodable Reader 24

Strategic Intervention

Teacher-Led
Page DI · 29

- Blend and Read Words with e/e/
- **Read** Decodable Reader 24

Advanced

Teacher-Led
Page LR11

- Extend Word Reading
- **Read** Independent Leveled Reader K.4.6

ⓘ Independent Activities

While you meet with small groups, have the rest of the class...

- Read self-selected reading
- Complete Practice Book K.4 pp. 59, 60
- Visit the Literacy Centers
- Write in their journals

DAY 5

On-Level

Teacher-Led
Pages 372–374

- Word Reading, Sets A and B
- Check Phonics
- Check Comprehension

Strategic Intervention

Teacher-Led
Pages 372, 374, DI · 30

- Check Phonics
- Check Comprehension
- Alternate Assessment

Advanced

Teacher-Led
Pages 372–374

- Word Reading, Set B
- Sentence Reading, Set C
- Monitor Comprehension

ⓘ Independent Activities

While you meet with small groups, have the rest of the class...

- Read self-selected reading
- Visit the Literacy Centers
- Write in their journals

ELL

Grouping Group English language learners by their reading ability in English.

Take It to the NET ONLINE
PearsonSuccessNet.com

P. David Pearson
For research on effective teaching practices, see the article "Looking Inside Classrooms" by B. Taylor, Scott Foresman author P. D. Pearson, and others.

TEACHER TALK

Explicit instruction is teaching in which the teacher explains a skill (what it is and when and why to use it), models how to perform it, guides practice, and offers independent practice.

Be sure to schedule time for children to work on the theme project *"Remember When* Album." This week children should help bind books with ribbon or yarn. Then they may present theirs to the class.

Looking Ahead

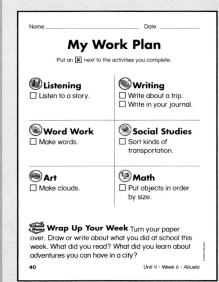

Name _____ Date _____

My Work Plan

Put an ☒ next to the activities you complete.

Listening
☐ Listen to a story.

Writing
☐ Write about a trip.
☐ Write in your journal.

Word Work
☐ Make words.

Social Studies
☐ Sort kinds of transportation.

Art
☐ Make clouds.

Math
☐ Put objects in order by size.

Wrap Up Your Week Turn your paper over. Draw or write about what you did at school this week. What did you read? What did you learn about adventures you can have in a city?

40   Unit 4 · Week 6 · Abuela

▲ **Group-Time Survival Guide** p. 40, Weekly Contract

Abuela **321**

☑ Customize Your Plan *by Strand*

ORAL LANGUAGE

Concept Development

What kind of adventures can you have in the city?

 to build oral vocabulary

abuela	flock	airport
adventure	city	harbor

BUILD

- ❑ **Question of the Week** Use the Message Board to introduce and discuss the question of the week. This week children will talk, sing, read, and write about adventures people can have. **DAY 1** *326*

- ❑ **Let's Talk** Use the Talk with Me Chart to introduce Amazing Words in a visual context. **DAY 1** *327*

- ❑ **Let's Listen** Use the Sing with Me/Background Building Audio CD to build background, vocabulary, and concepts. **DAY 1** *327*

- ❑ **Let's Sing** Use the Sing with Me Chart to sing a song about city adventures. **DAY 1** *327*

**Talk with Me,
Sing with Me Chart 24A**

**Talk with Me,
Sing with Me Chart 24B**

DEVELOP

- ❑ **Question of the Day/Week** Use the questions in the Message Boards to discuss lesson concepts and how they relate to the unit theme, Let's Explore. **DAY 2** *336*, **DAY 3** *351*, **DAY 4** *360*, **DAY 5** *368*

- ❑ **Let's Talk** Use the Talk with Me Chart to build background, vocabulary, and concepts. **DAY 2** *337*, **DAY 3** *352*, **DAY 4** *361*, **DAY 5** *369*

- ❑ **Let's Sing** Use the Sing with Me Chart to sing a song about city adventures. Ask children to sing along with you, listening for the Amazing Words as they sing. **DAY 2** *337*, **DAY 3** *352*, **DAY 4** *361*, **DAY 5** *369*

CONNECT

- ❑ **Wrap Up Your Week!** Connect concepts and vocabulary to next week's lesson. **DAY 5** *376*

CHECK

- ❑ **Check Oral Vocabulary** To informally assess children's oral vocabulary, have children use each word in a complete sentence. **DAY 5** *369*

PHONEMIC AWARENESS

TEACH

- ❑ **Reteach** /e/ Reteach and discriminate /e/. **DAY 1** *330*

PRACTICE/APPLY

- ❑ **Listen for Sounds** Use the Phonics Songs and Rhymes Chart to listen for /e/. **DAY 2** *346*

- ❑ **Practice** /e/ Identify /e/. **DAY 3** *354*

**Phonics Songs and
Rhymes Chart 24**

RETEACH/REVIEW

- ❑ **Review** Review /g/. **DAY 4** *363*

- ❑ **Review** Review /e/. **DAY 5** *371*

- ❑ **Reteach Lesson** If necessary, reteach /e/. **DAY 5** *DI·36*

❶ Use assessment data to determine your instructional focus.

❷ Preview this week's instruction by strand.

❸ Choose instructional activities that meet the needs of your classroom.

PHONICS

↻ CONNECT /e/ to Ee

TEACH

☐ **Connect /e/ to Ee** Reteach *Ee*/e/. **DAY 1** *331*

PRACTICE/APPLY

☐ **Connect /e/ to Ee** Practice *Ee*/e/.
DAY 2 *346*, **DAY 3** *354*

☐ **Phonics Story** Practice reading words with *Ee*/e/ in context. **DAY 2** *347*

☐ **Kindergarten Student Reader K.4.6** Practice reading words with *Ee*/e/ in context. **DAY 3** *356*

☐ **Decodable Reader 24** Practice reading words with *Ee*/e/ in context. **DAY 4** *364*

☐ **Homework** Practice Book K.4, pp. 53, 58.
DAY 1 *331*, **DAY 3** *354*

☐ **Word Work Center** Have children make words. **ANY DAY** *324*

Phonics Story

Kindergarten Student Reader K.4.6

Decodable Reader 24

RETEACH/REVIEW

☐ **Review** Review words with this week's phonics skill. **DAY 5** *371*

☐ **Reteach Lesson** If necessary, reteach *Ee*/e/. **DAY 5** *DI·36*

☐ **Spiral REVIEW** Review previously taught phonics skills.
DAY 1 *332*, **DAY 2** *347*, **DAY 3** *355*, **DAY 4** *363*

ASSESS

☐ **Word and Sentence Reading** Assess children's ability to read words with *Ee*/e/. **DAY 5** *372–373*

HIGH-FREQUENCY WORDS

HIGH-FREQUENCY WORDS
here   *go*   *from*

TEACH

☐ **Reteach** Reteach last week's high-frequency words. **DAY 1** *331*

PRACTICE/APPLY

☐ **Words in Context** Read high-frequency words in the context of the Phonics Story and Decodable Reader 24.
DAY 2 *347*, **DAY 4** *364*

☐ **Word Wall** Use the Word Wall to review and practice high-frequency words throughout the week. **DAY 3** *355*
DAY 4 *364*, **DAY 5** *371*

☐ **Kindergarten Student Reader K.4.6** Practice this week's high-frequency words in context of reader.
DAY 3 *355–356, DI·28*

☐ **Differentiated Text** Practice this week's high-frequency words in the context of differentiated text. **DAY 1** *DI·26*, **DAY 4** *LR11*

☐ **Homework** Practice Book K.4, p. 54.
DAY 2 *347*

Phonics Story

Decodable Reader 24

Kindergarten Student Reader K.4.6

Listen to Me Reader K.4.6

Independent Leveled Reader K.4.6

RETEACH/REVIEW

☐ **Spiral REVIEW** Review previously taught high-frequency words.
DAY 2 *347*, **DAY 3** *355*, **DAY 4** *364*, **DAY 5** *371*

ASSESS

☐ **Word Reading** Assess children's ability to read this week's high-frequency words. **DAY 5** *372–373*

☑ **Customize Your Plan** *by Strand*

COMPREHENSION

🎯 **SKILL SETTING** The setting is when and where the story happens.

TEACH

❏ **Skill Lesson** Introduce and model *setting*. **DAY 1** *329*

PRACTICE/APPLY

❏ **Skill in Context** Model how to identify *setting*. Then read *Abuela*, guiding children as they identify *setting*. **DAY 2** *338-345*

❏ **Skill in Context** Reread *One Little Mouse* and apply *setting*. **DAY 4** *362*

❏ **Leveled Text** Apply *setting* to leveled text. **DAY 4** *LR11*

Trade Book

Big Book

Independent Leveled Reader K.4.6

ASSESS

❏ **Check** Read "Apple Juice Tea." Then have children practice *setting*. **DAY 5** *370*

❏ **Assess** Use the blackline master on p. 374 to assess children's understanding of *setting*. **DAY 5** *370, 374*

Read Aloud Anthology

RETEACH/REVIEW

❏ **Review Realism and Fantasy** Review definition of *realism* and *fantasy* and apply to *Abuela*. **DAY 3** *353*

❏ **Reteach Lesson** If necessary, reteach *setting*. **DAY 5** *DI·36*

WRITING

TEACH

❏ **Write Together** Engage children in writing activities that develop language, grammar, and writing skills and practice phonics skills. Include independent writing as an extension of group writing activities.

Shared Writing
❏ **Connect to Grammar** DAY 1 *333*
❏ **This Week We...** DAY 5 *375*

Modeled Writing
❏ **Respond to Literature** DAY 2 *348*
❏ **Connect to Phonics** DAY 3 *357*

Interactive Writing
❏ **Connect to Phonics** DAY 4 *365*

PRACTICE/APPLY

❏ **Daily Journal Writing** Have children write about concepts and literature in their journals. **EVERY DAY** *318-319*

❏ **Writing Center** Have children complete sentence frames. **ANY DAY** *325*

① Use assessment data to determine your instructional focus.

② Preview this week's instruction by strand.

③ Choose instructional activities that meet the needs of your classroom.

GRAMMAR

TEACH

❏ **Introduce** Introduce pronoun *I*. DAY 1 *333*

PRACTICE/APPLY

❏ **Practice** Practice pronoun *I*. DAY 2 *348*, DAY 4 *365*

❏ **Daily Fix-It** Have children find and correct errors in capitalization and punctuation. DAY 1 *333*, DAY 2 *348*, **DAY 3** *357*, DAY 4 *365*, DAY 5 *375*

REVIEW

❏ **Review** Review last week's grammar skill, uppercase letters and periods. **DAY 3** *357*

❏ **Review** Review pronoun *I*. DAY 5 *375*

SPEAKING AND LISTENING

TEACH

❏ **Listen to Poems** Introduce and model listening to poems. DAY 1 *334*

PRACTICE/APPLY

❏ **Practice** Have children practice listening to poems. DAY 3 *358*, DAY 4 *366*

REVIEW

❏ **Review** Review listening to poems. Then have children listen to and illustrate poems. DAY 5 *376*

INQUIRY PROJECT

TEACH

❏ **Unit Inquiry Project** Allow time for children to work on the theme project "*Remember When* Album." Have children bind their books with ribbon or yarn. Then have them present them to the class. **ANY DAY** *xxiii*

Resources for Differentiated Instruction

Emergent

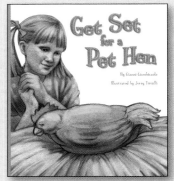

Listen to Me Reader

▶ **Oral Language**
Develop oral vocabulary.

▶ **Phonemic Awareness**
/e/ in initial and medial position

▶ **Decodable Words**
get   set   met   Ted
Hen   pet   pen   fed
bed   Meg

▶ **High-Frequency Words**
here   go   is
a   look

On-Level

Kindergarten Student Reader

▶ **Connected Text**
Realistic Fiction

▶ **Phonics: Ee/e/**
get   set   Ben
tells   gets

▶ **High-Frequency Words**
here   go   from

▶ **Spiral Review: Decodable Words**
Mom   in   cab   Dad
at   Big   Dig   Spot
can   it   did   and

High-Frequency Words
to   they   the   see
we   you   look   one

Independent

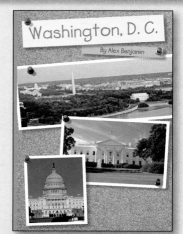

Leveled Reader K.4.6
Independent Leveled Reader

▶ **Comprehension: Setting**
Identify and describe setting.

▶ **Concept**
Adventures you can have in the city

▶ **Social Studies Standards**
National symbols

Leveled Reader, TE, LR12

ELL Resources

- ELL Poster 24
- ELL and Transition Handbook
- ELL Notes in Teacher's Edition, pp. 326–377

ELL Poster 24

ELL and Transition Handbook

My Sidewalks
Early Reading Intervention

For students who need intensive intervention

- Effectiveness proved by scientific research
- Instruction focused on early reading success predictors
- 30 minutes of daily small-group instruction

ONLINE

PearsonSuccessNet.com

Use the Online Database of over 600 books to

- Download and print additional copies of this week's leveled readers
- Listen to the readers being read online
- Search for more titles focused on this week's skills, topic, and content

Readers' Theater Anthology

Readers' Theater Anthology

- Six scripts to build fluency
- Poetry for oral interpretation

Homework

- Family Times Newsletter

Take-Home Books

- Kindergarten Student Readers
- Decodable Readers
- Listen to Me Readers
- Independent Leveled Readers

Literacy Centers

Listening

Let's Read
Along

- *Abuela*
- AudioText CD

Audio CD

Journal Writing

- **Day One** Draw or write about something you might see in a city.

- **Day Two** Dictate, illustrate, or write three words that rhyme with *bed*. Use one in a sentence.

- **Day Three** Dictate or write four words that rhyme with *bell*. Draw a picture of one of them.

- **Day Four** Dictate or write three short *e* words.

- **Day Five** Draw or write about an adventure you have had with a family member.

Word Work

Grab
Bag

MATERIALS
brown paper bag, index cards or construction paper, writing paper, writing utensils

Make a Word
1. On individual index cards or construction paper, write the following word parts: *p, b, t, l, f, -ell, -eg, -ed.* Place the word parts in a bag.
2. Working in pairs, have children take turns pulling out two cards each from the bag.
3. Children should work together, sharing their cards to sound out the letters and decide if the cards make a word.
4. Children should copy any words they make onto their papers and place the cards back into the bag and play Grab Bag again.

 Phonics Activities CD This interactive CD provides additional practice.

CENTER TIP You may wish to have a list of words that could be made from the word parts in the bag available for students.

Art

Cloud
Sculpting

MATERIALS
cotton balls, blue construction paper, white chalk, glue

Make Clouds
1. Encourage children to make clouds that look like familiar objects like the clouds seen in the story. Have children use chalk to draw an outline of a cloud on their paper.
2. Have children glue cotton balls within the shape to make their clouds.
3. Have children label their artwork *cloud*.

CENTER TIP You may wish to have children look at the sky to observe actual clouds.

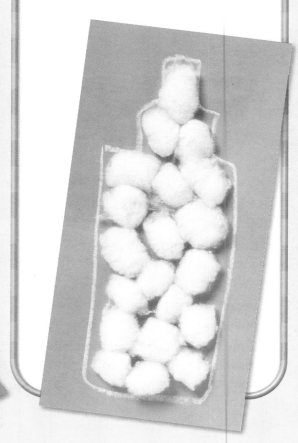

Scott Foresman Reading Street Centers Survival Kit

Use the *Abuela* materials from the Reading Street Centers
Survival Kit to organize this week's centers.

 Writing

 Social Studies

 Math

If I Could Fly!

MATERIALS
sentence prompt, writing
paper, writing utensils, crayons

Write About a Trip

1. Have the following sentence frame on the board or on paper at the center: *If I could fly, I would go*

   _____.

2. Have students copy the sentence onto their own papers.

3. Children can either write or dictate to finish the sentence about where they would go if they could fly like Rosalba and Abuela in the story.

4. Children should then draw a picture of the place they would go if they could fly.

Land, Water, or Air

MATERIALS
Picture Cards: *cloud, lake, playground*; *Abuela*; construction paper; writing utensils; crayons

Classify Transportation

1. Display the words *Land, Water,* and *Air* with the corresponding Picture Card next to each word.

2. Divide paper into three parts for each child. Children should write each of the three words on a section of the paper.

3. Children should use the story *Abuela* to pick out one mode of transportation, such as bicycle, airplane, and boat, and draw a picture of the mode of transportation that corresponds with the setting.

4. Remind children to use picture clues such as trees, water, and clouds to help others understand the setting of their picture.

Above the City

MATERIALS
construction paper, crayons, scissors, glue

Make Buildings

1. Remind children that the characters in the story flew over the city and saw many different buildings. Have children choose three different colors of construction paper, along with one piece of white paper.

2. Ask children to cut the construction paper into three building shapes, making each one a different size.

3. Have children glue the building shapes onto the white paper, starting with the smallest and moving to the largest shape. Children can decorate their building shapes with windows and other designs using crayons.

4. Have children label the pictures 1, 2, and 3, with 1 being the smallest building and 3 being the largest.

If I could fly, I would go to the park.

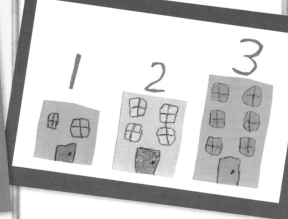

ALL CENTERS

Day 1
AT A GLANCE

Materials

- Calendar
- Talk with Me, Sing with Me Chart 24A, 24B
- Sing with Me/Background Building Audio CD
- Trade Book *Abuela*
- Big Books *Animal ABCs, One Little Mouse*
- AudioText CD
- Alphabet Cards: *Bb, Cc, Ee, Ff, Gg, Kk, Ll, Mm, Tt*
- Decodable Reader 23
- Picture Cards: p. 330
- Daily Fix-It Transparency 24

Calendar

Name the day and date
Point to today's date on the calendar and say the day, month, date, and year. Have children read the day, month, date, and year with you.

Identify pattern
Ask a volunteer to find today's date on the calendar. Point to Monday on the calendar. Point to Tuesday on the calendar. Which day comes after Tuesday? Name the days of the week with me.

Message Board

Question of the week
Tell children that they will have an opportunity to talk, sing, read, and write about adventures people can have.

Write and read the question as you track the print. Encourage children to respond in complete sentences.

> ## What kind of adventures can you have in the city?

Build Background Use the Day 1 instruction on ELL Poster 24 to assess knowledge and develop concepts.

ELL Poster 24

Build Background

LET'S TALK

Build concept
Display Talk with Me Chart 24A. Point to the pictures. These pictures show what it looks like to fly over a city. Look at this picture of airplanes. What else do you see here that can fly high in the air? What else do you see in the pictures? Prompt children to respond in complete sentences.

Build oral vocabulary
This week we will be talking about adventures in the city. We are going to learn six new words. Listen as I say the words; you may know some of them: *abuela, adventure, flock, city, airport,* and *harbor.*

Talk with Me, Sing with Me Chart

LET'S LISTEN

Share Background Building Audio
Play the CD that features children discussing relationships with their grandmothers.

Sing with Me/Background Building Audio CD

LET'S SING/PHONOLOGICAL AWARENESS

Sing "To the City We Will Go"
Display Sing with Me Chart 24B. Tell children that they are going to sing a song about city adventures. Read the title and describe the pictures. Sing the song several times to the tune of "Ring Around the Rosie." Encourage children to sing along with you.

Count syllables
Have children clap and count the syllables in the words *city, Abuela,* and *go.*

Sing with Me/Background Building Audio CD

To the City We Will Go

To the city we will go,
I love the bus, you know,
Abuela, Abuela,
An adventure for you and me!

Talk with Me, Sing with Me Chart

Amazing Words to build oral vocabulary

- abuela
- flock
- airport
- adventure
- city
- harbor

Options Before Reading

Activate Prior Knowledge

What Can You Do in the City? Ask children to discuss what they know about the city.

- What are some things you would see in the city?
- What are some things to do in the city?
- How would you get to the city?

Oral Language

What Happened? Ask children to recall a time they visited a city.

- What was the city like?
- What did you do there?
- What made it an adventure?

Develop Story Concepts

Make a Story Display the cover of *Abuela.* Create an adventurous story about flying over a city.

Comprehension

MODEL READING STRATEGIES

Preview and predict

Display *Abuela.* Look at the cover and tell me what you see.

 It looks like a girl and her grandmother are flying over a city. They look like they are happy.

The title of this book is *Abuela. Abuela* is the Spanish word for "grandmother." We will learn many Spanish words in this book. They are printed in special letters. At the end there is a page called a glossary with all the Spanish words and their meanings. What do you think this story will be about? Let's read to find out.

LET'S READ *Abuela*

Model fluent reading

Read the story with expression for enjoyment.

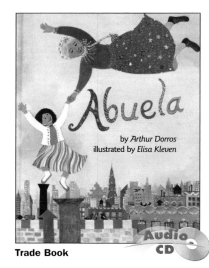

Trade Book

AudioText CD

Shared Reading

ROUTINE

Day 1	**Day 2**	**Day 3**	**Day 4**	**Day 5**
Preview and make predictions about *Abuela*. Read the whole book for enjoyment. Introduce comprehension skill, setting.	**Reread** *Abuela*. Use the Shared Reading Notes to engage children in a conversation about the story. Apply comprehension skill, setting.	**Reread** *Abuela*. Develop oral vocabulary by learning about new places and things. Review comprehension skill, realism and fantasy.	**Reread** *One Little Mouse*. Apply comprehension skill, setting.	**Read** "Apple Juice Tea" in the *Read Aloud Anthology*. Assess comprehension skill, setting.

Text to Self READER RESPONSE

Respond to literature

Invite children to sit on the floor in a group. Ask children to tell about an experience they had with someone special in their lives.

Text to World STRATEGY Predict

Check predictions

• What did you think the story would be about?

• What are some of the places Abuela and Rosalba visited?

Use the following questions to guide discussion.

• What place in the story did you like best?

• Why did you like that place?

 INTRODUCE SKILL Setting

Define Setting

• As you listen to a story, think about where and when the story takes place.

• Where and when the story takes place is called the ***setting.***

> **Think Aloud** Rosalba and Abuela had an adventure on a sunny day in the city.

Recall setting

Display *One Little Mouse.* Help children identify the setting.

• The little mouse visited many animal homes while looking for a new home. All of the animals lived in the woods. The woods is where the story *One Little Mouse* took place.

Relate setting to everyday life

We can think about where and when things happen in our daily routine also. Where do we come together to learn? (classroom in school) When do we come to school? (morning/afternoon) Where do we spend our evenings? (home)

OBJECTIVES

- Respond to literature.
- Check predictions.
- Introduce setting.

Skills Trace
Setting

Introduce/Teach	TE: K.1 79, 88; K.2 77, 86; K.4 329, 338; K.6 265, 274
Practice	TE: K.1 101, 110, 118; K.2 90, 99, 108, 116; K.4 353, 362, 370; K.6 287, 296, 304 PB: K.1 17, 19; K.2 17, 19; K.4 57, 59; K.6 47, 49
Reteach/Review	TE: K.1 165, 229, 353, DI-46; K.2 225, DI-46; K.4 227, DI-50; K.6 DI-49
Assess	TE: K.1 122, 380–382; K.2 120, 376–378; K.4 374, 380–382; K.6 308, 378–380; Unit 2 Benchmark Test

ELL

Access Content Display the book *Abuela.* Picture walk through the story. Ask children to identify the time of day and location.

Text to Self

OBJECTIVES

• Reteach /e/.
• Discriminate /e/.

Skills Trace

⊙ Short *e*

Introduce/Teach	TE: K.4 268–269
Practice	TE: K.4 282, 290, 293, 301, 346, 354, 357, 365; K.6 154, 162, 165, 173 PB: K.4 43, 45–46, 48, 53, 55–56, 58
Reteach/Review	TE: K.4 307, 330–331, 346, 354, 371, DI-35, DI-36; K.5 47; K.6 140–141, 179, 235, DI-33
Assess	TE: K.4 308–309, 372–373, 380–382; K.6 180–181, 378–380; Unit 4 Benchmark Test

Materials

• Trade Book *Abuela*
• Big Book *Animal ABCs*
• Alphabet Cards: *Bb, Cc, Ee, Ff, Gg, Kk, Ll, Mm, Tt*
• Decodable Reader 23
• Picture Cards:

bag	bed	box
desk	doll	drum
hat	hen	hose
jug	jam	jet

ELL

Support Phonemic Awareness
In many languages, short vowel sounds may not exist or may only have approximations. English language learners may have a hard time hearing the differences in these sounds. Provide additional phonemic awareness activities to help children hear and pronounce words with short vowel sounds.

Phonemic Awareness

RETEACH /e/

Reteach /e/
Listen carefully to this sound; it is one you know: /e/, /e/, /e/. Say it with me: /e/, /e/, /e/. Say these words with me and listen for /e/; /e/ can be first or in the middle of the word: *elbow, elephant, jet,* and *hen.*

Discriminate /e/
I am going to say two words. Tell me which word has /e/ in the middle. Listen carefully: *pen, pan.* Which word has /e/ in the middle, *pen* or *pan? Pen* has /e/ in the middle. *Pan* has /a/ in the middle. Continue with the following word pairs: *bag, beg; peg, pig; Don, den; pet, pot; sit, set;* and *met, mat.*

Substitute initial sounds
Listen to this word: *Meg,* /m/ /e/ /g/. What word would we have if we change the /m/ to /l/? /l/ /e/ /g/, *leg.* The word is *leg.* Let's try another word: *tell,* /t/ /e/ /l/. Change the /t/ to /b/. What is our new word? Continue changing initial phonemes with the following words to create the words in parentheses: *net (met), sell (yell), neck (deck), bed (red),* and *jet (vet).*

Listen for /e/
Teach children "Ten Red Hens," sung to the tune of "Row, Row, Row Your Boat."

**Ten little red hens
are sitting on their nests.
Meg yells, "Look at the time; it's ten o'clock."
"Girls, it's time to rest!"**

Sing the song several times. Then have children identify the /e/ words.

Monitor Progress — Check Sound Fluency

Listen for /e/ Display Picture Cards *bed, bag,* and *box.* Which word has /e/ in the middle? Continue with the following Picture Cards: *desk, doll, drum; hat, hen, hose;* and *jug, jam, jet.*

If... children cannot identify /e/,

then... say the words, emphasizing initial or medial /e/. Have them echo you.

SUCCESS PREDICTOR

▶ Day 1	Day 2	Day 3	Day 4	Day 5
Check Sound Fluency	Check Retelling/ Letter-Sound Knowledge	Check High-Frequency Words/ Word Reading	Check Phoneme Segmentation	Check Oral Vocabulary/ Assess Progress

Phonics

 CONNECT /e/ to *Ee*

Reteach *Ee*/e/

Display page 5 of *Animal ABCs*. Point to the word *elephant*. This is the word *elephant*. The word *elephant* begins with the letter *e*. The sound for *e* is /e/: /e/, /e/, *elephant*.

Alphabet Card

Recognize *Ee*

Encourage children to point to the letter *Ee* on your classroom Alphabet Chart or Alphabet Card.

Connect /e/ to *Ee*

Write the word *Ed*. What word is this? *Ed* begins with /e/. What is the letter for /e/? Yes, *E* is the letter for /e/. Have children trace the letters *Ee* in the palms of their hands.

Review letter names and sounds

Use *Animal ABCs* to review letter names and sounds. What is the name of this letter? *(e)* What is the sound of this letter? *(/e/)* Continue the routine with the following letters: *Bb, Cc, Ff, Gg, Kk, Ll, Mm,* and *Tt*.

Big Book

BLEND SOUNDS

Blend *e*/e/ words

Write *Peg* on the board. *Peg* has three sounds. I am going to blend the sound of each letter together to say this word: /p/ /e/ /g/. The word is *Peg*.

Say the sounds with me: /p/ /e/ /g/. Now blend the three sounds with me as I point to each letter: /p/ /e/ /g/, *peg*. The word is *peg*. Continue blending practice with *leg, bell, pet, red, tent, mess,* and *ten*.

Word Wall HIGH-FREQUENCY WORDS

Reteach *here, go, from*

Display *go*. This is the word *go*. Let's read it together: *go*. Continue with the words *here* and *from*. Can you find the words on the Word Wall? Let's look in the book *Abuela* to find *go, here,* and *from*.

 go   here   from

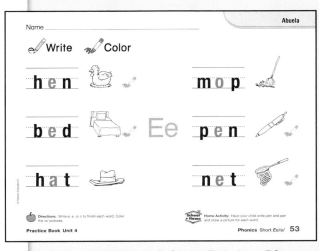

▲ **Practice Book 4** Short *Ee*/e/, p. 53

Sound Fluency
SUCCESS PREDICTOR

OBJECTIVES

- Review blending words.
- Write uppercase and lowercase *Ee*.

Group Time

On-Level

Reread Decodable Reader 23. Use the Small Group Reading **Routine**.

Strategic Intervention

Read Listen to Me Reader K.4.6. More practice with *Ee*/e/, p. DI·26.

Advanced

Reread Independent Leveled Reader K.4.5. Use the reading routine on p. DI·26. Reread to build fluency.

ELL

Group English language learners by their reading ability in English.

i Independent Activities

Self-Selected Reading See pp. TR14–15 for a bibliography of books related to the weekly concept.

Practice Book Short *Ee*/e/, p. 53

Centers Use the center activities on pp. 324–325 to practice this week's skills.

Journal Writing Draw or write about something you might see in a city.

Spiral REVIEW — PREPARE TO READ

Review words Review these words from last week's Decodable Reader 23 *Red Hen*:

Ben	get	hen	can
red	hid	did	not
Ken	in	ran	pen
got	Len		

Review high-frequency words Write the word *go* on the board. This is the word *go*. What is this word? Continue with the words *here*, *the*, and *from*.

Small Group Reading

Decodable Reader

1. **Model Fluent Reading** Have children finger point as you read a page.

2. **Read Chorally** Have children finger point as they chorally read the page. Continue reading page by page, repeating steps 1 and 2.

3. **Read Individually** Have children read aloud a page in their group.

4. **Reread and Monitor Progress** As you listen to individual children reread, monitor progress and provide support.

HANDWRITING

Write *E* and *e* Write *Eldon Elephant* on the board. This is the uppercase *E*. We use uppercase letters at the beginning of sentences and for the first letter in a person's name. *Eldon* begins with *E*. Watch as I trace the uppercase *E* with my finger. Follow the stroke instructions pictured below. Now you trace the *E* on your paper. Repeat the routine to write the lowercase *e* in *Elephant*.

D'Nealian™	Ball and Stick

Shared Writing

GRAMMAR Pronoun *I*

Introduce pronoun *I*

The word *I* is a special little word. **Write *I am little* on the board.** You use the word *I* when you are talking about yourself.

Identify pronoun *I*

When we use the letter *I* to talk about ourselves, it is always an uppercase letter, even if it is in the middle of a sentence. **Write *You and I can go* on the board.** Did I make the *I* an uppercase letter?

LET'S WRITE Connect to Grammar

Use pronoun *I*

Have children dictate a complete sentence about something they like to do. Write it on the board.

I play ball.

I like to go to the park.

I read books.

Revise and edit

The first word in a sentence begins with an uppercase letter. Did I do that? A telling sentence should end with a period. Did I do that? **Write three more sentences with children.**

Independent writing

Have children write or dictate their own sentences using *I* or copy a sentence the class wrote together. Then have them illustrate their sentences.

OBJECTIVES

- Introduce pronoun *I*.
- Use pronoun *I* in sentences.

DAILY FIX-IT

i can go to see you

(I can go to see you.)

This week's practice sentences appear on Daily Fix-It Transparency 24.

Writing ROUTINE

Day 1 **Shared Writing** Connect to grammar.

Day 2 **Modeled Writing** Respond to literature.

Day 3 **Modeled Writing** Connect to phonics.

Day 4 **Interactive Writing** Connect to phonics.

Day 5 **Shared Writing** Write about this week's literature.

OBJECTIVE

● Introduce listening to poems.

Access Content Recite *Mary Had a Little Lamb.* Have children identify rhyming words.

Speaking and Listening

LISTEN TO POEMS

Discuss listening to poems

Today we are going to listen to a poem. A poem is a story that might rhyme or might not rhyme. A poem has a rhythm, like clapping to a beat. A person who writes a poem chooses words carefully because poems usually have fewer words than books.

Model listen to poems

As I read the poem, try to figure out what the poem is about. Listen for rhyming words and a beat.

Flying Over New York
I flew over New York one day.
It was so big and I was so small.
I flew over New York one day
and saw a lady so tall.

Discuss listen to poems

• What do you think the poem was about?

• What are some rhyming words you heard?

Let's clap a beat as I read the poem again.

Wrap Up Your Day!

✓ **Oral Language** Today we read about a little girl named Rosalba and her adventure in the city. Have you ever gone on a fun adventure with someone you loved?

✓ **Comprehension** Every story takes place somewhere. In the story *Abuela,* the author takes us on a journey to the city.

✓ **Grammar** Today we used the word *I* to talk about ourselves. What did you do today?

PREVIEW Day 2

Tomorrow we will read *Abuela* **again.**

Homework Send home this week's Family Times newsletter.

EXTEND Your Day

Scenes from Our City

Materials Trade Book *Abuela,* map of your local city, construction paper, drawing tools

Overhead View Take a picture walk through *Abuela.* Point out the places Rosalba and Abuela visit.

Discuss things to see in your local city or town.

- What would it look like if you could fly over our town?
- What types of buildings would you see?
- What other places that you know about are in our city?
- What types of transportation are in our city?

Have children pretend they are flying over their town or city. Remind them that they will see only the tops of things as they look down from the sky. Guide them to describe who and what they can see. Have children draw what they imagine.

Time for
SOCIAL
STUDIES

Grammar
Write a Poem

Cinquains Have children write a cinquain *(sin-kain).* A cinquain is a five-line poem that fits a special pattern of length. Help children to follow this pattern:

Line 1: Child's name

Line 2: Two describing words about the child

Line 3: Three action words describing something the child likes to do

Line 4: Complete the sentence *I love to* _____.

Line 5: One describing word

> Olivia
> happy, healthy
> jumps, skates, soars
> she loves to race
> wonderful

Literature
Poetry

Rhyming Words As a class try to write a simple rhyming poem. Brainstorm to make a list of rhyming words that could be used in a poem, such as *Ted, red, Ned, fed* and *bed,* or *hop, top, mop,* and *pop.* Then work together to create a simple poem.

> **Corn can pop, pop, pop.**
> **I can hop, hop, hop.**
> **You can mop, mop, mop.**
> **Then we stop, stop, stop.**

Day 2
AT A GLANCE

Oral Language and Vocabulary
Calendar
Message Board
Build Background

Shared Reading
Trade Book *Abuela*
Strategy Recall and Retell
Skill Setting

Word Work

Phonemic Awareness
Listen for /e/

Phonics
Connect /e/ to *Ee*
Blend Sounds
H/F Words *here, go, from*
Phonics Story *Ted and the Pet*

Read
Group Time < Differentiated Instruction

Language Arts
Grammar: Pronoun *I*
Modeled Writing: Write About
City Adventures
Speaking and Listening:
Review Oral Vocabulary

Materials
- Calendar
- Talk with Me, Sing with Me Chart 23A, 24A, 24B
- Sing with Me/Background Building Audio CD
- Trade Book *Abuela*
- AudioText CD
- Phonics Songs and Rhymes Chart 24
- Phonics Songs and Rhymes Audio CD
- Alphabet Cards: *Aa, Bb, Cc, Dd, Ee, Gg, Mm, Nn, Pp, Tt,* keyboard
- Phonics Story *Ted and the Pet*

Calendar

Name the day and date
Ask a volunteer to find today's date on the calendar. Have children say the day, month, date, and year together.

Last week and next week
Show children this month's calendar and explain that it contains full and partial weeks. Show them last week and next week on the calendar. Explain that some weeks may be in more that one month if they are the first or last week of the month.

Message Board

Question of the day
Write and read the question as you track the print. Encourage children to respond in complete sentences.

> ## How is the city the same as or different from here?

Review high-frequency words
Have children find high-frequency words they know in the question of the day. Circle them and say them together.

Build Background Use the Day 2 instruction on ELL Poster 24 to practice the Develop Vocabulary words.

ELL Poster 24

Build Background

LET'S TALK/LET'S SING

Develop oral vocabulary

Display Talk with Me Chart 24A. Point to the photograph of a girl and her grandmother sitting on a park bench.

Talk with Me, Sing with Me Chart

To the City We Will Go

To the city we will go,
I love the bus, you know,
Abuela, Abuela,
An adventure for you and me!

- Who is sitting on this bench? It is a girl and her grandmother. The Spanish word for "grandmother" is *abuela*. This girl is sitting with her *abuela*.

- People in these hot-air balloons are going on an *adventure*. What kind of an *adventure* have you been on?

Sing "To the City We Will Go"

Display Sing with Me Chart 24B. The words *abuela* and *adventure* are in the song "To the City We Will Go." Ask children to listen for the words as you sing the song. Then ask children to name the places Abuela goes to in the song.

 Sing with Me/Background Building Audio CD

LET'S LEARN AMAZING WORDS

Oral Vocabulary   abuela   adventure

DAY 2 ROUTINE

1 **Introduce** *Abuela* is the Spanish word for "grandma." Remember that a grandma is the mother of your mommy or daddy. What is our new word for "grandma?"

Demonstrate *Abuela* is older than Mommy and Daddy. She is much older than we are. Does *Abuela* look older than Rosalba?

2 **Introduce** When we do something exciting, we can call it an *adventure*. Taking a trip to the zoo can be an *adventure*. What is our new word for doing something exciting?

Demonstrate Going to the city can be an *adventure*. When you travel somewhere new, it can be an *adventure*. Have you ever had an *adventure*?

3 **Review** We talked about two words today: *abuela* and *adventure*. Which word is another name for a "grandma," *abuela* or *adventure*? Which word names "something exciting we do," *abuela* or *adventure*?

4 **Apply** Have children use *abuela* and *adventure* in complete sentences. Have children use *abuela* instead of "grandma" for the rest of the day.

OBJECTIVES
- Build background.
- Develop oral vocabulary.

Amazing Words to build oral vocabulary

- abuela
- flock
- airport
- adventure
- city
- harbor

ELL

Activate Prior Knowledge Ask children which words in their home languages are used for the words *grandma* and *adventure*.

OBJECTIVES

- Recall story events.
- Recognize setting.
- Distinguish letters and words.

Materials

- Trade Book *Abuela*

ELL

Access Content Encourage children to retell the adventure of Rosalba and Abuela. If they have difficulty with English words, supply words and prompt children to use them.

TEACHING TiP

Using a Map Use a map or globe to show children where New York City is. Point out where the Statue of Liberty stands and explain its significance to immigrants arriving in America.

Comprehension

MODEL READING STRATEGY
Recall and Retell

Retell the story

Using the pictures as prompts, invite children to retell the story.

Open to the first page. We see a little girl named Rosalba and her abuela. What are they doing? Do you remember some of the places they visit?

Trade Book

SKILL Setting

Model identifying setting

Remind children to think about where and when a story takes place. *Abuela* takes place in New York City during the day.

> **Think Aloud** Rosalba and Abuela have adventures in the city. They aren't wearing heavy coats, so it must be warm. It is light outside; it looks like daytime.

CONCEPTS OF PRINT Letters and Words

Distinguish letters and words

Point to the word *grandma* on page 6 of *Abuela*. How many letters are in this word? Let's count together. There are seven letters in the word *grandma*. Remind children that words are made up of letters and words have spaces between them. Now let's count the number of words in this sentence. There are four words in this sentence. Continue with other words and sentences in the story.

LET'S READ *Abuela*

Reread the story

Ask children to identify the different places Rosalba and her abuela travel. Point out different kinds of buildings and forms of transportation. Use the Shared Reading Notes to prompt conversation about *Abuela*.

 **AudioText CD**

Shared Reading Notes

Page 5

Abuela takes me on the bus.
We go all around the city.

Read page 5 aloud. **What are these people getting on?** *Child may respond:* a bus

- The grandma and the little girl are getting on the bus. Have you ever ridden a city bus? What was it like? **distancing**

Pages 6–7

Abuela is my grandma.
She is my mother's mother.
Abuela means "grandma" in Spanish.
Abuela speaks mostly Spanish because
that's what people spoke where she grew up,
before she came to this country.
Abuela and I are always going places.

Who is the little girl with? *Child may respond:* her grandma

- The little girl is with her grandma. What kinds of places can you go on a bus? **open-ended**

Develop Vocabulary grandma

Pages 8–9

Today we're going to the park.
"El parque es lindo," says Abuela.
I know what she means.
I think the park is beautiful too.

"Tantos pájaros," Abuela says
as a flock of birds surrounds us.
So many birds.
They're picking up the bread we brought.

What are Rosalba and Abuela doing? *Child may respond:* feeding the birds

- The girl and Abuela are feeding the birds. What are other people doing at the park? *wh-* **question**

Develop Vocabulary park, bread

Shared Reading Notes

What is the little girl doing in this picture? *Child may respond:* flying

- The little girl is flying. Can she really fly? **open-ended**

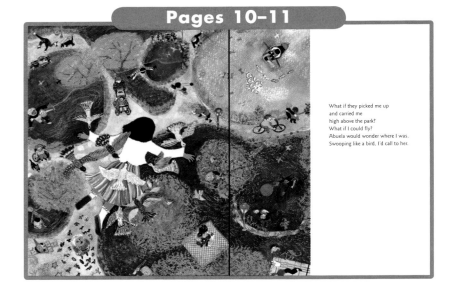

Pages 10–11

What if they picked me up
and carried me
high above the park?
What if I could fly?
Abuela would wonder where I was.
Swooping like a bird, I'd call to her.

Read page 12 aloud. What is Abuela doing now? *Child may respond:* flying

- Now Abuela is flying too. Where do you think they will fly on their adventure? **open-ended**

Expand Vocabulary leaped

Activate Prior Knowledge Ask children what places they have visited before. Allow English language learners to use expressions in their own language before translating into English.

Pages 12–13

Then she'd see me flying.
Rosalba the bird.
"*Rosalba el pájaro,*" she'd say.
"*Ven, Abuela. Come, Abuela,*" I'd say.
"*Sí, quiero volar,*" Abuela would reply
as she leaped into the sky
with her skirt flapping in the wind.

What are they flying over? *Child may respond:* the city

- Abuela and Rosalba are flying over the city. The city has many people. What are some of these people doing?
  wh- question

Expand Vocabulary soared

Pages 14–15

We would fly all over the city.
"*Mira,*" Abuela would say, pointing.

And I'd look, as we soared
over parks and streets, dogs and people.

Pages 16-17

We'd wave to the people waiting for the bus.
"*Buenos días*," we'd say.
"*Buenos días*. Good morning," they'd call
up to us.
We'd fly over factories and trains . . .

Pages 18-19

and glide close to the sea.
"*Cerca del mar*," we'd say.
We'd almost touch the tops of waves.

Abuela's skirt would be a sail.
She could race with the sailboats.
I'll bet she'd win.

Pages 20-21

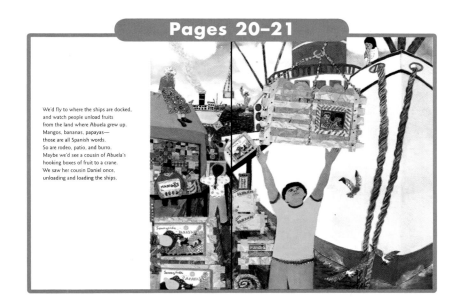

We'd fly to where the ships are docked,
and watch people unload fruits
from the land where Abuela grew up.
Mangos, bananas, papayas—
those are all Spanish words.
So are rodeo, patio, and burro.
Maybe we'd see a cousin of Abuela's
hooking boxes of fruit to a crane.
We saw her cousin Daniel once,
unloading and loading the ships.

Shared Reading Notes

What are Rosalba and Abuela doing now? *Child may respond:* waving to people

- Rosalba and Abuela are waving to people waiting for the bus. Have you ever looked down from the sky? **distancing**

Where are Rosalba and Abuela now? *Child may respond:* by the sea

- Rosalba and Abuela are by the sea. Who do they see? *wh-* **question**

What are Rosalba and Abuela looking at? *Child may respond:* boxes of fruit and ships

- Rosalba and Abuela are looking at boxes of fruit. What kind of fruit would you like the ship to bring? **distancing**

Shared Reading Notes

Where are they now? *Child may respond:* at the Statue of Liberty

- Rosalba and Abuela are flying by the Statue of Liberty. The Statue of Liberty was a gift to the United States from France. Do you know which city has the Statue of Liberty? **wh- question**

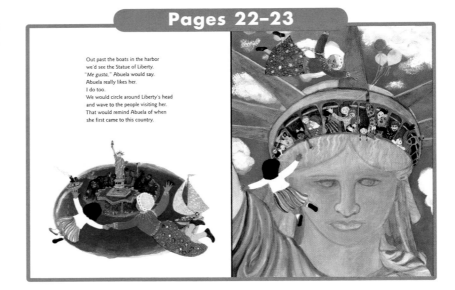

Pages 22–23

Out past the boats in the harbor
we'd see the Statue of Liberty.
"*Me gusta,*" Abuela would say.
Abuela really likes her.
I do too.
We would circle around Liberty's head
and wave to the people visiting her.
That would remind Abuela of when
she first came to this country.

Where did Rosalba and Abuela fly next? *Child may respond:* to the airport

- Rosalba and Abuela flew to the airport next. How many planes do you see at the airport? **wh- question**

Access Content Many words in this story are translated into Spanish for the readers. Walk through the pages and have children repeat the Spanish words with you.

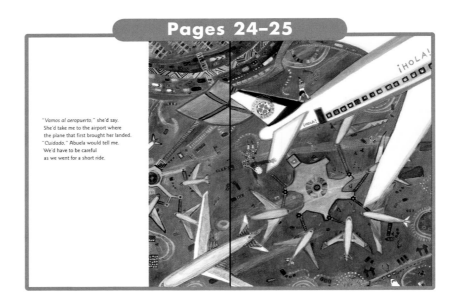

Pages 24–25

"*Vamos al aeropuerto,*" she'd say.
She'd take me to the airport where
the plane that first brought her landed.
"*Cuidado,*" Abuela would tell me.
We'd have to be careful
as we went for a short ride.

What are they doing now? *Child may respond:* drinking lemonade

- Rosalba and Abuela stopped for something to drink. Why did they stop flying? **open-ended**

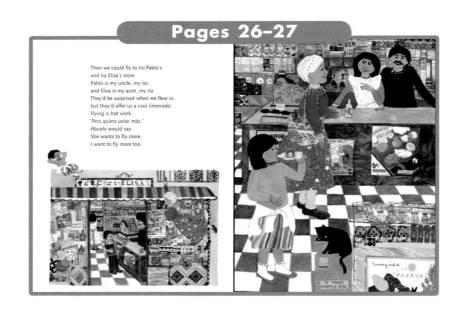

Pages 26–27

Then we could fly to *tío* Pablo's
and *tía* Elisa's store.
Pablo is my uncle, my *tío,*
and Elisa is my aunt, my *tía.*
They'd be surprised when we flew in,
but they'd offer us a cool *limonada.*
Flying is hot work.
"*Pero quiero volar más.*"
Abuela would say.
She wants to fly more.
I want to fly more too.

Shared Reading Notes

Pages 28–29

We could fly to *las nubes,* the clouds.
One looks like a cat, *un gato.*
One looks like a bear, *un oso.*
One looks like a chair, *una silla.*
"*Descansemos un momento,*"
Abuela would say.
She wants to rest a moment.
We would rest in our chair,
and Abuela would hold me in her arms,
with the whole sky
our house, *nuestra casa.*

Where are Abuela and Rosalba sitting?
Child may respond: on a cloud

• They are sitting on the clouds. I see some shapes in the clouds. What do you see? ***wh-* question**

Develop Vocabulary clouds

Pages 30–31

We'd be as high as airplanes,
balloons, and birds,
and higher than the tall buildings downtown.
But we'd fly there too
to look around.

What other things do you see in the sky?
Child may respond: balloons, planes, birds

• There are birds, balloons, and an airplane in the sky. They have been many places today. What is down below Abuela and Rosalba? ***wh-* question**

Pages 32–33

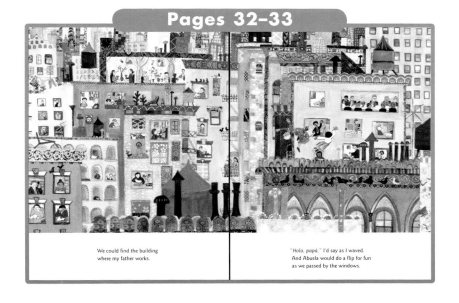

We could find the building
where my father works.

"*Hola, papá,*" I'd say as I waved.
And Abuela would do a flip for fun
as we passed by the windows.

What are some of the people in the buildings doing? *Child may respond:* typing, working, sleeping, eating, talking

• The people in the buildings are typing, talking, sleeping, and working. Who do they see in the window? ***wh-* question**

Shared Reading Notes

Where are Rosalba and Abuela? *Child may respond:* at the park, where they started

• Rosalba and Abuela are back in the park where they started. What do they see in the park? **open-ended**

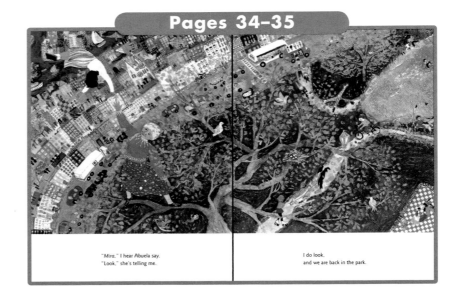
Pages 34–35

"*Mira,*" I hear Abuela say.
"Look," she's telling me.

I do look.
and we are back in the park.

What does Abuela want to do now? *Child may respond:* go for a boat ride

• Abuela wants to go for a boat ride. What is one thing Rosalba loves about Abuela? **recall**

Pages 36–37

We are walking by the lake.
Abuela probably wants to go for a boat ride.
"*Vamos a otra aventura,*" she says.
She wants us to go for another adventure.
That's just one of the things I love
about Abuela.
She likes adventures.

Where are Abuela and Rosalba going? *Child may respond:* on a boat ride

• Abuela and Rosalba are going for a boat ride. What kinds of things will they see on the lake? **open-ended**

Pages 38–39

Abuela takes my hand.
"*Vamos,*" she says.
"Let's go."

Page 40

Glossary

Abuela (ah-BWEH-lah)   Grandmother
Buenos días (BWEH-nohs DEE-ahs)   Good day
Cerca del mar (SEHR-kah dehl mahr)   Close to the sea
Cuidado (kwee-DAH-doh)   Be careful
Descansemos un momento (dehs-kahn-SEH-mohs oon moh-MEHN-toh)
   Let's rest a moment
El parque es lindo (ehl PAHR-kay ehs LEEN-doh)
   The park is beautiful
Hola, papá (OH-lah, pah-PAH)   Hello, papa
Las nubes (lahs NOO-behs)   The clouds
Limonada (lee-moh-NAH-dah)   Lemonade
Me gusta (meh GOO-stah)   I like
Mira (MEE-rah)   Look
Nuestra casa (NWEH-strah CAH-sah)   Our house
Pero quiero volar más (PEH-roh key-EH-roh boh-LAR mahs)
   But I would like to fly more
Rosalba el pájaro (roh-SAHL-bah ehl PAH-hah-roh)
   Rosalba the bird
Sí, quiero volar (see, key-EH-roh boh-LAR)
   Yes. I want to fly
Tantos pájaros (TAHN-tohs PAH-hah-rohs)   So many birds
Tía (TEE-ah)   Aunt
Tío (TEE-oh)   Uncle
Un gato (oon GAH-toh)   A cat
Un oso (oon OH-soh)   A bear
Una silla (OON-ah SEE-yah)   A chair
Vamos (BAH-mohs)   Let's go
Vamos al aeropuerto (BAH-mohs ahl ah-ehr-oh-PWEHR-toh)
   Let's go to the airport
Vamos a otra aventura (BAH-mohs ah OH-trah ah-behn-TOO-rah)
   Let's go on another adventure
Ven (behn)   Come

   The capitalized syllable is stressed in pronunciation

Shared Reading Notes

This page is called the glossary. What is it called? **(glossary)**

This glossary tells us what the Spanish words in the story mean in English.

Monitor Progress   Check Retelling *Abuela*

Picture Walk and Retell Help children use the pictures in *Abuela* to retell the story.

If... children have difficulty retelling the story,
then... use the Retelling Rubric to help them move toward fluent retelling.

 SUCCESS PREDICTOR

Day 1
Check Sound
Fluency

▶ **Day 2**
Check Retelling/
Letter-Sound
Knowledge

Day 3
Check High-
Frequency Words/
Word Reading

Day 4
Check Phoneme
Segmentation

Day 5
Check Oral
Vocabulary/
Assess Progress

Scoring Rubric   Retelling

Rubric 4 3 2 1	**4**	**3**	**2**	**1**
Setting	describes time and location	identifies time and location	omits time and location	is unable to identify time and location
Character	describes main character(s) and character development	identifies main character(s)	omits or inaccurately identifies characters	unable to identify character
Events	describes events in sequence with details	tells most events in sequence with some detail	retells first and last events but omits middle with few details	is unable to retell events

Retelling Plan
☑ Week 1 assess Advanced students.
☑ Week 2 assess On-Level students.
☑ Week 3 assess Strategic Intervention students.
☑ Week 4 assess Advanced students.
☑ Week 5 assess On-Level students.
☑ **This week assess Strategic Intervention students.**

 Retelling **SUCCESS PREDICTOR**

WORD WORK

- Practice initial and medial /e/.
- Listen for /e/.
-  Connect /e/ to *Ee*.

Materials

- Phonics Songs and Rhymes Chart 24
- Phonics Story *Ted and the Pet*
- Alphabet Cards: *Aa, Bb, Cc, Dd, Ee, Gg, Mm, Nn, Pp, Tt,* keyboard

ELL

Access Content Explain that *vet* is short for *veterinarian*, meaning "a doctor for animals."

Phonemic Awareness

PRACTICE /e/

Listen for /e/
Display Phonics Songs and Rhymes Chart 24. We are going to learn a new song today. Listen carefully to the song. Play the CD or sing the song to the tune of "Baa, Baa, Black Sheep" several times. Encourage children to join in.

Discriminate /e/ words
Replay the song. This time raise your hand each time you hear a word that has /e/ in it. Play the CD several times, identifying words with initial or medial /e/: *get, set, ten, pets, met, vet, rest, yet, jet, help, fed, Em,* and *bed.*

Get Set, Ten Pets!
Get set, ten pets!
Have you met the vet?
Don't rest just yet—
Here's our jet.

We'll help you get on,
We'll make sure you're fed.
Em the vet is set to get
All ten tucked in bed!

Phonics Songs and Rhymes Audio CD

Phonics Songs and Rhymes Chart

Phonics

 CONNECT /e/ to *Ee*

Recognize *E*
Ask children to identify *E* on the keyboard card.

Identify *Ee*
Display the chart. Remember we learned a new song. There were many words with *Ee*/e/. Have children circle words on the chart that contain *Ee*/e/.

Connect /e/ to *Ee*
Write *e* on the board. What is the name of this letter? *(e)* What is the sound for this letter? *(/e/)* Repeat the routine with *E*.

Monitor Progress | **Check Letter-Sound Knowledge**

Connect /e/ to *Ee* Have children write the letter *e* on a piece of paper. This is the letter *e*. The sound for *e* is /e/. I am going to say a word. If you hear /e/ in the word, hold up your *e*. Say these words: *Meg, mat, peg, cat, leg, tell, fish,* and *fun.*

If... children cannot connect /e/ to *Ee*,
then... practice segmenting words to identify /e/.

SUCCESS PREDICTOR

Day 1
Check Sound Fluency

▶**Day 2**
Check Retelling/ Letter-Sound Knowledge

Day 3
Check High-Frequency Words/ Word Reading

Day 4
Check Phoneme Segmentation

Day 5
Check Oral Vocabulary/ Assess Progress

 **BLEND SOUNDS**

Review letter names and sounds

Spell and blend words

PHONICS ACTIVITY MAT

Use the Alphabet Cards to review these letter names and sounds: *Aa, Bb, Cc, Dd, Ee, Gg, Mm, Nn, Pp,* and *Tt.*

Listen to the three sounds in *bed:* /b/ /e/ /d/. What is the first sound in *bed?* (/b/) What is the letter for that sound? *(b)* Write *b* on the board. Now you write *b* on your papers. Continue with the remaining sounds.

Help me blend the sounds together to read this word: /b/ /e/ /d/. The word is *bed.*

Continue spell and blend practice with the following words: *Ted, pet, big, fed, met, tent, can, am, nest,* and *in.*

PREPARE TO READ

Review high-frequency words

Write *here* on the board. This is the word *here.* What is this word? Continue the word reading routine with *go, I, have, is, a, my, the, to, has, see,* and *do.*

Small Group Reading

DAY 2 ROUTINE

1 **Model Fluent Reading** Have children finger point as you read a page.

2 **Read Chorally** Have children finger point as they chorally read the page. Continue reading page by page, repeating steps 1 and 2.

3 **Read Individually** Have children read aloud a page in their group.

4 **Reread and Monitor Progress** As you listen to individual children reread, monitor progress and provide support.

Practice Book 4 Phonics Story, pp. 55–56

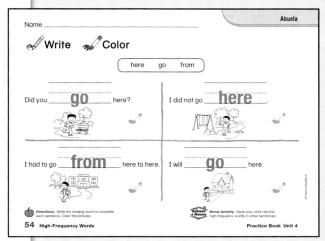

▲ **Practice Book 4** High-Frequency Words, p. 54

Group Time

On-Level

Read Phonics Story *Ted and the Pet.* Use the Small Group Reading **Routine.**

Strategic Intervention

Read Phonics Story *Ted and the Pet.* More practice with *Ee*/e/, p. DI·27.

Advanced

Read Decodable Reader 24. Use the reading routine on p. DI·27. Apply phonics skills.

ELL

Group English language learners by their reading ability in English.

i **Independent Activities**

Self-Selected Reading See pp. TR14–15 for books related to the weekly concept.

Practice Book High-Frequency Words, p. 54

Centers Use the center activities on pp. 324–325.

Journal Writing Dictate, illustrate, or write three words that rhyme with *bed.* Use one in a sentence.

Letter-Sound Knowledge

SUCCESS PREDICTOR

OBJECTIVES

- Practice pronoun *I*.
- Write about city adventures.

Materials

- Trade Book *Abuela*
- Talk with Me, Sing with Me Chart 23A

DAILY FIX-IT

i go to the park

(I go to the park.)

Writer's Checkup

✔ The first word in a sentence begins with an uppercase letter. Did I do that?

✔ A sentence should end with a period. Did I do that?

✔ A sentence should make sense. Does my sentence make sense?

✔ A good writer uses his or her best handwriting. Did I do that?

Modeled Writing

GRAMMAR Pronoun *I*

Practice pronoun *I*

Remember, when we talk about ourselves, we can use the letter *I* instead of our name. When I want to tell you what color I like, I would not say, *Ms. Sanchez likes yellow;* I would say, *I like yellow*. What is your favorite color? Answer the question in a complete sentence using the word *I*.

Identify pronoun *I*

Display page 8 of *Abuela*. Guide children to find places where the writer uses the pronoun *I*. Ask children who *I* is in *Abuela*.

Text to Self LET'S WRITE
Respond to Literature

Discuss *Abuela*

Discuss *Abuela*. Ask children to describe the places they see. Encourage children to use complete sentences and descriptive adjectives. Ask children if they have ever seen tall buildings or gone to the zoo.

Model writing a sentence

Abuela takes her granddaughter to fun and exciting places in the city. I like to take the train and see new things. Have you ever had an adventure in a city? What would you like to do? Would you play in the park, or shop in the stores? I would like to go to the zoo. I'm going to write:

I like to go to the zoo.

Independent writing

Have children write or dictate their own sentences about *Abuela* or copy one of the sentences the class wrote together. Then have them illustrate their sentences.

Speaking and Listening

LET'S REVIEW AMAZING WORDS

Display Talk with Me Chart 23A. Review these Amazing Words from last week.

Oral Vocabulary   Antarctica   continent

DAY 2 ROUTINE

1 **Introduce** *Antarctica* is a continent. It is very cold and covered with ice and snow. What is the name of the continent covered with ice and snow?

Demonstrate Remember, *Antarctica* is near the South Pole. Very few people live there because it is so cold. What else can you remember about *Antarctica?*

2 **Introduce** A *continent* is a large piece of land surrounded by oceans. We live on the North American *continent.* What is the name of a large piece of land surrounded by oceans?

Demonstrate There are seven *continents* in the world. Can you remember any of the seven *continents?* Can you point one out on the globe?

3 **Review** We talked about two words today: *Antarctica* and *continent.* Which word names a very cold place, *Antarctica* or *continent?* Which word is "a large piece of land," *Antarctica* or *continent?*

4 **Apply** Have children use *Antarctica* and *continent* in complete sentences. Have them locate *Antarctica* and another *continent* on a globe.

Wrap Up Your Day!

✓ **Oral Language** Today we read about an abuela on an adventure. What does *abuela* mean?

✓ **Grammar** Remember we use the word *I* when we talk about ourselves. What do you like to do after school?

✓ **Homework Idea** Have children take their Phonics Story home to share with their families.

 **PREVIEW Day 3**

Tomorrow we will read about Abuela again. What adventures would you like to have in the city?

EXTEND Your Day

Traveling

Materials paper, pencils, drawing tools

City Adventures Talk to children about the many adventures we can have in the city. Use these ideas to encourage discussion:

- go to the aquarium on a bus
- go to a museum in a taxi
- ride to the park on a bicycle
- take the train downtown to go shopping
- go to the top of a tall building in an elevator

Write the ideas on the board, along with the following sentence: *When I go to _____, I ride in a _____.*

Write a Sentence Children should write and illustrate the sentences about where they would go on an adventure and how they would get there.

Time for SOCIAL STUDIES

When I go to the park, I ride a bike.

Comprehension

Settings

Materials mural paper, crayons, markers

Create a Setting As a class, think of different possible settings for a story (locations, times of the day or year, or even other planets). Select two settings and have children discuss what they would see and what things they would need there, such as jackets for the snowy mountain. Divide the class into two groups, each to draw one of the settings. Have each group explain their setting and show their pictures.

Grammar

Pronoun *I*

Interviews Explain to children that in an interview, one person asks another person questions about him- or herself. Give these sample questions: *What do you like to do? Where do you live?* and *What do you like to eat?*

Ask volunteers to model interviewing each other for the class. Then have children interview each other, making sure to answer in complete sentences using the pronoun *I.* If needed, write the questions on the board.

Illustrate Pronoun *I* After the interviews are over, have children write or dictate one of their answers, such as *I like to ride my bike, I like to eat apples,* or *I live in the city.*

I go to the zoo.

Calendar

Name the day and date

Point to today's date on the calendar and read the day, month, date, and year. Have children say them after you.

Yesterday, today, tomorrow

Ask children to name the days of the week for today, tomorrow, and yesterday. Repeat and confirm that yesterday was Tuesday, today is Wednesday, and tomorrow will be Thursday.

Message Board

Question of the day

Write and read the question as you track the print. Encourage children to respond in complete sentences.

> ## Did you ever go on a city adventure?

Review phonics

- Which word in the question begins with /e/? *(ever)*
- What is the letter for /e/? *(e)*

Extend Language Use the Day 3 instruction on ELL Poster 24 to extend and enrich language.

ELL Poster 24

Oral Language and Vocabulary

Calendar
Message Board
Build Background

Shared Reading

Trade Book *Abuela*
Skill Realism and Fantasy
Skill Setting

Word Work

Phonemic Awareness
Identify /e/

Phonics
Connect /e/ to *Ee*
Blend Words
H/F Words *here, go, from*
Kindergarten Student Reader K.4.6

Read

Group Time < Differentiated Instruction

Language Arts

Grammar: Uppercase Letters and Periods
Modeled Writing: Write About Adventures in the City
Speaking and Listening: Listen to Poems

Materials

- Calendar
- Talk with Me, Sing with Me Chart 24A, 24B
- Sing with Me/Background Building Audio CD
- Trade Book *Abuela*
- AudioText CD
- Picture Cards: p. 354
- Alphabet Cards: *Aa, Bb, Cc, Dd, Ee, Gg, Hh, Ii, Ll, Mm, Nn, Oo, Pp, Ss, Tt, Yy*
- Kindergarten Student Reader K.4.6
- AlphaBuddy
- Big Book *Animal ABCs*

Build Background

Amazing Words to build oral vocabulary

- abuela
- adventure
- flock
- city
- airport
- harbor

Access Content Ask children what words in their home languages are used for *flock* and *city*.

LET'S TALK

Develop oral vocabulary

Display Talk with Me Chart 24A. Point to the picture of the birds.

- A group of birds is called a *flock* of birds. Where could this *flock* be flying?
- This picture shows a lot of buildings in a *city*. Do you know about any *cities*?

Talk with Me, Sing with Me Chart

LET'S SING

Sing "To the City We Will Go"

Display Sing with Me Chart 24B. Remind children that yesterday they sang "To the City We Will Go." Today we are going to listen for the words *flock* and *city*. Ask children to clap when they hear the words *flock* and *city*.

 Sing with Me/Background Building Audio CD

LET'S LEARN AMAZING WORDS

Oral Vocabulary flock city

DAY ROUTINE

1 **Introduce** When birds travel together in a group, the group of birds is called a *flock*. What's our new word for a group of birds?

Demonstrate In our story, a *flock* of birds surrounded the girl and her grandmother in the park. Have you ever seen a *flock* of birds fly in the sky or land together on the ground?

2 **Introduce** In a *city*, many people live and work. Some buildings in the *city* are very tall, and most buildings are close together. What's our new word for a place where many people live and work?

Demonstrate Many people go to the *city* to visit parks or museums. Did you ever go to a park or museum in a big *city*?

3 **Review** We talked about two words today: *flock* and *city*. Which word means "a group of birds," *flock* or *city*? Which word means "a place where many people live and work," *flock* or *city*?

4 **Apply** Have children use *flock* and *city* in complete sentences. Have them pretend to be a *flock* of birds flying over a big *city*.

Comprehension

OBJECTIVES
- Review realism and fantasy.
- Practice setting.

Materials
- Trade Book *Abuela*

REVIEW SKILL Realism and Fantasy

Review realism and fantasy

Remind children that a realistic story tells about something that could happen in real life. A fantasy is make-believe.

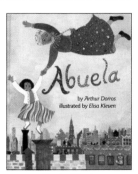

Trade Book

Apply realism and fantasy

- Could Rosalba and her abuela fly over the city in real life?
- Could they land in places and sit on clouds in real life?
- Could the story *Abuela* really happen or is it make-believe?

LET'S READ *Abuela*

Develop vocabulary

Reread *Abuela*. Develop vocabulary by having children tell about places in the story. Encourage children to relate their own experiences in a big city or with a grandparent.

 AudioText CD

SKILL Setting

Practice setting

Remind children to think about where and when the story happens. Use these questions to discuss the setting in *Abuela*.

- What do you think you would see on a city bus?
- What were some of the things the girl saw in the park?
- What other people and things could you see in a city?

Text to World

Monitor Progress

Setting

If... children have difficulty identifying a setting,	then... show a set of pages from the book and offer choices: "Is it in the park or on the beach?"

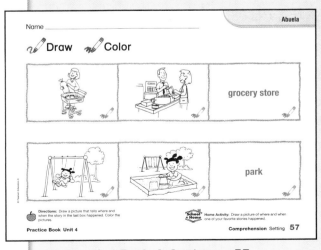

▲ **Practice Book 4** Setting, p. 57

3

Phonemic Awareness

PRACTICE /e/

Identify initial /e/

Display the *egg* Picture Card. What is the first sound in *egg*? Say the word with me: /e/, /e/, /e/, *egg*. *Egg* begins with /e/. Continue reviewing the following words: *elf, Ed,* and *end*.

Identify medial /e/

Display the *jet* Picture Card. What is the middle sound in *jet*? Say the word with me: *jet*. The middle sound in *jet* is /e/. Continue reviewing the following words: *sell, peg,* and *beg*.

Phonics

◎ CONNECT /e/ to *Ee*

Connect /e/ to *Ee*

Write a lowercase *e* on the board. What is the name of this letter? *(e)* What is the sound for this letter? *(/e/)* Repeat with *E*.

Substitute medial sounds

Write *peg* on the board. Say the three sounds with me: /p/ /e/ /g/, *peg*. We can make a new word by changing the middle sound. Change the *e* to *i.* Say the sounds with me: /p/ /i/ /g/, *pig*. What is the new word? The new word is *pig*. Continue changing letters with the following words to form the words in parenthesis: *bell (bill), beg (big), got (get), ten (tan),* and *pen (pin)*.

Identify e's

Write the song "Ten Red Hens" on chart paper or the board. Sing the song to the tune of "Row, Row, Row Your Boat" several times. Then invite children to come up to circle the *e*'s in the song.

Ten Red Hens

**Ten little red hens,
are sitting on their nests.
Meg yells, "Look at the time; it's ten o'clock."
"Girls, it's time to rest."**

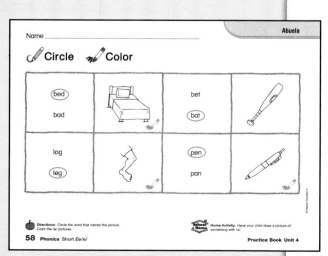

▲ **Practice Book 4** Short *Ee*/e/, p. 58

BLEND SOUNDS

Review letter names and sounds

Display the *Ee* Alphabet Card. What is the name of this letter? What is the sound for this letter? Review the following letters: *Aa, Bb, Cc, Dd, Gg, Hh, Ii, Ll, Mm, Nn, Oo, Pp, Ss, Tt,* and *Yy.*

Blend sounds

Write *Ben* on the board. I am going to blend the sound of each letter together to say this word: /b/ /e/ /n/.

B e n

The word is *Ben.* Say the sounds with me: /b/ /e/ /n/. Now blend the sounds with me as I point to each letter. Continue blending the following words: *Mom, get, set, in, cab, Dad, at, tells, big, dig,* and *spot.*

Word Wall HIGH-FREQUENCY WORDS

Practice high-frequency words

Write the word *go* on the board. This is the word *go.* What is this word? Repeat with *here, to, go, they, the, see, we, you, look, one,* and *from.*

Monitor Progress | **High-Frequency Words/Word Reading**

High-Frequency Words Write *here, from, go, they,* and *one* on the board. Have children take turns reading the words.

Blend Sounds to Read Words Write *cab* on the board. I am going to blend the sound of each letter together to say this word: /k/ /a/ /b/, *cab.* Blend the sounds with me: /k/ /a/ /b/. The word is *cab.* Continue with *Ben, get, set, red, Mom, Dad, dig, yell, big, spot, tells,* and *did.*

If... children cannot read high-frequency words,
then... write missed words on cards so they can practice reading at home.

If... children cannot blend sounds to read the words,
then... provide practice blending the words in chunks, /k/ -ab.

If... children can successfully blend sounds to read the words,
then... have them read Kindergarten Student Reader K.4.6 *Get Set, Go!*

 SUCCESS PREDICTOR

Group Time

Read Kindergarten Student Reader K.4.6. Use the Small Group Reading **Routine.**

Strategic Intervention

Read Kindergarten Student Reader K.4.6. More practice with *Ee*/e/, p. DI·28.

Advanced

Read Kindergarten Student Reader K.4.6. Use the reading routine on p. DI·28. Extend word reading.

Group English language learners by their reading ability in English.

....

i **Independent Activities**

Self-Selected Reading See pp. TR·14–15 for a bibliography of books related to the weekly concept.

Practice Book Setting, p. 57; Short *Ee*/e/, p. 58

Centers Use the center activities on pp. 324–325 to practice this week's skills.

Journal Writing Dictate or write four words that rhyme with *bell.* Draw a picture of one of them.

 Spiral REVIEW

● Reviews previously taught high-frequency words.
● Reviews previously taught letters and sounds.

Day 1
Check Sound Fluency

Day 2
Check Retelling/ Letter-Sound Knowledge

▶ **Day 3**
Check High-Frequency Words/ Word Reading

Day 4
Check Phoneme Segmentation

Day 5
Check Oral Vocabulary/ Assess Progress

 **Word Reading**

SUCCESS PREDICTOR

3

Access Content Ask children to point out naming words such as *Ben*, *Mom*, *Dad*, and *cab*. Have children act out the action words *see*, *tells*, and *dig*.

PREPARE TO READ

Introduce Kindergarten Student Reader K.4.6

Display the title page. We are going to read a new story. Point to the title. What is the title of this story? *Get Set, Go!* was written by Nuala White. This story was illustrated by Linda Bittner.

Small Group Reading

DAY 3 ROUTINE

1 **Model Fluent Reading** Have children finger point as you read a page.

2 **Read Chorally** Have children finger point as they chorally read the page. Continue reading page by page, repeating steps 1 and 2.

3 **Read Individually** Have children read aloud a page in their group.

4 **Reread and Monitor Progress** As you listen to individual children reread, monitor progress and provide support.

Kindergarten Student Reader

Ben and Mom get set to go.
They get in the cab.
2

Ben and Mom see Dad.
Ben and Mom look at Dad.
3

Dad tells the cab to go.
We go from here to the Big Dig Spot.
Get set, go!
4

The cab gets to the Big Dig Spot.
Can you see it?
5

Look here, Ben. You can dig.
You can dig and dig and dig.
Get set, go!
6

Did you get one, Ben?
Dig, Ben, dig.
Look! Ben can get one.
7

Ben, Mom, and Dad get set to dig and dig.
Get set, go!
8

Modeled Writing

REVIEW **GRAMMAR**
Uppercase Letters and Periods

Review uppercase letters and periods

Remind children that there are clues in reading and writing that help us. One clue is an uppercase letter, and another clue is a period. Ask children which clue shows the beginning of a sentence and which clue shows the end of the sentence.

Identify uppercase letters and periods

Write *i ride the bus* on the board with no capitalization or punctuation. Ask children which word should begin with an uppercase letter. Ask where the period should go.

LET'S WRITE Connect to Phonics

Review letters and sounds

Display page 5 of *Animal ABCs.* What is the name of this picture? (elephant) What sound do you hear at the beginning of *elephant?* What letter stands for /e/? Point out the words *Get* and *Set* in the title of Kindergarten Student Reader K.4.6. These words have /e/ in the middle spelled with the letter *e.* Have children find other words in the story that have *e*/e/.

Write sentences

In the story, Ben had an adventure in the city. Let's write a sentence about the city using words that have /e/.

Meg rides on the train.

Independent writing

Have children write or dictate a sentence about an adventure in the city. Have them illustrate their sentences.

Meg rides on the train.

OBJECTIVES

- Review uppercase letters and periods.
- Review letters and sounds.
- Write about adventures in the city.

Materials

- Big Book *Animal ABCs*
- Kindergarten Student Reader K.4.6

DAILY FIX-IT

you can dig here
(You can dig here.)

EXTEND SKILLS

Handwriting Remind children that uppercase letters go all the way to the top line, twice as high as most lowercase letters.

Writer's Checkup

- ✔ The first word in a sentence begins with an uppercase letter. Did I do that?
- ✔ A sentence should end with a period. Did I do that?
- ✔ A sentence should make sense. Does my sentence make sense?
- ✔ A good writer uses his or her best handwriting. Did I do that?

PREVIEW
Day 4

OBJECTIVE

• Practice listening to poems.

E L L

Access Content Have children think of a poem they know, such as a nursery rhyme.

Speaking and Listening

LISTEN TO POEMS

Practice listening to poems

Today I'm going to read a poem to you. A poem is different from a story because it is usually shorter. It can sound a little like a song. Sometimes it has rhyming words. Have AlphaBuddy tip from side to side as you recite "Humpty Dumpty." Then ask children whether "Humpty Dumpty" is a song or a poem.

Humpty Dumpty

**Humpty Dumpty sat on a wall.
Humpty Dumpty had a great fall.
All the king's horses,
And all the king's men,
Could not put Humpty together again.**

Did you hear words that rhyme in "Humpty Dumpty"? Let's listen again. When you hear rhyming words, raise your hand. Raise AlphaBuddy up when the rhyming words are spoken.

Connect listening to poems

You probably know many poems because poems are often the words to a song. Invite children to suggest and recite the words to a few songs, such as "Twinkle, Twinkle Little Star" or "Mary Had a Little Lamb," and have AlphaBuddy dance with the rhythm. Then have volunteers recite the words in front of the class.

Wrap Up Your Day!

✓ **Respond to Literature** Today we read about Ben and his mom and dad. They went to a museum. Have you ever visited a museum?

✓ **Grammar** Ask children whether a sentence begins with an uppercase letter or a lowercase letter. Have them find an example of a sentence in *Get Set, Go!*

✓ **Homework Idea** Have children write and illustrate three objects at home that begin with /e/ or have middle /e/.

PREVIEW
Day 4

Tomorrow we will read about a little mouse.

EXTEND Your Day

Ways to Travel

Materials pictures of forms of transportation, world map or globe

Land, Water, or Air? People use many ways to travel on land, over water, and in the air. People walk, but they cannot get very far that way. Machines help people move from one place to another quickly.

Hold up a transportation picture and ask children to tell you whether the vehicle travels on land, over water, or in the air. Record the information in a chart as shown.

Which Way Is Best?

If I wanted to go on a trip across an ocean, what would be the best machine to use? Use a map to trace a route from your location across the ocean. What is another way I could travel across the ocean? Continue this process, asking for the best way to get to a friend's house, school, and other destinations.

Land	Air	Water
bus	plane	boat
bike	helicopter	ship
car		

Comprehension
Real or Imaginary

City Bus Play Arrange the children in chairs in two rows with a middle aisle, as if they were sitting on a bus. As you pretend to drive, call out real and imaginary stops, such as "Next stop, the grocery store." After announcing a stop, ask the children whether it is a real place or a make-believe place for a bus to go. After describing the place, ask children if it could really happen or if it is make-believe.

Phonics
Organize Words

Materials web graphic organizer (one copy per child), pencils, crayons

***E* in the Middle** Write *pig, men, ten, hen, red, mop,* and *pet* on the board.

Make a web organizer on the board or use Graphic Organizer 18. Model how to write *e* in the center circle and an /e/ word in each of the other circles. Children may illustrate their /e/ words if they wish.

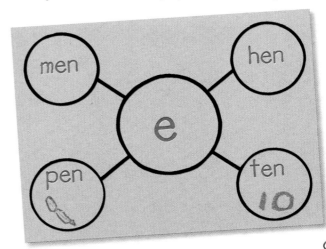

Oral Language and Vocabulary

Calendar
Message Board
Build Background

Shared Reading

Big Book *One Little Mouse*
Skill Setting

Word Work

Phonemic Awareness
Review /g/

Phonics
Blend Sounds
H/F Words *here, go, from*
Decodable Reader 24

Read

Group Time < Differentiated Instruction

Language Arts

Grammar: Pronoun *I*
Interactive Writing: Write
  Sentences Using /e/
Speaking and Listening: Listen
  to Poems

Materials

- Calendar
- Talk with Me, Sing with Me Chart 24A, 24B
- Sing with Me/Background Building Audio CD
- Big Book *One Little Mouse*
- Trade Book *Abuela*
- AudioText CD
- Picture Cards: p. 363
- Alphabet Cards: *Aa, Bb, Dd, Ee, Ff, Gg, Hh, Ii, Mm, Nn, Oo, Pp, Tt*
- Decodable Reader 24

Calendar

Name the day and date
Ask a volunteer to find today's date on the calendar. Have children say the day, month, date, and year together.

Identify pattern
Help children identify the pattern of the days of the week by asking what day always comes after Monday, what day is always in the middle of a school week, and what days we are usually at home.

Message Board

Question of the day
Write and read the question as you track the print. Encourage children to respond in complete sentences.

> ## How can you get to the city?

Review grammar
Have children give answers to the question using the pronoun *I,* such as *I can take a train.*

Access Content Use the Day 4 instruction on ELL Poster 24 to support children's use of English to communicate about lesson concepts.

ELL Poster 24

Build Background

LET'S TALK

Discuss city adventures

Display Talk with Me Chart 24A. Point to the picture of the airplanes.

- Where are the airplanes in this picture? (an airport) Planes fly in and out of an *airport.* Have you ever been to an *airport?*

- These boats are in a *harbor.* Boats stay in the *harbor* when they are not taking people on a trip. Have you ever seen a *harbor?*

Talk with Me, Sing with Me Chart

LET'S SING

Sing "To the City We Will Go"

Display Sing with Me Chart 24B. Recall that yesterday they sang "To the City We Will Go." Encourage children to listen for the words *airport* and *harbor* as you sing the song.

 Sing with Me/Background Building Audio CD

LET'S LEARN AMAZING WORDS

Oral Vocabulary airport harbor

DAY 4 ROUTINE

1 **Introduce** An *airport* is a place where airplanes and jets take off and land. What is our new word for the place where planes take off and land?

Demonstrate An *airport* is usually large, since many people go there to get on airplanes. What are some things you may see at an *airport?*

2 **Introduce** A *harbor* is where boats stay in the water to stay safe. What is our new word for the place where boats stay when they are not being used?

Demonstrate A *harbor* is a place where boats can park and unload people or things. A *harbor* has docks that people walk on to get out to the boats. Have you ever seen a *harbor?*

3 **Review** We talked about two words today: *airport* and *harbor.* Which word means "a place where airplanes take off and land," *airport* or *harbor?* Which word means "a place to park a boat," *airport* or *harbor?*

4 **Apply** Have children use *airport* and *harbor* in complete sentences. Have them pretend to be a plane flying into an *airport* or a boat floating into a *harbor.*

 **to build oral vocabulary**

- abuela
- flock
- airport
- adventure
- city
- harbor

Access Content Ask children how they say *airport* and *harbor* in their home languages.

OBJECTIVE

⊙ Apply setting.

Materials

● Big Book *One Little Mouse*

Extend Language Have children recall names of animals from *One Little Mouse*.

Comprehension

LET'S READ *One Little Mouse*

Review *One Little Mouse*

Display *One Little Mouse.* Read the title of the book as you point to the words. Then read the author's name and ask children to tell what an author does.

- What are some things you remember about this book?

Reread *One Little Mouse*

Reread the book and ask children to tell all the places Mouse looked to find a new home. Make a list of the settings on the board.

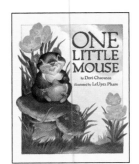

Big Book

AudioText CD

⊙ SKILL Setting

Apply setting to *One Little Mouse*

In this story, the mouse visits many different places. Remember that, as we read, we can think about where and when the story takes place.

Practice setting

After reading, ask:

- Which animal house did you like best?
- What kinds of places do we see in this book?
- How is the woodland the same or different from the city?

Have children act like the mouse in one of the settings.

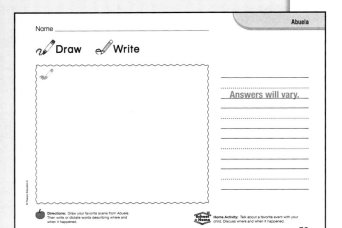

▲ **Practice Book 4** Setting, p. 59

Phonemic Awareness

REVIEW PRACTICE /g/

Isolate initial and final /g/

Display the *gum* Picture Card. What is the first sound in *gum*? Say it with me: /g/, /g/, *gum*. Continue with *garden* and *goat*.

Display the *egg* Picture Card. Say *egg* with me: /e/ /g/, *egg*. What sound do you hear at the end of /e/ /g/, *egg*? Repeat with *jug*.

Differentiate final sounds

Say *mug* and *mutt*. Compare final sounds /g/ in *mug* and /t/ in *mutt*. Continue to differentiate final sounds with these pairs: *bet, beg; Meg, mess; bus, bug;* and *tug, tub.*

Monitor Progress | Check Phoneme Segmentation

Check Segmentation I am going to say a word. Please tell me all of the sounds in the word. Say these words: *pet, hen, did, not, pen, got, bed,* and *nap.*

If... children cannot successfully identify all phonemes in each word,
then... guide them to move counters as they segment the phonemes.

SUCCESS PREDICTOR

Day 1	Day 2	Day 3	▶ Day 4	Day 5
Check Sound Fluency	Check Retelling/ Letter-Sound Knowledge	Check High-Frequency Words/ Word Reading	Check Phoneme Segmentation	Check Oral Vocabulary/ Assess Progress

Phonics

Spiral REVIEW BLEND SOUNDS

Review letter names and sounds

Use Alphabet Cards to review the following letter names and sounds: *Aa, Bb, Dd, Ee, Ff, Gg, Hh, Ii, Mm, Nn, Oo, Pp,* and *Tt.*

Blend sounds

Write *Peg* on the board. I am going to blend the sound of each letter together to say this word: /p/ /e/ /g/.

The word is *Peg*. Say the three sounds with me: /p/ /e/ /g/. Blend the sounds as I point to each letter: /p/ /e/ /g/, *Peg*. Continue with *met, Ned, got, pet, hen, did, let, pen, not, bed, get, in, fed,* and *nap.*

OBJECTIVES
- Review /g/.
- Blend sounds.

Materials
- Picture Cards:
  egg   garden   goat
  gum   jug
- Decodable Reader 24
- Alphabet Cards: *Aa, Bb, Dd, Ee, Ff, Gg, Hh, Ii, Mm, Nn, Oo, Pp, Tt*

Phoneme Segmentation

SUCCESS PREDICTOR

OBJECTIVES

- Recognize high-frequency words.
- Read decodable text.

Word Wall HIGH-FREQUENCY WORDS

Practice high-frequency words

Write the word *go* on the board. This is the word *go*. What is this word? Continue with *here, from, a, is,* and *have*. Look for these words in the story that we read today.

PREPARE TO READ

Introduce Decodable Reader 24

Display Decodable Reader 24 *A Pet Hen.* Today we will read *A Pet Hen.* Point to the title. What is the title of the story? Point to the names of the author and illustrator. *A Pet Hen* is written by Fran Quinn. This story is illustrated by Jason Edwards.

Group Time

On-Level

Read Decodable Reader 24. Use the Small Group Reading **Routine.**

Strategic Intervention

Read Decodable Reader 24. More practice with *Ee/e/,* p. DI·29.

Advanced

Read Independent Leveled Reader K.4.6. Use Leveled Reader lesson, p. LR11. Extend word reading.

Group English language learners by their reading ability in English.

. . . .

(*i*) Independent Activities

Self-Selected Reading See pp. TR14–15 for a bibliography of books related to the weekly concept.

Practice Book Setting, p. 59; Pronoun *I*, p. 60

Centers Use the center activities on pp. 324–325 to practice this week's skills.

Journal Writing Dictate or write three short *e* words.

Small Group Reading

① Model Fluent Reading Have children finger point as you read a page.

② Read Chorally Have children finger point as they chorally read the page. Continue reading page by page, repeating steps 1 and 2.

③ Read Individually Have children read aloud a page in their group.

④ Reread and Monitor Progress As you listen to individual children reread, monitor progress and provide support.

Decodable Reader

Interactive Writing

GRAMMAR Pronoun *I*

Identify pronoun *I*

Remember that when we talk about ourselves, we use the word *I*: *I like the color yellow; I like to ski; I am your teacher.* Now you try. Answer these questions using the word *I.*

• What do you like to eat?

• What sports do you play?

Sometimes when we are telling someone about our day or a favorite vacation, we have to use the word *I* many times. **Write** on the board: *I went to the park.* What are some things you would do at the park? **Write** all of the responses on the board.

LET'S WRITE Connect to Phonics

Review letters and sounds

Display the *Ee* Alphabet Card. What is the name of this picture? (escalator) What sound does *escalator* begin with? What letter stands for /e/? Continue reviewing the following letters: *Aa, Bb, Dd, Ff, Gg, Hh, Ii, Mm, Nn, Oo, Pp, Tt.*

Write sentences

Write the following sentence frame on the board.

Ten little _____ are in the _____.
(hens, nest)

Have children help you complete the sentence with words that have middle /e/. Ask volunteers to write the words in the blanks. Then read the sentence together.

Independent writing

Have children write or dictate their own sentences using words with /e/. Then have them illustrate their sentences.

EXTEND SKILLS

Spelling If children fill in the blank after *ten little* with a singular noun, review that most words that mean "more than one" of something end with the letter *s.*

DAILY FIX-IT

i look like Abuela
(I look like Abuela.)

E L L

Support Writing Allow children with the same home language to share their ideas in that language and discuss how to express them in English before writing.

▲ **Practice Book 4** Pronoun *I*, p. 60

Speaking and Listening

OBJECTIVE

● Practice listening to poems.

ELL

Access Content Let children know that *get set* is another way to say "get ready" and *yet* means "now."

Speaking and Listening

LISTEN TO POEMS

Review listening to poems

This week we have been learning about listening to poems. What are some poems you know? Remember that a poem is usually shorter than a story. The author carefully chooses words for feeling and meaning. It can rhyme, but it doesn't have to. Poems have a beat or rhythm.

Display Phonics Songs and Rhymes Chart 24. Sometimes a song can be read like a poem. Do you remember our phonics song from this week? Is this a story or a poem? *Get Set, Ten Pets* can be read like a poem. Listen for the rhyming words and how I read the poem. **Read the poem with emphasis on the rhythm.**

Ask children to identify the rhyming words in the poem. Did you notice the rhyming words? Did you notice that I read the poem a little like a song? Try reading it with me.

Practice listening to poems

Recite each line and allow children to echo you. Start with one line, then two, and then have children recite the entire poem with you. Then have volunteers recite the poem in front of the class.

Get Set, Ten Pets!
Get set, ten pets!
Have you met the vet?
Don't rest just yet—
Here's our jet.

We'll help you get on,
We'll make sure you're fed.
Em the vet is set to get
All ten tucked in bed!

Phonics Songs and Rhymes Chart

Wrap Up Your Day!

✓ **Oral Language** Today we read about *One Little Mouse* looking for a place to sleep. Do you remember where the mouse visited?

✓ **Speaking and Listening** Ask children to think of a song that sounds like a poem and say it together.

✓ **Homework Idea** Write a sentence using the pronoun *I* about what you do on Saturday.

PREVIEW Day 5

Tomorrow we will read a story called "Apple Juice Tea." What do you think it will be about?

EXTEND Your Day

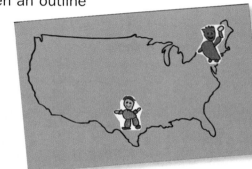

Time for **SOCIAL STUDIES**

National Symbols

Materials Patterns Book p. 61: *U.S. map;* pictures of the Statue of Liberty, the Liberty Bell, and the U.S. flag

Introduce National Symbols Explain to children that Rosalba and Abuela fly around a national symbol on their adventure in New York. Discuss these facts:

- A statue is a figure made of wood, metal, or stone.
- The Statue of Liberty is over 100 years old, over 300 feet tall, and very heavy.
- When people came to the United States long ago they often came by boat. The Statue of Liberty on Liberty Island seemed to welcome them to New York Harbor.

- The Statue of Liberty was given to our country from the country of France a long time ago.

Show children pictures of the Liberty Bell, the U.S. flag, and the Statue of Liberty. On a map, show children where the Liberty Bell and the Statue of Liberty are located in relation to their hometown and discuss how they would travel to visit Lady Liberty. Give children an outline map of the United States. Have them locate where they are and where the Statue is Liberty is by drawing pictures on the map.

Phonics

Initial and Final *Gg*

Make a List With children's help, write a list of words that have initial or final *g*. If children have difficulty, supply words from this list: *peg, tag, leg, get, go, garden, mug, rug, goat, goose, gum, jug, bug, egg,* and *flag.*

Write these labels on the board and have children label each side of a sheet of paper: *Begin with g* and *End with g.* Direct children to copy words that begin with *g* on one side and words that end with *g* on the other side.

Begin with g
go
get
got

End with g
tag
leg
dog

Comprehension

Settings

One Little Mouse Take a picture walk through *One Little Mouse.* Have children name the animal homes they see throughout the story. Write two separate lists, homes and animals, on the board. Have half of the children draw and label a home and the other half draw and label an animal.

Choose an animal home. Have children with that home stand with their pictures. Have children with the corresponding animal bring their pictures and stand next to the appropriate home. Have children say the following sentence together, filling in the blanks: *The _____ sleeps in the _____.*

Oral Language and Vocabulary
Calendar
Message Board
Build Background

Shared Reading
Read Aloud Anthology "Apple Juice Tea"
◉ **Skill** Setting

Word Work
Phonemic Awareness
Review /e/

Phonics
◉ Connect /e/ *to Ee*
H/F Words *here, go, from*

Read
Group Time < Differentiated Instruction

Monitor Progress

Language Arts
Grammar: Pronoun *I*
Shared Writing:
   This Week We . . .
Speaking and Listening: Listen to Poems

Materials
- Calendar
- Talk with Me, Sing with Me Chart 24A, 24B
- Sing with Me/Background Building Audio CD
- *Read Aloud Anthology* "Apple Juice Tea"
- Picture Cards: p. 371
- Decodable Reader 24
- Kindergarten Student Reader K.4.6
- Phonics Story *Ted and the Pet*
- Phonics Songs and Rhymes Chart 24
- Trade Book *Abuela*

Calendar

Name the day and date
Point to today's date on the calendar and read the day, month, date, and year. Have children read them after you.

Months of the year
What month is it? What is the first month of the year? What is the last month of the year? Let's say the names of the twelve months of the year in order.

Message Board

Question of the week
Remind children that this week they talked about and drew pictures of adventures people can have in a city.

> ## What kind of adventures can you have in the city?

Review oral vocabulary
Encourage children to use oral vocabulary words *abuela, adventure, flock, city, airport*, and *harbor* in their responses. Remind children to respond in complete sentences.

Assess Vocabulary Use the Day 5 instruction on ELL Poster 24 to monitor children's progress with oral vocabulary.

ELL Poster 24

Build Background

LET'S TALK

Discuss city adventures

Display Talk with Me Chart 24A. Point to the picture of the birds.

- This is a group of birds. What do we call a group of birds? (flock)

- This girl is sitting on the park bench with her grandma. What's the Spanish word for grandma that we learned? (abuela)

- Where are the planes in this picture? (airport)

- What do we call the place where the boats are? (harbor)

- We talked about different kinds of *adventures* you can have in the *city*. What kind of an *adventure* would you like to go on?

Talk with Me, Sing with Me Chart

LET'S SING

Sing "To the City We Will Go"

Display Sing with Me Chart 24B. Remind children that the words *abuela, adventure, flock, city, airport,* and *harbor* are in the song.

Talk with Me, Sing with Me Chart

 **Sing with Me/Background Building Audio CD**

OBJECTIVES

- Build background.
- Review oral vocabulary.

 **to build oral vocabulary**

- abuela
- flock
- airport
- adventure
- city
- harbor

Monitor Progress | **Check Oral Vocabulary**

Demonstrate Word Knowledge Prompt children to demonstrate knowledge of oral vocabulary words *abuela, adventure, flock, city, airport,* and *harbor*. Encourage them to use complete sentences.

If... children cannot demonstrate knowledge of oral vocabulary,
then... review words using Talk with Me Chart 24A or *Abuela*.

SUCCESS PREDICTOR

Day 1	Day 2	Day 3	Day 4	▶ Day 5
Check Sound Fluency	Check Retelling/ Letter-Sound Knowledge	Check High-Frequency Words/ Word Reading	Check Phoneme Segmentation	Check Oral Vocabulary/ Assess Progress

Oral Vocabulary

SUCCESS PREDICTOR

Comprehension

READ ALOUD

Read "Apple Juice Tea"

Tell children that you are going to read them a story about a girl and a visit from her grandma. Ask them to listen carefully for where the story happens. Listen carefully. I am going to read you a story, and then I will ask you where it happens and when it happens.

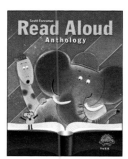

Read Aloud Anthology

🎯 CHECK SKILL Setting

Practice setting in "Apple Juice Tea"

After you read the story, ask children to tell where and when it happens.

- Where do Polly and her parents go to get Gran? (to the airport)
- When they all go out together, where do they go? (to the zoo)
- Where do they go after the zoo? (back home)
- When Mama and Daddy go out, Gran baby-sits Polly. What setting are Polly and Gran in now? (at home and going for a walk to the corner at night)
- What is the setting for Gran and Polly's tea party? (under the big table)

🎯 ASSESS SKILL Setting

Assess setting

Use the blackline master found on page 374. Copy one page for each child. Have children draw the setting for each of the three scenes pictured.

OBJECTIVE

🎯 Practice setting.

Materials

- *Read Aloud Anthology* "Apple Juice Tea"

ELL

Access Content Before reading aloud, introduce children to the setting of the story. Then use words and gestures to explain these key story words: *Gran* (another name for grandma) and *yoo-hoo* (a way to get someone's attention).

Monitor Progress

🎯 **Setting**

| **If...** children cannot identify the setting, | **then...** reteach using page DI·36. |

▲ **Teacher's Edition 4** Setting, p. 374

Phonemic Awareness

OBJECTIVES

- Review /e/.
- Discriminate medial sounds.
- Connect /e/ to *Ee*.

Materials

- Kindergarten Student Reader K.4.6
- Decodable Reader 24
- Phonics Story *Ted and the Pet*
- Picture Cards:
  mop   net

REVIEW /e/

Isolate /e/

What is the first sound in *egg*? (/e/) *Egg* begins with /e/. Continue with *end* and *elf*. What is the middle sound in *let*? (/e/) Continue with: *Ted, bed, Ned, beg,* and *peg.*

Discriminate medial sounds

Display Picture Cards *net* and *mop*. I am going to say a word. If the word has /o/ in the middle, point to the *mop*. If the word has /e/ in the middle, point to the *net.* Say these words: *red, hop, fed, led, pot, job, Meg, leg, tell, top, fell,* and *top.*

Phonics

 REVIEW *Ee*/e/

Connect /e/ to *Ee*

Say the word *bell*. What is the middle sound in *bell?* The middle sound is /e/. What letter makes /e/? Encourage children to add different consonants to the ending *-ell*, such as *t, d, f, w,* and *s.*

Word Wall HIGH-FREQUENCY WORDS

Practice high-frequency words

Write the word *here* on the board. This is the word *here*. Let's use the word *here* in a sentence. What is this word? Continue the routine with *go* and *from.*

Spiral REVIEW READ

Apply phonics in familiar text

Have children reread one of the readers that applies the target letter sound. You may wish to review the decodable words and the high-frequency words that appear in each reader prior to rereading.

Kindergarten Student Reader

Decodable Reader

Phonics Story in Practice Book

OBJECTIVE

◎ Assess: connect /e/ to *Ee*.

Group Time

On-Level

Sets A and B

Strategic Intervention

**Monitor Progress:
Check Phonics
Alternate Assessment, p. DI·30**

Advanced

Sets B and C

. . . .

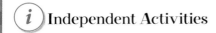 **Independent Activities**

Self-Selected Reading See pp. TR14–15 for a bibliography of books related to the weekly concept.

Centers Use the center activities on pp. 324–325 to practice this week's skills.

Journal Writing Draw or write about an adventure you have had with a family member.

Support Phonics For guidance in teaching phonics to English language learners, see the *ELL and Transition Handbook.*

PHONICS /e/ to *Ee*

Group assessment

Have children number a sheet of paper from 1 to 6. Read the list of words below. For each word, have children write *e* next to the corresponding number if the word contains medial /e/ or *X* if it does not.

1. bed	**3. pin**	**5. mop**
2. Ted	**4. sell**	**6. Meg**

Monitor Progress	Assess Progress
If... a child cannot complete the group assessment,	**then...** use the Reteach lesson on page DI·36.
If... a child correctly identifies several of the four words with /e/,	**then...** assess word reading Sets A and B on page 373.
If... a child correctly labels all four /e/ words,	**then...** assess word and sentence reading with Sets B and C on page 373.

ASSESS PHONICS

**Set A:
Read words**

Have children take turns reading the words. We're going to read some words. I'll do the first one and you do the rest. The first word is *Ted:* /t/ /e/ /d/. The first word is *Ted.* For each child, record any decoding problems.

Set B: Read more words

Have children take turns reading the words. We're going to read some words. I'll do the first one and you do the rest. The first word is *bell:* /b/ /e/ /l/. The word is *bell.* For each child, record any decoding problems.

Set C: Read sentences

For a cumulative assessment of phonics and high-frequency words, have each child read one or two sentences.

READ THE WORDS

Set A

Ted   leg

sled   send

READ MORE WORDS

Set B

bell   melt   send

spend   help   step

READ THE SENTENCES

Set C

1. I can ring my bell from here.

2. I have a little red hen.

3. Ned will come to see me.

4. My pet can look here.

5. Tell Ted to go with you.

Note to Teacher Set A: Children read each word. Set B: Children read each word.
Set C: Children read one or two sentences.

Abuela

Monitor Progress

SUCCESS PREDICTOR

SETTING

Draw where each part of the story happens.

Polly and her parents wait for Gran at the airport.

Gran and Polly take a walk.

Gran and Polly have a tea party.

Note to Teacher Have children fill in the setting in each picture by drawing the background for each of the three scenes.

Monitor Progress

REPRODUCIBLE PAGE • See also Assessment Handbook, p. 203

Shared Writing

GRAMMAR Pronoun *I*

Review pronoun *I*

What special little word do we use when we want to talk about our-selves? We use the word *I*. Who remembers how to write *I*? **Write *I am Meg* on the board.**

Identify pronoun *I*

When we use the letter *I* to talk about ourselves, we always write an uppercase letter, even if it is in the middle of a sentence. **Write *Sam and I played today*.** Did I make the word *I* an uppercase letter?

 **Text to Text** **LET'S WRITE** This Week We...

Recall literature

Display the following items: *Abuela; Get Set, Go!; A Pet Hen;* Sing with Me Chart 24B; and Phonics Songs and Rhymes Chart 24. We have read three new books this week and we sang two new songs. Which book or song was your favorite?

Write sentences

Today we will write about an adventure we've been on with some-one special. Remember to use the word *I*. I will start.

My class and I went to the zoo.

I went to the city with Ned.

Meg and I went to see the Statue of Liberty.

Continue the list with all children. Then have children echo read the complete list. Make sure children dictate complete sentences, checking for uppercase letters and periods.

Independent writing

Have children copy the sentence they dictated and draw the setting where their adventure took place.

OBJECTIVES

- Recognize pronoun *I*.
- Write about an adventure with someone.

Materials

- Trade Book *Abuela*
- Kindergarten Student Reader K.4.6
- Decodable Reader 24
- Talk with Me, Sing with Me Chart 24B
- Phonics Songs and Rhymes Chart 24

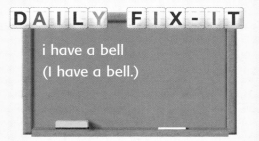

DAILY FIX-IT

i have a bell
(I have a bell.)

ELL

Support Writing Supply English words as children write or dictate their sentence.

OBJECTIVE
- Review listening to poems.

Speaking and Listening

LISTEN TO POEMS

Review listening to poems

Today we are going to listen to a poem. A poem is a story that can rhyme or not rhyme. Many songs are rhymes that we sing. We are going to listen to a poem that rhymes.

Flying Free

Way up high in the sky,
I am free to be me.

I look around without a sound.
Way below, you must know,
someone waits for me.

Connect listening to poems

Check that children understand what they have heard. Read "Flying Free" and other poems several times, and then have the children illustrate the poem they liked best.

Wrap Up Your Week!

 Phonics This week we learned about the letter *Ee.* What is the sound for *Ee?* Name a word that begins with /e/.

 Shared Reading What was your favorite book or song this week?

 High-Frequency Words Write *here, go,* and *from* on the board. Read these words to me.

PREVIEW Next Week

Next week we will read about a bunny taking a train. What do you think the story will be about?

You've learned

006 Amazing Words
this week!

You've learned
144 Amazing Words
so far this year!

EXTEND Your Day

TIME + FOR MATH

Graphing

Materials *Bunny Day, My Lucky Day, One Little Mouse, Goldilocks and the Three Bears, If you Could Go to Antarctica,* and *Abuela;* construction paper; crayons

Recall Favorite Adventure Display each book and have children recall the story. I am going to hold up a book about an adventure. Stand up when I hold up the book that you think had the best adventure. You can only stand up for one book, so decide now which one is your favorite adventure.

Graph the Results Hold up *Bunny Day* and count the number of children standing. Record the results on a graph. Continue with the other books and discuss the results. Why was that story your

favorite adventure? Have children illustrate their favorite adventure story.

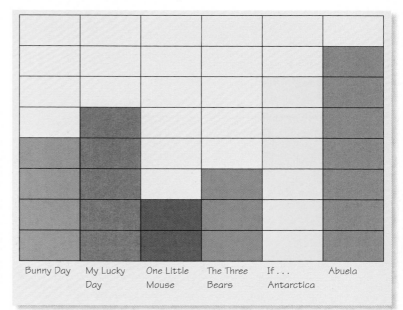

| Bunny Day | My Lucky Day | One Little Mouse | The Three Bears | If . . . Antarctica | Abuela |

American Flag

Time for SOCIAL STUDIES

Materials U.S. flag, large white construction paper, red and blue crayons, star stickers

National Symbol Show children the U.S. flag. Explain that the thirteen stripes represent the thirteen original colonies that our country began as and that the fifty stars represent the fifty states that are now part of the country. Tell children that the number of stars has changed over the years. In the beginning, there were thirteen, but each time our country grew and a state was added, a new flag was designed with more stars.

Draw a Flag Instruct children to draw a picture of the flag. Have them count the number of red stripes. Help them draw a box for their stars. After they color it blue, they can stick the stars in the box.

Transportation Collage

Time for SOCIAL STUDIES

Materials chart paper, construction paper, drawing tools, scissors, glue

Ways to Move Review the definition of a *form of transportation:* anything that moves a person from one place to another. Ask children to draw pictures of transportation on construction paper. Have them cut out the pictures and glue them to the chart paper. Invite children to tell about their part of the collage.

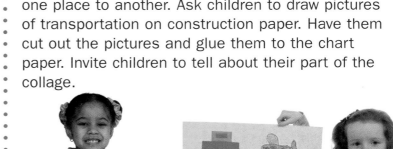

Unit 4
Wrap-Up

OBJECTIVES

- Discuss the unit theme.
- Connect content across selections.
- Combine content and skills in meaningful activities that build literacy.
- Respond to unit selections through a variety of modalities.

LET'S EXPLORE

Discuss the Big Idea

Where will our adventures take us?

Help children relate the theme question for this unit to the selections and their own experiences. Prompt discussion with questions such as the following:

- **What adventures did the people and animals in this unit have?**

- **Tell about adventures that you have had. Are they the same as any people or animal adventures you have read about?**

Project Wrap-Up

Remember When Album

- **What was your favorite part of the project?**

- **After hearing about your classmates' adventures, where would you like to go next?**

- **What is the best memory in your album?**

Adventure Hats

Exploring We Will Go Children can make hats to tell about an adventure they would like to take. Children can construct hats using paper, cardboard, or fabric. Then they can decorate their hats to give more detail about the adventure.

Explore Locations

Adventure Mural Working in groups, have children decide on a location they would like to explore. Each group will pick one type of adventure to depict in a mural. Murals should include details such as landforms, buildings, weather, or people. Murals can be displayed throughout the classroom, and groups can take turns presenting their adventure.

Character Adventures

Character Cut-Outs Have children, in groups or partners, choose a character from one of the stories in this unit that had an adventure. On a large piece of cardboard, have students draw the character, and assist them in cutting a hole for the head. Children should dress the character for the adventure and include details from the story. They can present their characters to the class, telling of the adventure while standing behind the board.

Day 5 Assessment Chart

Unit 4

	Record Assessment Data and Calculate Score		Reteach ✓	Reassess
	Total Possible	Child's Number Correct		
Week 1 *Bunny Day*				
A Read the Words	4			
B Read More Words	6			
C Read the Sentences	5			
Week 2 *My Lucky Day*				
A Read the Words	4			
B Read More Words	6			
C Read the Sentences	5			
Week 3 *One Little Mouse*				
A Read the Words	4			
B Read More Words	6			
C Read the Sentences	5			
Week 4 *Goldilocks and the Three Bears*				
A Read the Words	4			
B Read More Words	6			
C Read the Sentences	5			
Week 5 *If You Could Go to Antarctica*				
A Read the Words	4			
B Read More Words	6			
C Read the Sentences	5			
Week 6 *Abuela*				
A Read the Words	4			
B Read More Words	6			
C Read the Sentences	5			
	90			

- **RECORD SCORES** In the Child's Number Correct column, record scores for the set(s) of the Day 5 Assessment used.
- **RETEACH SKILLS** If a child is unable to successfully complete Sets A and/or B, then reteach the skills using the Reteach lessons on pp. DI·31–DI·36.

- **REASSESS** Use the same set of assessments or an easier set for reassessment.

REPRODUCIBLE PAGE • See also Assessment Handbook, p. 204

Unit 4
Assess and Regroup

FYI In Kindergarten there are opportunities for regrouping every six weeks—at the end of Units 2, 3, 4, and 5. These options offer sensitivity to each child's progress, although some teachers may prefer to regroup less frequently.

Regroup for Unit 5

To make regrouping decisions at the end of Unit 4, consider children's end-of-unit scores for

- Unit 4 Day 5 Assessments
- Unit 4 Benchmark Assessment

Group Time

On-Level	Strategic Intervention	Advanced
To continue On-Level or to move into the On-Level group, children should	**Children would benefit from Strategic Intervention if they**	**To move to the Advanced group, children should**
• score 80% or better on their cumulative Unit Scores on the Day 5 Assessment	• score 60% or lower on their cumulative Unit Scores on the Day 5 Assessment	• score 100% on their cumulative Unit Scores for the Day 5 Assessment
• score Developing on 3 or 4 skill strands of the Unit 4 Benchmark Assessment	• score Emerging on 2 or more skill strands of the Unit 4 Benchmark Assessment	• score Proficient on at least 4 skill strands of the Unit 4 Benchmark Assessment
• be capable of working in the On-Level group based on teacher judgment	• are struggling to keep up with the On-Level group based on teacher judgment	• read above grade level material fluently. You may try them out on the Independent Leveled Reader.
		• be capable of handling the work of the Advanced group based on teacher judgment
		• score 4 on retelling in this unit and demonstrate ease of language in their retellings

QUESTIONS TO CONSIDER

- What types of test questions did the child miss? Are they specific to a particular skill or strategy?
- Does the child have adequate background knowledge to understand the test passages or selections for retelling?

- Has the child's performance met expectations for daily lessons and assessments with little or no reteaching?
- Is the child performing more like children in another group?
- Does the child read for enjoyment, different purposes, and with varied interests?

Unit Scores

Weighted	
100% =	**90**
80% =	**72**
60% =	**54**

Name _____ Date _____

Unit 4 Literacy Development Checklist

	Unit 1	Unit 2	Unit 3	Unit 4	Unit 5	Unit 6
Concepts of Print						
• knows how to hold a book						
• knows the parts of a book (front cover, back cover)						
• knows the difference between letters and words						
• knows the difference between author and illustrator						
• tracks print from top to bottom and left to right						
• understands that print represents spoken language and conveys meaning						
• knows that letters make up words						
Phonological/Phonemic Awareness						
• can identify rhyming words						
• can produce rhyming words						
• knows that words are made up of syllables						
• knows that words are made up of letters						
• can isolate phonemes						
• can identify initial phonemes in words						
• can identify final phonemes in words						
• segments and blends phonemes in words						
Phonics and Decoding						
• identifies the letters of the alphabet, both upper- and lowercase						
• recognizes own name in print						
• can connect sound to letter—consonants						
• can connect sound to letter—vowels						
• uses letter-sound knowledge to read words						
Listening to Literature						
• retells stories with story structure, including setting, characters, and plot						
• uses illustrations to understand stories						
• predicts what will happen next						
• connects concepts from literature to own life						
Writing						
• writes own name—first and last						
• is moving from scribble writing to random letters and letter strings						
• uses knowledge of letter-sounds to write words						
• can dictate a story and "read" it back						

Key

+	Proficient
✓	Developing
–	Emerging

Leveled Readers

Table of Contents

SEQUENCE

RECALL/RETELL

Fish Can Swim

SUMMARY This informational text tells about fish. This selection supports and extends the unit theme of adventures by illustrating and telling about what happens to some fish over a period of time.

INTRODUCE THE BOOK

BUILD BACKGROUND Remind children that there are many kinds of fish. Explain that fish have fins that help them swim. Encourage children to share what they know about fish. Where do fish live? Can you name different kinds of fish?

PREVIEW/PICTURE WALK Have children preview the book by looking at the pictures. Based on this preview, ask children what they think the selection will be about.

READ THE BOOK

SMALL GROUP READING
1. **Model Fluent Reading** Have children finger point as you read each page.
2. **Read Chorally** Have children finger point as they chorally read each page.
3. **Read Individually** Have children read aloud a favorite page in their group.
4. **Reread and Monitor Comprehension** As you listen to individual children reread, monitor progress and provide support.

TARGETED SKILL AND STRATEGY

SEQUENCE Remind children that in some selections, something happens first, something happens next, and something happens last. Ask children to tell what the fish did first in this selection. What did they do next? What did they do last?

RECALL/RETELL Have children retell the events of the selection in correct order.

Use the following questions to support comprehension.

PAGES 2–5 Why do you think the fish do not like the net? *(Possible answer: They do not want to get caught.)*

PAGE 6 How do the fish get food? *(They dig in the sand and push the food out.)*

PAGES 7–8 What happens at the end of the story? *(Fish eggs hatch into baby fish, and then they all swim away.)*

TEXT-TO-SELF QUESTION

Ask children the following: If you were a fish, where would you swim? What kind of adventure would you have?

RESPONSE OPTIONS

DRAMA Assign children the roles of fish and the man with a fishing pole. Have children act out that part of the selection as you reread it.

CONTENT CONNECTIONS

MATH Reread or retell the last page of this selection. Then have children draw five or more baby fish. Have children count how many fish they draw and write the appropriate number on their paper. If possible, display children's pictures by number, that is, all pictures that show six fish are grouped together.

Name _____

 Write.  Color.

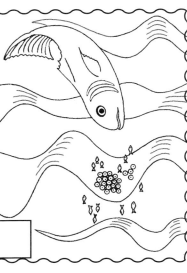

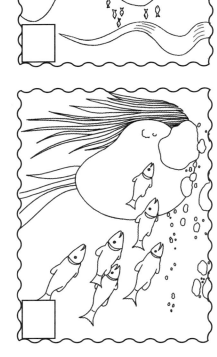

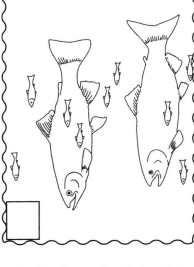

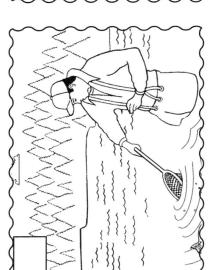

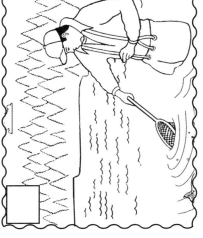

Directions Put the pictures in order. Write the numbers in the boxes. Color the pictures.

49 **Unit 4 Comprehension:** Sequence 49

🔊 **CAUSE AND EFFECT**

🔊 **RECALL/RETELL**

A Pig's Life

SUMMARY This informational text tells about pigs. This selection supports and extends the unit theme of adventures by illustrating and telling about what pigs can do.

INTRODUCE THE BOOK

BUILD BACKGROUND Tell children that a pig is a farm animal. Encourage children to share what they know about pigs. Tell children that a pig is a four-footed animal with short legs, large ears, a short tail, and a nose that is called a snout.

PREVIEW/PICTURE WALK Have children preview the book by looking at the pictures. Based on this preview, ask children what they think the selection will be about.

READ THE BOOK

SMALL GROUP READING
1. **Model Fluent Reading** Have children finger point as you read each page.
2. **Read Chorally** Have children finger point as they chorally read each page.
3. **Read Individually** Have children read aloud a favorite part in their group.
4. **Reread and Monitor Comprehension** As you listen to individual children reread, monitor progress and provide support.

TARGETED SKILL AND STRATEGY

🔊 **CAUSE AND EFFECT** Remind children that as they read or listen to a selection, they should think about things that happen and why those things happen. Ask what happens because the pigs take a mud bath. (They are safe from the hot sun.)

🔊 **RECALL/RETELL** Have children retell what happened in the selection in their own words.

Use the following questions to support comprehension.

PAGES 2–3 Where do pigs live? (They live in a pen.)

PAGES 4–5 Why do the pigs get in the mud? (The pigs are hot, and the mud keeps them safe from the sun.)

PAGE 8 Can you name the parts of a pig? (snout, ears, tail, hoof)

TEXT-TO-SELF QUESTION

Remind children that the pigs in the story got in the mud to cool off. Ask: What do you do to keep cool?

RESPONSE OPTIONS

WRITE Have children complete this sentence: A pig can _____ .

CONTENT CONNECTIONS

SCIENCE Explain to children that baby animals are not always called by the same name as their mothers. Help children name some baby animals.

Ask what a baby pig is called (piglet); baby cat (kitten); baby dog (puppy); baby cow (calf); baby bear (cub); baby duck (duckling); and baby frog (tadpole).

Name _____

 Draw a line.

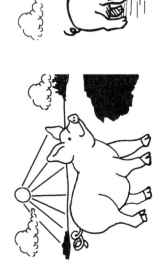

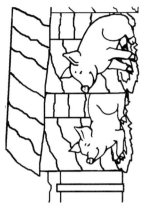

Directions Look at the pictures on the top. Draw a line to the picture on the bottom to show what will happen next.

51 **Unit 4 Comprehension:** Cause and Effect **51**

The Path to Frog's New Home

🔘 **SEQUENCE**

🔘 **RECALL/RETELL**

SUMMARY This informational text tells about a frog. This selection supports and extends the unit theme of adventures by illustrating and telling about the exciting things that happen to a frog while it looks for a new home.

INTRODUCE THE BOOK

BUILD BACKGROUND Explain that a frog is a small animal. Encourage children to share what they already know about frogs. Where do frogs live? How does a frog move from place to place? What sound does it make?

PREVIEW/PICTURE WALK Have children preview the book by looking at the pictures. Based on this preview, ask children what they think the selection will be about.

READ THE BOOK

SMALL GROUP READING
1. **Model Fluent Reading** Have children finger point as you read each page.
2. **Read Chorally** Have children finger point as they chorally read each page.
3. **Read Individually** Have children read aloud a favorite page in their group.
4. **Reread and Monitor Comprehension** As you listen to individual children reread, monitor progress and provide support.

TARGETED SKILL AND STRATEGY

🔘 **SEQUENCE** Remind children that in some selections, something happens first, something happens next, and something happens last. Ask children to tell what happened to the frog first. Ask what else the frog saw and in what order it saw them.

🔘 **RECALL/RETELL** Have children retell the events of the selection in the correct order. If they need help, have them look at the selection again.

Use the following questions to support comprehension.

PAGES 2–3 What kind of home was the frog looking for? *(The frog was looking for a home with shade.)*

PAGES 4–5 What animals did the frog see in the lake? *(The frog saw three ducks in a lake.)*

PAGE 8 Why is this pond a good home? *(It has shade, sun, and moths.)*

TEXT-TO-TEXT QUESTION

Say the following to the children: What did the pig in last week's story, *A Pig's Life,* do to stay safe from the sun? How did it stay cool? What does the frog do to stay cool? (It finds a pond with shade.)

RESPONSE OPTIONS

ART Have children draw a picture of the frog in its new home. Call on volunteers to tell about their picture.

CONTENT CONNECTIONS

MATH Have children write the number to answer each question.

How many nuts fell on the path? (1)
How many snakes did the frog see? (2)
How many ducks did the frog see? (3)
How many bits of trash were there? (4)

Name _____

 Write.  Color.

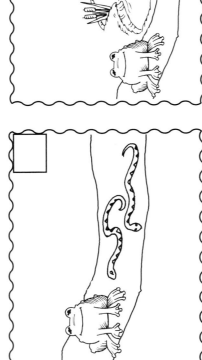

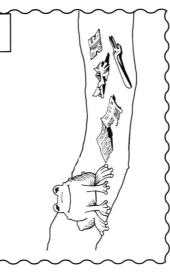

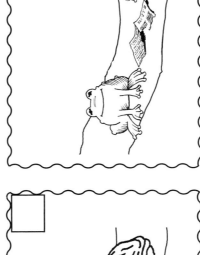

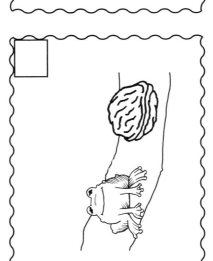

Directions Put the pictures in order. Write the numbers in the boxes. Color the pictures.

53 **Unit 4 Comprehension:** Sequence 53

© Pearson Education K

Five Bears All in a Den

Five Bears All in a Den

By Suzi Jones
Illustrated by Daniel J. Mahoney

⊙ **CHARACTER**

⊙ **RECALL/RETELL**

SUMMARY This realistic story tells about a family of bears. This selection supports and extends the unit theme of adventures by illustrating and telling about the bears' adventures.

INTRODUCE THE BOOK

BUILD BACKGROUND Explain that a bear is a wild animal that lives in the woods. Encourage children to share what they already know about bears. How many have ever seen a bear at the zoo? Where do bears live in the wild? What is a baby bear called?

PREVIEW/PICTURE WALK Have children preview the book by looking at the pictures. Based on this preview, ask children what they think the story will be about.

READ THE BOOK

SMALL GROUP READING

1. **Model Fluent Reading** Have children finger point as you read each page.
2. **Read Chorally** Have children finger point as they chorally read each page.
3. **Read Individually** Have children read aloud a favorite part in their group.
4. **Reread and Monitor Comprehension** As you listen to individual children reread, monitor progress and provide support.

TARGETED SKILL AND STRATEGY

⊙ **CHARACTER** Remind children that characters are people or animals in stories. Ask children who the characters are in this story. What kinds of things do the cubs like to do in the story?

⊙ **RECALL/RETELL** Have children retell the story in their own words. Prompt them as needed.

Use the following questions to support comprehension.

PAGES 2–3 What do you call a bear family's home? *(a den)*

PAGES 4–5 Why do the bears go to the river? *(They go to the dam to trap (catch) and eat fish.)*

PAGES 6–8 Where do the bears go to sleep? How many bears are there? *(Mom and Dad nap by the water. There are five bears.)*

TEXT-TO-WORLD QUESTION

Say the following to the children: A bear is a wild animal that lives in the woods. What other wild animals do you know about?

RESPONSE OPTIONS

WRITING Have children write a word or sentence telling one thing a bear can do. Children can illustrate their writing.

CONTENT CONNECTIONS

MATH Distribute two-color counters or cubes to each child. Children can use their counters or cubes to show the answers to questions such as the following: How many bears are in the story? How many are grown-up bears? How many are cubs? How many paws does Dad lift? How many fish does Mom trap?

Name _____

 Color.

Directions Color the pictures that show what the characters do in the story.

55 **Unit 4 Comprehension:** Character 55

A Walk in Antarctica

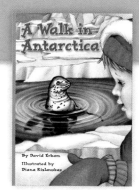

🔅 **CLASSIFY AND CATEGORIZE**

🔅 **RECALL/RETELL**

SUMMARY This realistic story tells about a boy who lives in Antarctica. This story supports and extends the unit theme of adventures by illustrating and telling about the adventure of living in Antarctica.

INTRODUCE THE BOOK

BUILD BACKGROUND Explain to children that Antarctica is a part of the world that is very cold. Tell them that not many people live there because it is so cold, but a few animals, such as whales, seals, and penguins, live there.

PREVIEW/PICTURE WALK Have children preview the book by looking at the pictures. Based on this preview, ask children what they think the story will be about.

READ THE BOOK

SMALL GROUP READING

1. **Model Fluent Reading** Have children finger point as you read each page.
2. **Read Chorally** Have children finger point as they chorally read each page.
3. **Read Individually** Have children read aloud a favorite page in their group.
4. **Reread and Monitor Comprehension** As you listen to individual children reread, monitor progress and provide support.

TARGETED SKILL AND STRATEGY

🔅 **CLASSIFY AND CATEGORIZE** Remind children that some things or animals can make up a group. Ask why seals, whales, and penguins can go together. How are these animals alike? (They all can live in Antarctica.)

🔅 **RECALL/RETELL** Have children retell the events of the story in their own words. Prompt them as needed.

Use the following questions to support comprehension.

PAGES 2–3 What does the boy do? *(He goes on a walk and then sits on a rock.)*

PAGES 4–5 What animals does the boy see? *(He sees a seal and whales.)*

PAGES 6–8 Why do you think the boy likes this place of snow and ice? *(Accept all reasonable responses such as: He likes the animals that live there.)*

TEXT-TO-SELF QUESTION

Ask children the following: How is Antarctica different from the place where you live?

RESPONSE OPTIONS

ART Have children use black construction paper and white chalk or paint to make snow pictures.

CONTENT CONNECTIONS

TIME FOR Science

SCIENCE Help children see how water changes in its different stages. Display a bowl of snow (or crushed ice) and have children note the amount. Come back to the bowl at intervals throughout the day and help children observe how the snow's amount and appearance change as it melts.

Name _____

✏️ Draw a line.

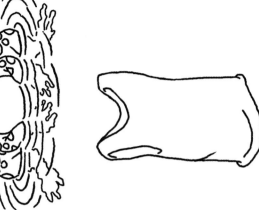

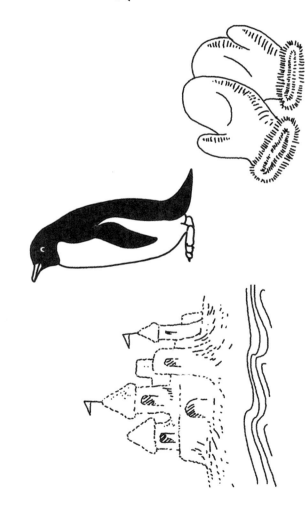

Directions Draw a line from the sun to the pictures that go with hot weather. Draw a line from the snowflakes to the pictures that go with cold weather.

57 Unit 4 Comprehension: Classify/Categorize 57

Independent Leveled Reader

◎ **SETTING**

◎ **RECALL/RETELL**

Washington, D.C.

SUMMARY This informational text tells about Washington, D.C., our nation's capital. This selection supports and extends the unit theme of adventures by illustrating and telling about the different places and things to do in Washington, D.C.

INTRODUCE THE BOOK

BUILD BACKGROUND If possible, point to Washington, D.C., on a map. Explain that this is an important place because our president and lawmakers are there. If any of the children have visited this place, discuss what they saw.

PREVIEW/PICTURE WALK Have children preview the book by looking at the pictures. Based on this preview, ask children what they think the selection will be about.

READ THE BOOK

SMALL GROUP READING
1. **Model Fluent Reading** Have children finger point as you read each page.
2. **Read Chorally** Have children finger point as they chorally read each page.
3. **Read Individually** Have children read aloud a favorite part in their group.
4. **Reread and Monitor Comprehension** As you listen to individual children reread, monitor progress and provide support.

TARGETED SKILL AND STRATEGY

◎ **SETTING** Remind children that when they read or listen to a story, they should think about where the story happens. Ask children if this story happens in a place that is real or make believe.

◎ **RECALL/RETELL** Have children retell the selection in their own words. Remind them to name the different places shown in the selection.

Use the following questions to support comprehension.

PAGES 2–3 How can you get around Washington, D.C.? *(You can take the subway.)*

PAGES 4–7 Name some of the places you could see in Washington, D.C. *(the Mall, Washington Monument, the Wall)*

PAGE 8 What would you see if you visited Washington, D.C., in the spring? *(flowering cherry blossom trees)*

TEXT-TO-SELF QUESTION

Say to children: Think about where you live. What special places are near your home?

RESPONSE OPTIONS

ART Have each child decorate a large square of drawing paper as a kite. Help children add "tails" to one corner of their paper.

CONTENT CONNECTIONS

SOCIAL STUDIES Tell children that sometimes we show we respect people who have helped our country by building a monument to honor them. Show pictures of and describe other monuments. Include information about who the monument honors and why.

Time for SOCIAL STUDIES

Name _____

 Write.  Color.

Washington Monument   city   subway

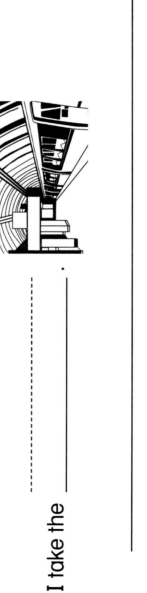

I take the _____.

The _____ is tall.

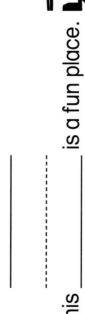

This _____ is a fun place.

Directions Read each sentence. Look at the picture. Then write the word that completes the sentence and tells about the setting. Color the pictures.

59 Unit 4 Comprehension: Setting 59

© Pearson Education K

Fish Can Swim   LR2

The boxes should be numbered across. Row 1: 1, 4, 3; Row 2: 2, 5

A Pig's Life   LR4

Children draw a line from the 1st picture on top to picture 2 on the bottom.

Children draw a line from the 2nd picture on top to picture 4 on the bottom.

Children draw a line from the 3rd picture on top to picture 1 on the bottom.

Children draw a line from the 4th picture on top to picture 3 on the bottom.

The Path to Frog's New Home   LR6

Children write 2 in the 1st box.

Children write 3 in the 2nd box.

Children write 1 in the 3rd box.

Children write 4 in the 4th box.

Children write 5 in the 5th box.

Five Bears All in a Den   LR8

Children should color the den, the tree with beehive, and the river with fish.

A Walk in Antarctica   LR10

Draw a line from the sun to the sandcastle, the tank top, the frog.

Draw a line from the snowflake to the penguin, the mittens, the snowman.

Washington, D.C.   LR12

Children should write *subway* in sentence 1.

Children should write *Washington Monument* in sentence 2.

Children should write *city* in sentence 3.

Differentiated Instruction

Table of Contents

Daily Group Time Lessons

Unit 4
Group Time

Strategic Intervention

ROUTINE

1 Phonemic Awareness

Isolate /h/ Display the *hammer* Picture Card. This is a hammer. *Hammer* begins with /h/. Say it with me: /h/, /h/, /h/, *hammer*. Repeat with *hat, hen,* and *hose.*

2 Phonics

Connect /h/ to Hh Display the *Hh* Alphabet Card. The name of this letter is *h*. The sound for this letter is /h/. Have children echo you.

Blend Sounds Write *Hap* on the board. Have children blend the sound of each letter to read the word. Continue with *can, hop, sit, bit, nap, hot,* and *not.*

H a p

Review High-Frequency Words Write *that* on the board. This is the word *that.* Name the letters with me: *t, h, a, t, that.* Continue with *a, are, you,* and *do.*

3 Read Decodable Text

Read Listen to Me Reader K.4.1 Display the book. The title of this story is *Hap is Hot.* It is written by Kevin Reese. It is illustrated by Chad Thompson. Follow along with your finger as I read, and then we will take turns reading each page. Reread the book several times, giving children opportunities to read the story. Provide support as necessary.

Listen to Me Reader K.4.1

Advanced

ROUTINE

1 Phonics

Connect /h/ to Hh Display the *Hh* Alphabet Card. What is the name of this letter? What is the sound for this letter?

Blend Sounds Write *hop* on the board. Help me blend the sounds in this word to read it: /h/ /o/ /p/. The word is *hop.* Continue with *hip, hit, hat, hot,* and *had.*

2 Oral Language

Build Background Remind children that a chameleon is a lizard that changes colors so it cannot be seen. Chameleons can hide in flower beds or in dirt and mud. Encourage children to share what they know about chameleons. Have you ever seen a chameleon at the zoo? Do you know anyone who has a chameleon for a pet?

3 Reread Leveled Text

Reread Independent Leveled Reader K.3.6 Have children take turns reading *Can You Spot It?* for their group.

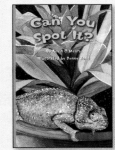

Reread for Fluency Model reading fluently for children. I will read one sentence at a time. I will read just the way I speak. I want you to read each sentence together after me. Try to read just as if you are speaking.

Independent Leveled Reader K.3.6

Use your oral reading to model reading with an appropriate pace. Then have children practice reading orally with a partner. Listen to them read and provide feedback regarding their oral reading and their use of the blending strategy.

Unit 4
Group Time

Strategic Intervention

ROUTINE

1 Phonemic Awareness

Discriminate /h/ Display Phonics Songs and Rhymes Chart 19. Sing the song several times. Ask children to clap when they hear /h/ words.

2 Phonics

Connect /h/ to Hh Display page 8 of *Animal ABCs*. What is the name of this letter? What is the sound for this letter? This is a *hawk*. What letter does *hawk* begin with? What is the sound for that letter?

Blend Sounds Write *hat* on the board. Have children blend the sound of each letter to read the word. Continue with *hit, on, it, can,* and *hop.*

h a t
▶ ▶ ▶
━━━━━━▶

Review High-Frequency Words Write *that* on the board. This is the word *that.* Name the letters with me: *t, h, a, t, that.* Continue with *I, have, a, the, is, little, my, me, you, with,* and *like.*

3 Read Decodable Text

Read Phonics Story Display the story. The title of this story is *I Have!* Follow along with your finger as I read, and then we will take turns reading this page. Reread the book several times giving children opportunities to read the story. Provide support as necessary.

Phonics Story

Advanced

ROUTINE

1 Build Fluency

Blend Sounds Write *Hob* on the board. Help me blend the sounds in this word to read it, /h/ /o/ /b/. The word is *Hob.* Continue with *man, Dan, can, hit, it, fan, Pam, Sam, did, not, hot, had, hat,* and *pop.*

Review High-Frequency Words Write *that* on the board. This is the word *that.* Say the letters with me: *t, h, a, t, that.* Repeat with *is, do, see,* and *a.*

2 Read Decodable Text

Read Decodable Reader 19 The title of this story is *Hob Can Hit.* The author is Roy Kass. The illustrator is Ryan Bines. Let's read the story together. Follow the Small Group Reading Routine.

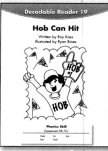

Decodable Reader 19

• **Model Fluent Reading**

• **Read Chorally**

• **Read Individually**

• **Reread and Monitor Progress**

Unit 4
Group Time

ROUTINE

1 Phonemic Awareness

Isolate /h/ Display the *house* Picture Card. This is a house. What is the first sound in *house*? The first sound is /h/. Repeat this routine with the following words: *head, helicopter, help, hippo, horse,* and *hug*.

2 Phonics

Connect /h/ to *Hh* Write *Hh* on the board. What is the name of this letter? What is the sound for this letter? Name some words that begin with /h/.

Blend Sounds Write *hit* on the board. Have children blend the sound of each letter to read the word. Continue with *Nan, and, Nat, can, top, bin, it, tin, hot, fan, nap, man, at,* and *sip*.

PHONICS ACTIVITY MAT

Review High-Frequency Words Write *are* on the board. This is the word *are*. Name the letters with me: *a, r, e, are*. Continue with *that, do, you, see, the, of, a, they,* and *look*.

Introduce Rebus Words Write *stand*. This is the word *stand*. Name the letters with me: *s, t, a, n, d, stand*. Look for this word in our story today.

3 Read Decodable Text

Read Kindergarten Student Reader K.4.1 Display the book. The title of this story is *All in a Day*. The author is Ann Rossi. The illustrator is Jaime Smith. Let's read this story together. Follow the Small Group Reading Routine.

Kindergarten Student Reader K.4.1

- **Model Fluent Reading**
- **Read Chorally**
- **Read Individually**
- **Reread and Monitor Progress**

ROUTINE

1 Build Fluency

Blend Sounds Write *Nat* on the board. Blend the sounds in this word to read it: /n/ /a/ /t/. What is this word?

Review High-Frequency Words Write *are* on the board. This is the word *are*. Say the letters with me: *a, r, e, are*. Repeat with *that, do, you, see, the, of, a, they,* and *look*.

Introduce Rebus Words Write *stand* on the board. This is the word *stand*. Name the letters with me: *s, t, a, n, d, stand*. Look for this word in our story today.

2 Read Decodable Text

Read Kindergarten Student Reader K.4.1 Show the cover of the story. The title of this story is *All in a Day*. Read the first page for children. Have volunteers reread the page.

Kindergarten Student Reader K.4.1

Reread for Fluency Use echo reading to model reading fluently for children. I will read one sentence at a time. I will read the words with no mistakes. I want you to read the sentences together after me. Try to read them just the way I do.

After modeling, have children continue to practice reading orally with a partner. Listen to children read, and provide feedback regarding their oral reading and their use of the blending strategy.

Unit 4
Group Time

ROUTINE

DAY 4

1 Phonemic Awareness

Isolate /h/ Display the *hippopotamus* Picture Card. This is a hippo. What is the first sound in *hippo?* The first sound is /h/. Repeat this routine with the following words: *head, helicopter, help, horse,* and *hug.*

Discriminate /h/ Teach children the following song sung to the tune of "Mary Had a Little Lamb":

> Henry Hippo hops to town,
> Hops to town, hops to town.
> Henry Hippo hops to town.
> Hopping with his hard hat on!

Have children sing with you several times. Then have them clap when they hear a /h/ word.

2 Phonics

Connect /h/ to *Hh* Write *Hh* on the board. What is the name of this letter? What is the sound for this letter? Name some words that begin with /h/.

Blend Sounds Write *hit* on the board. Have children blend the sound of each letter to read the word.

Continue with *man, Dan, can, it, fan, Pam, Sam, did, not, hot, had, hat,* and *pop.*

3 Build Fluency

Review High-Frequency Words Write *are* on the board. This is the word *are.* Name the letters with me: *a, r, e, are.* Continue with *that, is, a, do,* and *see.*

4  Decodable Text

Read Decodable Reader 19 Display the story. The title of this story is *Hob Can Hit.* Follow along with your finger as I read, and then we will take turns reading this page. Reread the book several times, giving children opportunities to read the story. Provide support as necessary.

Decodable Reader 19

Unit 4
Group Time

ROUTINE

DAY 5

1 Phonemic Awareness

Listen for /h/ Tell children you will tell them a story and they should listen for /h/. When you say a word that begins with /h/, the children should hop and repeat the word. Tell a simple story, emphasizing the initial /h/ words and pausing to give children a chance to hop and repeat the word. *Hope likes to hop. She hops all around her house. Hope hops and hops until she is hot. Hopping makes Hope happy. Hop! Hop! Hop!*

2 Phonics

Connect /h/ to *Hh* Write *Hh* on the board. What is the name of this letter? What is the sound for this letter?

Discriminate *h* Words Give each child an *h* Finger Tracing Card. I am going to say some words. I want you to listen carefully. If the word begins with /h/, raise your *h* card. Listen carefully: *Henry Hippo.* Did you hold your card up two times? *Henry* and *Hippo* both begin with *h.* Let's try some more. Use the following words: *garden hose, Hugh hums, happy hens, green helicopters,* and *brown horses.*

3 Alternate Assessment

Build Words Give each child the following letter tiles: *a, i, o, d, h, p,* and *t.* I am going to say a word, and you are going to use your tiles to build the word. Listen to the sounds in *hot.* What is the first sound in *hot*? The first sound is /h/. What is the letter for /h/? Place your *h* tile in front of you. Repeat this routine for the *o* and *t.* Then have children blend the sounds to read the word. Make note of children who seem to struggle connecting the sound to the letter. Continue the assessment with the following words: *hat, had, hip, hop, dot, did,* and *dad.*

Unit 4
Group Time

Strategic Intervention

ROUTINE

DAY 1

1 Phonemic Awareness

Isolate /l/ Display the *ladybug* Picture Card. This is a ladybug. *Ladybug* begins with /l/. Say it with me: /l/, /l/, /l/, *ladybug.* Repeat with *lake, lamp,* and *leaf.*

2 Phonics

Connect /l/ to Ll Display the *Ll* Alphabet Card. The name of this letter is *l.* The sound for this letter is /l/. Have children echo you.

Blend Sounds Write *Lin* on the board. Have children blend the sound of each letter to read the word. Continue with *at, Lib, sad, mad, it, Rob, had, lap,* and *nap.*

Review High-Frequency Words Write *that* on the board. This is the word *that.* Name the letters with me: *t, h, a, t, that.* Continue with *look, is, do, you, see, are,* and *a.*

3 Read Decodable Text

Read Listen to Me Reader K.4.2 Display the book. The title of this story is *A Rainy Day.* It is written by Donna Latham. It is illustrated by Aleksey Ivanov. Follow along with your finger as I read, and then we will take turns reading this page. Reread the book several times, giving children opportunities to read the story. Provide support as necessary.

Listen to Me Reader K.4.2

Advanced

ROUTINE

DAY 1

1 Phonics

Connect /l/ to Ll Display the *Ll* Alphabet Card. What is the name of this letter? What is the sound for this letter?

Blend Sounds Write *lit* on the board. Help me blend the sounds in this word to read it: /l/ /i/ /t/. The word is *lit.* Continue with *led, lug, lip,* and *lab.*

2 Oral Language

Build Background Remind children that fish dig in sand to look for food and lay their eggs in thick grass. Encourage children to share what they know about a home for a fish. In what kinds of places do fish live? Do you know anyone who has a fish for a pet?

3 Reread Leveled Text

Reread Independent Leveled Reader K.4.1 Have children take turns reading *Fish Can Swim* for their group.

Independent Leveled Reader K.4.1

Reread for Fluency After children read, model reading fluently for them. I am going to read this selection aloud. I will read the words with no mistakes. I want you to read it aloud with me. Try to read the words just as I do.

Use echo reading of Independent Leveled Reader K.4.1 to model reading fluently. Use your oral reading to model for children where to pause, when to change pitch, and which words to stress. Then have children reread orally three to four times, or until they can read with few or no mistakes.

Unit 4
Group Time

Strategic Intervention

ROUTINE

1 Phonemic Awareness

Discriminate /l/ Display Phonics Songs and Rhymes Chart 20. Sing the song several times. Ask children to clap when they hear /l/ words.

2 Phonics

Connect /l/ to Ll Display page 12 of *Animal ABCs*. What is the name of this letter? What is the sound for this letter? This is a *lion*. What letter does *lion* begin with? What is the sound for that letter?

Blend Sounds Write *Lad* on the board. Have children blend the sound of each letter to read the word. Continue with *hit, on, lap, lot,* and *hop.*

Review High-Frequency Words Write *that* on the board. This is the word *that*. Name the letters with me: *t, h, a, t, that.* Continue with *is, my, little, do, you, like, I, a, the, we, are.*

3 Read Decodable Text

Read Phonics Story Display the story. The title of this story is *Lad and Me.* Follow along with your finger as I read, and then we will take turns reading this page. Reread the book several times giving children opportunities to read the story. Provide support as necessary.

Phonics Story

Advanced

ROUTINE

1 Build Fluency

Blend Sounds Write *Tab* on the board. Help me blend the sounds in this word to read it, /t/ /a/ /b/. The word is *Tab.* Continue with *sat, on, lap, Kit, did, not, Lil, lit, it, had, can, bat, in, lid,* and *fit.*

Review High-Frequency Words Write *that* on the board. This is the word *that*. Say the letters with me: *t, h, a, t, that.* Repeat with *a, do, you, see, the, they,* and *are.*

2 Read Decodable Text

Read Decodable Reader 20 The title of this story is *Can It Fit?* The author is Myleen Rush. The illustrator is Gloria Leek. Let's read the story together. Follow the Small Group Reading Routine.

- **Model Fluent Reading**
- **Read Chorally**
- **Read Individually**
- **Reread and Monitor Progress**

Decodable Reader 20

Unit 4
Group Time

Strategic Intervention

ROUTINE

1 Phonemic Awareness

Isolate /l/ Display the *doll* Picture Card. This is a doll. What is the last sound in *doll*? The last sound is /l/. Repeat this routine with the following words: *pail, seal,* and *snail.*

2 Phonics

Connect /l/ to Ll Write *Ll* on the board. What is the name of this letter? What is the sound for this letter? Name some words that end with /l/.

Blend Sounds Write *lid* on the board. Have children blend the sound of each letter to read the word. Continue with *sit, and, Nat, Lin, Rob, can, tap, rap, bam, on, pot, tan, pan, hit, Nan,* and *dad.*

Review High-Frequency Words Write *me* on the board. This is the word *me*. Name the letters with me: *m, e, me*. Continue with *with, you, we, like, to, the,* and *look.*

Introduce Rebus Words Write *play* on the board. This is the word *play*. Say the word with me: *play.*

3 **Read** Decodable Text

Read Kindergarten Student Reader K.4.2 Display the book. The title of this story is *A Musical Adventure.* The author is Ann Rossi. The illustrator is Jaime Smith. Let's read this story together. Follow the Small Group Reading Routine.

- **Model Fluent Reading**
- **Read Chorally**
- **Read Individually**
- **Reread and Monitor Progress**

Kindergarten Student Reader K.4.2

Advanced

ROUTINE

1 Build Fluency

Blend Sounds Write *Nat* on the board. Blend the sounds in this word to read it: /n/ /a/ /t/. What is this word?

Why did I use uppercase *N* at the beginning of the word *Nat*? (*Nat* is a name.)

Review High-Frequency Words Write *look* on the board. This is the word *look*. Say the letters with me: *l, o, o, k, look*. Repeat with *with, you, we, like, to, the,* and *me.*

Introduce Rebus Words Write *play* on the board. This is the word *play*. Name the letters with me: *p, l, a, y, play*. Look for this word in our story today.

2 **Read** Decodable Text

Read Kindergarten Student Reader K.4.2 Show the cover of the book. The title of this story is *A Musical Adventure*. Read the first page for children. Have volunteers reread the page.

Kindergarten Student Reader K.4.2

Reread for Fluency After reading with children, model reading fluently for them. I am going to read this story aloud. I will read the words with no mistakes. I want you to read it aloud with me. Try to read the words just as I do.

Use echo reading of Kindergarten Student Reader K.4.2 to model reading fluently. Use your oral reading to model for children where to pause, when to change pitch, and which words to stress. Then have children reread orally three to four times, or until they can read with few or no mistakes.

Unit 4
Group Time

ROUTINE

DAY 4

1 Phonemic Awareness

Isolate /l/ Display the *leaf* Picture Card. This is a leaf. What is the first sound in *leaf*? The first sound is /l/. Repeat this routine with the following words: *lid, lamp,* and *loaf.*

Discriminate /l/ Teach children the following song sung to the tune of "London Bridge":

Lions like to live by lakes,
Live by lakes, live by lakes.
Lions like to live by lakes,
And seals like it too.

Have children sing with you several times. Then have them clap when they hear a word that begins with /l/.

2 Phonics

Connect /l/ to Ll Write *Ll* on the board. What is the name of this letter? What is the sound for this letter? Name some words that begin or end with /l/.

Blend Sounds Write *Tab* on the board. Have children blend the sound of each letter to read the word.

T a b
→ → →
→

Continue with *sat, on, lap, Kit, did, not, Lil, lit, it, had, can, bat, in, lid,* and *fit.*

3 Build Fluency

Review High-Frequency Words Write *the* on the board. This is the word *the.* Name the letters with me: *t, h, e, the.* Continue with *I, am, little, a, to, have, is we, my, like, he, for, me, with, she, see, look, they, you, of, are, that,* and *do.*

4 Read Decodable Text

Read Decodable Reader 20 Display the story. The title of this story is *Can It Fit?* Follow along with your finger as I read, and then we will take turns reading this page. Reread the book several times, giving children opportunities to read the story. Provide support as necessary.

Decodable Reader 20

Unit 4
Group Time

DAY 5

Strategic Intervention

ROUTINE

1 Phonemic Awareness

Listen for /l/ Tell children you will tell them a story and they should listen for /l/. When you say a word that begins with /l/, the children should pat their legs and repeat the word. Tell a simple story, emphasizing the initial /l/ words and pausing to give children a chance to pat their legs and repeat the word. *Lucy likes lemons. She loves to lick lots of lemons until her lips look puckered up. Lucy really likes lemons!*

2 Phonics

Connect /l/ to Ll Write *Ll* on the board. What is the name of this letter? What is the sound for this letter?

Discriminate l Words Give each child an *l* Finger Tracing Card. I am going to say some words. I want you to listen carefully. If the word begins with /l/, raise your *l* card. Listen carefully: *little, lemon.* Did you hold your card up two times? *Little* and *lemon* both begin with *l.* Let's try some more. Use the following words: *laughing lion, many trees, lovely ladybug,* and *last letter.*

3 Alternate Assessment

Build Words Give each child the following letter tiles: *a, i, o, l, t, d,* and *p.* I am going to say a word, and you are going to use your tiles to build the word. Listen to the sounds in *lad.* What is the first sound in *lad*? The first sound is /l/. What is the letter for /l/? Place your *l* tile in front of you. Repeat this routine for the *a* and *d.* Then have children blend the sounds to read the word. Make note of children who seem to struggle connecting the sound to the letter. Continue the assessment with the following words: *lot, lap, lip,* and *lid.*

Group Time

DAY 1

ROUTINE

1 Phonemic Awareness

Isolate Initial Blends Display the *playground* Picture Card. This is a playground. *Playground* begins with the blend /pl/. Say it with me: /pl/, /pl/, /pl/, *playground*. Repeat with *flag, cloud,* and *sled.*

2 Phonics

Connect /pl/ to *Pp* and *Ll* Using Finger Tracing Cards, have children trace the letters *p* and *l*. The sound for these letters together is /pl/. Have children echo you. Repeat the routine with /cl/, /fl/, and /sl/.

Blend Sounds Write *flop* on the board. Have children blend the sounds of the letters to read the word. Continue with *spins, slid, plop,* and *spot.*

Review High-Frequency Words Write *one* on the board. This is the word *one*. Name the letters with me: *o, n, e, one.* Continue with *two, three, four,* and *five.*

3 Read Decodable Text

Read Listen to Me Reader K.4.3 Display the book. The title of this selection is *One, Two, Three, Four, Five!* It is written by Susan Yuen. Follow along with your finger as I read, and then we will take turns reading this page. Reread the book several times, giving children opportunities to read the text. Provide support as necessary.

Listen to Me Reader K.4.3

DAY 1

ROUTINE

1 Phonics

Connect /pl/ to *Pp* and *Ll* Using Finger Tracing Cards, have children trace the letters *p* and *l*. What is the sound for these letters together? Repeat the routine with /cl/, /fl/, and /sp/.

Blend Sounds Write *flap* on the board. Help me blend the sounds in this word to read it: /fl/ /a/ /p/. The word is *flap*. Continue with *flip, clap, flag,* and *spin.*

2 Oral Language

Build Background Remind children that a pig is a farm animal that often lives in a pen. Pigs take mud baths to keep them safe from the sun. Encourage children to act out sniffing for food with their "snouts" and shaking off after taking a mud bath.

3 Reread Leveled Text

Reread Independent Leveled Reader K.4.2 Have children take turns reading *A Pig's Life* for their group.

Reread for Fluency Model reading fluently for children. I am going to read this story aloud. I will read the words with no mistakes. I want you to read it aloud with me. Try to read the words just as I do.

Independent Leveled Reader K.4.2

Use echo reading to model reading fluently. Use your oral reading to model for children where to pause, when to change pitch, and which words to stress. Then have children reread orally three to four times, or until they can read with few or no mistakes.

Unit 4
Group Time

Strategic Intervention

1 Phonemic Awareness

Discriminate Blends Display Phonics Songs and Rhymes Chart 21. Sing the song several times. Ask children to clap when they hear words beginning with a blend.

2 Phonics

Recognize Blends List the words *clap*, *slid*, and *plop* on chart paper. Circle the beginning blend in each word. What are the names of these letters? What are the sounds of these letters together? This word is *clap*. What two letters does *clap* begin with? What is the sound for that blend?

Blend Sounds Write *clip* on the board. Have children blend the sound of the letters to read the word. Continue with *trap*, *spot*, *crab*, and *trip*.

Review High-Frequency Words Write *two* on the board. This is the word *two*. Name the letters with me: *t, w, o, two*. Continue with *I*, *have*, *one*, *is*, *like*, *you*, *three*, and *do*.

3 Read Decodable Text

Read Phonics Story Display the story. The title of this story is *My Words*. Follow along with your finger as I read, and then we will take turns reading this page. Reread the book several times, giving children opportunities to read the story. Provide support as necessary.

Phonics Story

Advanced

1 Build Fluency

Blend Sounds Write *spin* on the board. Help me blend the sounds in this word to read it, /sp/ /i/ /n/. The word is *spin*. Continue with *flop, slam, drop, land, plop,* and *stop.*

Review High-Frequency Words Write *one* on the board. This is the word *one*. Say the letters with me: *o, n, e, one*. Repeat with *two, three, four, five,* and *a.*

2 Read Decodable Text

Read Decodable Reader 21 The title of this story is *One to Five*. The author is Heather Leavy. The illustrator is Kris Pool. What do the author and illustrator do? (write the words and draw the pictures) Let's read the story together. Follow the Small Group Reading Routine.

Decodable Reader 21

- **Model Fluent Reading**
- **Read Chorally**
- **Read Individually**
- **Reread and Monitor Progress**

Unit 4
Group Time

Strategic Intervention

ROUTINE

1 Phonemic Awareness

Isolate Initial Blends Display the *cloud* Picture Card. This is a cloud. Do you hear a blend in *cloud*? The first sound is /cl/. Repeat this routine with the following words: *clock, flash,* and *slide.*

2 Phonics

Recognize Blends Supply children with the *a, i, m, d, s,* and *k* letter tiles. Use the *m, a, s,* and *k* letter tiles to spell the word *mask.* Hold up the *s* and *k.* What are the names of these letters? What is the sound of these letters together? Continue the routine with the words *disk, skim, skid,* and *ask.*

Blend Sounds Write *skip* on the board. Have children blend the sounds of the letters to read the word. Continue with *and, Nan, hop, Nat, stop, Flap, cat, claps, can, sip, drops, spot, dots, on, him, sit, in,* and *lap.*

s k i p

Review High-Frequency Words Write *three* on the board. This is the word *three.* Name the letters with me: *t, h, r, e, e, three.* Continue with *one, two, four, five, for, the, I, do, you, like, to,* and *my.*

3 Read Decodable Text

Read Kindergarten Student Reader K.4.3 Display the book. The title of this story is *A Home for Flap the Cat.* The author is Susi Jones. Let's read this story together. Follow the Small Group Reading Routine.

Kindergarten Student Reader K.4.3

- **Model Fluent Reading**
- **Read Chorally**
- **Read Individually**
- **Reread and Monitor Progress**

Advanced

ROUTINE

1 Build Fluency

Blend Sounds Write *clap* on the board. Blend the sounds in this word to read it: /cl/ /a/ /p/. What is this word?

cl a p

Continue with the words *skip* and *stop.*

Review High-Frequency Words Write *one* on the board. This is the word *one.* Say the letters with me: *o, n, e, one.* Repeat with *two, three, four, five,* and *a.*

2 Read Decodable Text

Read Kindergarten Student Reader K.4.3 Show the cover of the book. The title of this story is *A Home for Flap the Cat.* Read the first page for children. Have volunteers reread the page.

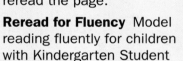

Kindergarten Student Reader K.4.3

Reread for Fluency Model reading fluently for children with Kindergarten Student Reader K.4.3. I will read one sentence at a time. I will read just the way I speak. I want you to read each sentence together after me. Try to read just as if you are speaking.

Use your oral reading to model reading with an appropriate pace. Then have children practice reading orally with a partner. Listen to them read, and provide feedback regarding their oral reading and their use of the blending strategy.

Unit 4
Group Time

DAY 4

ROUTINE

1 Phonemic Awareness

Isolate Final Blends Display the *desk* Picture Card. This is a desk. *Desk* ends with the blend /sk/. What is the last sound in *desk*? The last sound is /sk/. Repeat this routine with the following words: *sand, list, land, milk, fast,* and *mask*.

Discriminate Blends Say the following rhyme for children several times. Then have them clap when they hear an initial blend.

> Clip and clop,
> Clip and clop,
> Feet are marching,
> Never stop.

2 Phonics

Connect Sounds to Letters Write *Cc* and *Ll* on the board. What are the names of these letters? What sounds do these letters make when they are blended together? Name some words that begin with /cl/.

Blend Sounds Write *spin* on the board. Have children blend the sound of each letter to read the word.

s p i n

Continue with *sat, on, mat, ran, pan, hid, lid, land, lap,* and *top*.

3 Build Fluency

Review High-Frequency Words Write *four* on the board. This is the word *four*. Name the letters with me: *f, o, u, r, four.* Continue with *one, two, three, five,* and *a*.

4 Read Decodable Text

Read Decodable Reader 21 Display the story. The title of this story is *One to Five*. Follow along with your finger as I read, and then we will take turns reading this page. Reread the book several times, giving children opportunities to read the story. Provide support as necessary.

Decodable Reader 21

Unit 4
Group Time

ROUTINE

DAY 5

1 Phonemic Awareness

Listen for Blends Tell children you will tell them a story and they should listen for initial blends. When you say a word with two-letter blends, children should clap and repeat the word. Tell a simple story, emphasizing the initial blend words and pausing to give children a chance to clap and repeat the word. *Clare plans to take a trip. She puts on her pretty blue dress. On her trip, Clare gets to climb at a playground. She plays on the slide and swings. When it is time to fly back to Cleveland, Clare cleans up slowly. It has been a fun trip!*

2 Phonics

Connect /sl/ to Ss and Ll Write the letters *Ss* and *Ll* on the board. What are the names of these letters? What is the sound when these letters are blended together?

Discriminate Blends I am going to say some words. I want you to listen carefully. If the words begin with a blend, nod your head "yes" twice. If not, shake your head "no" twice. Listen carefully: *Clarence Clown.* Did you nod your head twice? *Clarence* and *Clown* both begin with a blend. Let's try some more. **Use the following words:** *drops dripping, big balloons, sitting down,* and *slipping slowly.*

3 Alternate Assessment

Listen for Blends Give each child the following letter tiles: *c, l, s, f, t,* and *r.* I am going to say a word, and you are going to use your tiles to tell me the blend the word begins with. Listen to the beginning of *trip.* What is the first sound in *trip?* The first sound is /tr/. What are the letters for /tr/? Place your *t* and *r* tiles in front of you. Continue the routine with the words *flip, stop, slip,* and *clown.*

Unit 4
Group Time

Strategic Intervention

ROUTINE

DAY 1

1 Phonemic Awareness

Isolate /g/ Display the *garden* Picture Card. This is a garden. *Garden* begins with /g/. Say it with me: /g/, /g/, /g/, *garden.* Repeat with *goat, goose,* and *gum.*

2 Phonics

Connect /g/ to Gg Display the *Gg* Alphabet Card. The name of this letter is *g.* The sound for this letter is /g/. Have children echo you.

Blend Sounds Write *Gib* on the board. Have children blend the sound of each letter to read the word. Continue with *got, it,* and *Gil.*

Review High-Frequency Words Write *one* on the board. This is the word *one.* Name the letters with me: *o, n, e, one.* Continue with *two, three, four,* and *five.*

3 Read Decodable Text

Read Listen to Me Reader K.4.4 Display the book. The title of this story is *Gib Got It.* It is written by Carmie Rosario. Follow along with your finger as I read, and then we will take turns reading this page. Reread the book several times, giving children opportunities to read the story. Provide support as necessary.

Listen to Me Reader K.4.4

Advanced

ROUTINE

DAY 1

1 Phonics

Connect /g/ to Gg Display the *Gg* Alphabet Card. What is the name of this letter? What is the sound for this letter?

Blend Sounds Write *gap* on the board. Help me blend the sounds in this word to read it: /g/ /a/ /p/. The word is *gap.* Continue with *get, got,* and *gas.*

2 Oral Language

Build Background Remind children that a frog needs to live in a quiet, moist place that has sun and shade. Picture walk through *The Path to Frog's New Home* and discuss what Frog encounters along the path. Why was the lake a bad home for Frog? Why might bits of trash be bad for Frog?

3 Reread Leveled Text

Reread Independent Leveled Reader K.4.3 Have children take turns reading *The Path to Frog's New Home* for their group.

Reread for Fluency After the children read, model reading fluently for them. I am going to read this selection aloud. I will read the words with no mistakes. I want you to read it aloud with me. Try to read the words just as I do.

Independent Leveled Reader K.4.3

Use echo reading of Independent Leveled Reader K.4.3 to model reading fluently. Use your oral reading to model for children where to pause, when to change pitch, and which words to stress. Then have children reread orally three to four times, or until they can read with few or no mistakes.

Unit 4
Group Time

DAY 2

Strategic Intervention

ROUTINE

1 Phonemic Awareness

Discriminate /g/ Display Phonics Songs and Rhymes Chart 22. Sing the song several times. Ask children to clap when they hear /g/ words.

2 Phonics

Connect /g/ to Gg Display page 7 of *Animal ABCs.* What is the name of this letter? What is the sound for this letter? This is a gorilla. What letter does *gorilla* begin with? What is the sound for that letter?

Blend Sounds Write *dog* on the board. Have children blend the sound of each letter to read the word. Continue with the word *at.*

d o g

Review High-Frequency Words Write *do* on the board. This is the word *do.* Name the letters with me: *d, o, do.* Continue with *you, see, one, I, two, three, four, five, look,* and *that.*

3 Read Decodable Text

Read Phonics Story Display the story. The title of this story is *How Many?* Follow along with your finger as I read, and then we will take turns reading this page. Reread the book several times, giving children opportunities to read the story. Provide support as necessary.

Name
How Many?

Lin and Hap can see one dog.

Phonics Story

Advanced

ROUTINE

1 Build Fluency

Blend Sounds Write *Gil* on the board. Help me blend the sounds in this word to read it: /g/ /i/ /l/. The word is *Gil.* Continue with *got, pop, sad, mom, had, plan, flag,* and *not.*

Review High-Frequency Words Write *one* on the board. This is the word *one.* Say the letters with me: *o, n, e, one.* Repeat with *two, three, four, five, a,* and *is.*

2 Read Decodable Text

Read Decodable Reader 22 The title of this story is *Gil Got One.* The author is William Dillberts. The illustrator is Hillary Gem. Let's read the story together. Follow the Small Group Reading Routine.

Decodable Reader 22

Gil Got One

Written by William Dillberts
Illustrated by Hillary Gem

Phonics Skill
Consonant Gg /g/

- **Model Fluent Reading**
- **Read Chorally**
- **Read Individually**
- **Reread and Monitor Progress**

Decodable Reader 22

Unit 4
Group Time

Strategic Intervention
ROUTINE

1 Phonemic Awareness

Isolate /g/ Display the *goat* Picture Card. This is a goat. What is the first sound in *goat*? The first sound is /g/. Repeat this routine with the following words: *goose* and *gum*.

2 Phonics

Connect /g/ to Gg Write *Gg*. What is the name of this letter? What is the sound for this letter? Name some words that begin with /g/.

Blend Sounds Write *big* on the board. Have children blend the sound of each letter to read the word. Continue with *am, Sam, stops, at, Nat, and, Nan, hop, on, Lin, skips, on, Gil, Gab, Dad, Sal, can, not, Ann, Dan, Kim, Tim, has, lots, dots, Kip, kids,* and *flag.*

Review High-Frequency Words Write *with*. This is the word *with*. Name the letters with me: *w, i, t, h, with.* Continue with *I, my, one, for, two, little, three, four, of, five, the, they, he,* and *to*.

Introduce Rebus Words Write *bus*. This is the word *bus*. Name the letters with me: *b, u, s, bus.* Look for this word in our story today.

3 Read Decodable Text

Read Kindergarten Student Reader K.4.4 Display the book. The title of this story is *Five Stops*. The author is Carolyn Kelly. The illustrator is Jaime Smith. Let's read this story together. Follow the Small Group Reading Routine.

Kindergarten Student Reader K.4.4

- **Model Fluent Reading**
- **Read Chorally**
- **Read Individually**
- **Reread and Monitor Progress**

Advanced
ROUTINE

1 Build Fluency

Blend Sounds Write *Gil* on the board. Blend the sounds in this word to read it: /g/ /i/ /l/. What is this word?

Continue with the following words: *big, stop, hop, skips,* and *flag.*

Review High-Frequency Words Write *five* on the board. This is the word *five*. Say the letters with me: *f, i, v, e, five.* Repeat with the word *they.*

Introduce Rebus Words Write *school* on the board. This is the word *school*. Name the letters with me: *s, c, h, o, o, l, school.* Repeat with the word *bus.* Look for these words in our story today.

2 Read Decodable Text

Read Kindergarten Student Reader K.4.4 Show the cover of the story. The title of this story is *Five Stops*. Read the first page for children. Have volunteers reread the page.

Kindergarten Student Reader K.4.4

Reread for Fluency Use echo reading to model fluent reading with Kindergarten Student Reader K.4.4. I will read one sentence at a time. I will read the words with no mistakes. I want you to read the sentences together after me. Try to read them just the way I do.

Use your oral reading to model for children where to pause, when to change pitch, and which words to stress. Then have children reread orally three to four times, or until they can read with few or no mistakes.

Unit 4
Group Time

ROUTINE

DAY 4

1 Phonemic Awareness

Isolate /g/ Display the *gum* Picture Card. This is a piece of gum. What is the first sound in *gum*? The first sound is /g/. Repeat this routine with the following words: *garden* and *goose*.

Discriminate /g/ Teach children the following song, sung to the tune of "Row, Row, Row Your Boat":

Gil got a little goat,
He got a goose as well,
He gave the goat some green, green grapes,
The goose got some as well!

Have children sing with you several times. Then have them clap when they hear a /g/ word.

2 Phonics

Connect /g/ to Gg Write *Gg* on the board. What is the name of this letter? What is the sound for this letter? Name some words that begin with /g/.

Blend Sounds Write *sad* on the board. Have children blend the sound of each letter to read the word.

s a d

Continue with *got, pop, Gil, mom, had, plan, flag,* and *not*.

3 Build Fluency

Review High-Frequency Words Write *five* on the board. This is the word *five*. Name the letters with me: *f, i, v, e, five.* Continue with *one, two, three, four, a,* and *is.*

4 Read Decodable Text

Read Decodable Reader 22 Display the story. The title of this story is *Gil Got One.* Follow along with your finger as I read, and then we will take turns reading this page. Reread the book several times, giving children opportunities to read the story. Provide support as necessary.

Decodable Reader 22

Goldilocks and the Three Bears   **DI•19**

Unit 4
Group Time

ROUTINE

DAY 5

1 Phonemic Awareness

Listen for /g/ Tell children you will tell them a story and they should listen for /g/. When you say a word that begins or ends with /g/, children should clap their hands and repeat the word. Tell a simple story, emphasizing the /g/ words and pausing to give children a chance to clap and repeat the word. *Gayle gave Meg a new bag because Meg was being a good girl. Meg was happy she got a new bag. She took the tag off the bag and put her books in the bag.*

2 Phonics

Connect /g/ to Gg Write *Gg* on the board. What is the name of this letter? What is the sound for this letter?

Discriminate /g/ Words Give each child a *g* Finger Tracing Card. I am going to say some words. I want you to listen carefully. If the word begins with /g/, raise your *g* card. Listen carefully: *Gil.* Did you hold your card up? *Gil* begins with G. Let's try some more. Use the following words: *garden, goose, happy, green,* and *peanut.*

3 Alternate Assessment

Build Words Give each child the following letter tiles: *a, e, i, g, b, p,* and *t.* I am going to say a word, and you are going to use your tiles to build the word. Listen to the sounds in *get.* What is the first sound in *get?* The first sound is /g/. What is the letter for /g/? Place your *g* tile in front of you. Repeat this routine for the *e* and *t.* Then have children blend the sounds to read the word. Make note of children who seem to struggle connecting the sound to the letter. Continue the assessment with the following words: *big, tag, gap,* and *pig.*

Unit 4
Group Time

Strategic Intervention

ROUTINE

1 Phonemic Awareness

Isolate /e/ Display the *egg* Picture Card. This is an egg. *Egg* begins with /e/. Say it with me: /e/, /e/, /e/, *egg.* Repeat with *bed, desk,* and *net.*

2 Phonics

Connect /e/ to Ee Display the *Ee* Alphabet Card. The name of this letter is *e*. The sound for this letter is /e/. Have children echo you.

Blend Sounds Write *red* on the board. Have children blend the sound of each letter to read the word. Continue with *Nan, hen, in, pen, spots, Ken, not, can,* and *get.*

Review High-Frequency Words Write *is* on the board. This is the word *is.* Name the letters with me: *i, s, is.* Continue with *a, she, he, to, here, go,* and *from.*

3 Read Decodable Text

Read Listen to Me Reader K.4.5 Display the book. The title of this story is *Nan the Red Hen!* It is written by Jebb McFlickers. It is illustrated by Philomena O'Neil. Follow along with your finger as I read, and then we will take turns reading this page. Reread the book several times, giving children opportunities to read the story. Provide support as necessary.

Listen to Me Reader K.4.5

Advanced

ROUTINE

1 Phonics

Connect /e/ to Ee Display the *Ee* Alphabet Card. What is the name of this letter? What is the sound for this letter?

Blend Sounds Write *pet* on the board. Help me blend the sounds in this word to read it: /p/ /e/ /t/. The word is *pet.* Continue with *ten* and *hen.*

2 Oral Language

Build Background Remind children that bears are wild animals that sleep in dens during the winter. Encourage children to pretend to be the bears stretching after a long nap. Have them make up a conversation between two bears about what they want to do now.

3 Reread Leveled Text

Reread Independent Leveled Reader K.4.4 Have children take turns reading *Five Bears All in a Den* for their group.

Reread for Fluency Model reading fluently for children. I will read one sentence at a time. I will read just the way I speak. I want you to read each sentence together after me. Try to read just as if you are speaking.

Independent Leveled Reader K.4.4

Use echo reading of Independent Leveled Reader K.4.4 to model reading fluently. Use your oral reading to model reading with an appropriate pace. Then have children practice reading the story orally with a partner. Listen to them read, and provide feedback regarding their oral reading and their use of the blending strategy.

Unit 4
Group Time

ROUTINE

DAY 2

① Phonemic Awareness

Discriminate /e/ Display Phonics Songs and Rhymes Chart 23. Sing the song several times. Ask children to clap when they hear /e/ words.

② Phonics

Connect /e/ to Ee Display page 5 of *Animal ABCs.* What is the name of this letter? What is the sound for this letter? This is an elephant. What letter does *elephant* begin with? What is the sound for that letter?

Blend Sounds Write *pet* on the board. Have children blend the sound of each letter to read the word. Continue with *hen, can, ten, fat, red,* and *bell.*

Review High-Frequency Words Write *have* on the board. This is the word *have.* Name the letters with me: *h, a, v, e, have.* Continue with *I, a, do, you, see,* and *my.*

③ Read Decodable Text

Read Phonics Story Display the story. The title of this story is *Ten, Ten, Ten!* Follow along with your finger as I read, and then we will take turns reading this page. Reread the book several times, giving children opportunities to read the story. Provide support as necessary.

Phonics Story

ROUTINE

DAY 2

① Build Fluency

Blend Sounds Write *Ben* on the board. Help me blend the sounds in this word to read it: /b/ /e/ /n/. The word is *Ben.* Continue with *get, Red, Hen, can, in, pen, ran, hid, did, not, Ken, Len,* and *got.*

Review High-Frequency Words Write *go* on the board. This is the word *go.* Say the letters with me: *g, o, go.* Repeat with *the, from,* and *here.*

② Read Decodable Text

Read Decodable Reader 23 The title of this story is *Red Hen.* The author is Nathan Aguilera. The illustrator is Samantha Johnson. Let's read the story together. Follow the Small Group Reading Routine.

- **Model Fluent Reading**
- **Read Chorally**
- **Read Individually**
- **Reread and Monitor Progress**

Decodable Reader 23

Unit 4
Group Time

DAY
3

ROUTINE

1 Phonemic Awareness

Isolate /e/ Display the *red* Picture Card. This is the color red. What is the sound in the middle of *red*? The middle sound is /e/. Repeat this routine with the following words: *web* and *vest*.

2 Phonics

Connect /e/ to Ee Write *Ee* on the board. What is the name of this letter? What is the sound for this letter? Name some words with /e/ in the middle.

Blend Sounds Write *Ken* on the board. Have children blend the sound of each letter to read the word. Continue with *Nan, Nat, Dad, gets, red, sleds, Ben, Sam, tells, Bill, Don, and, Dan, Ted, ten, at,* and *end*.

Review High-Frequency Words Write *look* on the board. This is the word *look*. Name the letters with me: *l, o, o, k, look*. Continue with *the, have, to, a, from, for, little, we, here,* and *go*.

3 Read Decodable Text

Read Kindergarten Student Reader K.4.5 Display the book. The title of this story is *Ten Red Sleds*. The author is Padraig George. Let's read this story together. Follow the Small Group Reading Routine.

Kindergarten Student Reader K.4.5

- **Model Fluent Reading**
- **Read Chorally**
- **Read Individually**
- **Reread and Monitor Progress**

DAY
3

ROUTINE

1 Build Fluency

Blend Sounds Write *sled* on the board. Blend the sounds in this word to read it: /sl/ /e/ /d/. What is this word?

s l e d

Continue with the following words: *get, ten, red, Bill, Ted,* and *Don*.

Review High-Frequency Words Write *the* on the board. This is the word *the*. Say the letters with me: *t, h, e, the*. Repeat with *have, to, a, go,* and *from*.

2 Read Decodable Text

Read Kindergarten Student Reader K.4.5 Show the cover of the story. The title of this story is *Ten Red Sleds*. Read the first page for children. Have volunteers reread the page.

Kindergarten Student Reader K.4.5

Reread for Fluency Have children read Kindergarten Student Reader K.4.5. Listen to children read and provide feedback regarding their use of the word reading strategy. Have them reread orally three to four times, or until they can read phrases with few or no mistakes.

Unit 4
Group Time

DAY **4**

ROUTINE

1 Phonemic Awareness

Isolate /e/ Display the *web* Picture Card. This is a web. What is the sound in the middle of *web*? The sound in the middle is /e/. Repeat this routine with the following words: *sled* and *hen.*

Discriminate /e/ Tell children the following rhyme several times:

> "Ned," said Ted,
> "I've found a shell."
> "Ted," said Ned,
> "that is just swell."

Then have them raise their hands when they hear a word with /e/ in the middle.

2 Phonics

Connect /e/ to *Ee* Write *Ee* on the board. What is the name of this letter? What is the sound for this letter? Name some words that have /e/ in the middle.

Blend Sounds Write *Len* on the board. Have children blend the sound of each letter to read the word.

Continue with *get, Red, Hen, can, in, pen, ran, hid, did, not, Ken, Ben,* and *got.*

3 Build Fluency

Review High-Frequency Words Write *go* on the board. This is the word *go.* Name the letters with me: *g, o, go.* Continue with *the, from,* and *here.*

4 Read Decodable Text

Read Decodable Reader 23 Display the story. The title of this story is *Red Hen.* Follow along with your finger as I read, and then we will take turns reading this page. Reread the book several times, giving children opportunities to read the story. Provide support as necessary.

Decodable Reader 23

Unit 4
Group Time

ROUTINE

DAY 5

1 Phonemic Awareness

Listen for /e/ Tell children you will tell them a story and they should listen for /e/. When you say a word with /e/, children should bend over at the waist and repeat the word. Tell a simple story, emphasizing the /e/ words and pausing to give children a chance to bend and repeat the word. *Ken has a pet hen. The name of the hen is Len. Len stays in a pen with ten other hens. Len the hen lays many eggs. Ken gets the eggs from Len and puts them in the den.*

2 Phonics

Connect /e/ to Ee Write *Ee* on the board. What is the name of this letter? What is the sound for this letter?

Discriminate /e/ Words Give each child an e Finger Tracing Card. I am going to say some words. I want you to listen carefully. If the word has /e/ in the middle, raise your e card. Listen carefully: *Ned*. Did you hold your card up? *Ned* has /e/ in the middle. Let's try some more. Use the following words: *red, flag, get, bed, mop,* and *win.*

3 Alternate Assessment

Build Words Give each child the following letter tiles: *e, g, n, b, d, l,* and *t.* Listen to the sounds in *leg.* What is the letter for /l/? Place your *l* tile in front of you. Repeat this routine for the *e* and *g.* Then have children blend the sounds to read the word. Make note of children who seem to struggle connecting the sound to the letter. Continue the assessment with the following words: *den, get, bed, let,* and *ten.*

Unit 4
Group Time

Strategic Intervention

1 Phonemic Awareness

Isolate /e/ Display the *bed* Picture Card. This is a bed. *Bed* has /e/ in the middle. Say it with me: /b/ /e/ /d/, *bed*. Repeat with *nest* and *ten*.

2 Phonics

Connect /e/ to Ee Display the *Ee* Alphabet Card. The name of this letter is *e*. The sound for this letter is /e/. Have children echo you.

Blend Sounds Write *set* on the board. Let's blend the sound of each letter to read the word: /s/ /e/ /t/. The word is *set*.

s e t

Continue with *get, Kim, met, Ted, can, hen, pet, pen, got, fed, in,* and *bed*.

Review High-Frequency Words Write *go* on the board. This is the word *go*. Name the letters with me: *g, o, go.* Continue with *here, is, a,* and *look*.

3 Read Decodable Text

Read Listen to Me Reader K.4.6 Display the book. The title of this story is *Get Set for a Pet Hen*. The author is Gianni Giambiccolo. The illustrator is Jerry Tiritilli. Follow along with your finger as I read. Then we will take turns reading this page. Reread the book several times, giving children several opportunities to read the text. Provide support with decoding as necessary.

Listen to Me Reader K.4.6

Advanced

1 Phonics

Connect /e/ to Ee Display the *Ee* Alphabet Card. What is the name of this letter? What is the sound for this letter? Ask children to name some /e/ words.

Blend Sounds Write *hen* on the board. Help me blend the sounds in this word to read it: /h/ /e/ /n/. The word is *hen*. Continue with *pet, den,* and *get*.

2 Oral Language

Build Background Remind children that Antarctica is a very cold place where seals, whales, and penguins live. Encourage children to describe what they might see or wear if they were to take a hike in Antarctica.

3 Reread Leveled Text

Reread Independent Leveled Reader K.4.5 Have children take turns reading *A Walk in Antarctica* for their group.

Reread for Fluency After the children read, model reading fluently for them. I am going to read this selection aloud. I will read the words with no mistakes. I want you to read it aloud with me. Try to read the words just as I do.

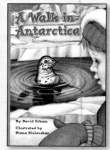

Independent Leveled Reader K.4.5

Use echo reading of Independent Leveled Reader K.4.5 to model reading fluently. Use your oral reading to model for children where to pause, when to change pitch, and which words to stress. Then have children reread orally three to four times, or until they can read with few or no mistakes.

Unit 4
Group Time

Strategic Intervention

ROUTINE

1 Phonemic Awareness

Discriminate /e/ Display Phonics Songs and Rhymes Chart 24. Sing "Get Set, Ten Pets!" to the tune of "Baa, Baa, Black Sheep" several times with children. Have children pretend to pet an animal when they hear an /e/ word.

2 Phonics

Connect /e/ to Ee Display page 5 of *Animal ABCs*. What is the name of this letter? What is the sound for this letter? This is an elephant. What letter does *elephant* begin with? What is the sound for that letter?

Blend Sounds Write *Ted* on the board. Have children blend the sound of each letter to read the word: /t/ /e/ /d/, *Ted*. Why did I write *Ted* with an uppercase *T*? *Ted* is a name, and names always begin with uppercase letters. Repeat the routine with the following words: *pet, met, in, tent, it, big, can, nest.*

Review High-Frequency Words Write *go* on the board. This is the word *go*. What word is this? Continue with the following words: *I, am, have, a, is, little, my, here, the, to, you, see, do.*

3 Read Decodable Text

Read Phonics Story Display the story. The title of this story is *Ted and the Pet.* Follow along with your finger as I read. Then we will take turns reading this page. Reread the book several times, giving children several opportunities to read the text. Provide support as necessary.

Phonics Story

Advanced

ROUTINE

1 Build Fluency

Connect /e/ to Ee Display the *Ee* Alphabet Card. What is the name of this letter? What is the sound for this letter? Ask children to name other words that have /e/ at the beginning or in the middle.

Blend Sounds Write *Peg* on the board. Have children blend the sound of each letter to read the word: /p/ /e/ /g/, *Peg. Peg* is a name, so it begins with uppercase *P*. Repeat the routine with the following words: *met, Ned, got, pet, Hen, did, pen, not, in, bed, get, fed, let, nap.*

Review High-Frequency Words Review the following high-frequency words with children: *a, from, here, is, have, go.*

2 Read Decodable Text

Read Decodable Reader 24 The title of this story is *A Pet Hen.* The author is Fran Quinn. The illustrator is Jason Edwards. Let's read the story together.

Follow the Small Group Reading Routine.

- **Model Fluent Reading**
- **Read Chorally**
- **Read Individually**
- **Reread and Monitor Progress**

Decodable Reader 24

Unit 4
Group Time

Strategic Intervention — ROUTINE

1 Phonemic Awareness

Isolate /e/ Display the *egg* Picture Card. What is this? This is an egg. *Egg* begins with /e/. Say it with me: /e/, /e/, /e/, *egg*. **Repeat** with *red* and *net*. Where do you hear /e/ in *red* and *net*? /e/ is in the middle of the words *red* and *net*.

2 Phonics

Connect /e/ to Ee Write *Ee* on the board. What is the name of this letter? What is the sound for this letter? Name some /e/ words.

Blend Sounds Write *Ben* on the board. Blend the sound of each letter to read the word: /b/ /e/ /n/, *Ben*.

B e n

Continue with *Mom, get, set, in, cab, Dad, at, tells, big, spot, can, it,* and *had*.

Review High-Frequency Words Write *with* on the board. This is the word *with*. Name the letters with me: *w, i, t, h, with*. Continue with *to, for, the, see, we, from, here, you, look, one,* and *a*.

3 Read Decodable Text

Read Kindergarten Student Reader K.4.6 Display the book. The title of this story is *Get Set, Go!* The author is Nuala White. Let's read this story together. Follow the Small Group Reading Routine.

Kindergarten Student Reader K.4.6

- **Model Fluent Reading**
- **Read Chorally**
- **Read Individually**
- **Reread and Monitor Progress**

Advanced — ROUTINE

1 Build Fluency

Blend Sounds Write *Ben* on the board. Blend the sound of each letter to read the word: /b/ /e/ /n/, *Ben*. What is this word?

B e n

Continue with *Mom, get, set, in, cab, Dad, at, tells, big, spot, can, it,* and *had*.

Review High-Frequency Words Write *with* on the board. This is the word *with*. Name the letters with me: *w, i, t, h, with*. Continue with *to, for, the, see, we, from, here, you, look, one,* and *a*.

2 Read Decodable Text

Read Kindergarten Student Reader K.4.6 Show the cover of the story. The title of this story is *Get Set, Go!* Read the first page for children. Have volunteers reread the page.

Kindergarten Student Reader K.4.6

Reread for Fluency Use echo reading to model fluent reading with Kindergarten Student Reader K.4.6. I will read one sentence at a time. I will read the words with no mistakes. I want you to read the sentences together after me. Try to read them just the way I do.

After modeling, have children continue to practice reading orally with a partner. Listen to them read, and provide feedback regarding their oral reading and their use of the blending strategy.

Unit 4
Group Time

Strategic Intervention

1 Phonemic Awareness

Discriminate /e/ I am going to say two words. Tell me which word begins with /e/. Listen carefully: *elbow, foot.* Say the words with me: *elbow, foot.* Which word begins with /e/? *Elbow* begins with /e/. *Foot* begins with /f/. **Continue with** *elevator, down; monkey, elephant; escalator, up;* and *toast, egg.*

Listen for /e/ Teach children the following rhyme. Have children recite the rhyme several times. When children are familiar with the rhyme, ask them to clap for the /e/ words.

> Five little elephants are at the water pool.
> Evelyn said, "The water is cool."
> Elbert said, "The water is deep."
> Ellen said, "I want to sleep."
> Eldon said, "I'll just put my trunk in."
> Ester yelled, "Watch out! Ed's going to jump in."
> Ed came running along the path.
> Splash! Five little elephants took a shower and bath!

2 Phonics

Connect /e/ to Ee Write *Ee* on the board. What is the name of this letter? What is the sound for this letter? Name some /e/ words.

Blend Sounds Write *Ned* on the board. Have children blend the sound of each letter to read the word.

N e d

Continue with *met, Peg, got, get, pet, hen, did, not, pen, not, in, bed, get, fed, let,* and *nap.*

3 Build Fluency

Review High-Frequency Words Write *the* on the board. This is the word *the.* Name the letters with me: *t, h, e, the.* Continue with *a, from, here, is, have,* and *go.*

4 Read Decodable Text

Read Decodable Reader 24 Display the story. The title of this story is *A Pet Hen.* Follow along with your finger as I read, and then we will take turns reading this page. Reread the book several times, giving children opportunities to read the story. Provide support as necessary.

Decodable Reader 24

Abuela **DI•29**

Group Time

DAY 5

ROUTINE

1 Phonemic Awareness

Listen for /e/ The word *leg* has /e/. Say it with me: *leg.* Where do you hear /e/? /e/ is in the middle of *leg.* I am going to tell you a story, and I want you to listen for /e/. When you hear a word that has /e/, I want you to shake your leg in the air and then repeat the word with /e/. **Tell this simple story, emphasizing the /e/ words and pausing to give children a chance to shake their legs and repeat the word.** *Meg* is going to *get* a new *pet* today. *Meg* is *letting Ben* and *Ken* come. *Meg begged* for her *pet,* the *pet* with four *legs* and a tail. *Meg* is all *set* for her *pet.* The *pet* will live in the *den.* The *den* is *ready* for her *pet.* Finally, *Meg met* the *pet* and she named the *pet Len. Len* the *pet* is for *Meg!*

2 Phonics

Review *Ee*/e/ Write *Ee* on the board. What is the name of this letter? What is the sound for this letter?

Connect /e/ to *Ee* Give each child an e Finger Tracing Card. I am going to say some words. I want you to listen carefully. If you hear /e/ in the word, raise your e card. Listen carefully: *Ned's pet.* Did you hold your e card for *Ned* and *pet*? Let's try some more. **Use the following words:** *big bed, fried eggs, big jet, Jen the hen, bird's nest,* and *red sled.*

3 Alternate Assessment

Build Words Give each child the following letter tiles: *e, b, d, g, n, p, l,* and *t.* I am going to say a word, and you are going to use your tiles to build the word. Listen to the sounds in *leg.* What is the first sound in *leg*? The first sound is /l/. What is the letter for /l/? Place your *l* tile in front of you. **Repeat this routine for the e and g. Then have children blend the sounds to read the word. Make note of children who seem to struggle connecting the sound to the letter.** Continue the assessment with the following words: *bed, net, get, peg, ten, den,* and *let.*

Word Work

Consonant *Hh*

1 DEVELOP PHONEMIC AWARENESS

Display the *hat* and *tub* Picture Cards. /h/, /h/, *hat;* /t/, /t/, *tub.* Which word begins with /h/, *hat* or *tub?* (*hat*)

Display the following Picture Cards in random order: *cat, five, hammer, hen, house, hippopotamus, man, nest.* Let volunteers take turns choosing a picture whose name begins with /h/.

Show children how to say /h/ by opening your mouth and forcing air from the back of your throat. Together say: /h/, /h/, *hop.*

Say and segment the word *ham:* /h/ /a/ /m/, *ham.* Listen again: /h/ /a/ /m/. What is the word? Continue the activity by segmenting the following words and asking children to tell which word they hear: *hat, him, hit, has.*

2 CONNECT SOUND TO LETTER

Open the Big Book *Animal ABCs* to *Hh.* Identify the hawk. *Hawk* begins with /h/. Point to *Hh.* This is the letter that stands for /h/. It is the letter *Hh:* *Hh,* /h/, *hawk.*

Give the *hat* and *hen* Picture Cards to two volunteers. Have them identify each picture. Then ask them to turn over the card and point to the letter *Hh* as they say the name of the picture. Repeat the activity with the following Picture Cards: *hammer, hippopotamus, hose, house.*

Comprehension

Sequence

1 TEACH

Distribute all of the Alphabet Cards to children. Remind children that the letters of the alphabet come in a special order. Review the order by singing "The Alphabet Song."

Let's put the letters in the right order to make the alphabet. Work with children to form the alphabet by having them stand in a line as they hold their letter cards. Ask questions, such as:

• Which letter comes first? *(Aa)*
• Which letter comes after *Mm?* *(Nn)*
• Which letter is last? *(Zz)*

Remind children that putting things in order is showing what comes first, next, and last.

2 PRACTICE

Show pictures in mixed order of a seed, a young plant without flowers, and a mature plant with flowers. Recall with children that they have learned about plants growing in gardens. Ask:

• How do plants start out? (as seeds)
• When do plants get flowers—right away when the plant grows out of the seed or after they have been growing for a while? (after they have been growing for a while)

Have children put the pictures in order to show the growth of a plant. Encourage them to use the words *first, next,* and *last.* Conclude by reminding children that this can happened in a story also. Things happen first, next, and last.

3 APPLY

Display the Big Book *Bunny Day.* Reread the story and then say: I am going to retell the story. I want you to tell me if I put everything in the right order. Retell events in the story, mixing up the order of some of the events. If children struggle to remember the order, display pictures to help them.

Word Work
Consonant *Ll*

1 DEVELOP PHONEMIC AWARENESS

Display the *lamp* and *leaf* Picture Cards. Name each picture. *Lamp* and *leaf* begin with /l/. Listen as I say each word: /l/, /l/, *lamp*; /l/, /l/, *leaf*.

Continue displaying the *lamp* and *leaf* Picture Cards. Display the *ladybug* Picture Card next to them. Name the cards and ask: Do all three words begin alike? Continue by adding each of the following Picture Cards: *lake, bat, lemon, egg, duck,* and *loaf.* If the words all begin with /l/, have children repeat the words. If they do not all begin with /l/, have children remove the card that does not belong.

Show children how to say /l/ by putting the front of your tongue against your upper front teeth and vibrating your vocal cords. Have children practice saying /l/ by repeating this silly sentence: *Little lambs love lollipops.*

Listen to this word. I am going to say it so you can hear /l/ at the beginning: /l/, /l/, *lip*; /l/ *-ip, lip.* What is this word? The word is *lip.* Repeat with *lad* and *lid.*

2 CONNECT SOUND TO LETTER

Display the Big Book *Animal* ABCs and open to *Ll.* Have children identify the picture of the *lion.* Listen to the word *lion.* It begins with /l/. Point to *Ll.* This is the letter *Ll.* It stands for /l/: *Ll,* /l/, *lion.*

Display the *Ll* Alphabet Card. Remind children that *Ll* stands for /l/. Then read words in the *Ll* section and have volunteers point to the *Ll* in each word. Help children notice that the letter *Ll* comes at the beginning of the word and so does /l/.

Comprehension
Cause and Effect

1 TEACH

Turn off the light and ask:

- What happened when I turned off the light? (It got darker.)
- What caused the darkness? (turning off the light)

When something happens, there is a *cause* for, or reason, why it happens. Turning off the light *caused* the room to get darker.

2 PRACTICE

Give children a situation and have them tell the reason why it is happening, or the cause.

- I see people holding umbrellas. Why? (It is raining.)
- I see all the children in class sitting quietly on the rug. Why? (It is story time.)
- I see people wearing shorts and wiping sweat off their faces. Why? (It is hot outside.)

Remind children that there is a *cause* for, or reason, why each of these things happens.

3 APPLY

Display the Trade Book *My Lucky Day.* Reread pages 3–9 and say:
- The fox is very happy to see the piglet at his door. Why? What causes him to be so happy? (He thinks he can eat the piglet.)

Reread pages 14–17 and say:
- The fox cooks for the piglet. Why? What causes him to cook for the piglet? (The piglet says he needs to be fattened up.)

Reread pages 24–27 and say:
- The fox falls asleep. Why? What causes him to fall asleep? (He is tired from washing, cooking for, and massaging the piglet.)

Word Work

Consonant Blends

1 DEVELOP PHONEMIC AWARENESS

Hold up the *pan* Picture Card. Name the picture as you show it to the class. Listen carefully to this sentence: *I have a plan to buy a pan.* What two words in that sentence sound alike? *Pan* and *plan* sound alike, but there is an extra sound in *plan.* Have children say *pan* and *plan.* Explain that some words—like *plan*—begin with two sounds that are blended together.

Say three words and have children tell you which two words have the same beginning sounds. Use the following sets of words: *crate, cat, crab; tie, try, trip; spot, pot, spy; flip, flop, lip.*

Model how to say these initial blends: /sl/, /pl/, /cl/, /fl/, /cr/, /dr/, /tr/, /st/, /sp/. Then use these tongue twisters to help children practice saying initial blends: *slide slick slugs; climb clean cliffs; stir sticky stew; drop dried dresses.*

Explain that blends can also come at the end of words. Ask children to listen to some words that end with blends. Say three words and have children tell you which two words have the same ending sounds. Use the following sets of words: *add, and, land; left, heft, let; milk, will, silk; ask, task, pass; sat, last, fast.*

2 CONNECT SOUND TO LETTER

Write each of the following letters and words on index cards: *f, l, r, s, t, flag, trash, step.*

Place the *t* and *r* cards in a pocket chart with space between them. Have children identify each letter. Put the letter cards together and say /tr/. Hold up the *trash* card and read it. Let a volunteer point to the *tr* in the word. Then put the word card beside the *t* and *r* in the pocket chart. Use the same procedure for *f, l,* and *flag* and for *s, t,* and *step.*

Comprehension

Sequence

1 TEACH

Write the numbers 1 through 10 on index cards. Distribute the cards to ten students. Review the order by counting to ten with the children.

Work with children to put the cards in numerical order by having them stand in a line as they hold the cards. Ask questions, such as:

- Which number comes first? (1)
- Which number comes right after 5? (6)
- Which number comes last? (10)

Remind children that putting things in order is showing what should come first, next, and last.

2 PRACTICE

Have one child pretend to wash dishes. Have another child pretend to set the table. Have a third child sit at a table and pretend to eat. They are washing dishes, setting the table, and eating dinner.

- When it is time for dinner, which of these things do we do first? (set the table)
- What do we do next? (sit down and eat)
- What do we do last? (wash the dishes)

Remind children that putting things in order means showing what happened first, next, and last.

3 APPLY

Display the Big Book *One Little Mouse.* Reread pages 6–13 and say: Mouse decided to look for a new house. He met three meadow frogs, four bobwhite quail, and two blackish moles.

- Whom did Mouse meet first? (two blackish moles)
- Whom did he meet next? (three meadow frogs)
- Whom did he meet last? (four bobwhite quail)

What words help us remember the order? *(two, three, and four)* When we tell what happens first, next, and last, we are talking about the order.

Word Work

Consonant *Gg*

1 DEVELOP PHONEMIC AWARENESS

Hold up the *goose* Picture Card and name it. The word *goose* begins with /g/, /g/, /g/, *goose*. Display the card where children can see it.

Hold up the *dog* and *goat* Picture Cards and name them. Which word begins like *goose, dog* or *goat*? (*goat*) Display the *goat* card next to *goose*. Continue with the following pairs of Picture Cards: *gum, carrot; rabbit, garden.*

Explain how to say /g/ by raising the back of your tongue against the back of the roof of your mouth (soft palate) and keeping the front of your tongue down. Have children put their hand between their chin and throat to feel the movement as they say /g/. Have children practice /g/ with the following sentence: *Goose gave Goat gold guitars.*

Display three different colored stacking blocks. Say and segment the word *got*: /g/ /o/ /t/, *got*. Repeat, setting a block down as you say each sound. Then blend the sounds together, pushing the blocks together as you say the sounds. Repeat the activity with the words *gap* and *gum*.

2 CONNECT SOUND TO LETTER

Display the Big Book *Animal ABCs* and open to *Gg*. Have a volunteer name the animal. The first sound in *gorilla* is /g/. Point to *Gg*. This is the letter that makes /g/. *Gg* is the first letter in *gorilla*: *Gg*, /g/, *gorilla*.

Write *Gg* on the board and have children name the letter. Who can find the letter *Gg* on our ABC Wall? Read some of the words found in the section. Have volunteers point to the *Gg* in the words you read.

Comprehension

Character: Actions/Traits

1 TEACH

Use a child's drawing that includes people. Let the child who created the picture tell about it. Ask:

- Who are the people and animals in this picture?
- What are they doing?

Let children use the picture to create a story. Remind children that the people and animals in a story are called the *characters*.

2 PRACTICE

Read the following nursery rhyme:

> **Hey diddle diddle,**
> **The cat and the fiddle,**
> **The cow jumped over the moon.**
> **The little dog laughed,**
> **To see such sport,**
> **And the dish ran away with the spoon.**

- Who are the characters in "Hey Diddle Diddle"? (the cat, fiddle, cow, dog, dish, and spoon)
- What did the cow do? (jumped over the moon)
- What did the dog do? (laughed)
- What did the dish do? (ran away with the spoon)

The animals and people in a story or rhyme are called the *characters*.

3 APPLY

Display the Trade Book *Goldilocks and the Three Bears*. Reread the story and ask:
- Who is the story about? (Goldilocks, a mother bear, a father bear, and a baby bear)
- What is Goldilocks like? (She is a little girl.)
- What does Goldilocks do? (She goes into the bears' home.)

Word Work

Short *Ee*

1 DEVELOP PHONEMIC AWARENESS

Show and name the *egg* and *olive* Picture Cards. Listen as I say these words: /e/, /e/, *egg;* /o/, /o/, *olive.* Show the pictures again and let a volunteer name them. Which word begins with /e/, *egg* or *olive*? (*egg*)

Show and name the *box* and *jet* Picture Cards. Sometimes /e/ does not come at the beginning of the word. /b/ /o/ /ks/, *box;* /j/ /e/ /t/, *jet.* Which word has /e/, *box* or *jet*? (*jet*)

Explain how to say /e/ by opening your mouth and teeth slightly and relaxing your face muscles. Practice saying these rhyming words with /e/ together: *get, met, let, wet, jet, net.*

Draw three squares on the board. Use the squares to help children listen for /e/. Segment the word *pen:* /p/ /e/ /n/, *pen.* As you segment the word a second time, shade the middle square as you say /e/. Point out that the shaded square shows where /e/ is heard. Have children repeat each sound. Blend the sounds together by drawing an arc from one square to the next as you say *pen.* Have children repeat the word *pen.* Continue the activity with the words *ten, let,* and *fed.*

2 CONNECT SOUND TO LETTER

Display the Big Book *Animal ABCs* and open to *Ee.* Have children identify the elephant. The first sound in *elephant* is /e/. Point to *Ee.* This is the letter that makes /e/: *Ee,* /e/, *elephant.*

Focus attention on the *Ee* section of the ABC Wall. Read some of the words and let children point to the letter *Ee.* Have volunteers find words in other sections that have /e/ in the middle. Let children point to the *e* as you read the words.

Comprehension

Classify and Categorize

1 TEACH

Write the headings *Big Things* and *Little Things* on the board. Read the headings. Explain that you want children to help you sort things in the room into two groups—things that are big and things that are little.

- What are some big things? (*Possible answers:* desk, bookcase, table, aquarium, bulletin board, door)
- What are some little things? (*Possible answers:* crayons, paper clips, pencils, scissors, erasers, chalk)

Remind children that we can put things together that are alike in some way.

2 PRACTICE

Write two colors (for example, *red* and *green*) on the board as headings.

Ask questions and list children's responses:
- What are some things in the room that are red? (*Possible answers:* flag, stripes, a shirt, a book)
- What are some things that are green? (*Possible answers:* a toy, plants, a drawing)

Extend the activity by adding columns for other colors.

3 APPLY

Display and reread the Big Book *If You Could Go to Antarctica.* Write the headings *In Antarctica* and *Not in Antarctica* on the board. Ask:

- What are some things we could find in Antarctica? (snow, ice, icebergs, penguins, seals)
- What are some things we could *not* find in Antarctica? (*Possible answers:* most plants, people who aren't scientists, kids)

Word Work
Short *Ee*

1 DEVELOP PHONEMIC AWARENESS

Show and name the *elbow* and *apple* Picture Cards. Listen carefully as I say *elbow* and *apple*: /e/, /e/, elbow; /a/, /a/, apple. Show the pictures again and let a volunteer name them. Which word begins with /e/, elbow or apple? *(elbow)*

Show and name the *nut* and *net* Picture Cards. Sometimes /e/ does not come at the beginning. Listen carefully: /n/ /u/ /t/, nut; /n/ /e/ /t/, net. Which word has /e/, nut or net? *(net)*

Remind children how to say /e/ by opening your mouth and teeth slightly and relaxing your face muscles. Practice saying these /e/ words together: *pet, desk, let, ten, wet, west, bed.*

Display three pens to help you segment the word *pen:* /p/ /e/ /n/, *pen.* As you segment the word a second time, place one pen on a table as you say each sound. Point out that each pen represents a sound in the word, and the middle pen stands for /e/. Have children repeat each sound. Push the pens together as you blend the sounds. Have children repeat the word *pen.* Continue the activity with the words *send, hen,* and *web.*

2 CONNECT SOUND TO LETTER

Display the *Ee* Alphabet Card. Have children identify the escalator. The first sound in *escalator* is /e/. Point to the *Ee.* This is the letter that stands for /e/: Ee, /e/, escalator.

Give the *elephant* and *elevator* Picture Cards to two volunteers. Have them identify each picture. Then ask them to turn over the card and point to the letter *Ee* as they name the picture. Repeat the activity with the *egg* and *elbow* Picture Cards.

Comprehension
Setting

1 TEACH

Talk to children about the setting of your classroom. Encourage multiple answers.

- Where are we right now? (*Possible answers:* on the story carpet; in our classroom; in the school)
- What time of day is it?

Remind children that stories happen in a certain time and place.

2 PRACTICE

Tell a short story, asking children to explain the various settings as you tell it.

- An astronaut buckles his seatbelt as he gets ready for takeoff. Where is this part of the story taking place? (in a spaceship) When is it taking place? (just before takeoff)
- The astronaut hears, "Three, two, one, blastoff!" as his rocket shoots into space. He looks out the window as he speeds away from Earth. Where is this part of the story taking place? (in outer space) When is it taking place? (just after takeoff)
- A few days later, the astronaut steps out of his rocket and onto the surface of the moon. Where is this part of the story taking place? (on the moon) When is it taking place? (a few days later)

3 APPLY

Display the Trade Book *Abuela.* Reread pages 5–7 and ask:
- Where are Rosalba and Abuela? (on the bus)
- Where are they going on the bus? (to the park) The bus and the park are places the story takes place.

Reread pages 14–17 and ask:
- Where are Rosalba and Abuela now? (flying over the city) The sky above the city is also a place where the story happens.

Providing children with reading materials they can and want to read is an important step toward developing fluent readers. A running record allows you to determine each child's instructional and independent reading level. Information on how to take a running record is provided on pp. DI•39–DI•40.

Instructional Reading Level

Only approximately 1 in 10 words will be difficult when reading a selection from the Student Edition for children who are at grade level. (A typical first-grader reads approximately 45–60 words correct per minute.)

- Children who are able to read the high-frequency words and decode CVC words can read from the Kindergarten Student Readers. Use the Kindergarten Student Readers and Decodable Readers, with teacher support as suggested in the Teacher's Edition.
- Children not yet reading connected text can read the Listen to Me Reader and the Decodable Readers. Instructional plans can be found in the Teacher's Edition.
- Children who are reading connected text can use the Independent Leveled Readers. Instructional plans can be found in the Teacher's Edition and the Leveled Reader Teaching Guide.

Independent Reading Level

Children should read regularly in independent-level texts. Factors that make a book accessible include the child's interest in the topic, the amount of text on a page, how well illustrations support meaning, and the complexity and familiarity of the concepts. Suggested books for self-selected reading are provided for each lesson on p. TR14 in this Teacher's Edition.

Guide children in learning how to self-select books at their independent reading level. As you talk about a book with children, discuss the challenging concepts in it, list new words children find in sampling the book, and ask children about their familiarity with the topic. A blackline master to help children evaluate books for independent reading is provided on p. DI•38.

Self-Selected/Independent Reading

Independent reading is of crucial importance to children's futures as readers and learners. Children need to develop their ability to read independently for increasing amounts of time.

- Schedule a regular time for sustained independent reading in your classroom. During the year, gradually increase the amount of time devoted to independent reading.
- More fluent readers may choose to read silently during independent reading time. Other children might read to a partner, to a stuffed animal, or to an adult volunteer.
- Help children track the amount of time they read independently and the number of pages they read in a given amount of time. Tracking will help motivate them to gradually increase their duration and speed. Blackline masters for tracking independent reading are provided on pp. DI•38 and TR15.

Choosing a Book to Read by Yourself

These questions can help you pick a book to read.

_____ 1. Is this book about something that I like?

_____ 2. This book may be about a real person, about facts, or a made-up story. Do I like reading this kind of book?

_____ 3. Have I read other things by this author? Do I like the author?

If you say "yes" to question 1, 2, or 3, go on.

_____ 4. Were there fewer than 5 hard words on the first page?

_____ 5. Does the number of words on a page look about right to me?

If you say "yes" to questions 4 and 5, the book is right for you.

Silent Reading

Write the date, the title of the book, and the number of minutes you read.

Date	Title	Minutes

Taking a Running Record

A running record is an assessment of a child's oral reading accuracy and oral reading fluency. Reading accuracy is based on the number of words read correctly. Reading fluency is based on the reading rate (the number of words correct per minute) and the degree to which a child reads with a "natural flow."

How to Measure Reading Accuracy

1. Choose a grade-level text of about 80 to 120 words that is unfamiliar to the child.

2. Make a copy of the text for yourself. Make a copy for the child or have the child read aloud from a book.

3. Give the child the text and have the child read aloud. (You may wish to record the child's reading for later evaluation.)

4. On your copy of the text, mark any miscues or errors the child makes while reading. See the running record sample on page DI·40, which shows how to identify and mark miscues.

5. Count the total number of words in the text and the total number of errors made by the child. Note: If a child makes the same error more than once, such as mispronouncing the same word multiple times, count it as one error. Self-corrections do not count as actual errors. Use the following formula to calculate the percentage score, or accuracy rate:

$$\frac{\text{Total Number of Words} - \text{Total Number of Errors}}{\text{Total Number of Words}} \times 100 = \text{percentage score}$$

Interpreting the Results

• A child who reads **95–100%** of the words correctly is reading at an **independent level** and may need more challenging text.

• A child who reads **90–94%** of the words correctly is reading at an **instructional level** and will likely benefit from guided instruction.

• A child who reads **89%** or fewer of the words correctly is reading at a **frustrational level** and may benefit most from targeted instruction with lower-level texts and intervention.

How to Measure Reading Rate (WCPM)

1. Follow Steps 1–3 above.

2. Note the exact times when the child begins and finishes reading.

3. Use the following formula to calculate the number of words correct per minute (WCPM):

$$\frac{\text{Total Number of Words Read Correctly}}{\text{Total Number of Seconds}} \times 60 = \text{words correct per minute}$$

Running Record Sample

Running Record Sample

Ming is on the job! He jumps on his
bike. Ming has work to do.

What is your (first) stop, Ming?
Good-bye! Race on, Ming! /rīd/

"What was that?" said Pam.

"What was that?" said Dad.

"It was Ming!" said Bob.

Ming zips past the park. Ming zips
past the batters. Race on, Ming! (sc) on

Ming is at his stop. Look at his face! H

"Hello, Ming!" said Ann.

Ann is glad to see Ming. Ming hands
Ann a small box. little

Hop back on, Ming! Where will Ming
race to next? Race home, Ming.

From *Ming the Messenger*
Independent Leveled Reader K.5.3

Symbols

Accurate Reading
The student reads a word correctly.

Omission
The student omits words or word parts.

Mispronunciation/Misreading
The student pronounces or reads a word incorrectly.

Insertion
The student inserts words or parts of words that are not in the text.

Self-Correction
The student reads a word incorrectly but then corrects the error. Do not count self-corrections as actual errors. However, noting self-corrections will help you identify words the student finds difficult.

Hesitation
The student hesitates over a word, and the teacher provides the word. Wait several seconds before telling the student what the word is.

Substitution
The student substitutes words or parts of words for the words in the text.

Running Record Results ▶	**Reading Accuracy** ▶	**Reading Rate—**WCPM
Total Number of Words: 91	$\frac{91-5}{91}$ x 100 = 94.5 = 95%	$\frac{95}{175}$ x 60 = 32.57 = 33 WCPM
Number of Errors: 5		
Reading Time: **175 sec**	Accuracy Percentage Score: **95%**	Reading Rate: **33** WCPM

Teacher Resources

Table of Contents

High-Frequency Words

ROUTINE

1 Display the word. Read it. Tell children they cannot blend the sounds in the word.

2 Have children say the letters in the word and repeat the word.

Example This is the word *little*. Say the letters with me: *l, i, t, t, l, e, little*.

Blend and Read

ROUTINE

1 Say the word and have children listen for the sounds.

2 Have children identify the first sound in the word.

3 Have children identify the letter for that sound and write it. Continue with the remaining sounds.

4 Blend the sound of each letter together to read the word.

Example Listen to the three sounds in *dot*: /d/ /o/ /t/. What is the first sound in *dot?* What is the letter for that sound? **Write *d* on the board.** Now you write *d* on your paper. **Continue the word with the remaining sounds.**

Help me blend the sound of each letter together to read this word: /d/ /o/ /t/. The word is *dot*.

HIGH-FREQUENCY WORDS

Unit 1

Weeks 1 and 2	**Weeks 3 and 4**	**Weeks 5 and 6**
I	the	to
am	little	a

Unit 2

Weeks 1 and 2	**Weeks 3 and 4**	**Weeks 5 and 6**
have	we	he
is	my	for
	like	

Unit 3

Weeks 1 and 2	**Weeks 3 and 4**	**Weeks 5 and 6**
me	see	they
with	look	you
she		of

Unit 4

Weeks 1 and 2	**Weeks 3 and 4**	**Weeks 5 and 6**
are	one	here
that	two	go
do	three	from
	four	
	five	

Unit 5

Weeks 1 and 2	**Weeks 3 and 4**	**Weeks 5 and 6**
yellow	what	where
green	said	come
blue	was	

WORDS TO BLEND

Unit 1 Consonant *m* and Consonant *t* are introduced.

Unit 2

Week 1	**Short *a***	am at mat				Tam	
Week 2	**Consonant *s***	sat				Sam	
Week 3	**Consonant *p***	pat	map sap tap			Pam Pat	
Week 4	**Consonant *c*/k/**	cap cat				Cam Mac	
Weeks 5 and 6	**Short *i***	it	pip sip tip	pit sit		Tim Pip Tip	

Unit 3

Week 1	**Consonant *b***	bam bat bib	bin bit	cab nab	tab ban	Bim Bin	Tab Tib
	Consonant *n*	nab nap nip	an ban can man pan tan	in bin pin tin		Nat Nan Bin	
Week 2	**Consonant *r***	ram ran rap rat	rib rim rip			Ric Rin Rip	Rap
Week 3	**Consonant *d***	dab did dim dip	ad bad dad fad mad pad sad	bid rid		Dan Tad Sid	
	Consonant *k*/k/	kid kin kiss kit				Kim Kip Kit	
Week 4	**Consonant *f***	fad fan fat	fib fin fit	if		Fab Fif Tif	
Weeks 5 and 6	**Short *o***	on	mob rob sob nod pod rod	sod mom bop mop pop top	cot dot not pot rot tot	Bob Rob Rod Mom Tom	Don Ron Bob Dot

WORDS TO BLEND

Unit 4

Week 1	Consonant *h*	had ham hat	hid him hip hit	hot hop			Hap Hob	
Week 2	Consonant *l* (Final –ll)	lab lad lap lid lip lit	lob lop lot	pal	ill dill fill hill mill pill doll		Lad Lib Lil Lill Lin	Al Hal Sal Bill
Week 3	Consonant Blends	blab crab drab scab slab small clam cram slam plan clap flap slap snap trap flat crib slid drill	skill spill still brim skim slim trim skin spin clip drip flip skip slip snip trip spit blob snob	clod drop flop plop stop plot spot raft camp damp lamp and band hand land sand stand ant pant	ask mask cast fast last mast past lift sift limp mint lint tint fist list mist		Flap Brad Spot Stan	
Week 4	Consonant *g*	gab gag gap gas gift glad grab	grim grin gob got bag lag nag	rag sag tag brag drag flag snag	big dig fig gig pig rig grim	dog frog log	Gab Gram Gib Gil Gip	
Weeks 5 and 6	Short *e*	egg elf elm end	bed fed fled led red sled left beg leg held bell fell sell smell	spell tell help belt felt melt hem den hen men pen ten bend blend	lend mend send bent dent rent sent tent pep step kept desk less mess	best nest rest test bet get let met net pet set	Ed Fred Ned Ted Greg Meg Peg	Reg Ben Ken

WORDS TO BLEND

Unit 5

Week 1

Consonant *w*	wag	wig	well	went	Wes
	web	win	will	wept	Will
	wed	wit		west	
	wet			wind	
				wisp	

Consonant *j*	jam	jig	jest		Jan
	jab	job			Jed
	jet	jog			Jeff
		jot			Jem
					Jen
					Jill
					Jim
					Jon

Week 2

Consonant *x*/ks/	ax	fix	box	next	Max
	fax	mix	fox		Lex
	lax	six	ox		Rex
	sax		pox		
	tax				
	wax				

Weeks 3 and 4

Short *u*	up	sud	bum	pup	plug	Gus
	us	cuff	gum	bus	slug	Bud
	cub	huff	hum	but	snug	
	dub	puff	mum	cut	drum	
	hub	bug	sum	hut	bump	
	nub	dug	bun	jut	dump	
	rub	hug	fun	nut	hump	
	sub	jug	pun	rut	jump	
	tub	mug	run	club	dust	
	dud	rug	sun	flub	just	
	mud	tug	cup	drug	must	

Week 5

Consonant *v*	van	vet	vast		Val	Bev
	vat		vent		Vic	
			vest		Vin	
					Von	

Consonant *z*	zap	jazz			
	zip	fizz			
	zest	buzz			
		fuzz			

Week 6

Consonant *y*	yak	yes			
	yam	yip			
	yell	yum			
	yet				

Consonant *qu*/kw/	quill				Quinn
	quit				
	quiz				

Oral Vocabulary Routine

ROUTINE

Oral Vocabulary	**Example**
1 **Introduce** the word and its meaning.	The bunnies do *chores. Chores* are jobs you do to make your home clean.
2 **Demonstrate** the meaning of the word.	Putting toys away is a *chore.* Playing with your toys is not a *chore.* What are some *chores* you do at home?
3 **Review** the word and its meaning.	We talked about *chores* today. What is the word that means "to clean up"?
4 **Apply** the word by having children demonstrate their understanding of the meaning.	Have children use *chores* in a complete sentence. Have them act out doing *chores.*

ABOUT ORAL VOCABULARY A child's oral vocabulary development is a predictor of future reading success. Oral vocabulary development now boosts children's comprehension as they become fluent readers. Oral vocabulary is informally assessed.

ORAL VOCABULARY WORDS

Unit 1		Amazing Words		Develop Vocabulary		Expand Vocabulary
Week 1	The Little School Bus	first second third	fourth fifth sixth	school bus	driver bus stop	sly wig
Week 2	Fix-It Duck	repair leak steep	ladder puddles shed	duck sheep	frog goat	bleats hitch
Week 3	Plaidypus Lost	platypus around lost	found market groceries	grandma lake	shirt swing	sink float
Week 4	Miss Bindergarten Takes a Field Trip with Kindergarten	bakery post office fire station	library park chaperone	teacher children	parent kindergarten	scrumptious splendid
Week 5	Julius	granddaddy sharing protect	crate scary sneaked	pig cat	dog towels	records imitations
Week 6	Dig Dig Digging	scooping swooshing squelching	gobbling spinning rumbling	trucks fire engines	helicopters machines	transporters bulldozers

Unit 2		Amazing Words		Develop Vocabulary		Expand Vocabulary
Week 1	Life in an Ocean	ocean world crab	shell fish seaweed	water animals	plants salt	shore kelp
Week 2	Armadillo's Orange	armadillo burrow tortoise	rattlesnake grubs insects	home orange	neighbors honeybees	orange grove soil
Week 3	Animal Babies in Grasslands	calf grassland cub	pup joey foal	zebra lion	kangaroo giraffe	prairie dog meerkat
Week 4	Bear Snores On	sleep winter cave	woods storm blustery	bear snores		lair
Week 5	A Bed for the Winter	meadow nest stump	tree trunk hive den	bed winter	burrow cave	dormouse coat
Week 6	Whose Garden Is It?	garden gardener plant	seed soil blossoms	rabbit nest	flowers rain	permission pollinate

REMEMBER that oral vocabulary is informally assessed.

ORAL VOCABULARY WORDS

Unit 3		Amazing Words		Develop Vocabulary		Expand Vocabulary
Week 1	Little Panda	weigh measure healthy	bamboo curious explore	panda paw	leg wobbly	fragile Chinese
Week 2	Little Quack	duckling pond paddle	plunged proud brave	water duck	nest	
Week 3	See How We Grow	twins newborn crawl	walk children babies	milk bottle	eat play	
Week 4	Farfallina and Marcel	goose gosling caterpillar	butterfly reflection cocoon	pond friend	game	solitary
Week 5	Seeds	seeds pod roots	stem pit sprouts	tree fruit plant	leaves bread grass	kernels ripe samaras moisture
Week 6	Hide, Clyde!	chameleon jungle pattern	skin hide scampered	brothers mother	window bumblebee	creatures

Unit 4		Amazing Words		Develop Vocabulary		Expand Vocabulary
Week 1	Bunny Day	tidy bustle race	story hungry chores	clock nap play	bunnies rabbit	peacefully artist
Week 2	My Lucky Day	piglet fox lucky	filthy cook scrubber	rabbit dinner	bath cookies	startled delicious
Week 3	One Little Mouse	woodland nest vale	hollow comfortable shadows	mouse frogs snakes	cottontails squirrels	moles bobwhite quail chickadees porcupine quills opossums
Week 4	Goldilocks and the Three Bears	bears porridge cottage	big middle-sized small	woods father	mother baby	delicious wandered
Week 5	If You Could Go to Antarctica	Antarctica continent icebergs	penguins seals whales	thunder		thickest scientists coast
Week 6	Abuela	abuela adventure flock	city airport harbor	grandma park	bread clouds	leaped soared

REMEMBER that oral vocabulary is informally assessed.

ORAL VOCABULARY WORDS

Unit 5		Amazing Words		Develop Vocabulary		Expand Vocabulary	
Week 1	Max Takes the Train	plane jetway subway	tunnel ferryboat sidecar	bus train		flight attendant	
Week 2	Mayday! Mayday!	rescue pilot yacht	sailor mechanic shimmering	boat taxi	swimmer yatch	radar fueled	turbines hoisted
Week 3	Messenger, Messenger	messenger delivery radios	pickup escalator eyeshades	sun wind rain tunnels	snow parking lots bike	squints	
Week 4	The Little Engine That Could	engine tracks passenger	roundhouse mountain valley	load sleeping cars wheels	dining-car switching dolls toys	berths freight	
Week 5	On the Move!	travel kayak llama	dogsled submarine double- decker bus	water land airplane	trail camel ocean	romp quest swamp	
Week 6	This Is the Way We Go to School	cable car trolley horse-and- buggy	skis Metro line vaporetto	school bus car	train bicycles radio	the El	

Unit 6		Amazing Words		Develop Vocabulary		Expand Vocabulary	
Week 1	Homes Around the World	home roof tools	apartment city country	mud grass sticks	wood stone water	suburb mobile materials	
Week 2	Old MacDonald had a Woodshop	saw drill hammer	screwdriver file chisel	sheep cat goat rooster	pig mouse cow dog	woodshop	
Week 3	Building Beavers	beaver lodge paddle	river stream lake	teeth trees mud	pond kits	balance webbed predators	herbivores grooming
Week 4	The Night Worker	engineer construction foreman	hard hat beacons street sweeper	delivery worker	policewoman machinery	concrete foundation hoists	mammoth survey
Week 5	The House That Tony Lives In	architect electricians plumbers	painters landscapers movers	construction workers	neighbors drivers	installed connected	
Week 6	Animal Homes	predators shelter shields	prey colony bark	safe pond cocoon	hibernate den	burrow amphibian damp mollusk	hollow larva roost

REMEMBER that oral vocabulary is informally assessed.

Position for Writing

Left-handed and right-handed writers slant their papers differently from one another, but they sit and hold their pencils the same way.

Body Position

- Children should sit tall, with both feet flat on the floor and arms relaxed on a table or desk.

- Children should hold their papers with their non-writing hand.

Paper Slant

- Paper should be positioned at a slant that is approximately parallel to the writing arm.

- For left-handed children, the paper should slant from the right at the top to the left at the bottom.

- Right-handed children should slant the paper from the left at the top to the right at the bottom.

Pencil Grip

- Children should grasp the pencil lightly between the thumb and index finger, usually about an inch above the pencil point.

- For a child who grasps the pencil too close to the point, a simple remedy is to wrap a rubber band around the pencil about an inch above the point. Have the child hold the pencil above the rubber band.

Legibility

Legibility should be the goal of handwriting instruction. Children should be praised for writing legibly, even though their writing may deviate from a perfect model. Legibility is based on flexible but standard criteria for letter form, size, and slant, and for letter and word spacing.

Letter Form

- Standards for letter form enable each letter to be distinguished clearly from other letters.

- In the letter *a*, for example, the round part of the letter must be open, and the letter must be closed at the top. The letter *a* must not be confused with *u, d,* or *o*.

- The letters *t* and *f* must be crossed; the letters *i* and *j* dotted.

Letter Size

- Small letters sit on the bottom line and touch the middle line.

- Tall letters sit on the bottom line and touch the top line.

- Letters with descenders have tails that go down under the bottom line and touch the line below.

Letter Slant

- Letter slant should be consistent.

- All letters may slant to the right, to the left, or be straight up and down.

Letter and Word Spacing

- Letters in a word should be evenly spaced. They should not be written too close together or too far apart.

- There should be more space between words in a sentence than between letters in a word. This allows each word to stand out.

Hints for Handwriting Instruction

My Name

In kindergarten, it is very important for children to learn how to write their own names. You might want to give each child a model of his or her name, written on heavy paper or cardboard. It can be placed on the child's table for reference.

Handwriting Center

You may want to set up a handwriting center in your classroom. Include the following materials:

- many different colors and types of pencils

- many different colors and types of paper

- a picture file with a picture for each upper and lower-case letter

- write-on/wipe-off boards

- a sandbox or container of sand in which children can finger trace letters

- a chalkboard, with chalk and an eraser

Encouraging Neatness

From the beginning, encourage children to cross out incorrect letters instead of erasing them. Young children tend to erase long and hard. This makes for messy papers that sometimes end up with holes in them. This can be upsetting for the child. By simply crossing out letters, pupils have neater papers and can learn from the mistakes they have made.

D'Nealian™ Alphabet

a b c d e f g h i

j k l m n o p q r s t

u v w x y z

A B C D E F G

H I J K L M N O

P Q R S T U V

W X Y Z . , ' ?

1 2 3 4 5 6

7 8 9 10

Manuscript Alphabet

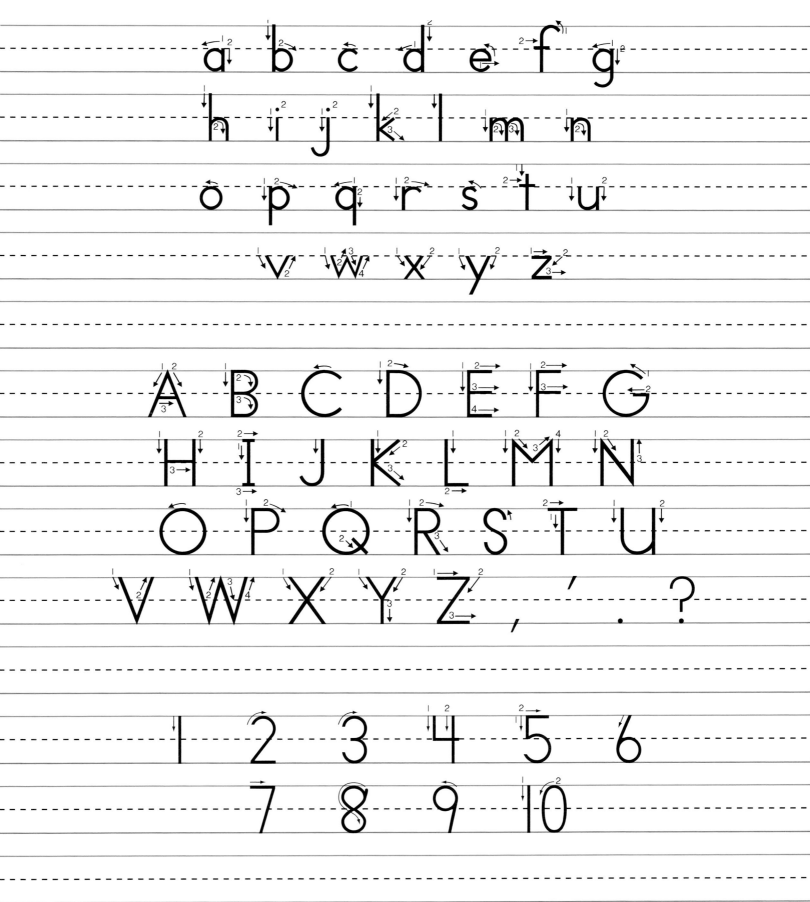

Unit 4 Let's Explore

To Read Aloud!	Below-Level	On-Level	Advanced

Bunny Day

Buzz
by Janet S. Wong (Harcourt, 2000) As his parents get ready for work, a child observes the household routine and the buzzing of a bee outside.

Just Like Daddy
by Frank Asch (Aladdin, 1981) A young bear describes all the activities he does during the day that are just like his daddy's.

10 Minutes till Bedtime
by Peggy Rathmann (Putnam, 1998) A boy's hamster leads an increasingly large group of hamsters on a tour of the boy's house and bedtime rituals, while his father counts down the minutes to bedtime.

Tales of Amanda Pig
by Jean Van Leeuwen (Penguin Books, 1983) Amanda Pig, her brother Oliver, and their parents share a busy day, working and playing together from breakfast to bedtime.

My Lucky Day

Suddenly!
by Colin McNaughton (Harcourt Brace, 1994) Time after time, Preston the pig unknowingly outwits a hungry wolf that is trying to catch and eat him.

Rosie's Walk
by Pat Hutchins (Simon & Schuster, 1968) Although unaware that a fox is after her as she walks around the farmyard, Rosie the hen still manages to lead him into one accident after another.

Fox Trot
by Molly Coxe (Golden Books, 1999) Fox's plans for a delicious dinner are spoiled by a band he hires to entertain his guests.

The Gruffalo
by Julia Donaldson (Dial, 1999) A clever mouse uses the threat of a terrifying creature to keep from being eaten by a fox, an owl, and a snake—only to have to outwit that creature as well.

One Little Mouse

A House Is a House for Me
by Mary Ann Hoberman (Puffin, 1982) In a rollicking rhyme, the author lists the dwellings of various animals and things.

Mouse Finds A House
by Karen Hoenecke (School Zone, 1997) After enquiring about living with various animals, a mouse finds her own special home.

The Best Nest
by P.D. Eastman (Random House, 1968) Mr. and Mrs. Bird set out to build a new, best nest, but they discover their old nest is really the best nest.

Animal Homes
by Sonia Black (Scholastic, 2001) In this easy-to-read science book, children learn about the homes of polar bears, turtles, ants, and more.

Goldilocks and the Three Bears

Leola and the Honeybears
by Melodye Benson Rosales (Scholastic, 1999) With rural Southern flavor, a classic nursery tale becomes a new adventure in an African American version of Goldilocks and the three bears.

Deep in the Forest
by Brinton Turkle (Puffin, 1992) In this variation of the classic, a bear cub explores a cabin in the forest, eats food, breaks chairs, and climbs into bed for a nap.

The Three Billy Goats Gruff
by Annette Smith (Rigby, 1997) Three Billy goats must cross a bridge that shelters a mean and hungry troll in order to get to their favorite pasture.

Somebody and The Three Blairs
by Marylin Tolhurst (Scholastic, 1994) In a reversal of the Goldilocks story, a bear explores the home of the three Blairs while they are out.

If You Could Go to Antarctica

Antarctic Antics: A Book of Penguin Poems
by Judy Sierra (Harcourt Brace, 1998) A collection of poems celebrating the habits and habitat of Emperor penguins.

Puffins Climb, Penguins Rhyme
by Bruce McMillan (Harcourt, 1995) Large photographs and rhyming word pairs present Atlantic puffins and southern gentoo penguins.

Follow the Polar Bears
by Sonia Black (Scholastic, 2000) This introduction to the lives of polar bears is written specifically for early readers.

Lionel in Winter
by Steven Krensky (Dial, 1994) Lionel pretends to be an Arctic explorer and engages in winter activities.

Abuela

Tar Beach
by Faith Ringgold (Crown, 1991) Eight-year-old Cassie Lightfoot dreams of flying above her Harlem home.

Lots of Grandparents
by Shelley Rotner and Sheila Kelly (Millbrook Press, 2001) This lovely photographic essay celebrates all of the wonderfully interesting and loving grandparents who relate to their grandkids.

Hairs/Pelitos
by Sandra Cisneros (Dragonfly Books, 1994) A child describes how each family member has hair that looks and acts differently.

Alison's Wings
by Marion Dane Bauer (Hyperion Books, 1996) In this easy chapter book, a girl dreams of growing wings so she can fly.

Unit 4 Reading Log

See also *Assessment Handbook*, p. 115

Name _____

Dates Read	Title and Author	What is it about?	How would you rate it?	Explain your rating.
From ___ to ___			Great 5 4 3 2 1 Awful	
From ___ to ___			Great 5 4 3 2 1 Awful	
From ___ to ___			Great 5 4 3 2 1 Awful	
From ___ to ___			Great 5 4 3 2 1 Awful	
From ___ to ___			Great 5 4 3 2 1 Awful	

Unit 4 Narrative Retelling Chart

Selection Title _____   Name _____   Date _____

Retelling Criteria/Teacher Prompt	Teacher-Aided Response	Student-Generated Response	Rubric Score (Circle one.)
Connections Did you like this book? Why or why not? How does this story remind you of other stories?			4 3 2 1
Author's Purpose What was the author trying to teach us?			4 3 2 1
Characters Describe _____ (character's name).			4 3 2 1
Setting Where and when did the story happen?			4 3 2 1
Plot Tell me what happened in the story.			4 3 2 1

Summative Retelling Score   4   3   2   1

Comments _____

See also *Assessment Handbook*, p. 110

Unit 4 Expository Retelling Chart

Selection Title _____   Name _____   Date _____

Retelling Criteria/Teacher Prompt	Teacher-Aided Response	Student-Generated Response	Rubric Score (Circle one.)
Connections Did this selection make you think about other selections?			4 3 2 1
Author's Purpose Why do you think the author wrote this selection?			4 3 2 1
Topic What was the selection about?			4 3 2 1
Important Ideas What is important for me to know about _____ (topic)?			4 3 2 1
Conclusions What did you learn from this selection?			4 3 2 1

Summative Retelling Score   4   3   2   1

Comments _____

Reading

Concepts of Print and Print Awareness	Pre-K	K	1	2	3	4	5	6
Develop awareness that print represents spoken language and conveys and preserves meaning	•	•	•					
Recognize familiar books by their covers; hold book right side up	•	•						
Identify parts of a book and their functions (front cover, title page/title, back cover, page numbers)	•	•	•					
Understand the concepts of letter, word, sentence, paragraph, and story	•	•	•					
Track print (front to back of book, top to bottom of page, left to right on line, sweep back left for next line)	•	•	•					
Match spoken to printed words	•	•	•					
Know capital and lowercase letter names and match them	•	• T	•					
Know the order of the alphabet	•	•	•					
Recognize first name in print	•	•	•					
Recognize the uses of capitalization and punctuation		•	•					
Value print as a means of gaining information	•	•	•					

Phonological and Phonemic Awareness	Pre-K	K	1	2	3	4	5	6

Phonological Awareness

	Pre-K	K	1	2	3	4	5	6
Recognize and produce rhyming words	•	•	•					
Track and count each word in a spoken sentence and each syllable in a spoken word	•	•	•					
Segment and blend syllables in spoken words			•					
Segment and blend onset and rime in one-syllable words		•	•					
Recognize and produce words beginning with the same sound	•	•	•					
Identify beginning, middle, and/or ending sounds that are the same or different	•	•	•					
Understand that spoken words are made of sequences of sounds	•	•	•					

Phonemic Awareness

	Pre-K	K	1	2	3	4	5	6
Identify the position of sounds in words		•	•					
Identify and isolate initial, final, and medial sounds in spoken words	•	•	•					
Blend sounds orally to make words or syllables		•	•					
Segment a word or syllable into sounds; count phonemes in spoken words or syllables		•	•					
Manipulate sounds in words (add, delete, and/or substitute phonemes)	•	•	•					

Phonics and Decoding	Pre-K	K	1	2	3	4	5	6

Phonics

	Pre-K	K	1	2	3	4	5	6
Understand and apply the *alphabetic principle* that spoken words are composed of sounds that are represented by letters	•	•	•					
Know letter-sound relationships	•	• T	• T	• T				
Blend sounds of letters to decode		•	• T	• T	• T			
Consonants, consonant blends, and consonant digraphs		•	• T	• T	• T			
Short, long, and r-controlled vowels; vowel digraphs; diphthongs; common vowel patterns			• T	• T	• T			
Phonograms/word families		•	•	•	•			

Word Structure

	Pre-K	K	1	2	3	4	5	6
Decode words with common word parts		•	• T	• T	• T	•	•	•
Base words and inflected endings			• T	• T	•	•	•	•
Contractions and compound words			• T	• T	• T	•	•	•
Suffixes and prefixes			• T	• T	• T	•	•	•
Greek and Latin roots						•	•	•
Blend syllables to decode words			• T	• T	• T	•	•	•

Decoding Strategies

	Pre-K	K	1	2	3	4	5	6
Blending strategy: Apply knowledge of letter-sound relationships to decode unfamiliar words		•	•	•	•			
Apply knowledge of word structure to decode unfamiliar words		•	•	•	•	•	•	•
Use context and syntax along with letter-sound relationships and word structure to decode	•	•	•	•	•	•	•	•
Self-correct		•	•	•	•	•	•	•

Fluency	Pre-K	K	1	2	3	4	5	6
Read aloud fluently with accuracy, comprehension, appropriate pace/rate; with expression/intonation (prosody); with attention to punctuation and appropriate phrasing			• T	• T	• T	• T	• T	• T
Practice fluency in a variety of ways, including choral reading, partner/paired reading, Readers' Theater, repeated oral reading, and tape-assisted reading		•	•	•	•	•	•	•

• instructional opportunity   T tested in standardized test format

	Pre-K	K	1	2	3	4	5	6
Work toward appropriate fluency goals by the end of each grade			•T	•T	•T	•T	•T	•T
Read regularly in independent-level material		•	•	•	•	•	•	•
Read silently for increasing periods of time		•	•	•	•	•	•	•

Vocabulary (Oral and Written)

	Pre-K	K	1	2	3	4	5	6
Word Recognition								
Recognize regular and irregular high-frequency words	•	•	•T	•T				
Recognize and understand selection vocabulary		•	•	•T	•	•	•	•
Understand content-area vocabulary and specialized, technical, or topical words			•	•	•	•	•	•
Word Learning Strategies								
Develop vocabulary through direct instruction, concrete experiences, reading, listening to text read aloud	•	•	•	•	•	•	•	•
Use knowledge of word structure to figure out meanings of words			•	•T	•T	•T	•T	•T
Use context clues for meanings of unfamiliar words, multiple-meaning words, homonyms, homographs			•	•T	•T	•T	•T	•T
Use grade-appropriate reference sources to learn word meanings	•	•	•	•	•T	•T	•T	•T
Use picture clues to help determine word meanings	•	•	•	•	•			
Use new words in a variety of contexts	•	•	•	•	•	•	•	•
Examine word usage and effectiveness		•	•	•	•	•	•	•
Create and use graphic organizers to group, study, and retain vocabulary			•	•	•	•	•	•
Extend Concepts and Word Knowledge								
Academic language	•	•	•	•	•	•	•	•
Classify and categorize	•	•	•	•	•	•	•	•
Antonyms and synonyms			•	•T	•T	•T	•T	•T
Homographs, homonyms, and homophones				•	•T	•T	•T	•T
Multiple-meaning words			•	•	•T	•T	•T	•T
Related words and derivations					•	•	•	•
Analogies					•	•		
Connotation/denotation						•	•	•
Figurative language and idioms			•	•	•	•	•	•
Descriptive words (location, size, color, shape, number, ideas, feelings)	•	•	•	•	•	•	•	•
High-utility words (shapes, colors, question words, position/directional words, and so on)	•	•	•	•				
Time and order words	•	•	•	•	•	•	•	•
Transition words						•	•	•
Word origins: Etymologies/word histories; words from other languages, regions, or cultures					•	•	•	•
Shortened forms: abbreviations, acronyms, clipped words			•	•	•	•	•T	

Text Comprehension

	Pre-K	K	1	2	3	4	5	6
Comprehension Strategies								
Preview the text and formulate questions	•	•	•	•	•	•	•	•
Set and monitor purpose for reading and listening	•	•	•	•	•	•	•	•
Activate and use prior knowledge	•	•	•	•	•	•	•	•
Make predictions	•	•	•	•	•	•	•	•
Monitor comprehension and use fix-up strategies to resolve difficulties in meaning: adjust reading rate, reread and read on, seek help from reference sources and/or other people, skim and scan, summarize, use text features				•	•	•	•	•
Create and use graphic and semantic organizers		•	•	•	•	•	•	•
Answer questions (text explicit, text implicit, scriptal), including *who, what, when, where, why, what if, how*	•	•	•	•	•	•	•	•
Look back in text for answers				•	•	•	•	•
Answer test-like questions				•	•	•	•	•
Generate clarifying questions, including *who, what, where, when, how, why,* and *what if*	•	•	•	•	•	•	•	•
Recognize text structure: story and informational (cause/effect, chronological, compare/contrast, description, problem/solution, proposition/support)	•	•	•	•	•	•	•	•
Summarize text		•	•	•	•	•	•	•
Recall and retell stories	•	•	•	•	•	•	•	•
Identify and retell important/main ideas (nonfiction)	•	•	•	•	•	•	•	•
Identify and retell new information			•	•	•	•	•	•
Visualize; use mental imagery		•	•	•	•	•	•	•
Use strategies flexibly and in combination			•	•	•	•	•	•

Comprehension Skills

Skill	Pre-K	K	1	2	3	4	5	6
Author's purpose			• T	• T	• T	• T	• T	• T
Author's viewpoint/bias/perspective					•	•	•	• T
Categorize and classify	•	•	•	•				
Cause and effect		•	• T	• T	• T	• T	• T	• T
Compare and contrast		•	• T	• T	• T	• T	• T	• T
Details and facts		•	•	•	•	•	•	•
Draw conclusions		•	• T	• T	• T	• T	• T	• T
Fact and opinion			• T	• T	• T	• T	• T	• T
Follow directions/steps in a process	•	•	•	•	•	•	•	•
Generalize					• T	• T	• T	• T
Graphic sources		•	•	•	•	• T	• T	• T
Main idea and supporting details		• T	• T	• T	• T	• T	• T	• T
Paraphrase			•	•	•	•	•	•
Persuasive devices and propaganda			•	•	•	•	•	•
Realism/fantasy		•	• T	• T	• T	•	•	•
Sequence of events		• T	• T	• T	• T	• T	• T	• T

Higher Order Thinking Skills

Skill	Pre-K	K	1	2	3	4	5	6
Analyze			•	•	•	•	•	•
Describe and connect the essential ideas, arguments, and perspectives of a text		•	•	•	•	•	•	•
Draw inferences, conclusions, or generalizations, support them with textual evidence and prior knowledge	•	•	•	•	•	•	•	•
Evaluate and critique ideas and text		•	•	•	•	•	•	•
Hypothesize						•	•	•
Make judgments about ideas and text		•	•	•	•	•	•	•
Organize and synthesize ideas and information		•				•	•	•

Literary Analysis, Response, & Appreciation

	Pre-K	K	1	2	3	4	5	6
Genre and Its Characteristics								
Recognize characteristics of a variety of genre	•	•	•	•	•	•	•	•
Distinguish fiction from nonfiction		•	•	•	•	•	•	•
Identify characteristics of literary texts, including drama, fantasy, traditional tales		•	•	•	•	•	•	•
Identify characteristics of nonfiction texts, including biography, interviews, newspaper articles		•	•	•	•	•	•	•
Identify characteristics of poetry and song, including nursery rhymes, limericks, blank verse	•	•	•	•	•	•	•	•
Literary Elements and Story Structure								
Character	•	• T	• T	• T	• T	• T	• T	•
Recognize and describe traits, actions, feelings, and motives of characters		•	•	•	•	•	•	•
Analyze characters' relationships, changes, and points of view		•	•	•	•	•	•	•
Analyze characters' conflicts				•	•	•	•	•
Plot and plot structure	•	• T	• T	• T	• T	• T	• T	•
Beginning, middle, end	•	•	•	•	•			
Goal and outcome or problem and solution/resolution		•	•	•	•	•	•	•
Rising action, climax, and falling action/denouement; setbacks						•	•	•
Setting	•	• T	• T	• T	• T	• T	•	•
Relate setting to problem/solution						•	•	•
Explain ways setting contributes to mood						•	•	•
Theme		•	• T	• T	•	•	•	•
Use Literary Elements and Story Structure	•	•	•	•	•	•	•	•
Analyze and evaluate author's use of setting, plot, character				•	•	•	•	•
Identify similarities and differences of characters, events, and settings within or across selections/cultures		•	•	•	•	•	•	•
Literary Devices								
Allusion								•
Dialect						•	•	•
Dialogue and narration	•	•	•	•	•	•	•	•
Exaggeration/hyperbole					•	•	•	•
Figurative language: idiom, jargon, metaphor, simile, slang			•	•	•	•	•	•

• instructional opportunity   **T** tested in standardized test format

	Pre-K	K	1	2	3	4	5	6
Flashback						•	•	•
Foreshadowing							•	•
Formal and informal language				•	•	•	•	•
Humor					•	•	•	•
Imagery and sensory words			•	•	•	•	•	•
Mood				•	•		•	•
Personification				•	•	•	•	•
Point of view (first person, third person, omniscient)					•	•	•	•
Puns and word play				•	•			
Sound devices and poetic elements	•	•	•	•	•	•	•	•
Alliteration, assonance, onomatopoeia	•	•	•	•	•	•	•	•
Rhyme, rhythm, repetition, and cadence	•	•	•	•	•	•	•	•
Word choice				•	•	•	•	•
Symbolism				•	•	•	•	•
Tone							•	•
Author's and Illustrator's Craft								
Distinguish the roles of author and illustrator	•	•	•	•				
Recognize/analyze author's and illustrator's craft or style				•	•	•	•	•
Literary Response								
Recollect, talk, and write about books	•	•	•	•	•	•	•	•
Reflect on reading and respond (through talk, movement, art, and so on)	•	•	•	•	•	•	•	•
Ask and answer questions about text	•	•	•	•	•	•	•	•
Write about what is read	•	•	•	•	•	•	•	•
Use evidence from the text to support opinions, interpretations, or conclusions				•	•	•	•	•
Support ideas through reference to other texts and personal knowledge				•	•	•	•	•
Locate materials on related topic, theme, or idea				•	•	•	•	•
Generate alternative endings to plots and identify the reason for, and the impact of, the alternatives	•	•	•	•	•	•	•	•
Synthesize and extend the literary experience through creative responses	•	•	•	•	•	•	•	•
Make connections: text to self, text to text, text to world	•	•	•	•	•	•	•	•
Evaluate and critique the quality of the literary experience				•	•	•	•	•
Offer observations, react, speculate in response to text				•	•	•	•	•
Literary Appreciation/Motivation								
Show an interest in books and reading; engage voluntarily in social interaction about books	•	•	•	•	•	•	•	•
Choose text by drawing on personal interests, relying on knowledge of authors and genres, estimating text difficulty, and using recommendations of others	•	•	•	•	•	•	•	•
Read a variety of grade-level appropriate narrative and expository texts		•	•	•	•	•	•	•
Read from a wide variety of genres for a variety of purposes	•	•	•	•	•	•	•	•
Read independently		•	•	•	•	•	•	•
Establish familiarity with a topic		•	•	•	•	•	•	•
Cultural Awareness								
Develop attitudes and abilities to interact with diverse groups and cultures	•	•	•	•	•	•	•	•
Connect experiences and ideas with those from a variety of languages, cultures, customs, perspectives	•	•	•	•	•	•	•	•
Understand how attitudes and values in a culture or during a period in time affect the writing from that culture or time period						•	•	•
Compare language and oral traditions (family stories) that reflect customs, regions, and cultures		•	•	•	•			•
Recognize themes that cross cultures and bind them together in their common humanness						•	•	•

Language Arts

Writing	Pre-K	K	1	2	3	4	5	6
Concepts of Print for Writing								
Develop gross and fine motor skills and hand/eye coordination	•	•	•					
Print own name and other important words	•	•	•					
Write using pictures, some letters, and transitional spelling to convey meaning	•	•	•					
Dictate messages or stories for others to write	•	•	•					

	Pre-K	K	1	2	3	4	5	6
Create own written texts for others to read; write left to right on a line and top to bottom on a page	•	•	•					
Participate in shared and interactive writing	•	•	•					

Traits of Writing

Focus/Ideas

	Pre-K	K	1	2	3	4	5	6
Maintain focus and sharpen ideas		•	•	•	•	•	•	•
Use sensory details and concrete examples; elaborate		•	•	•	•	•	•	•
Delete extraneous information			•	•	•	•	•	•
Rearrange words and sentences to improve meaning and focus			•	•	•	•	•	•
Use strategies, such as tone, style, consistent point of view, to achieve a sense of completeness						•	•	•

Organization/Paragraphs

	Pre-K	K	1	2	3	4	5	6
Use graphic organizers to group ideas		•	•	•	•	•	•	•
Write coherent paragraphs that develop a central idea			•	•	•	•	•	•
Use transitions to connect sentences and paragraphs			•	•	•	•	•	•
Select an organizational structure based on purpose, audience, length						•	•	•
Organize ideas in a logical progression, such as chronological order or by order of importance		•	•	•	•	•	•	•
Write introductory, supporting, and concluding paragraphs				•	•	•	•	•
Write a multi-paragraph paper				•	•	•	•	•

Voice

	Pre-K	K	1	2	3	4	5	6
Develop personal, identifiable voice and an individual tone/style			•	•	•	•	•	•
Maintain consistent voice and point of view						•	•	•
Use voice appropriate to audience, message, and purpose						•	•	•

Word Choice

	Pre-K	K	1	2	3	4	5	6
Use clear, precise, appropriate language		•	•	•	•	•	•	•
Use figurative language and vivid words			•	•	•	•	•	•
Select effective vocabulary using word walls, dictionary, or thesaurus		•	•	•	•	•	•	•

Sentences

	Pre-K	K	1	2	3	4	5	6
Combine, elaborate, and vary sentences		•	•	•	•	•	•	•
Write topic sentence, supporting sentences with facts and details, and concluding sentence			•	•	•	•	•	•
Use correct word order			•	•	•	•	•	•
Use parallel structure in a sentence							•	•

Conventions

	Pre-K	K	1	2	3	4	5	6
Use correct spelling and grammar; capitalize and punctuate correctly		•	•	•	•	•	•	•
Correct sentence fragments and run-ons					•	•	•	•
Use correct paragraph indention				•	•	•	•	•

The Writing Process

	Pre-K	K	1	2	3	4	5	6
Prewrite using various strategies	•	•	•	•	•	•	•	•
Develop first drafts of single- and multiple-paragraph compositions		•	•	•	•	•	•	•
Revise drafts for varied purposes, including to clarify and to achieve purpose, sense of audience, precise word choice, vivid images, and elaboration	•	•	•	•	•	•	•	•
Edit and proofread for correct spelling, grammar, usage, and mechanics		•	•	•	•	•	•	•
Publish own work	•	•	•	•	•	•	•	•

Types of Writing

	Pre-K	K	1	2	3	4	5	6
Narrative writing (such as personal narratives, stories, biographies, autobiographies)	•	•	• T	• T	• T	• T	• T	• T
Expository writing (such as essays, directions, explanations, news stories, research reports, summaries)		•	• T	• T	• T	• T	• T	• T
Descriptive writing (such as labels, captions, lists, plays, poems, response logs, songs)	•	•	• T	• T	• T	• T	• T	• T
Persuasive writing (such as ads, editorials, essays, letters to the editor, opinions, posters)		•	• T	• T	• T	• T	• T	• T

Writing Habits and Practices

	Pre-K	K	1	2	3	4	5	6
Write on a daily basis	•	•	•	•	•	•	•	•
Use writing as a tool for learning and self-discovery				•	•	•	•	•
Write independently for extended periods of time			•	•	•	•	•	•

ENGLISH LANGUAGE CONVENTIONS in WRITING and SPEAKING	Pre-K	K	1	2	3	4	5	6

Grammar and Usage in Speaking and Writing

Sentences

	Pre-K	K	1	2	3	4	5	6
Types (declarative, interrogative, exclamatory, imperative)	•	•	• T	• T	• T	• T	• T	• T
Structure (simple, compound, complex, compound-complex)	•	•	•	•	•	• T	• T	• T

• instructional opportunity   T tested in standardized test format

	Pre-K	K	1	2	3	4	5	6
Parts (subjects/predicates: complete, simple, compound; phrases; clauses)				•T	•	•T	•T	•T
Fragments and run-on sentences		•	•	•	•	•	•	•
Combine sentences, elaborate			•	•	•	•	•	•
Parts of speech: nouns, verbs and verb tenses, adjectives, adverbs, pronouns and antecedents, conjunctions, prepositions, interjections		•	•T	•T	•T	•T	•T	•T
Usage								
Subject-verb agreement		•	•T	•	•	•T	•T	•T
Pronoun agreement/referents			•T	•	•	•T	•T	•T
Misplaced modifiers						•	•T	•T
Misused words					•	•	•	•T
Negatives; avoid double negatives					•	•	•	•

Mechanics in Writing

	Pre-K	K	1	2	3	4	5	6
Capitalization (first word in sentence, proper nouns and adjectives, pronoun *I*, titles, and so on)	•	•	•T	•T	•T	•T	•T	•T
Punctuation (apostrophe, comma, period, question mark, exclamation mark, quotation marks, and so on)		•	•T	•T	•T	•T	•T	•T

Spelling

	Pre-K	K	1	2	3	4	5	6
Spell independently by using pre-phonetic knowledge, knowledge of letter names, sound-letter knowledge	•	•	•	•	•	•	•	•
Use sound-letter knowledge to spell	•	•	•	•	•	•	•	•
Consonants: single, double, blends, digraphs, silent letters, and unusual consonant spellings		•	•	•	•	•	•	•
Vowels: short, long, *r*-controlled, digraphs, diphthongs, less common vowel patterns, schwa		•	•	•	•	•	•	•
Use knowledge of word structure to spell			•	•	•	•	•	•
Base words and affixes (inflections, prefixes, suffixes), possessives, contractions and compound words			•	•	•	•	•	•
Greek and Latin roots, syllable patterns, multisyllabic words			•	•	•	•	•	•
Spell high-frequency, irregular words		•	•	•	•	•	•	•
Spell frequently misspelled words correctly, including homophones or homonyms			•	•	•	•	•	•
Use meaning relationships to spell					•	•	•	•

Handwriting

	Pre-K	K	1	2	3	4	5	6
Gain increasing control of penmanship, including pencil grip, paper position, posture, stroke	•	•	•	•				
Write legibly, with control over letter size and form; letter slant; and letter, word, and sentence spacing		•	•	•	•	•	•	•
Write lowercase and capital letters	•	•	•	•				
Manuscript	•	•	•	•	•	•	•	•
Cursive				•	•	•	•	•
Write numerals	•	•	•					

Listening and Speaking

Listening Skills and Strategies

	Pre-K	K	1	2	3	4	5	6
Listen to a variety of presentations attentively and politely	•	•	•	•	•	•	•	•
Self-monitor comprehension while listening, using a variety of skills and strategies	•	•	•	•	•	•	•	•
Listen for a purpose								
For enjoyment and appreciation	•	•	•	•	•	•	•	•
To expand vocabulary and concepts	•	•	•	•	•	•	•	•
To obtain information and ideas	•	•	•	•	•	•	•	•
To follow oral directions	•	•	•	•	•	•	•	•
To answer questions and solve problems	•	•	•	•	•	•	•	•
To participate in group discussions	•	•	•	•	•	•	•	•
To identify and analyze the musical elements of literary language	•	•	•	•	•	•	•	•
To gain knowledge of one's own culture, the culture of others, and the common elements of cultures	•	•	•	•	•	•	•	•
Recognize formal and informal language				•	•	•	•	•
Listen critically to distinguish fact from opinion and to analyze and evaluate ideas, information, experiences	•	•	•	•	•	•	•	•
Evaluate a speaker's delivery					•	•	•	•
Interpret a speaker's purpose, perspective, persuasive techniques, verbal and nonverbal messages, and use of rhetorical devices						•	•	•

Speaking Skills and Strategies

	Pre-K	K	1	2	3	4	5	6
Speak clearly, accurately, and fluently, using appropriate delivery for a variety of audiences, and purposes	•	•	•	•	•	•	•	•
Use proper intonation, volume, pitch, modulation, and phrasing		•	•	•	•	•	•	•
Speak with a command of standard English conventions	•	•	•	•	•	•	•	•
Use appropriate language for formal and informal settings	•	•	•	•	•	•	•	•

Speak for a purpose	Pre-K	K	1	2	3	4	5	6
To ask and answer questions	•	•	•	•	•	•	•	•
To give directions and instructions	•	•	•	•	•	•	•	•
To retell, paraphrase, or explain information			•	•	•	•	•	•
To communicate needs and share ideas and experiences	•	•	•	•	•	•	•	•
To participate in conversations and discussions	•	•	•	•	•	•	•	•
To express an opinion	•	•	•	•	•	•	•	•
To deliver dramatic recitations, interpretations, or performances	•	•	•	•	•	•	•	•
To deliver presentations or oral reports (narrative, descriptive, persuasive, and informational)	•	•	•	•	•	•	•	•
Stay on topic	•	•	•	•	•	•	•	
Use appropriate verbal and nonverbal elements (such as facial expression, gestures, eye contact, posture)	•	•	•			•	•	•
Identify and/or demonstrate methods to manage or overcome communication anxiety						•	•	•

Viewing/Media	Pre-K	K	1	2	3	4	5	6
Interact with and respond to a variety of print and non-print media for a range of purposes	•	•	•	•	•	•	•	•
Compare and contrast print, visual, and electronic media					•	•	•	•
Analyze and evaluate media			•	•	•	•	•	•
Recognize purpose, bias, propaganda, and persuasive techniques in media messages			•	•	•	•	•	•

Research and Study Skills

Understand and Use Graphic Sources	Pre-K	K	1	2	3	4	5	6
Advertisement			•	•	•	•	•	•
Chart/table	•	•	•	•	•	•	•	•
Diagram/scale drawing			•	•	•	•	•	•
Graph (bar, circle, line, picture)		•	•	•	•	•	•	•
Illustration, photograph, caption, label	•	•	•	•	•	•	•	
Map/globe	•	•	•	•	•	•	•	•
Order form/application						•	•	•
Poster/announcement	•	•	•	•	•	•	•	•
Schedule						•	•	
Sign	•	•	•	•		•		
Time line			•	•	•	•	•	•

Understand and Use Reference Sources	Pre-K	K	1	2	3	4	5	6
Know and use parts of a book to locate information	•	•	•	•	•	•	•	
Use alphabetical order			•	•	•	•		
Understand purpose, structure, and organization of reference sources (print, electronic, media, Internet)	•	•	•	•	•	•	•	•
Almanac						•	•	•
Atlas		•		•	•	•	•	•
Card catalog/library database				•	•	•	•	•
Dictionary/glossary		•	•	•	• T	• T	• T	• T
Encyclopedia				•	•	•	•	•
Magazine/periodical				•	•	•	•	•
Newspaper and Newsletter				•	•	•	•	•
Readers' Guide to Periodical Literature						•	•	•
Technology (computer and non-computer electronic media)		•	•	•	•	•	•	•
Thesaurus				•	•	•	•	•

Study Skills and Strategies	Pre-K	K	1	2	3	4	5	6
Adjust reading rate			•	•	•	•	•	•
Clarify directions	•	•	•	•	•	•	•	•
Outline				•	•	•	•	•
Skim and scan			•	•	•	•	•	•
SQP3R						•	•	•
Summarize		•	•	•	•	•	•	•
Take notes, paraphrase, and synthesize			•	•	•	•	•	•
Use graphic and semantic organizers to organize information		•	•	•	•	•	•	•

• instructional opportunity   **T** tested in standardized test format

Test-Taking Skills and Strategies	Pre-K	K	1	2	3	4	5	6
Understand the question, the vocabulary of tests, and key words			•	•	•	•	•	•
Answer the question; use information from the text (stated or inferred)		•	•	•	•	•	•	•
Write across texts				•	•	•	•	•
Complete the sentence				•	•	•	•	•

Technology/New Literacies	Pre-K	K	1	2	3	4	5	6
Non-Computer Electronic Media								
Audio tapes/CDs, video tapes/DVDs	•	•	•	•	•	•	•	
Film, television, and radio		•	•	•	•	•	•	•
Computer Programs and Services: Basic Operations and Concepts								
Use accurate computer terminology	•	•	•	•	•	•	•	•
Create, name, locate, open, save, delete, and organize files			•	•	•	•	•	•
Use input and output devices (such as mouse, keyboard, monitor, printer, touch screen)	•	•	•	•	•	•	•	•
Use basic keyboarding skills			•	•	•	•	•	•
Responsible Use of Technology Systems and Software								
Work cooperatively and collaboratively with others; follow acceptable use policies	•	•	•	•	•	•	•	•
Recognize hazards of Internet searches			•	•	•	•	•	•
Respect intellectual property					•	•	•	•
Information and Communication Technologies: Information Acquisition								
Use electronic web (non-linear) navigation, online resources, databases, keyword searches				•	•	•	•	•
Use visual and non-textual features of online resources	•	•	•	•	•	•	•	•
Internet inquiry			•	•	•	•	•	•
Identify questions			•	•	•	•	•	•
Locate, select, and collect information			•	•	•	•	•	•
Analyze information			•	•	•	•	•	•
Evaluate electronic information sources for accuracy, relevance, bias					•	•	•	•
Understand bias/subjectivity of electronic content (about this site, author search, date created)					•	•	•	•
Synthesize information					•	•	•	•
Communicate findings				•	•	•	•	•
Use fix-up strategies (such as clicking *Back, Forward,* or *Undo;* redoing a search; trimming the URL)			•	•	•	•	•	•
Communication								
Collaborate, publish, present, and interact with others		•	•	•	•	•	•	•
Use online resources (e-mail, bulletin boards, newsgroups)			•	•	•	•	•	•
Use a variety of multimedia formats			•	•	•	•	•	•
Problem Solving								
Select the appropriate software for the task	•	•	•	•	•	•	•	•
Use technology resources for solving problems and making informed decisions			•	•	•	•	•	•
Determine when technology is useful				•	•	•	•	•

The Research Process	Pre-K	K	1	2	3	4	5	6
Choose and narrow the topic; frame and revise questions for inquiry		•	•	•	•	•	•	•
Choose and evaluate appropriate reference sources				•	•	•	•	•
Locate and collect information	•	•	•	•	•	•	•	•
Take notes/record findings				•	•	•	•	•
Combine and compare information				•	•	•	•	•
Evaluate, interpret, and draw conclusions about key information		•	•	•	•	•	•	•
Summarize information		•	•	•	•	•	•	•
Make an outline				•	•	•	•	•
Organize content systematically		•	•	•	•	•	•	•
Communicate information		•	•	•	•	•	•	•
Write and present a report				•	•	•	•	•
Include citations						•	•	•
Respect intellectual property/plagiarism						•	•	•
Select and organize visual aids		•	•	•	•	•	•	•

Teacher's Edition

Text

Pages 25–29: *Bunny Day: Telling Time from Breakfast to Bedtime* by Rick Walton, illustrations by Paige Miglio. Text copyright © 2002 by Rick Walton. Illustrations copyright © 2002 by Paige Miglio. Published by arrangement with HarperCollins Children's Books, a division of HarperCollins Publishers Inc. All rights reserved.

Pages 87–92: *My Lucky Day* by Keiko Kasza. Copyright © 2003, Keiko Kasza. Published by arrangement with G.P. Putnam's Sons, a division of Penguin Young Readers Group, a member of Penguin Group (USA) Inc. All rights reserved.

Pages 151–155: *One Little Mouse* written by Dori Chaconas and illustrated by LeUyen Pham. Text copyright © 2002 by Dori Chaconas. Illustrations copyright © 2002 by LeUyen Pham. Published by arrangement with Viking Children's Books, a division of Penguin Young Readers Group, a member of Penguin Group (USA) Inc.

Pages 213–218: *Goldilocks and the Three Bears* as retold and illustrated by Valeri Gorbachev. Copyright © 2001 by Valeri Gorbachev. Reprinted by arrangement with North-South Books Inc., New York. All rights reserved.

Pages 277–280: *If You Could Go to Antarctica* by Fay Robinson © 2007 Pearson Education, Inc.

Pages 339–345: *Abuela* by Arthur Dorros. Text copyright © 1991 by Arthur Dorros. Illustrations copyright © 1991 by Elisa Kleven. Used by permission of Dutton Children's Books, a division of Penguin Young Readers Group.

Artists

Illustration

Cover Rob Hefferan

Unit 4 Opener Richard Bernal

Photographs

Every effort has been made to secure permission and provide appropriate credit for photographic material. The publisher deeply regrets any omission and pledges to correct errors called to its attention in subsequent editions.

Unless otherwise acknowledged, all photographs are the property of Scott Foresman, a division of Pearson Education.

Photo locators denoted as follows: Top (T), Center (C), Bottom (B), Left (L), Right (R), Background (Bkgd)

Page 2: ©Anne Walton/Rick Walton

Page 64: ©Keiko Kasza

Page 128: ©LeUyen Pham

Page 190: ©Valeri Gorbachev

Page 233: Getty Images

Page 254: ©Fay Robinson